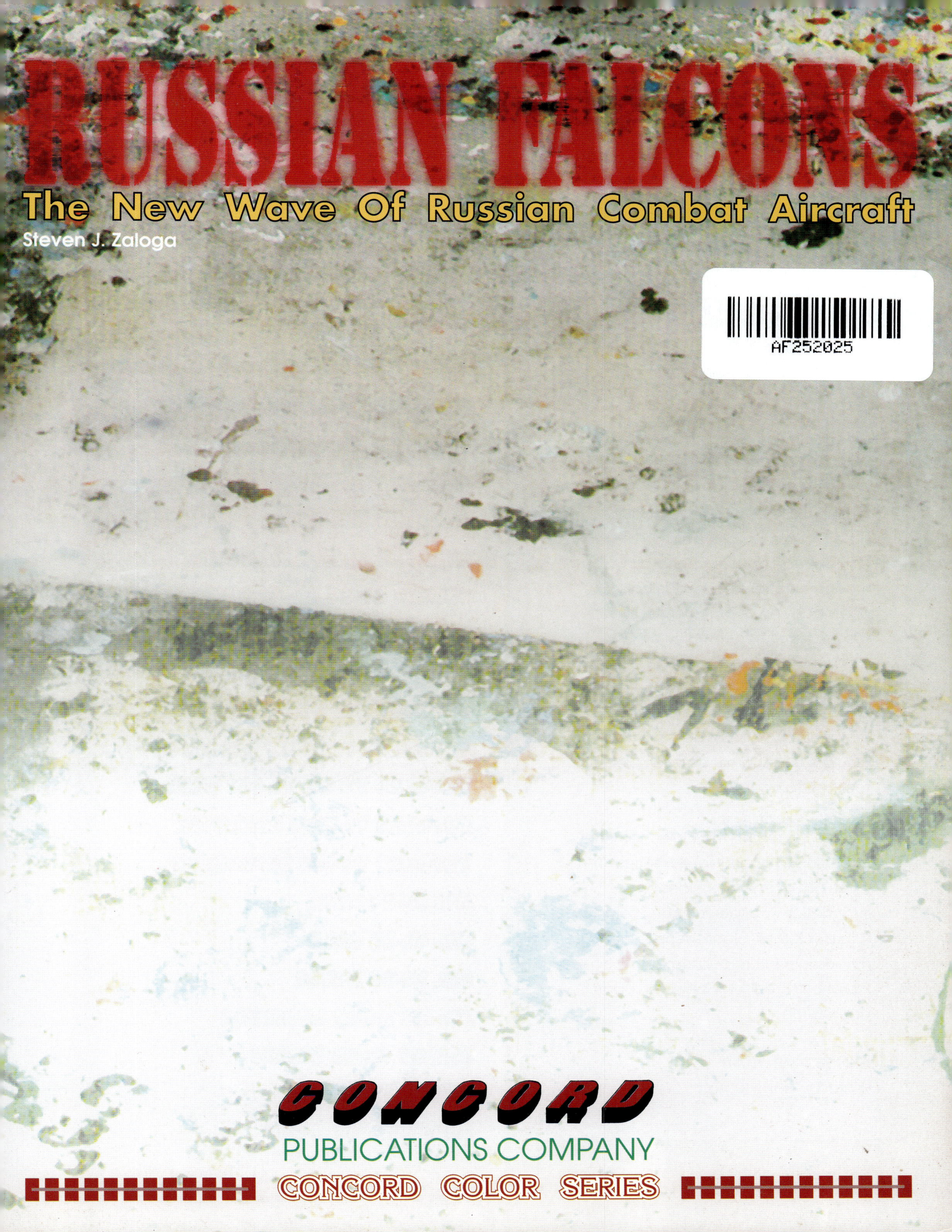

RUSSIAN FALCONS

The New Wave Of Russian Combat Aircraft

Steven J. Zaloga

CONCORD
PUBLICATIONS COMPANY

CONCORD COLOR SERIES

CONTENTS

INTRODUCTION

In 1992, the Armed Forces of the Russian Federation were formed on the basis of the former Soviet Armed Forces. The year 1992 also marked the first time that a major international air show was held in Moscow, called Mosaeroshow '92. The 1992 airshow held at Zhukovskiy air base was the first time many new Russian combat aircraft were displayed. Mosaeroshow was soon followed by a major display of additional Russian aircraft at the 1992 Farnborough Air Show in Britain. The aim of this book is to present a pictorial presentation of the many new Russian combat aircraft displayed in 1992 at these events.

Russian and the former Soviet Union has traditionally celebrated Aviation Day in August, in some cases with a big demonstration at Tushino, some years at Khodynka, and others at Kubinka. Last summer, the author was with one of the first groups allowed to visit the secret test center near the town of Ramenskoye, officially called Zhukovskiy Air Base. Zhukovskiy is better known in the west as Ramenskoye, and for many years, unidentified new Soviet aircraft were called RAM-A, etc. after they were first spotted there. Zhukovskiy is home of the LII, the Russian Experimental Flight Institute, which conducts all testing of new military and commercial aircraft. The neighboring area is still a restricted zone, as it is also home to TsAGI, the Central Aerodynamics Institute.

The 1992 Mosaeroshow was a remarkable event, providing the most detailed view behind the scenes of the Russian aviation industry. Manufacturers were far more open in discussing their programs than at any previous time. Many exhibitors, such as missile, electronic and weapons design bureaus, had been completely secret until the show. Although the Mosaeroshow included the largest single display of contemporary Russian aircraft ever held, some aircraft were not shown at the display. This was mainly due to the business decision that it would be better to wait until the Farnborough Air Show in September 1992 to reveal some of the latest combat types, such as the MiG-33, Su-35, and Yak-141.

The photos here attest to the wide variety of types displayed at these shows. The aim of this book is to provide heaviest coverage on the newest aircraft types: MiG-33, Su-35, MiG-29K, Su-27K, Ka-50 and IL-102. But the book also covers many other types of aircraft and missiles with a special emphasis on close-up detail shots of use to aviation modelers.

Ilyushin IL-102 Shturmovik

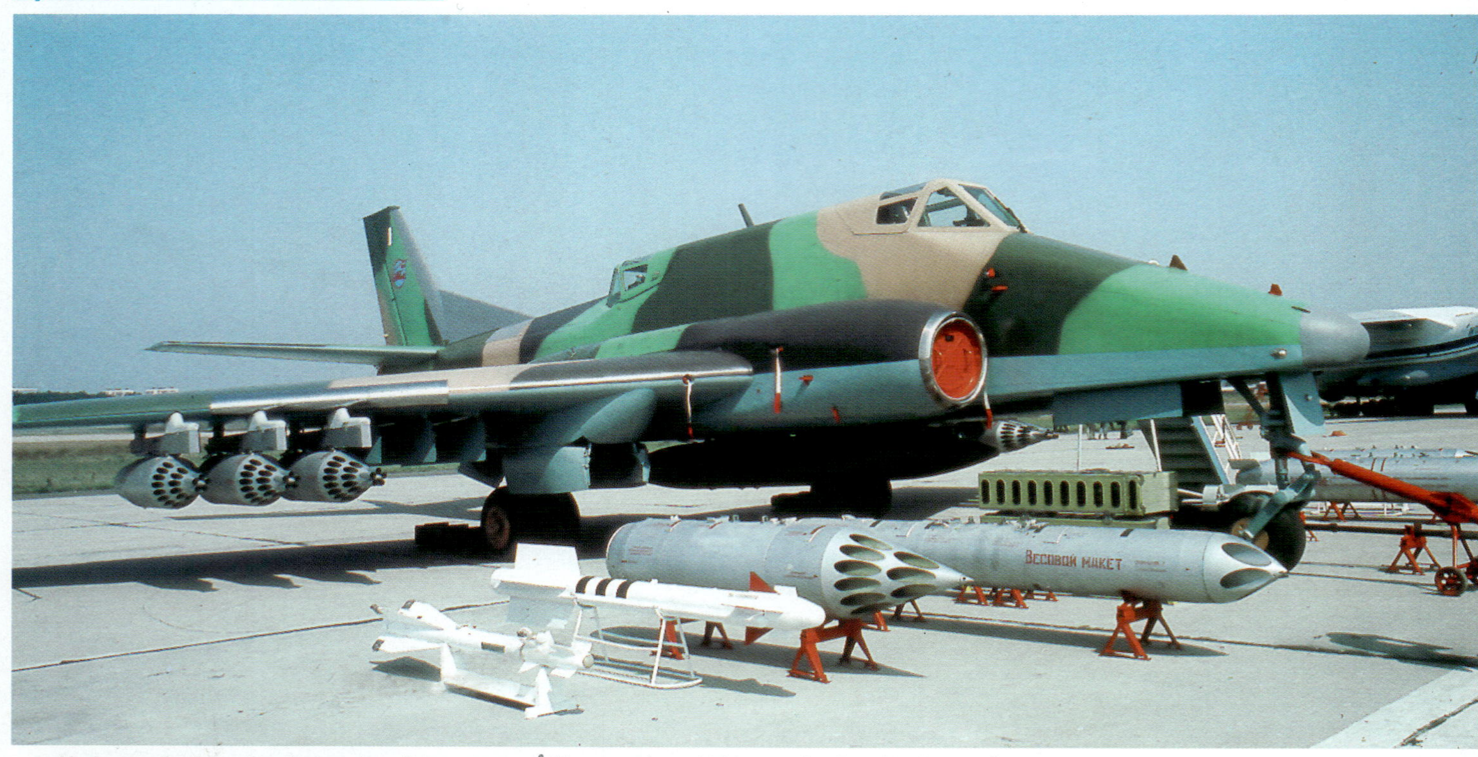

Undoubtedly the oddest new aircraft to appear at Mosaeroshow 1992 was the Ilyushin IL-102 Shturmovik II attack aircraft. Believe it or not, this dinosaur first flew in 1982! Design started in the late 1950s as a successor to the 1953-vintage IL-40 Brawny attack aircraft, intended as a jet replacement for the IL-10 *Shturmovik*. With the decision to adopt the Su-7B as the new strike fighter, the Ilyushin IL-40 was cancelled.

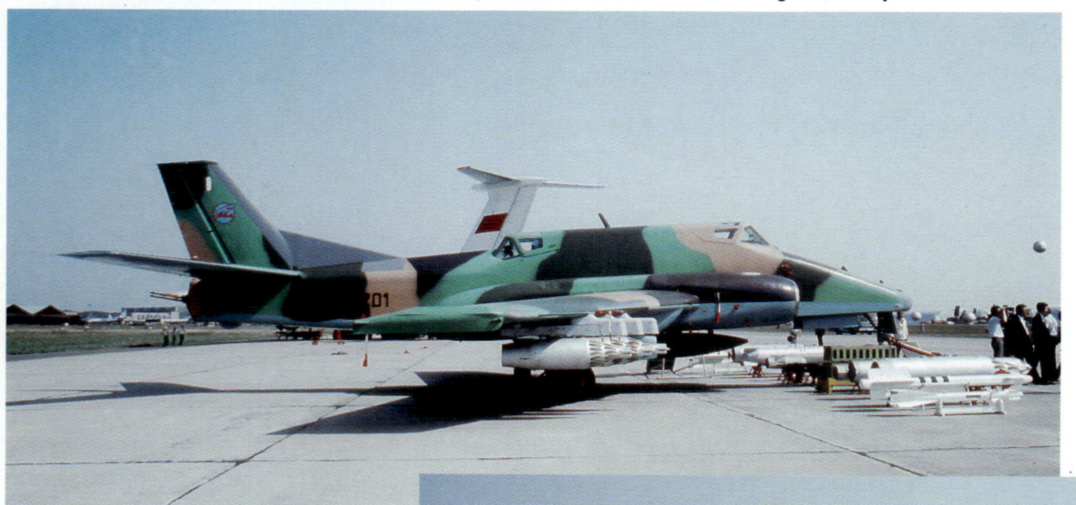

This side view shows the similarity of the IL-102 and the earlier IL-40. Apparently, the IL-40 program was resurrected in the late 1970s due to the Sukhoi Su-25 Frogfoot. The IL-102 still retained many hopelessly obsolete features, such as the rear defensive machine gun position. The main change between the IL-40 and IL-102 was the reconfiguration of the engine air intake from the unusual nose-mounted "pan-flute" style in the IL-40 to the more conventional wing root style in the IL-102. The engines in the IL-102 are the newer RD-33, the same type as in the MiG-29 fighter, but without afterburners.

The IL-102 has a crew of two, with the rear crewman operating the rear twin machine guns using an optical sight patterned on those found in the World War 2-vintage B-29 Superfortress bomber. Rear mounted tail guns disappeared in the late 1950s due to the advent of air-to-air missiles since such guns could no longer defend bombers against the longer ranged missiles.

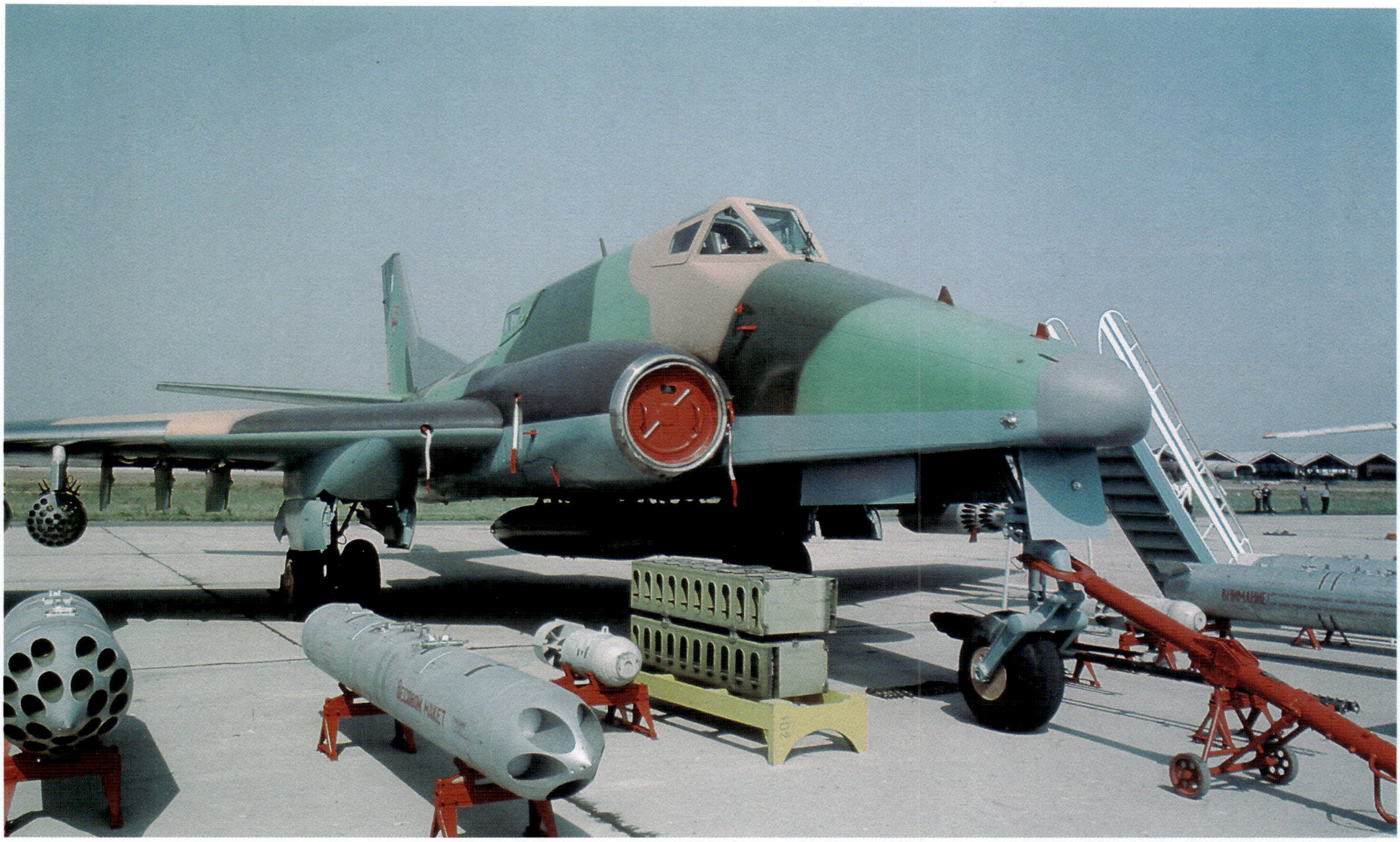

The IL-102 never entered production, but Ilyushin officials indicated the design could be put into production if there was foreign interest! Although the design is outdated, it has been designed to accept new ground attack ordnance such as the 80mm and 57mm rocket pods displayed in front of it. The green containers near the nose landing gear are submunition containers for the KMGU-500 cluster bomb.

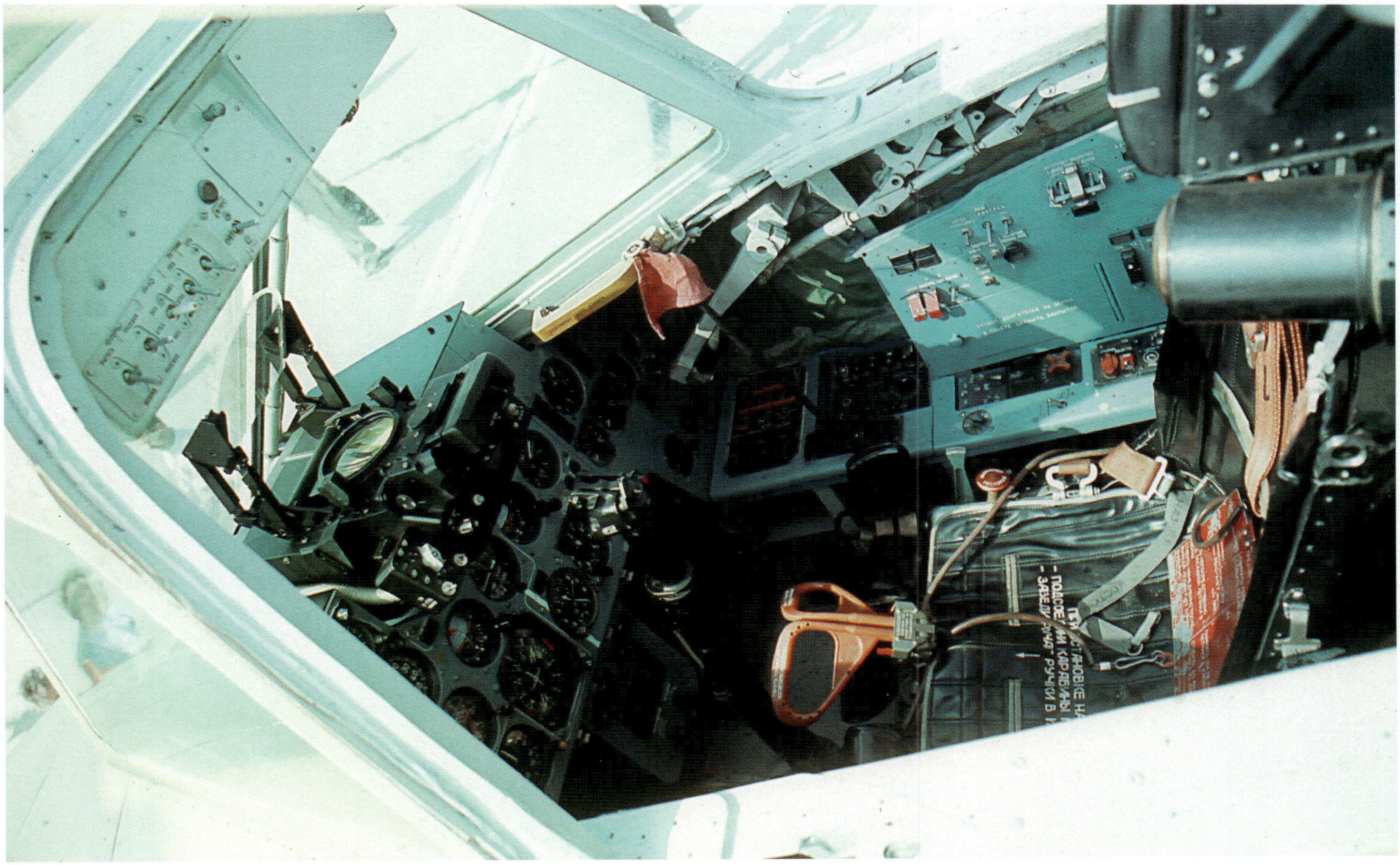

The cockpit interior of the IL-102 is very similar in general layout to contemporary Russian fighters, complete with a Heads-Up-Display.

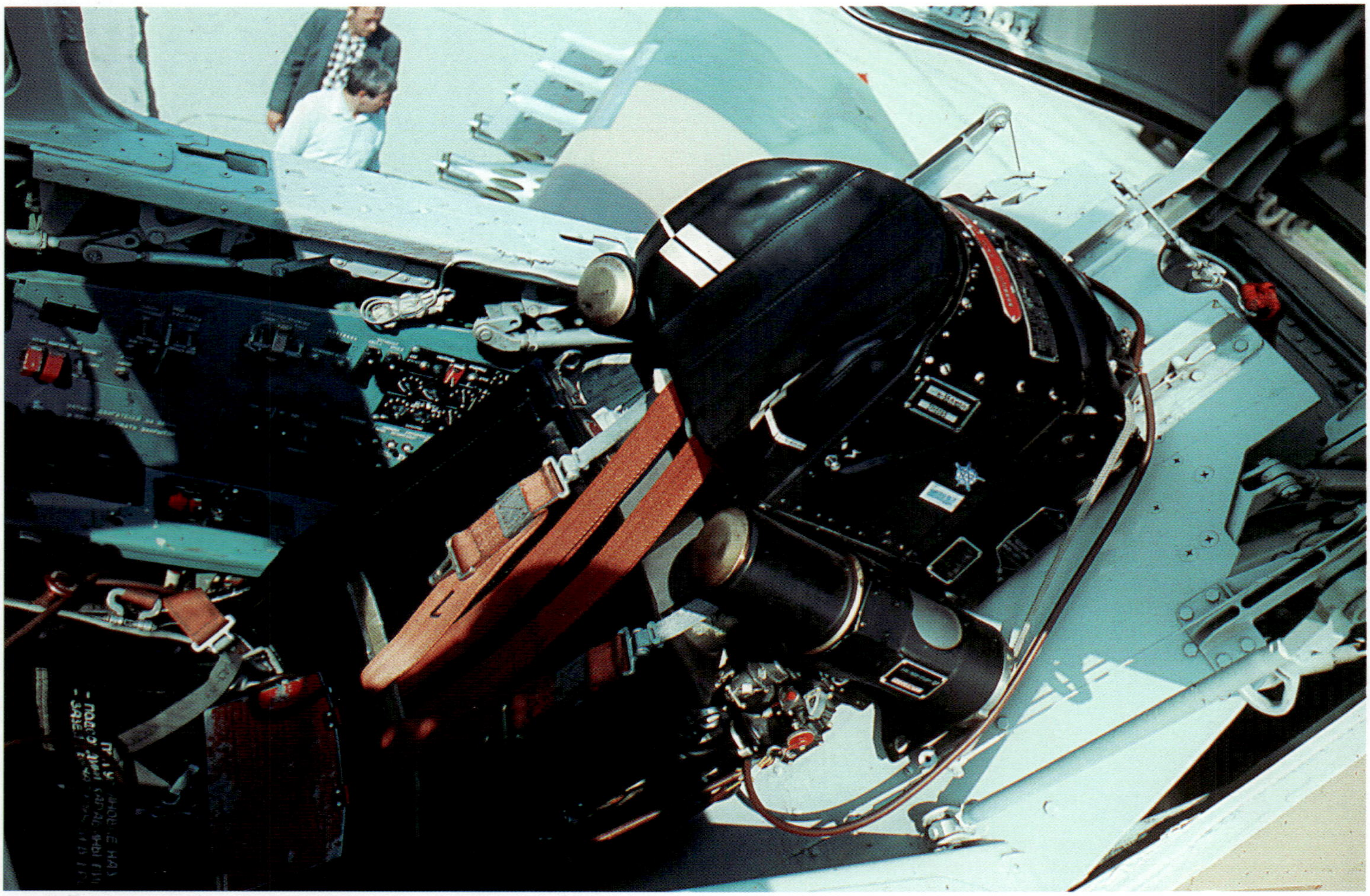

As a small concession to modernity, the IL-102 is fitted with a Severin K-36 ejection seat, like those fitted in other contemporary Russian fighters.

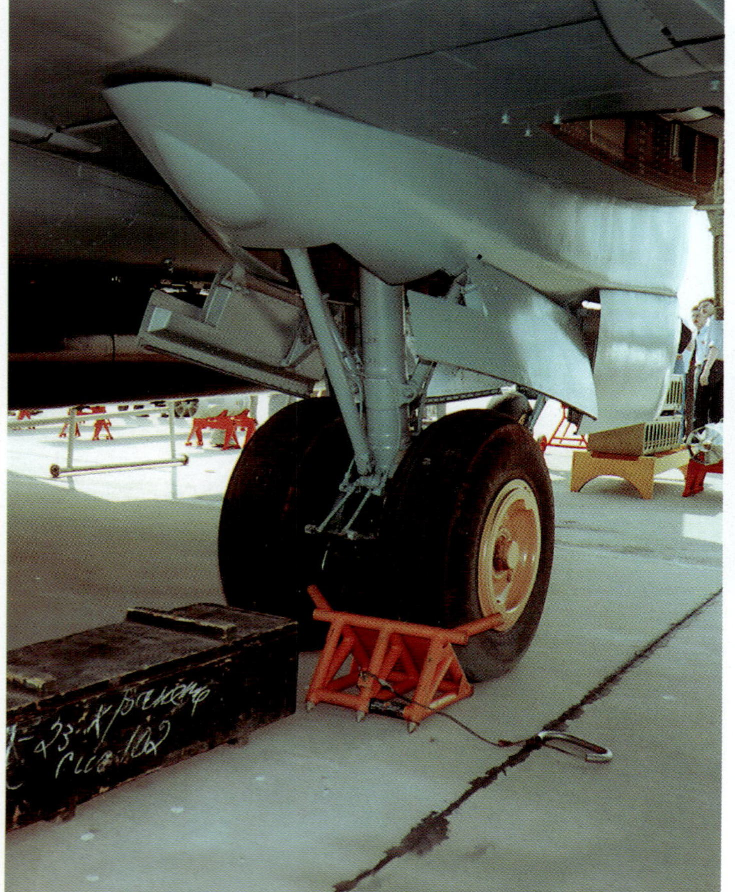

A close-up detail view of the main landing gear assembly on the IL-102 shturmovik.

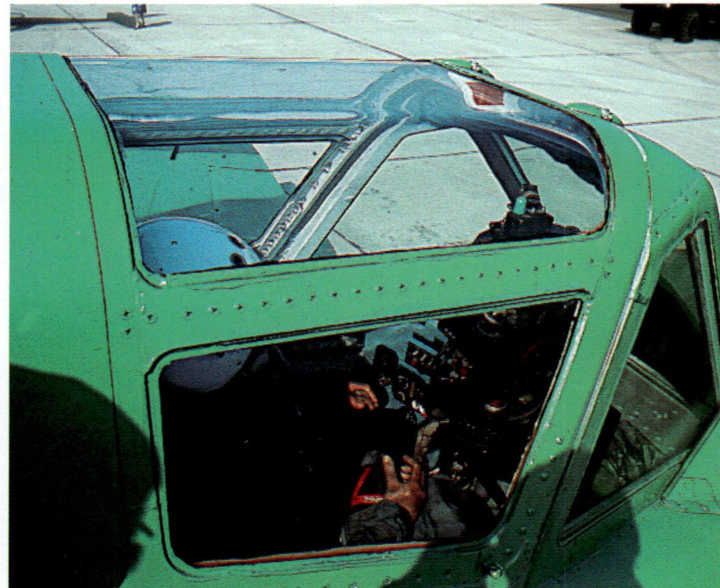

A close-up of the rear gunner's station. This feature is certainly one of the oddest of this aircraft, accenting its obsolete design roots.

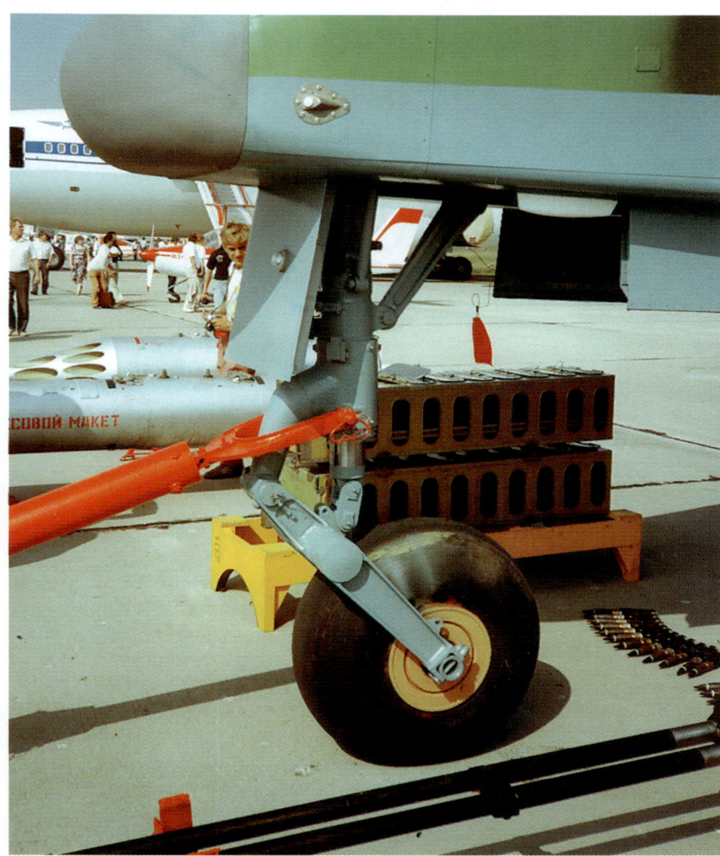

A detail view of the nose-wheel of the IL-102.

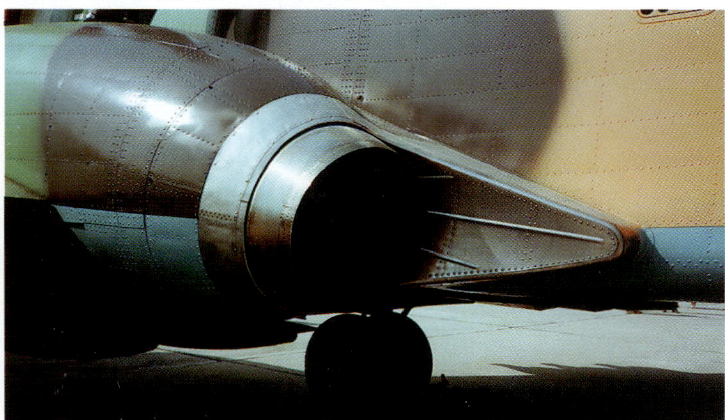

A detail view of the titanium exhaust cover and engine exhaust on the IL-102. This aircraft is powered by two RD-331 jet engines, the same type as in the MiG-29 fighter, but minus the afterburners.

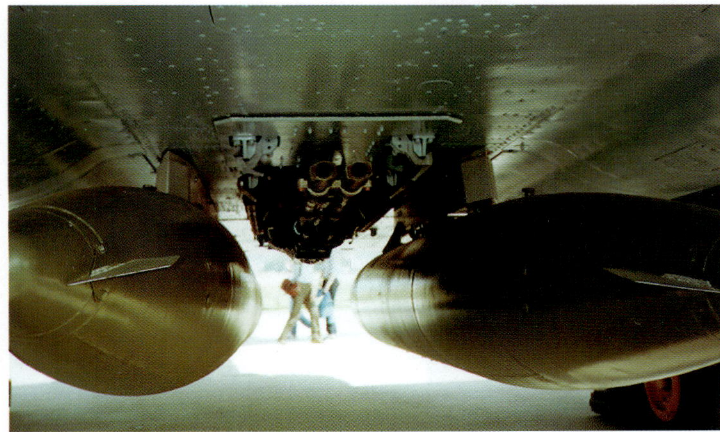

An underbelly view of the twin 30mm cannon on the IL-102. Reportedly, other gun packages could be fitted including a 45mm and 57mm cannon!

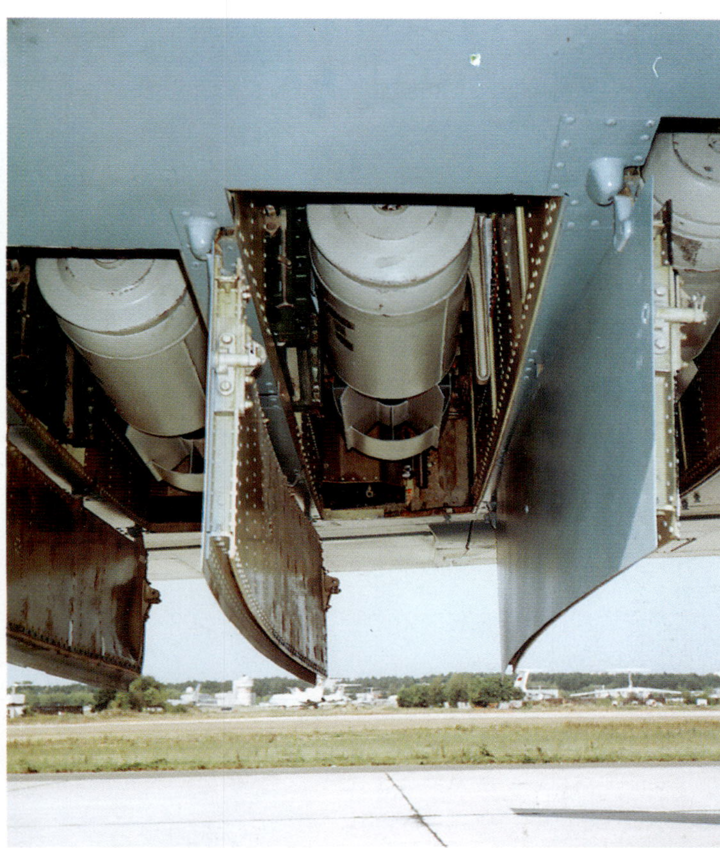

Another reminder of World War 2 shturmovik design is the provision of wing-mounted bomb-bays on the IL-102, much likes its ancestor, the legendary IL-2M *shturmovik*. This aircraft has a payload of 7.2 tons.

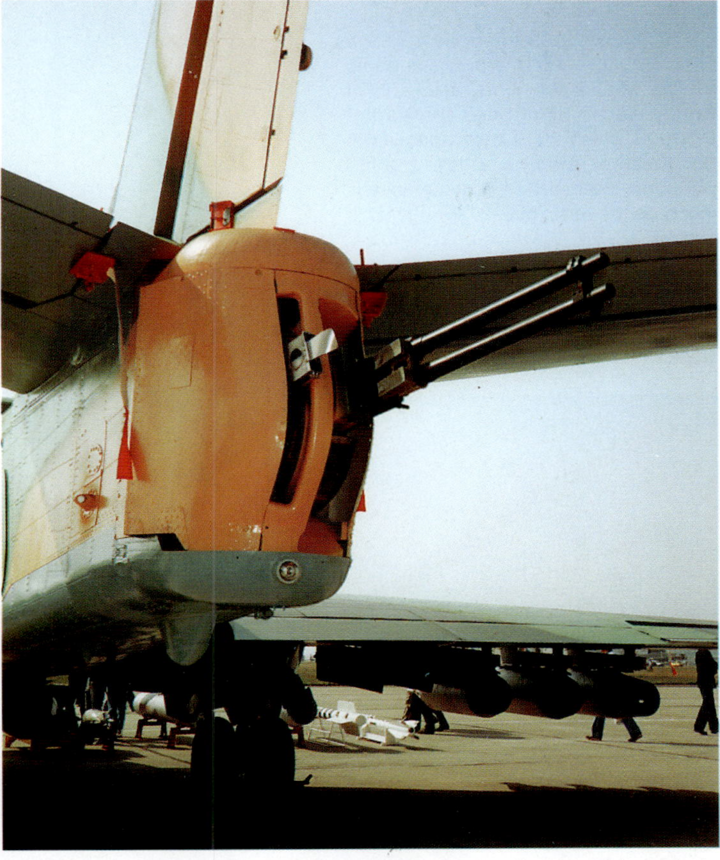

A detail view of the rear gun position on the IL-102. This archaic design feature is the strongest indication of how old the IL-102 design must be. Few modern aircraft have such positions since they cannot offer protection from missile-armed enemy fighters. The small device next to the two cannon is probably the remote television sight for the gun.

Mikoyan MiG-27M Flogger J

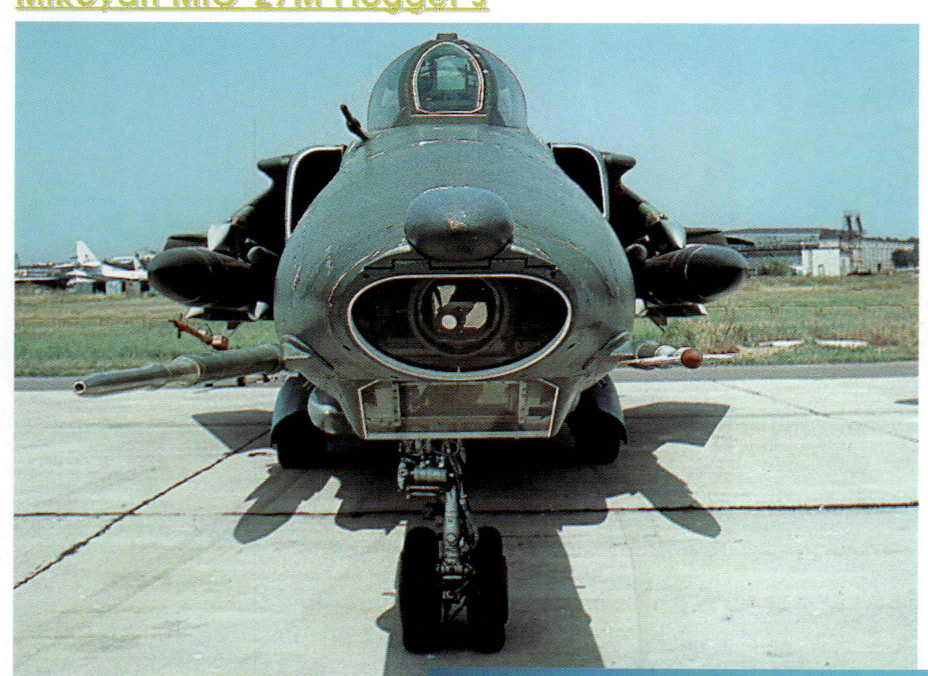

The Mikoyan MiG-27M Flogger J is the final member of this versatile strike fighter family and can be distinguished by its unique nose. The two optical ports are part of the PrNK-23M navigation/attack system and consist of a stabilized laser rangefinder and laser target designator.

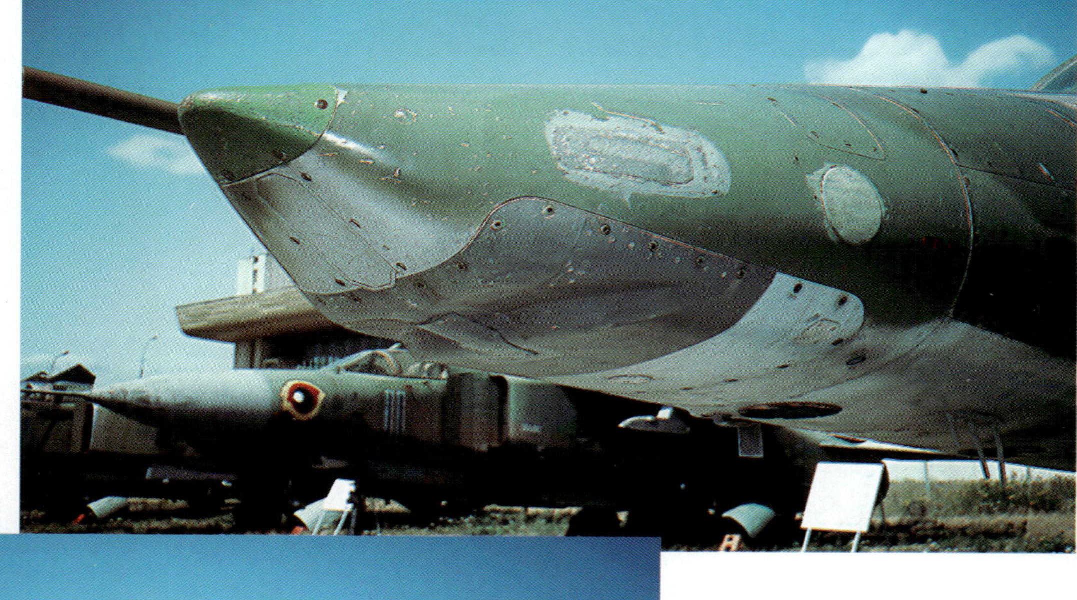

Compare this nose view of the basic MiG-23B with the previous photo of the MiG-27M. This aircraft, at Khodynka air field, uses the earlier PrNK-23 which lacks the capability to fire laser or electro-optical guided weapons. Essentially the same nose is found on the basic MiG-27 Flogger D.

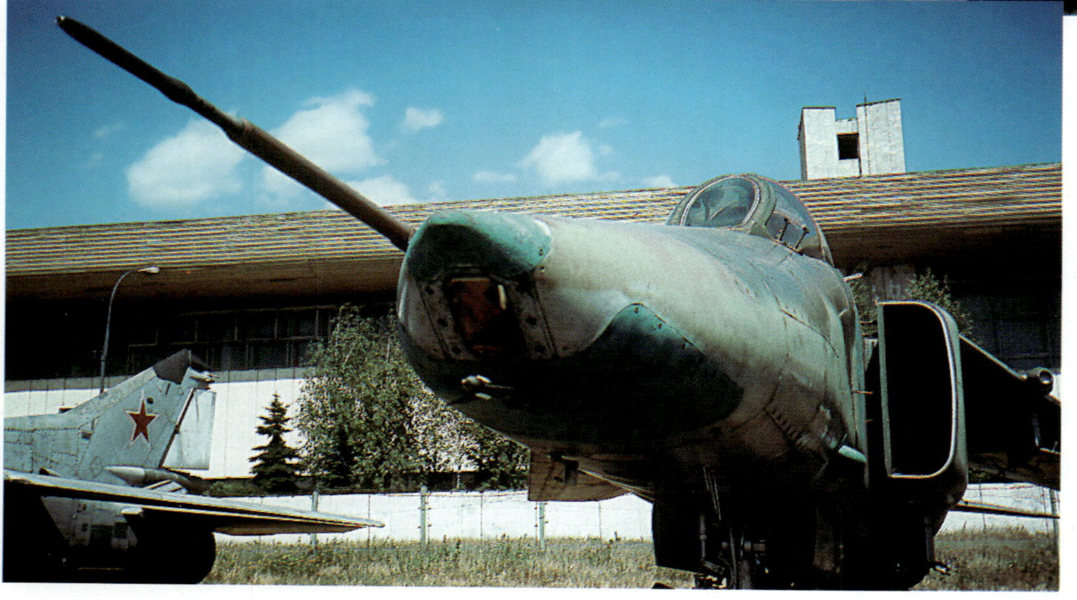

Another nose view of a MiG-27, this time the improved MiG-27K Flogger J. This aircraft uses the PrNK-23K *Klen* navigation/attack system and has a small optical port in the nose for a laser rangefinder. This nose is also found on the MiG-23BK.

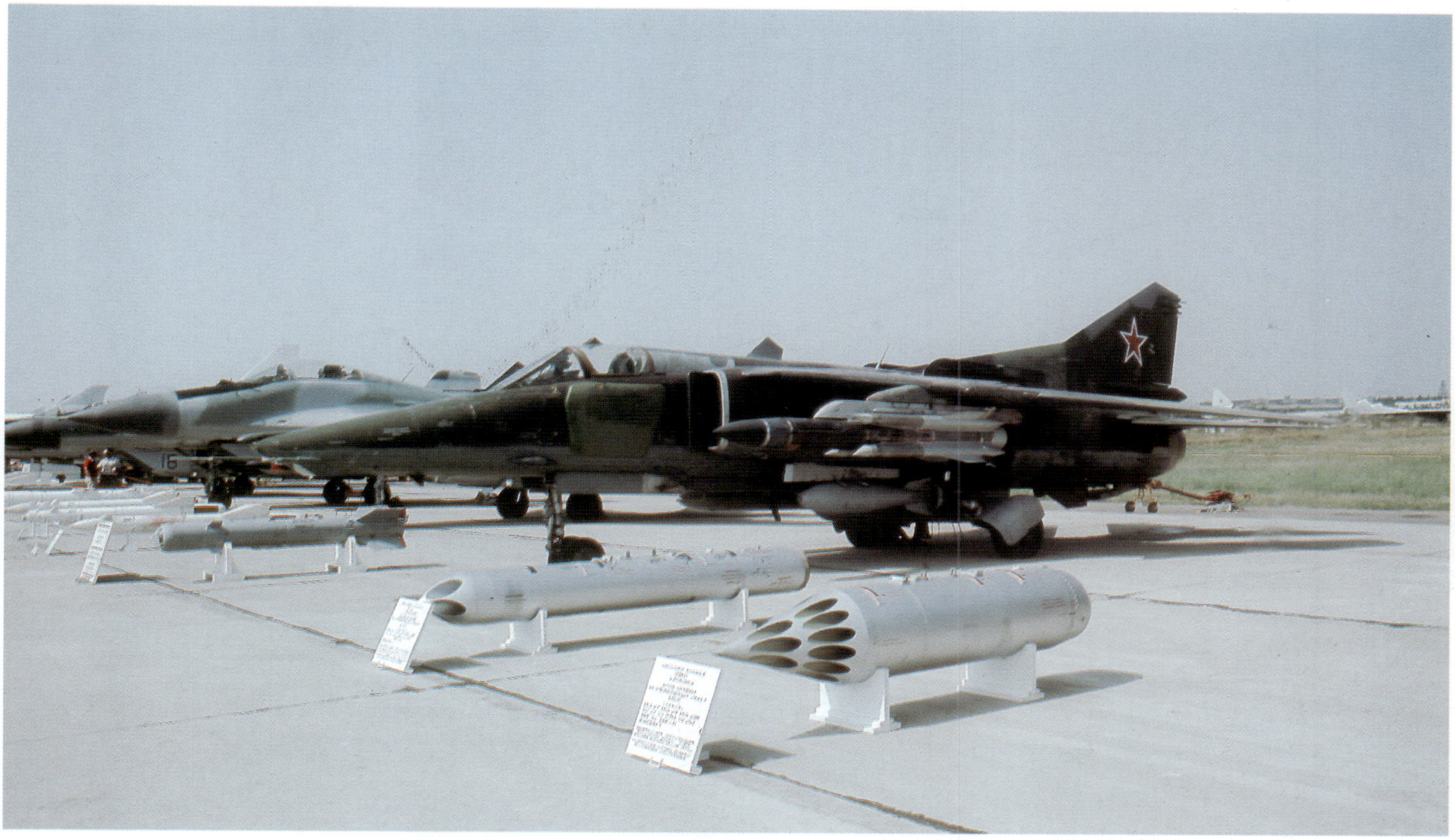

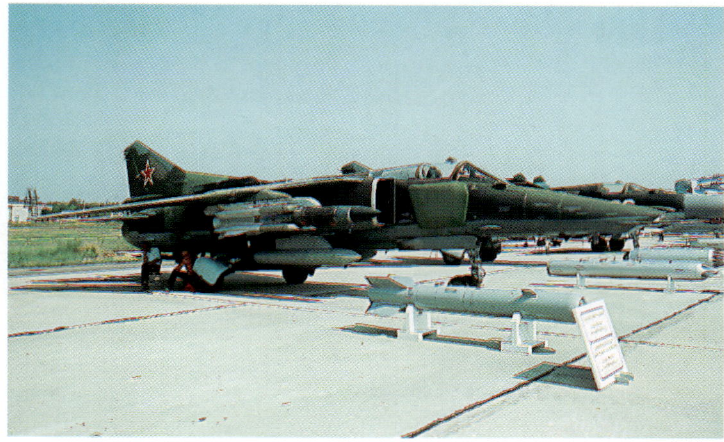

A left side view of the MiG-27M showing another Kh-31P anti-radiation missile under the wing pylon, and a FAB-500 bomb under the air-intake pylon. Interestingly enough, the applique armor on the side of the cockpit is painted in a lighter shade of green than the rest of the aircraft.

A right side view of the MiG-27M armed with a Kh-31P anti-radiation missile. When armed with such weapons, the host aircraft is fitted with an APK-8 pod, seen on the pylon under the missile, which contains electronic sensing equipment to acquire the radar target as well as a data link system. This system is used in lieu of the BA-58 belly pack seen on Su-22M4s fitted for the anti-radar role.

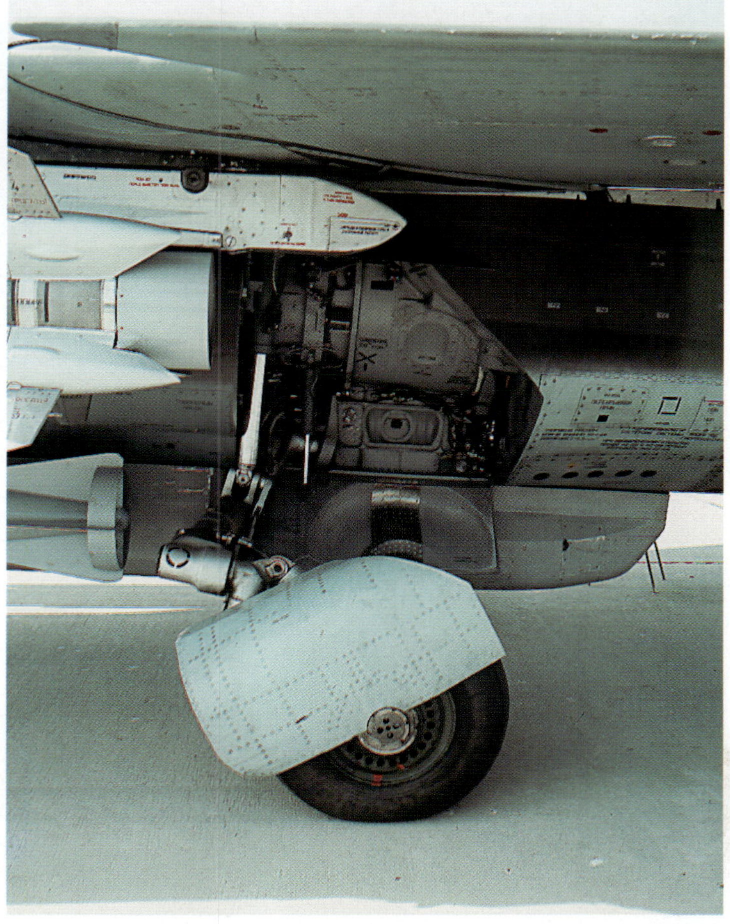

A detail view of the port wheel well of the MiG-27M, finished in the same blue-grey color as the undersurface color.

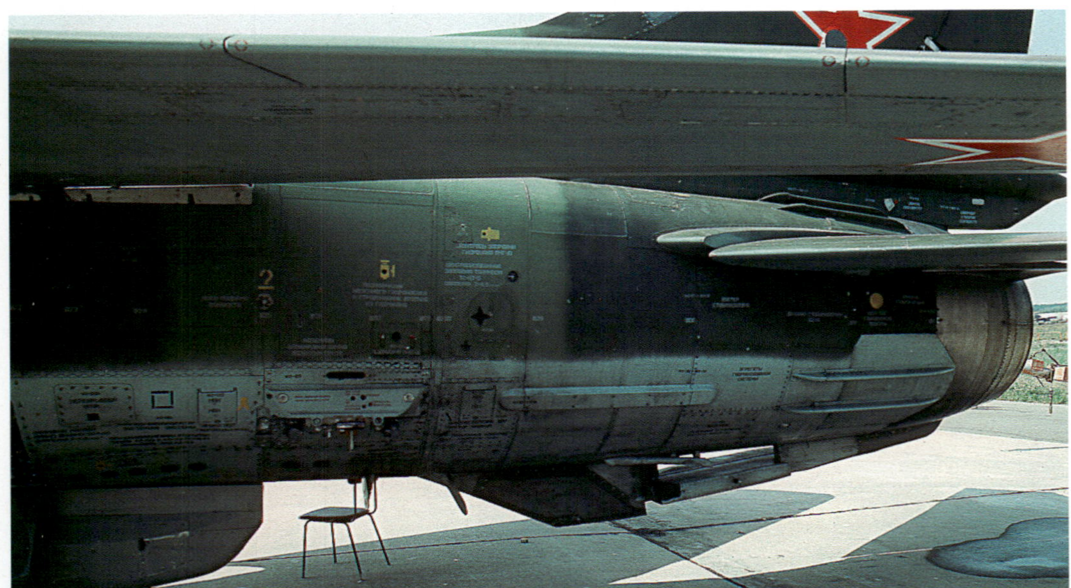

A detail view of the rear fuselage of the MiG-27M showing the proliferation of stenciling as well as the shackles for the unusual rear fuselage bomb rack.

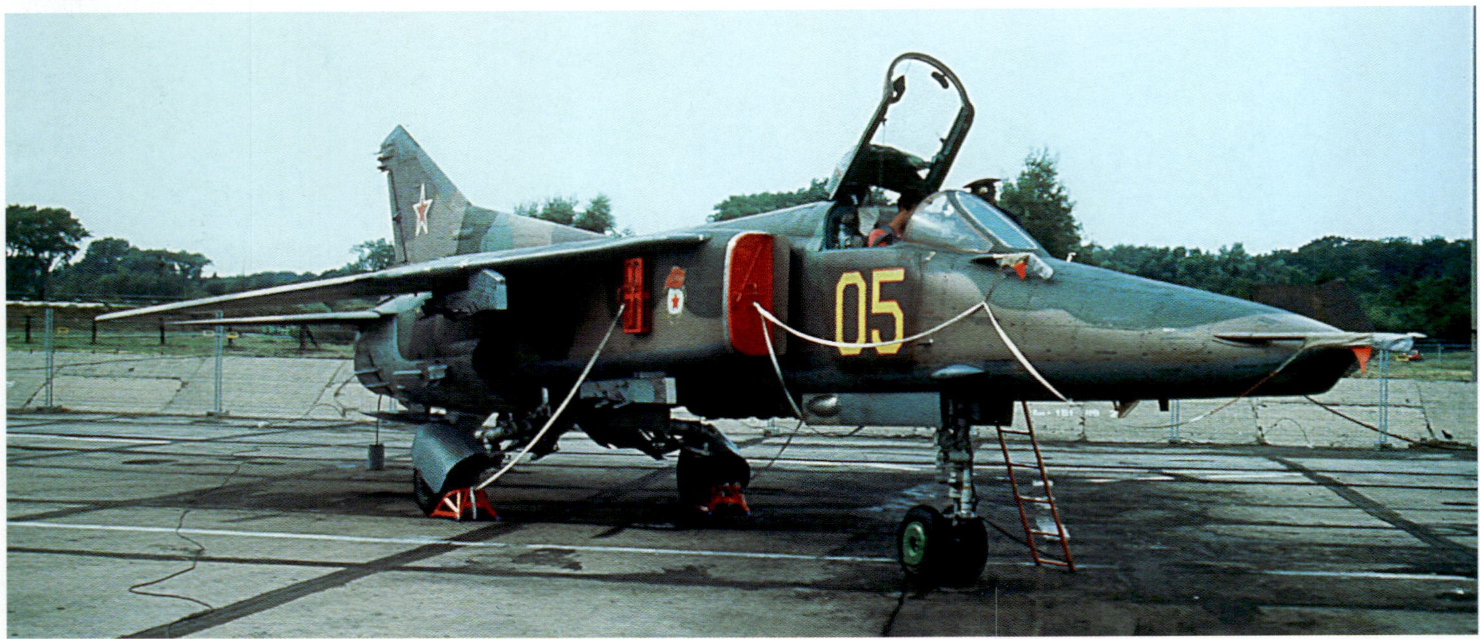

A MiG-27M, probably of the 125th Guards Fighter-Bomber Division, displayed at Damgarten in July 1992. The aircraft wears the traditional Guards emblem on the air intake, and carries its *bort* number in yellow on the fuselage applique armor panel. (Michael Jerchel)

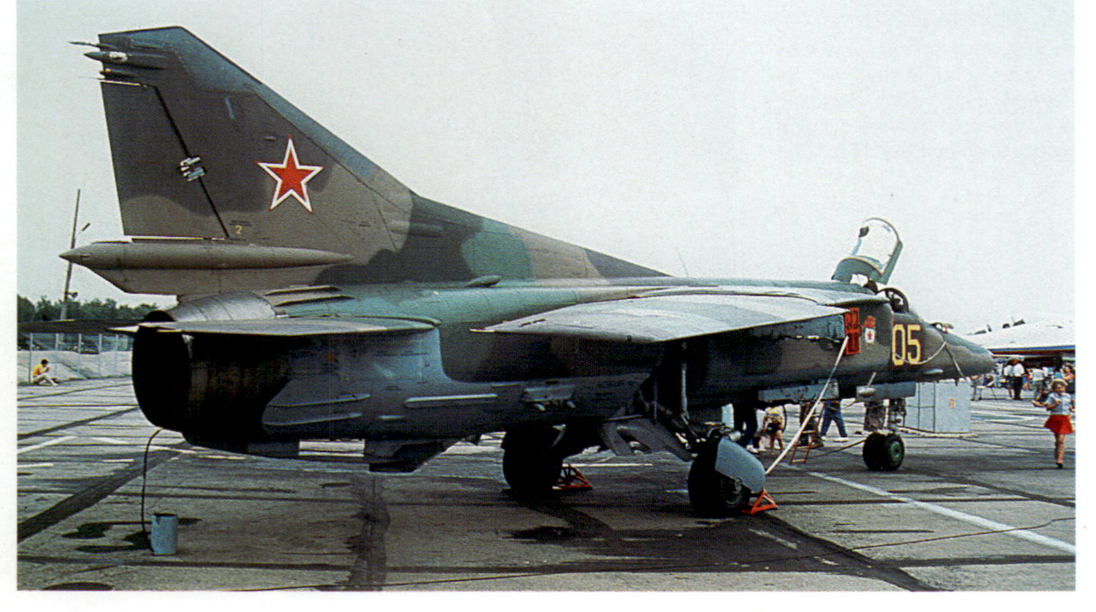

Another view of the MiG-27M showing the standard European strike fighter camouflage of earth brown, medium green and dark green. Compare this to the scheme of the MiG-27M displayed at Zhukovskiy. The reason for these variations in tactical camouflage patterns has never been made clear. (Michael Jerchel)

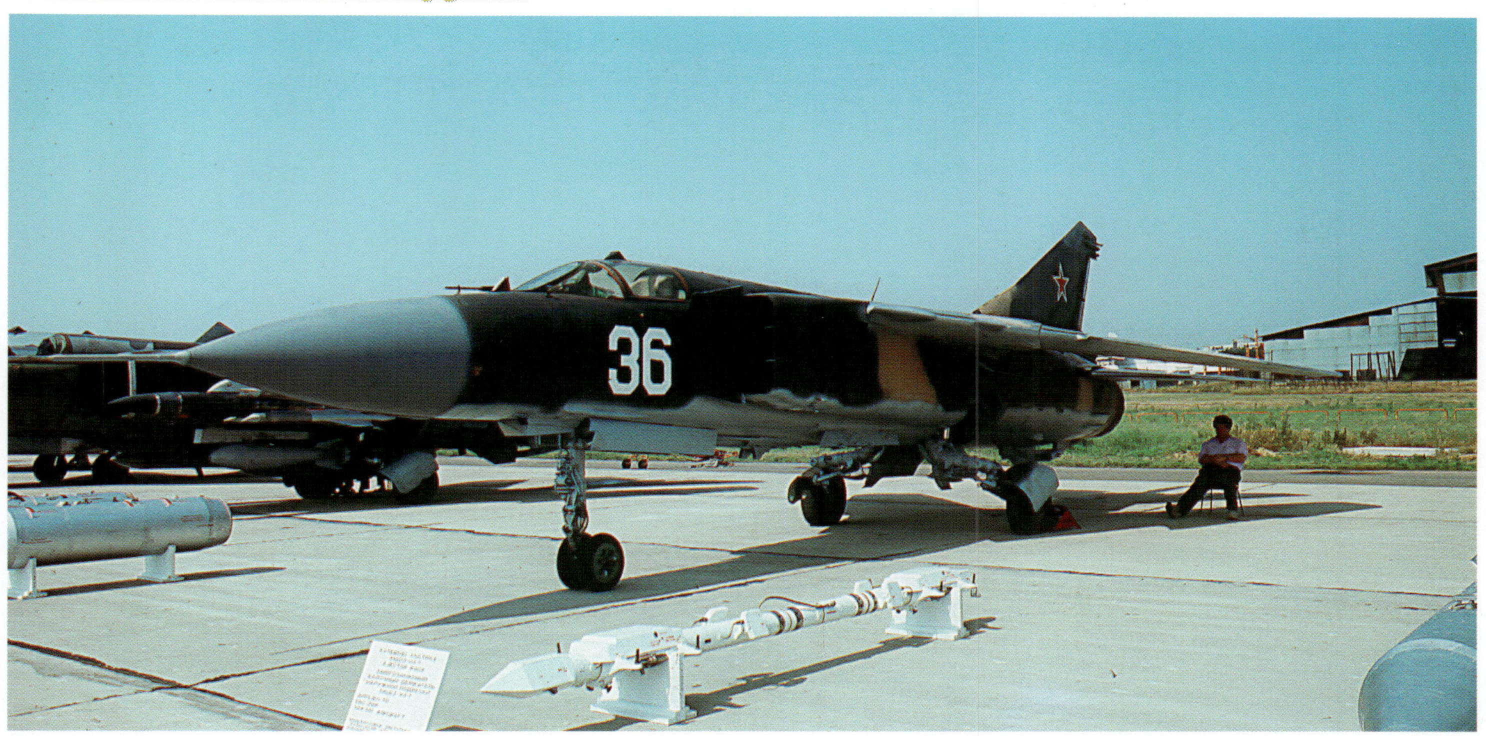

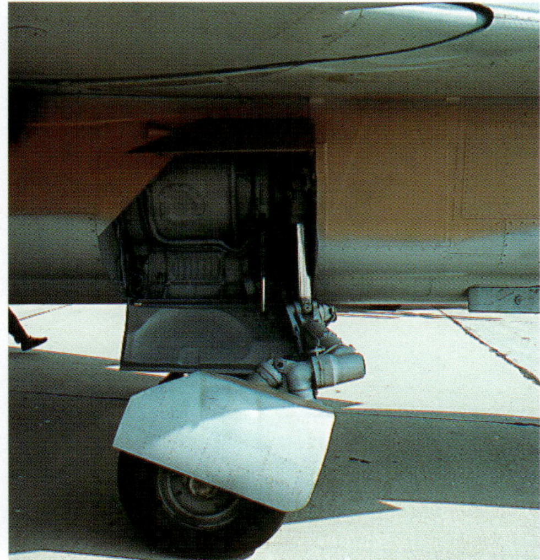

The final fighter version of the Flogger family is the MiG-23MLD Flogger K. This version can be distinguished by the dog-tooth leading edge at the wing root, added to improve air flow over the wing. The long white device on the ground is an MBD3-U4-T multiple ejector bomb rack.

A detail view of the starboard wheel well of the MiG-23MLD.

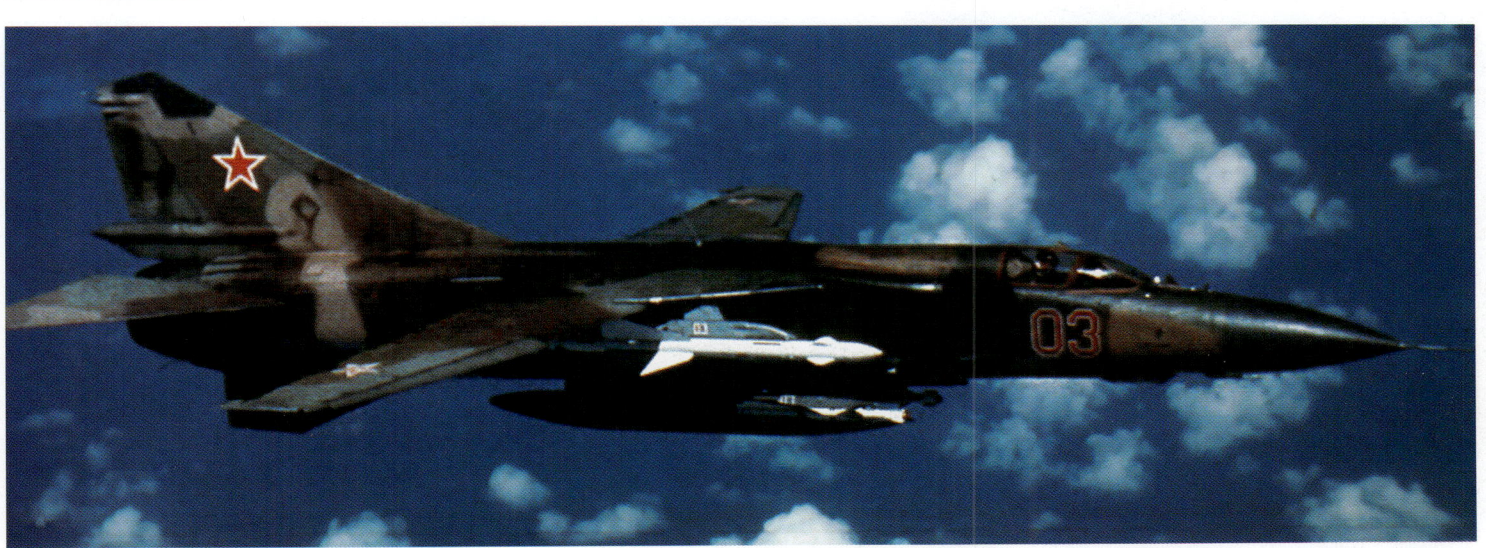

A MiG-23MLD Flogger K over the South China Sea in 1989. This aircraft was based at Cahm Ran Bay in Vietnam until the early 1990s when it was withdrawn back to Russia. The regiment used a shark insignia on the rudder, but on this aircraft, it has been painted over. (US Navy)

MIKOYAN MIG-25 FOXBAT

Mikoyan MiG-25RBK Foxbat D

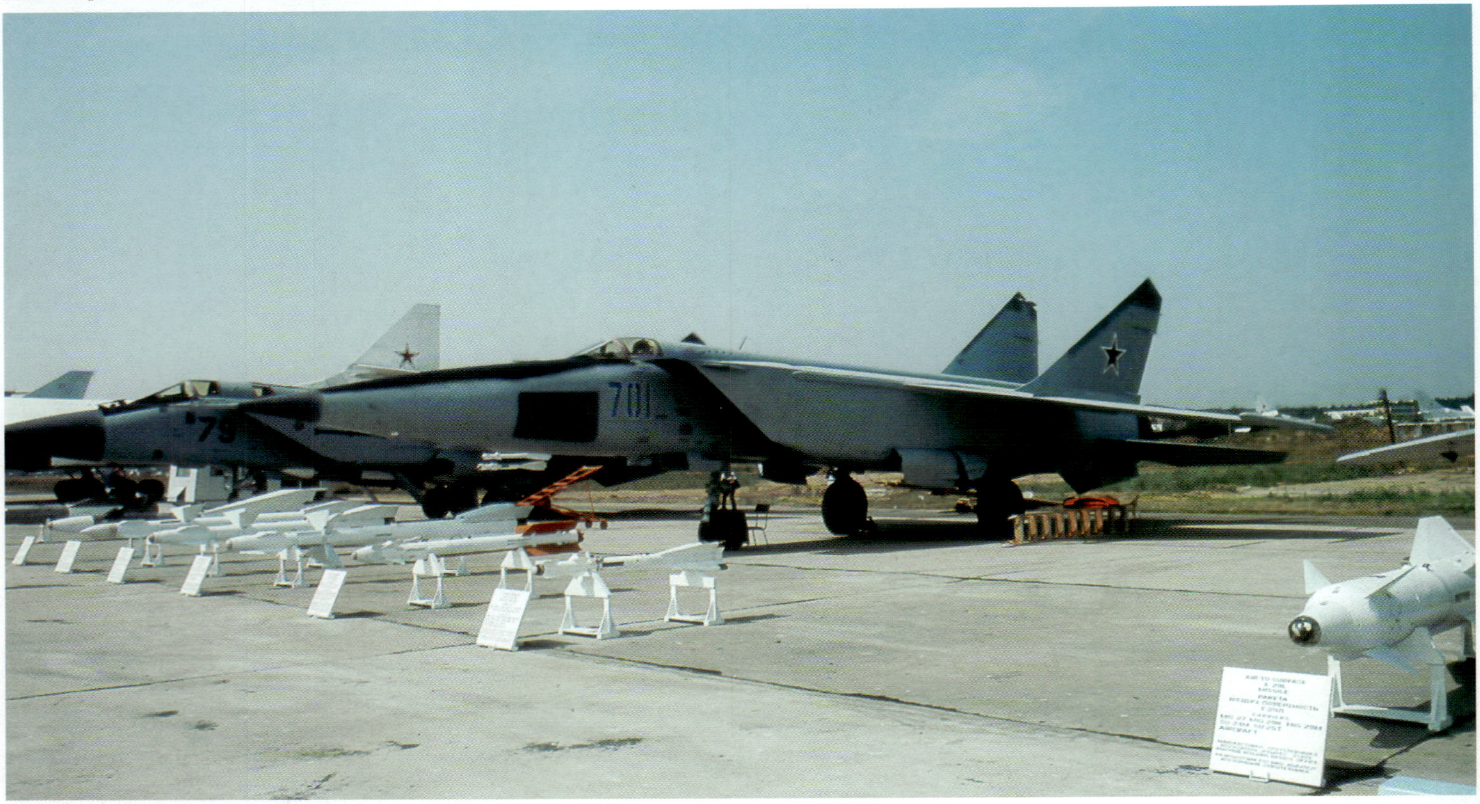

A Mikoyan MiG-25RBK Foxbat D reconnaissance fighter. This particular version of the Foxbat family has the *Kub* side-looking radar (SLAR), evident from the dark grey dielectric panel in front of the *bort* number 701.

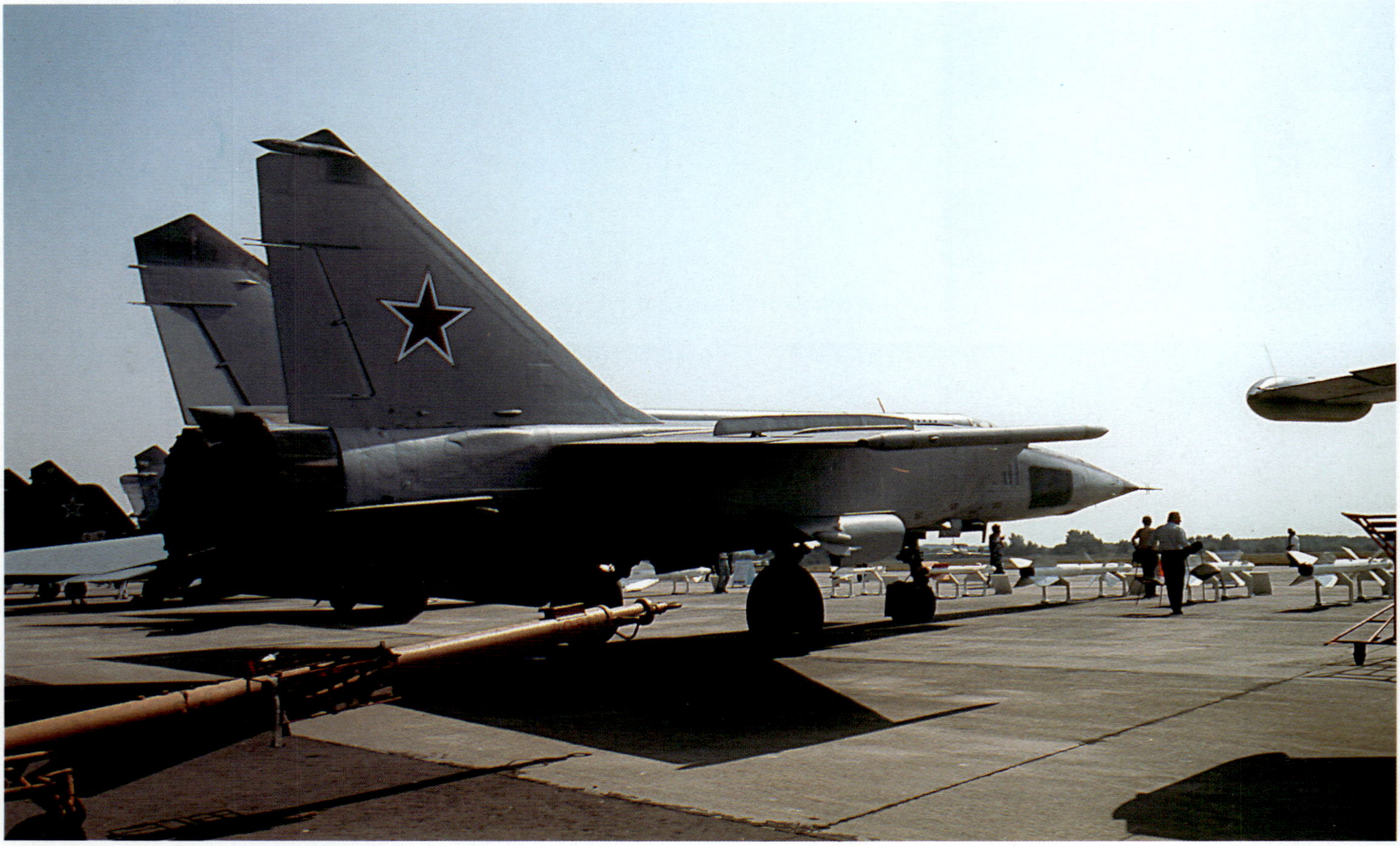

A starboard rear view of the MiG-25RBK. This version, unlike the earlier MiG-25RB, does not carry nose-mounted cameras. As displayed here, the aircraft is clean of any defensive armament.

Mikoyan MiG-29K

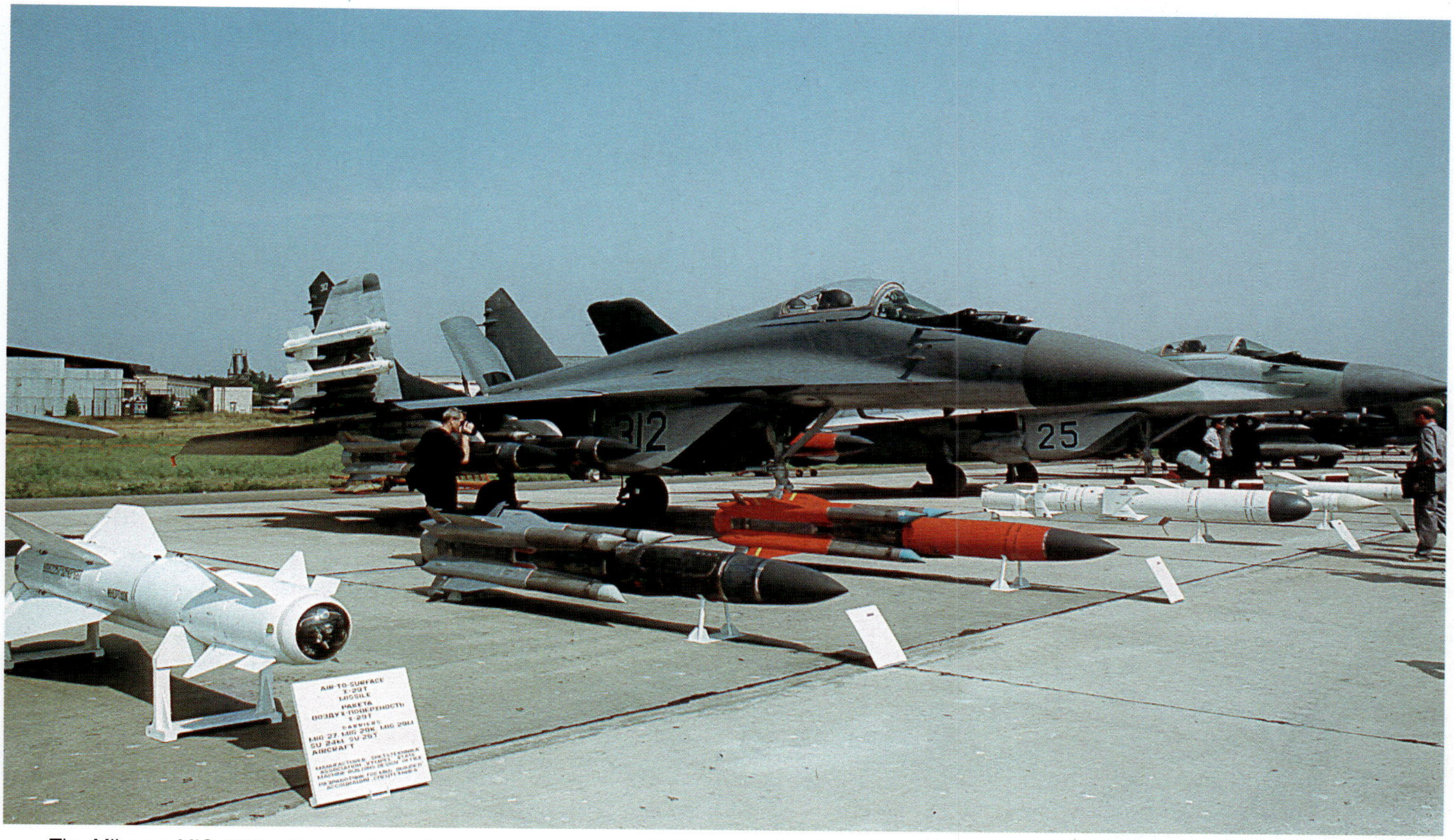

The Mikoyan MiG-29K is the navalized fighter version of the Fulcrum family. Compared to the basic MiG-29 (Obiekt 9.12), there are several obvious changes in the design, including the folding wings, rear fuselage speed brake, and modified hard-points for air-to-surface missiles.

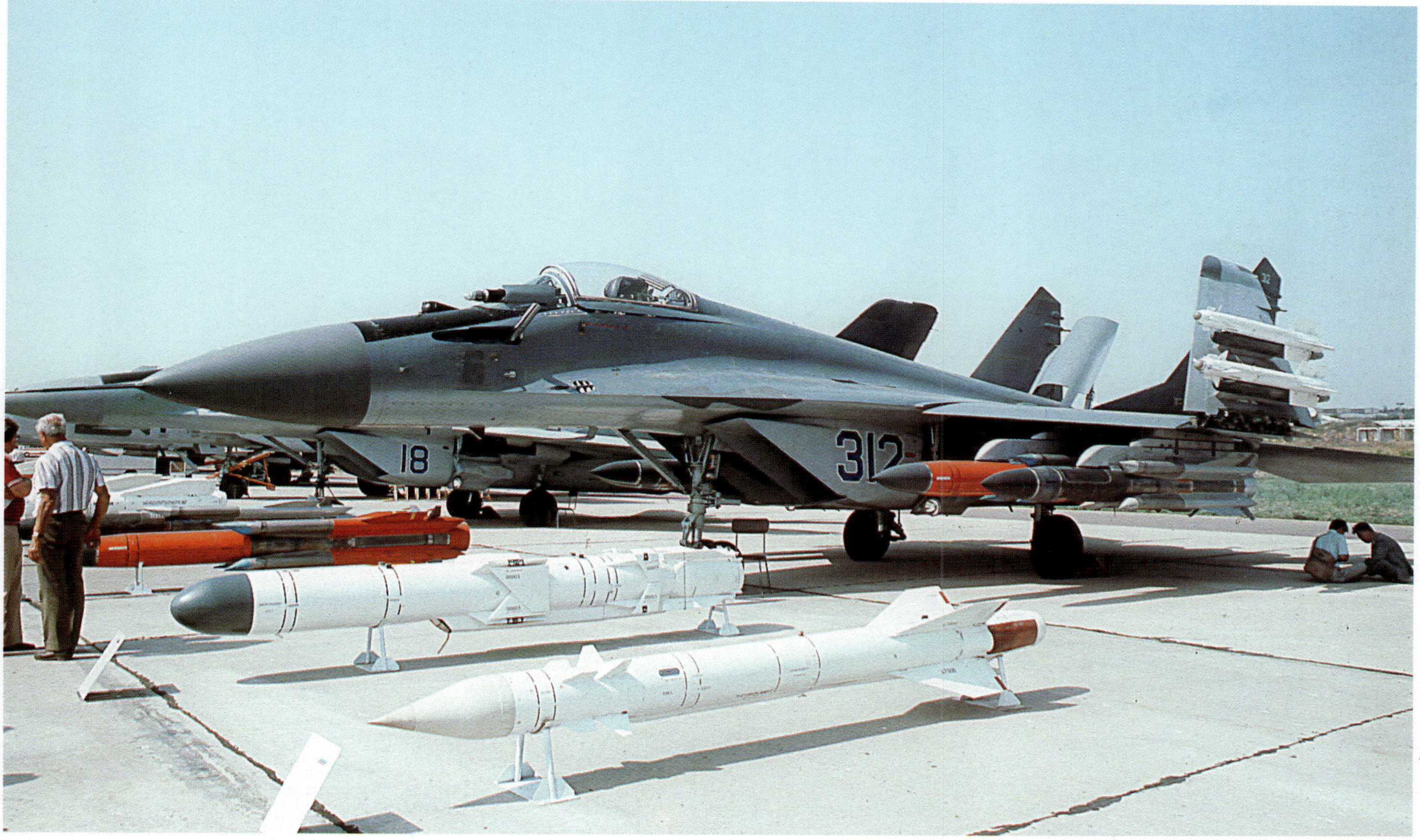

This port side view of the MiG-29K shows additional detail differences from earlier variants. Most noticeable is the refueling probe.

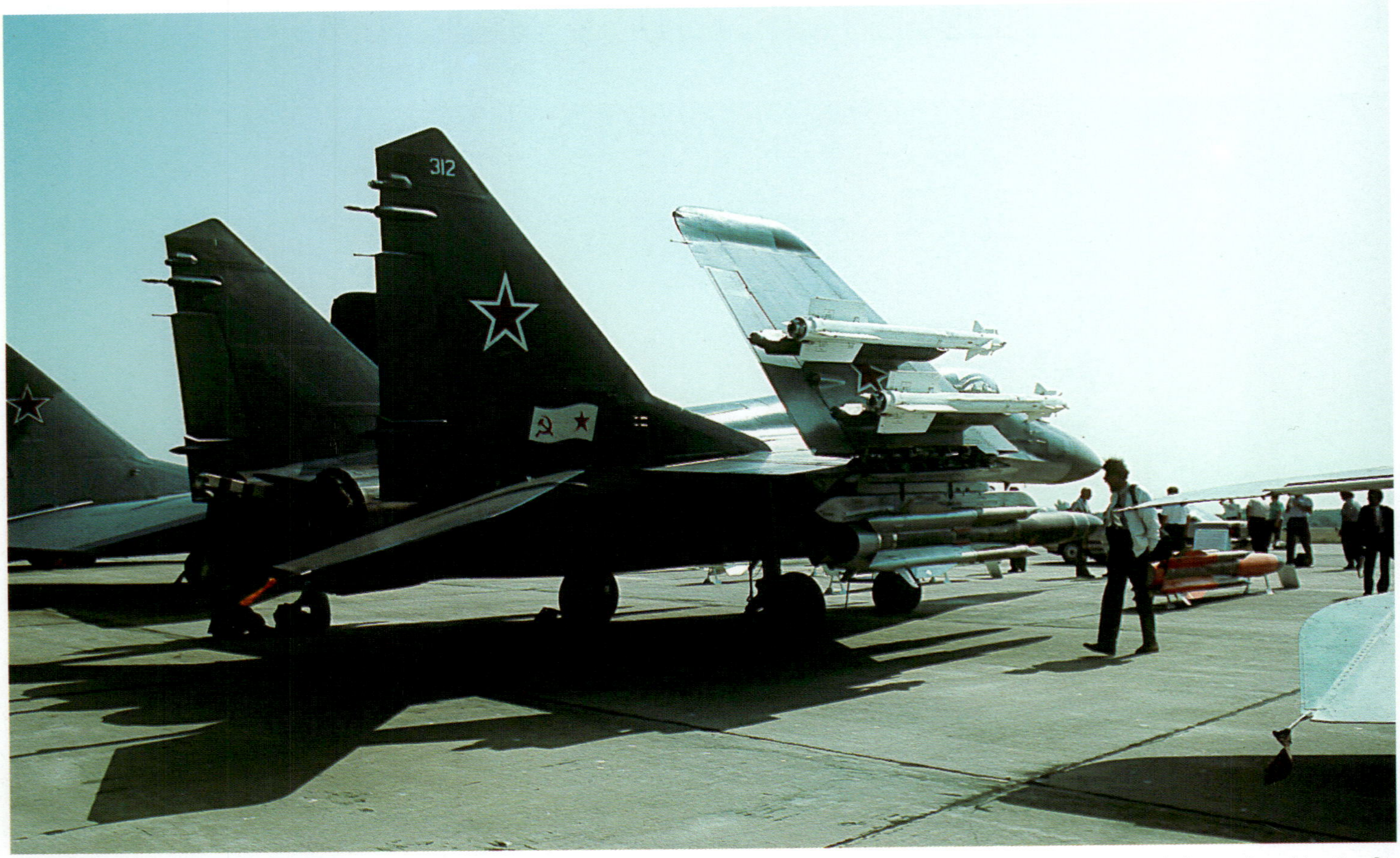

A rear-view of the MiG-29K with its wings folded. The flag on the tail is the traditional naval ensign of the Soviet Fleet, being replaced by the St. Andrew's Cross since August 1992.

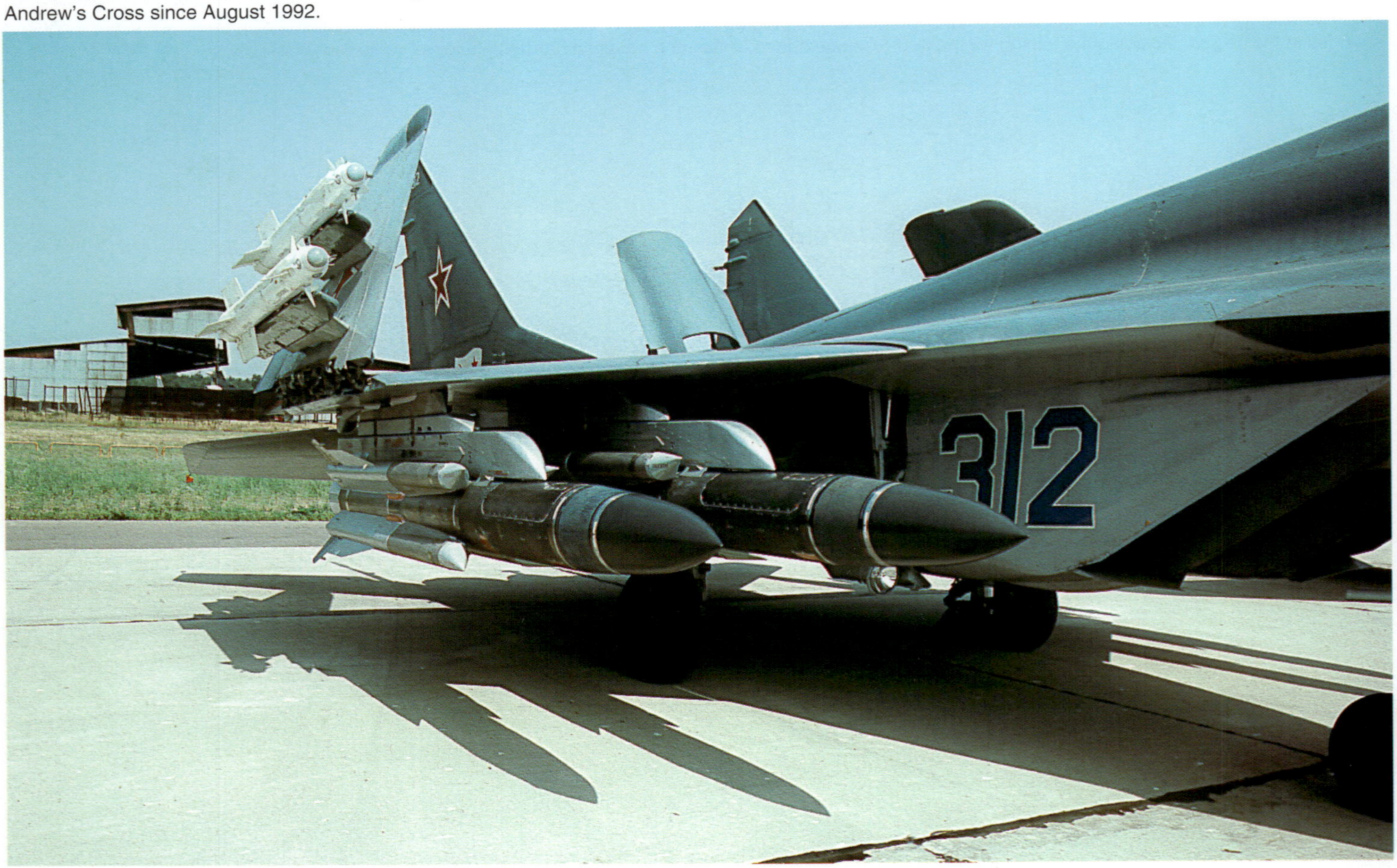

A detail view of the wing showing two Kh-31P anti-radar missiles under the inner wing , and two R-73 air-to-air missiles on the folded portion. The wing tip has dielectric panels for the aircraft's Gardeniya-1 ESM system, similar to the configuration on the land-based MiG-29S.

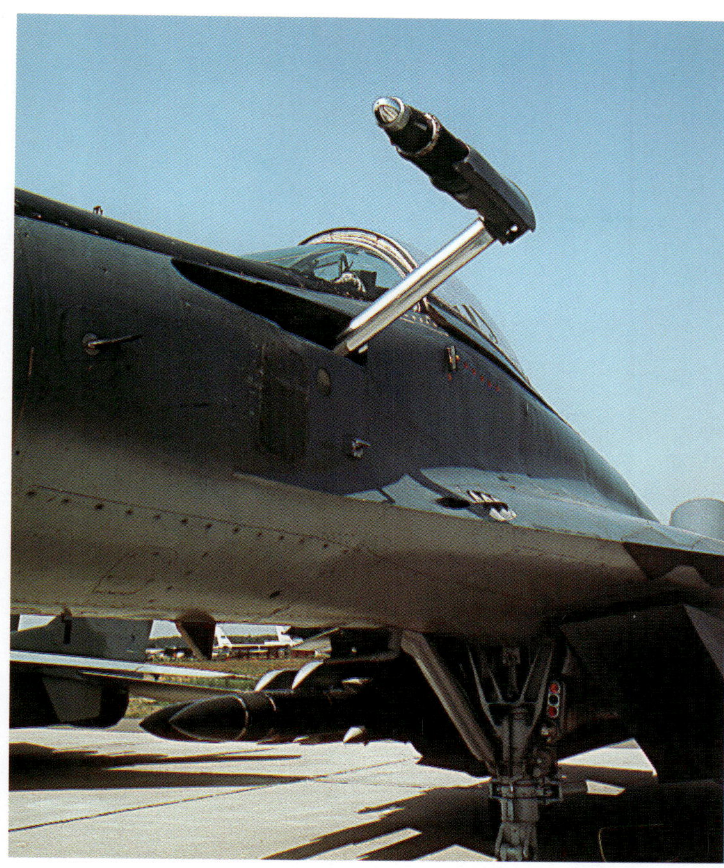

A detail view of the refueling probe on the port side of the nose. This was a critical addition for the naval version due to the MiG-29's poor range compared to its Su-27 competitor. It is still not clear whether the MiG-29K will be purchased in any numbers by the Russian Navy.

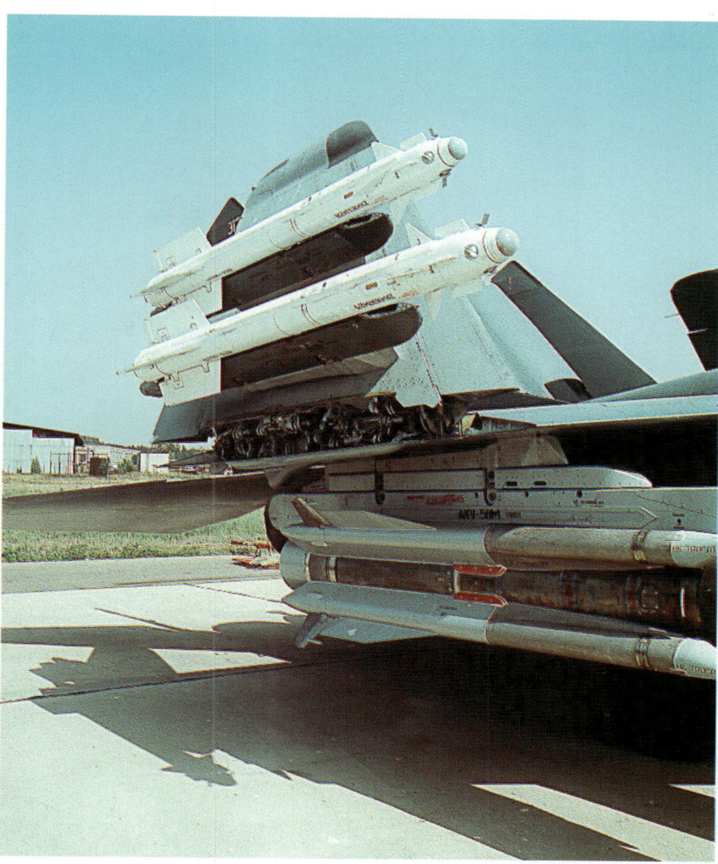

Another close-up view of the MiG-29K wing, showing additional details of the wing hinge area.

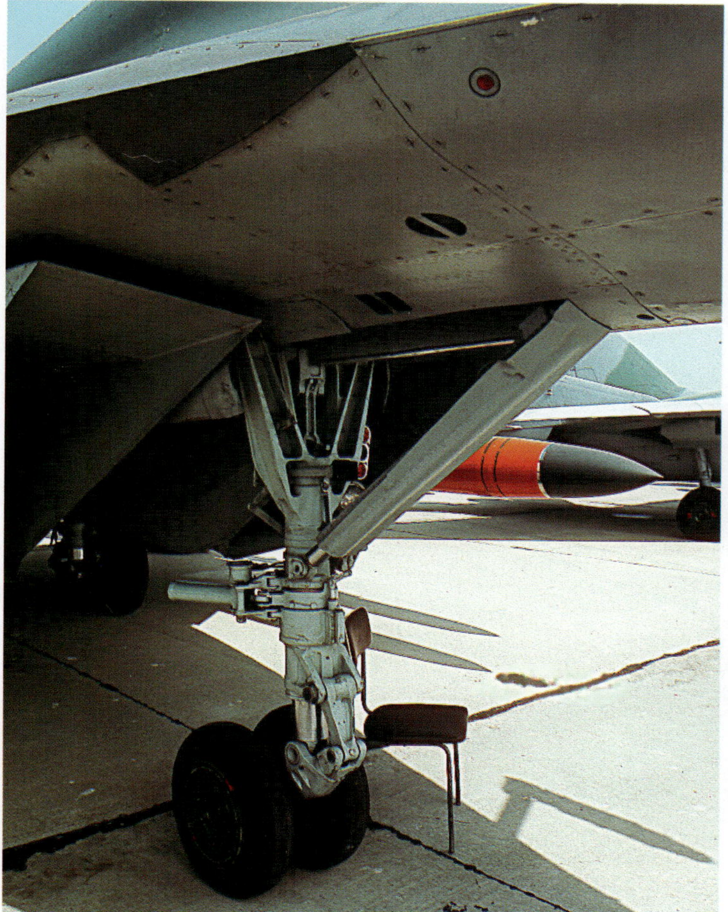

The reinforced forward landing gear of the MiG-29K naval fighter.

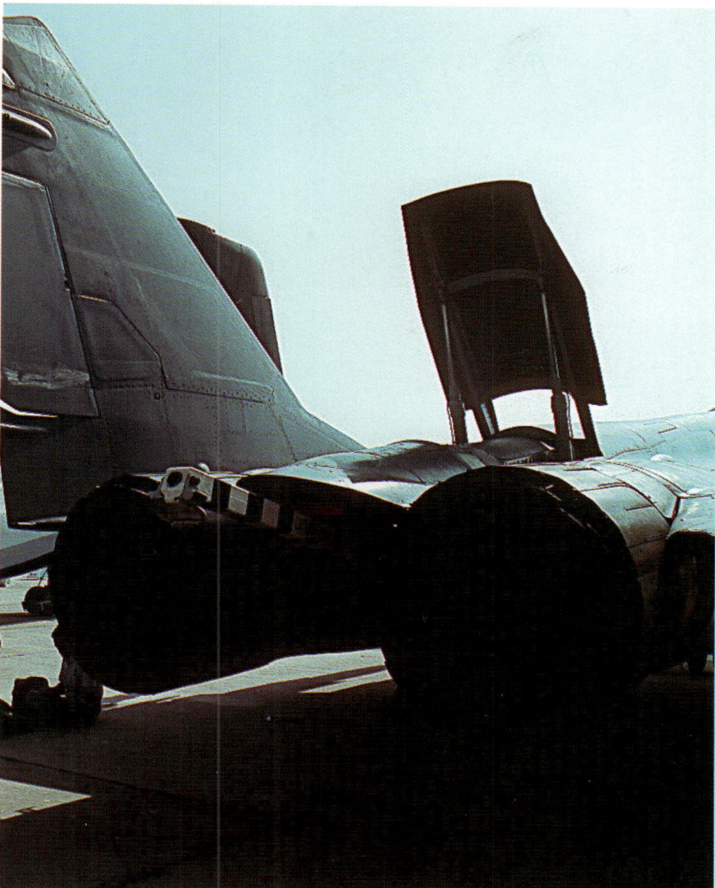

The MiG-29K is fitted with a large speed-brake instead of using braking parachutes as on the land-based versions. The rear of the fuselage has been reconfigured by the deletion of the brake parachute housing and the addition of the carrier arrestor hook.

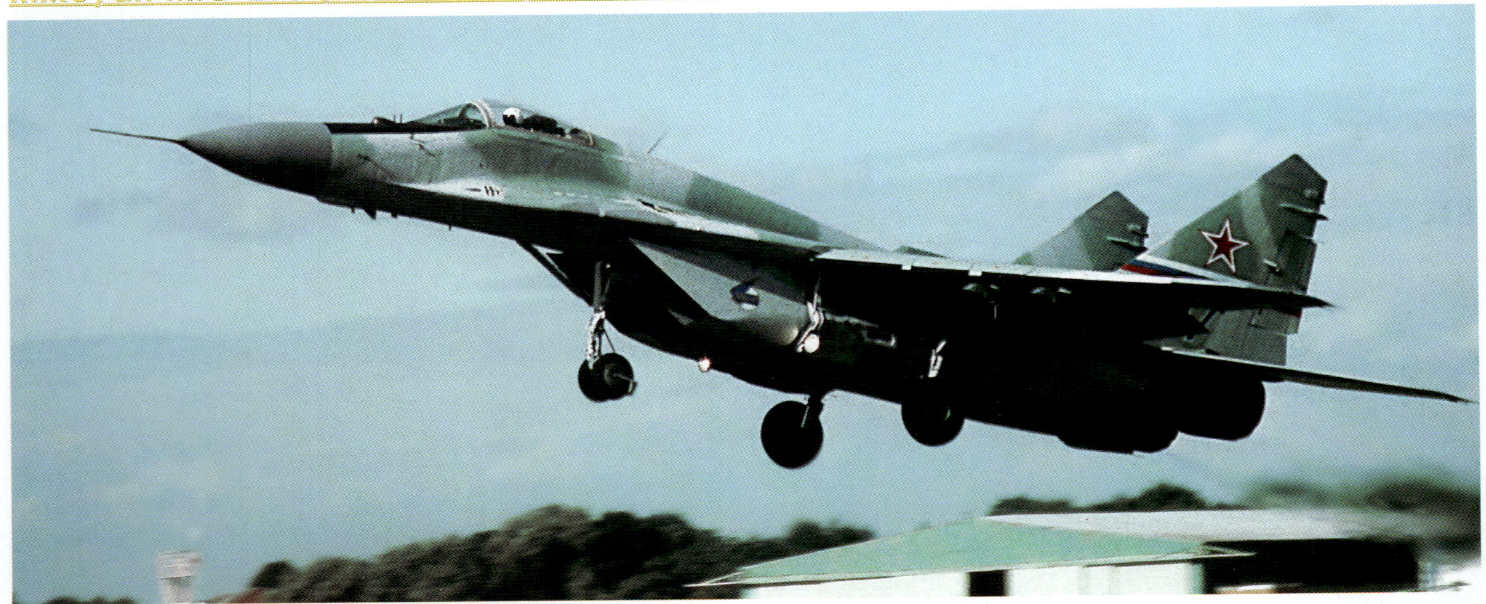

The Mikoyan MiG-29S (Obiekt 9.13) has sometimes been called the "Fat-back" as its aft fuselage spine is thicker than that on the earlier MiG-29A. Otherwise, both aircraft are very similar.

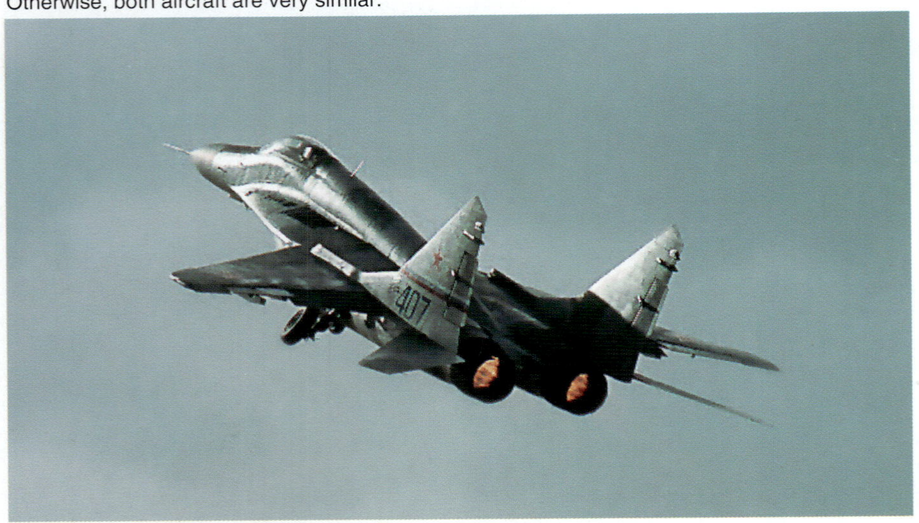

The fuselage aft the cockpit on the MiG-29S retains its full width further down the spine than did the fuselage of the MiG-29A.

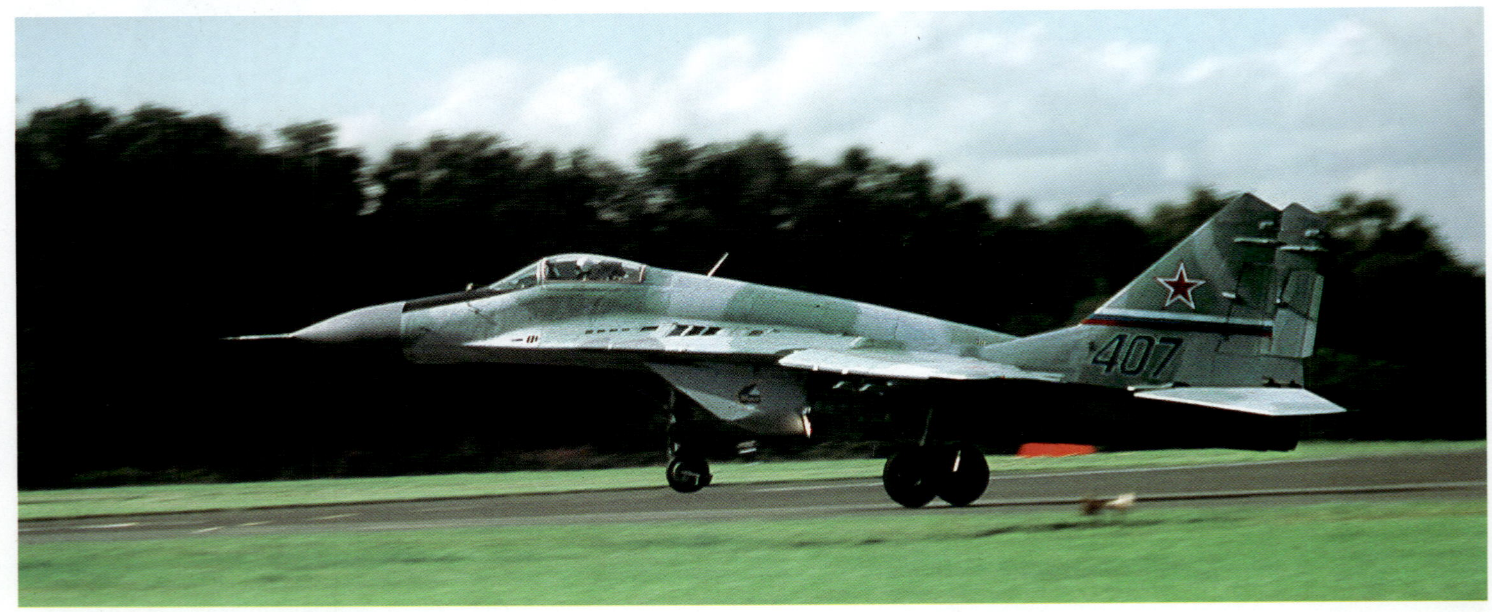

A similarity between the MiG-29S and the earlier MiG-29A is that they both use the upper surface air intake doors during take-off for FOD protection as is evident in this view. Notice that the MiG-29S displayed at Farnborough carries the white-blue-red national colors of the Russian Federation as a new style national marking.

One of the significant combat differences of the MiG-29S is that it has been modified to carry the new R-77 active radar air-to-air missile, an advanced weapon similar to the US AIM-120 AMRAAM.

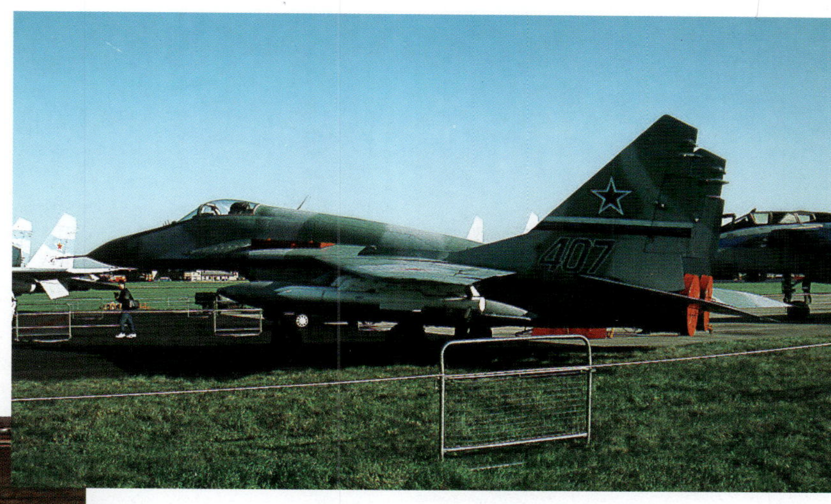

A view down along the spine of the MiG-29S showing the new shape. Note also that there are detail differences in the configuration of the FOD doors.

The cockpit interior of the MiG-29S is very similar to that in the earlier MiG-29A Fulcrum A.

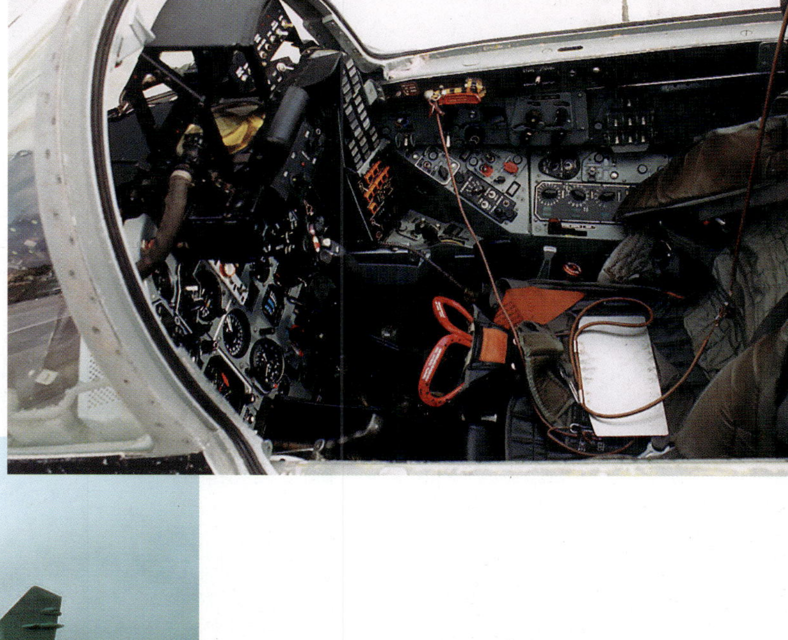

The thicker spine of the MiG-29S gives it a slightly "hump-backed" appearance from certain angles.

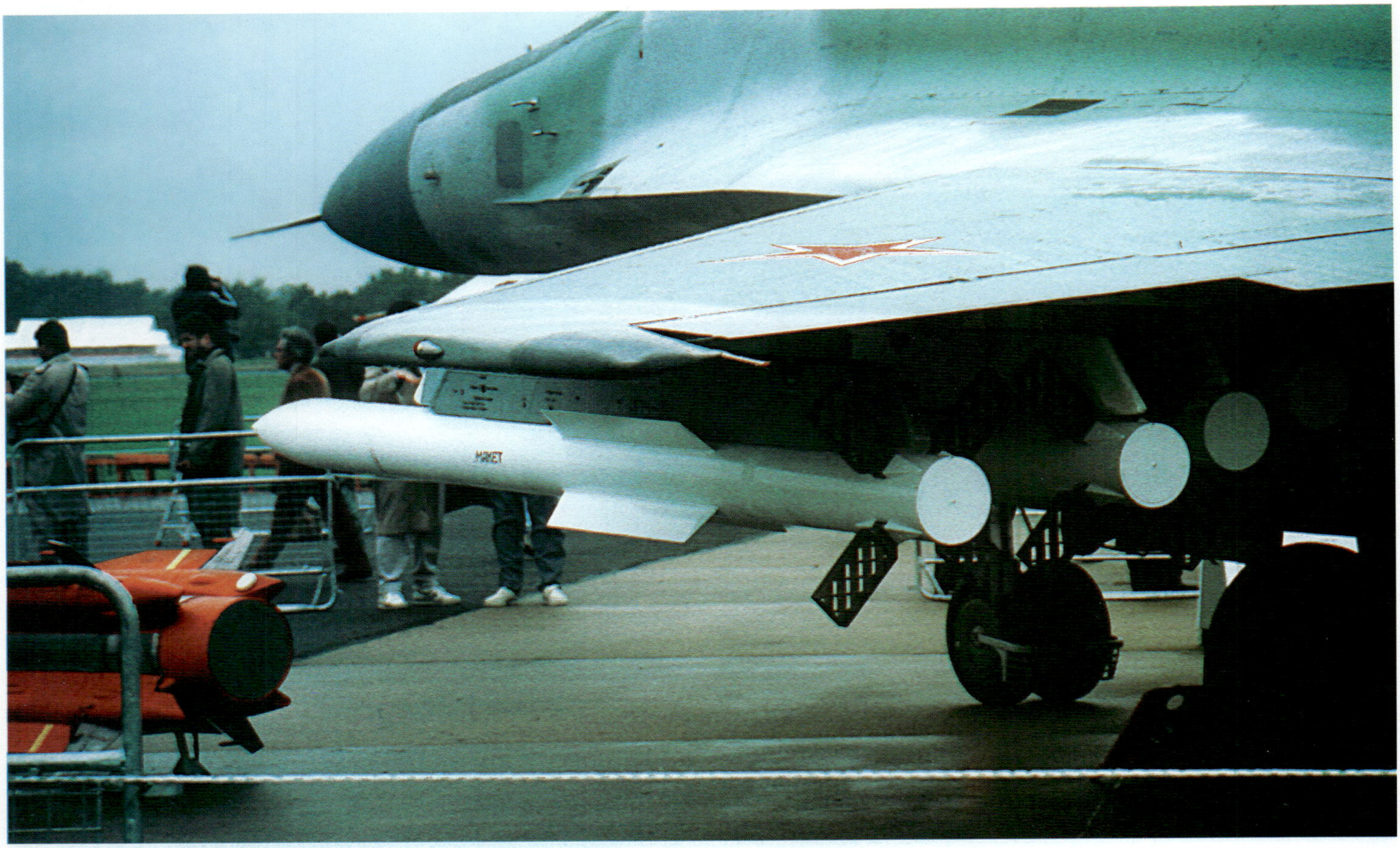

One of the more subtle changes between the MiG-29A and the MiG-29S has been the reconfiguration of the wing-tips to permit the incorporation of dielectric panels used in the Gardeniya-1 FUE electronic warfare system of the aircraft. This particular view is the wingtip of a MiG-29M (MiG-33), but this feature is common between both types.

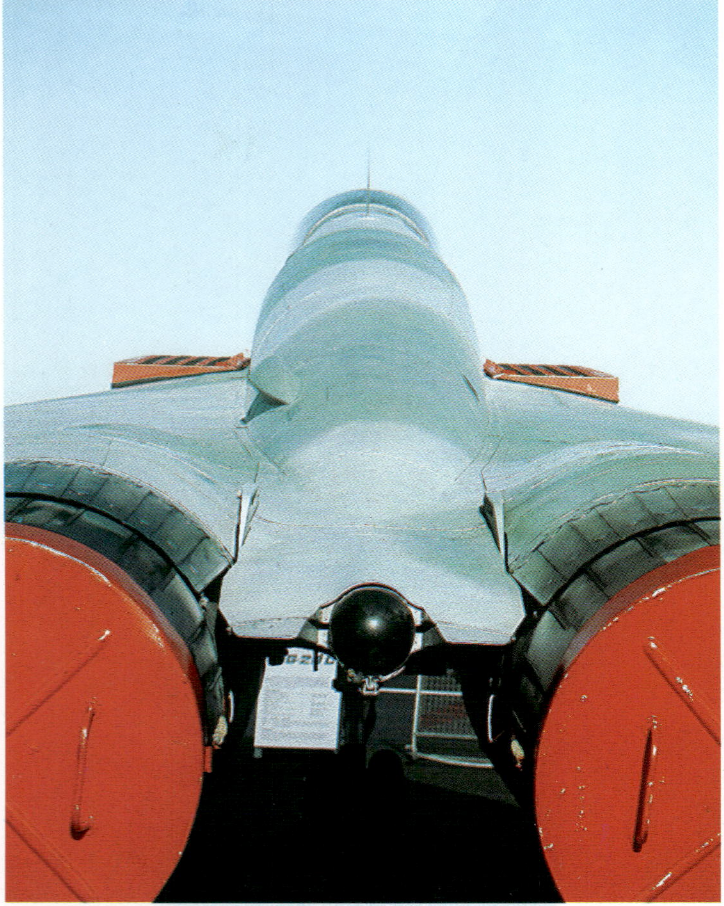

A view up the spine of the MiG-29S showing the revised shape.

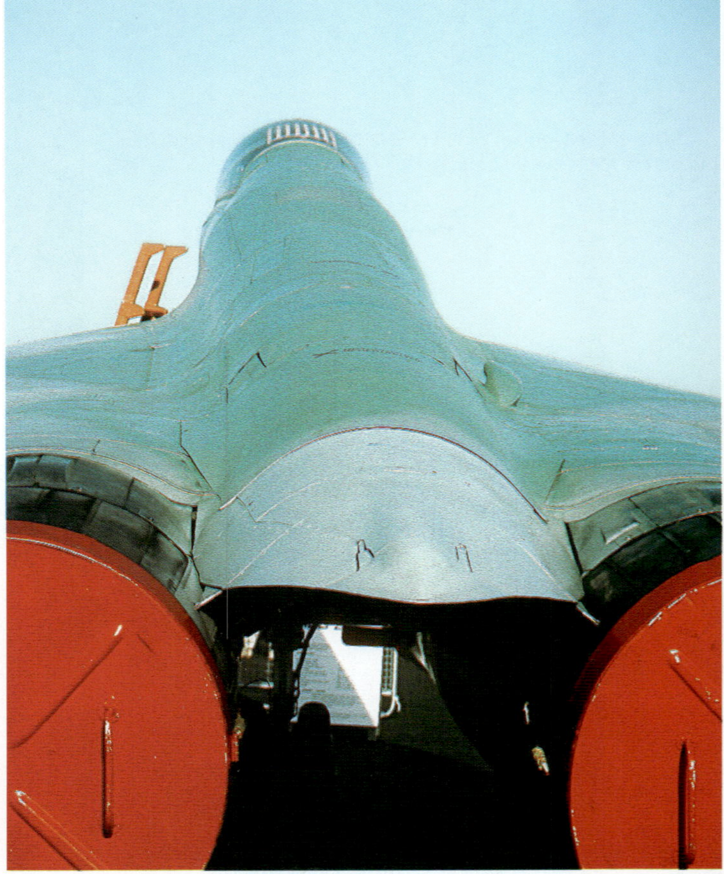

A comparative view of the spine of the MiG-29M (MiG-33) showing how the fuselage spine tapers all the way back to the new beaver tail.

The initial production versions of the MiG-29S Obiekt 9.13 were not adapted to carry some of the new weapons such as the R-77. This MiG-29S is in service with the 16th Fighter Division at Damgarten, Germany, July 1992. (Michael Jerchel)

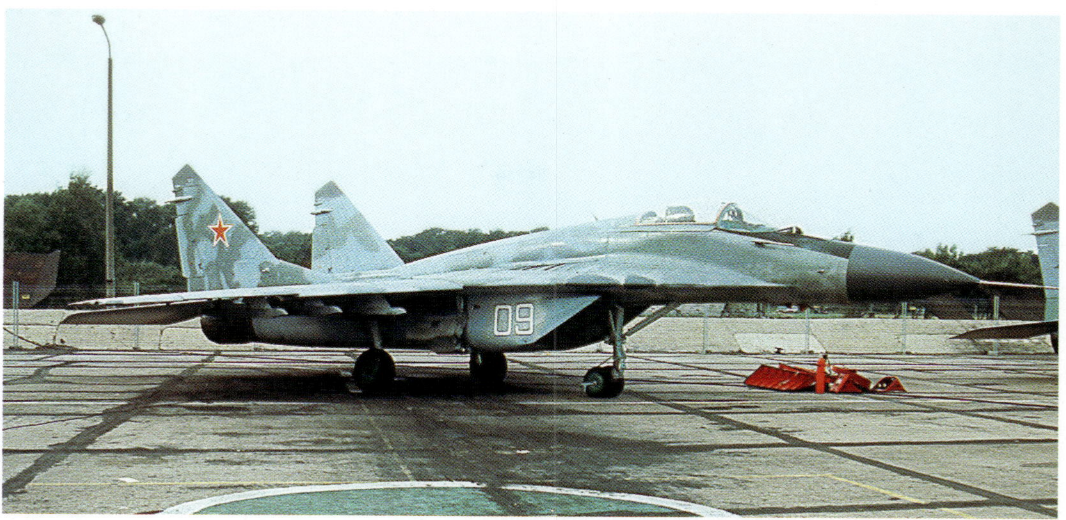

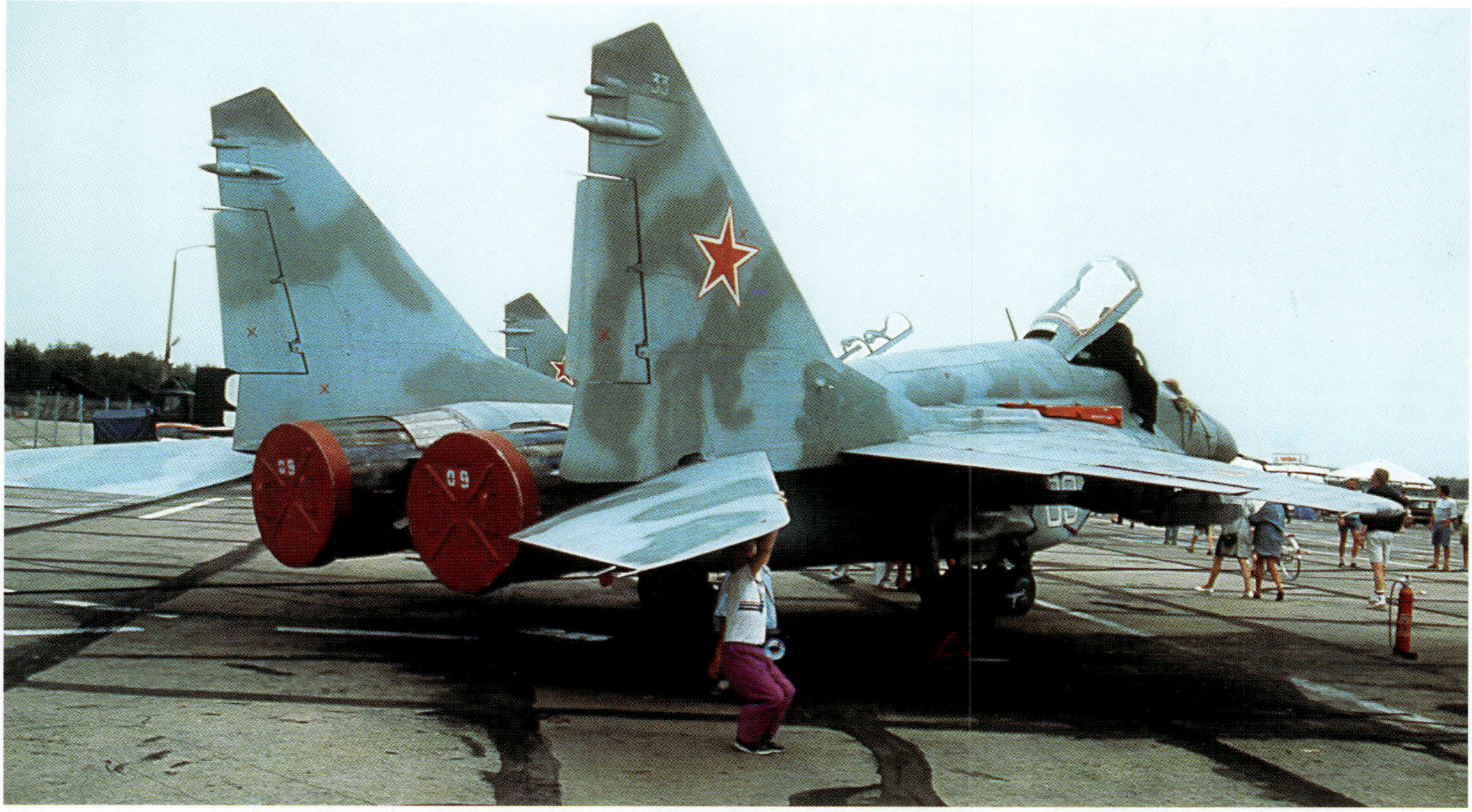

This MiG-29S of the 16th Fighter Division is finished in a non-standard camouflage pattern compared to the airshow aircraft. (Michael Jerchel)

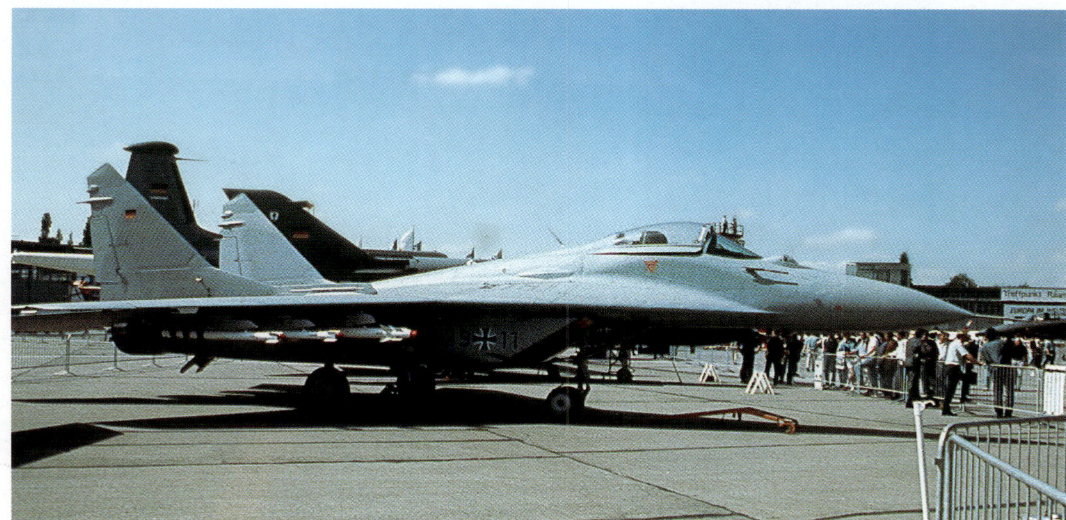

A MiG-29A (Obiekt 9.12) of the German Luftwaffe in the new air superiority grey scheme, displayed at the ILA show in Berlin in 1992.

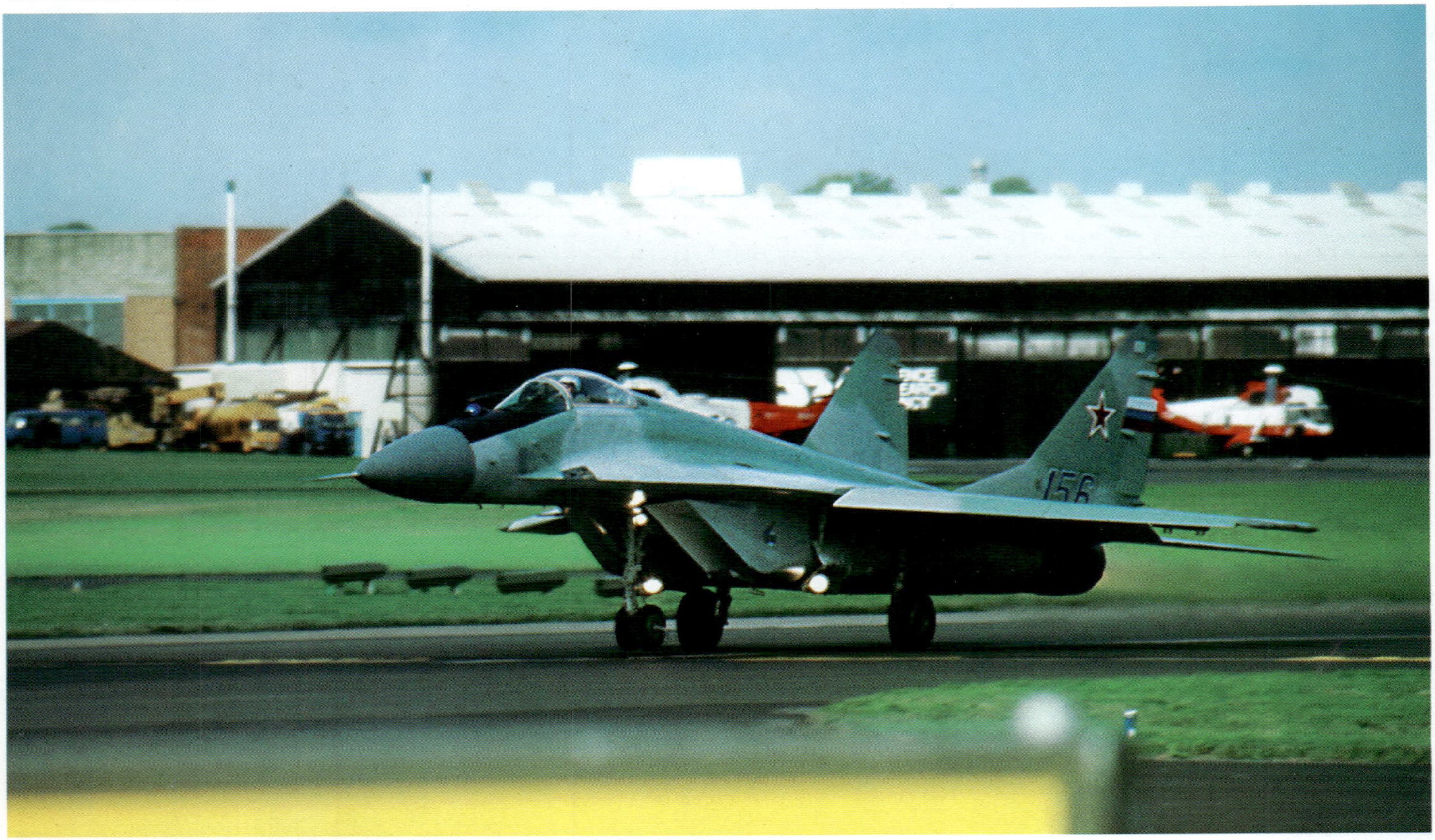

From the front, the MiG-33 closely resembles the MiG-29S. However, careful inspection of the wing-root will reveal that this version does not have the overhead anti-FOD air intake doors found on all previous versions of the MiG-29 fighter.

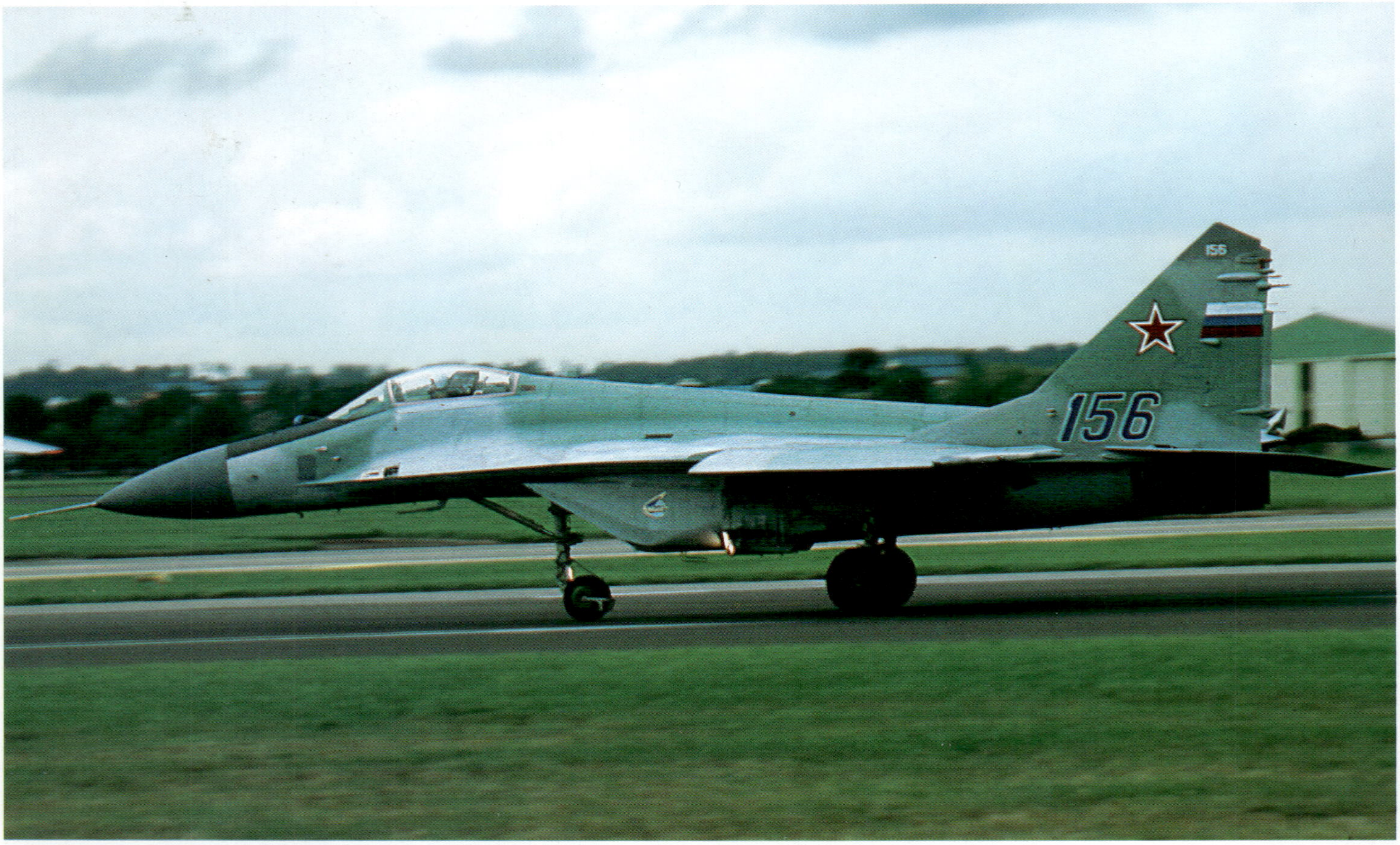

The spine of the MiG-33 is high, as on the MiG-29S. The MiG-33 is fitted with the simple rear fin, lacking the flare countermeasure dispenser strake at the front.

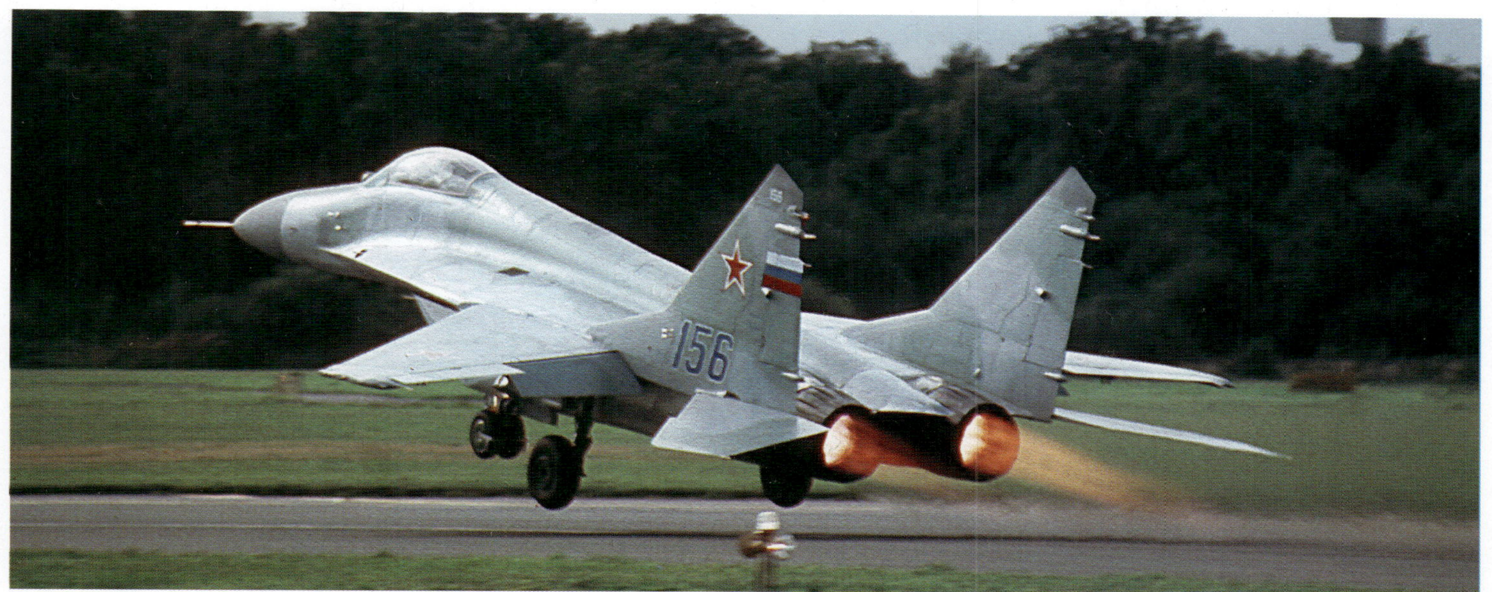

The MiG-33 was originally called the MiG-29M; its name was changed mainly for publicity purposes. As this take-off shot demonstrates, it has some significant changes in its tail area: a broader chord-tail with saw-tooth edge, a reconfigured trailing edge to the vertical tail fin, and a significantly reconfigured rear fuselage.

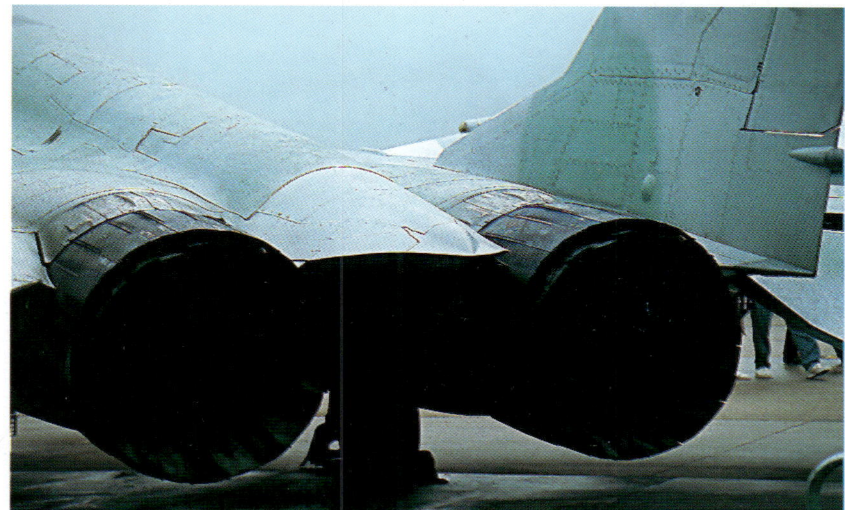

The fuselage spine has been thickened yet again on the MiG-33 to incorporate additional fuel and avionics. This has led to a reconfiguration of the rear tail area, resembling a beaver's tail without the usual small dome parachute cover seen on earlier models of this fighter.

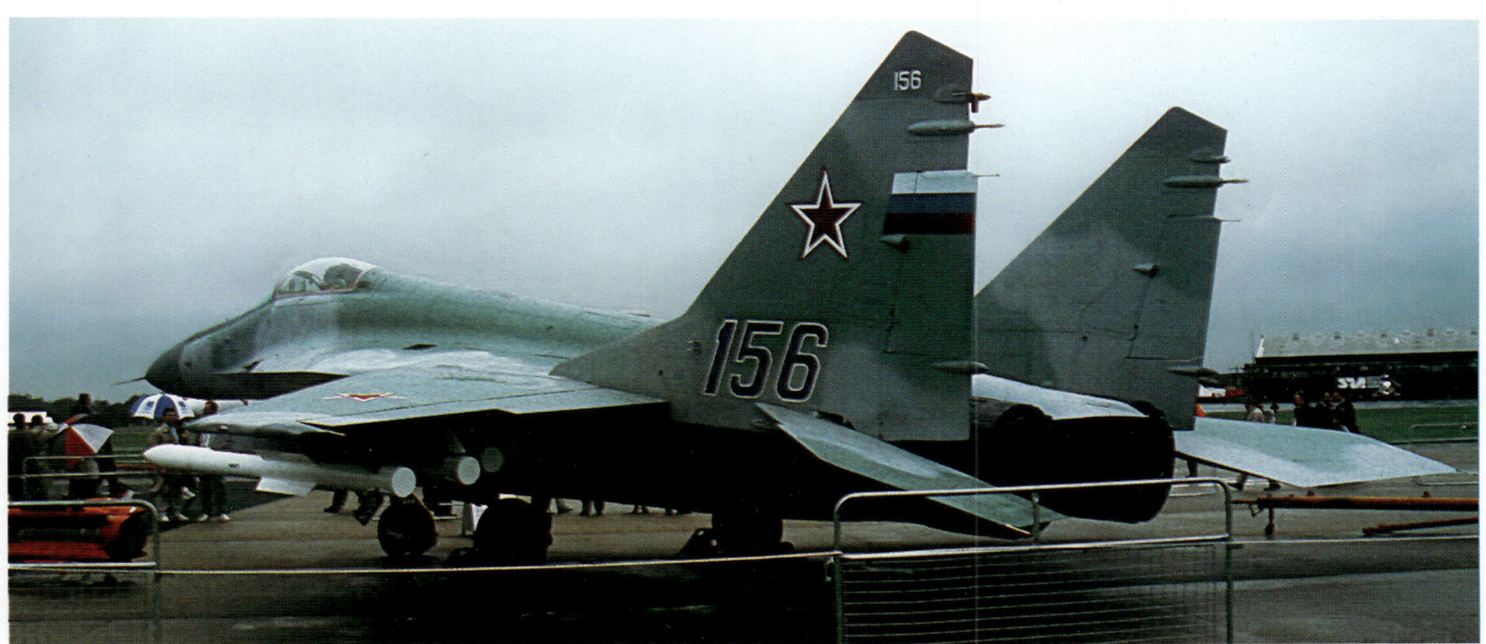

A rear view of the MiG-33 at Farnborough. Note that the aircraft is fitted with a broader-chord tail. This has necessitated the broadening of the base of the vertical tail so that the trailing edge is almost vertical under the rudder, and wider than on previous models of this fighter.

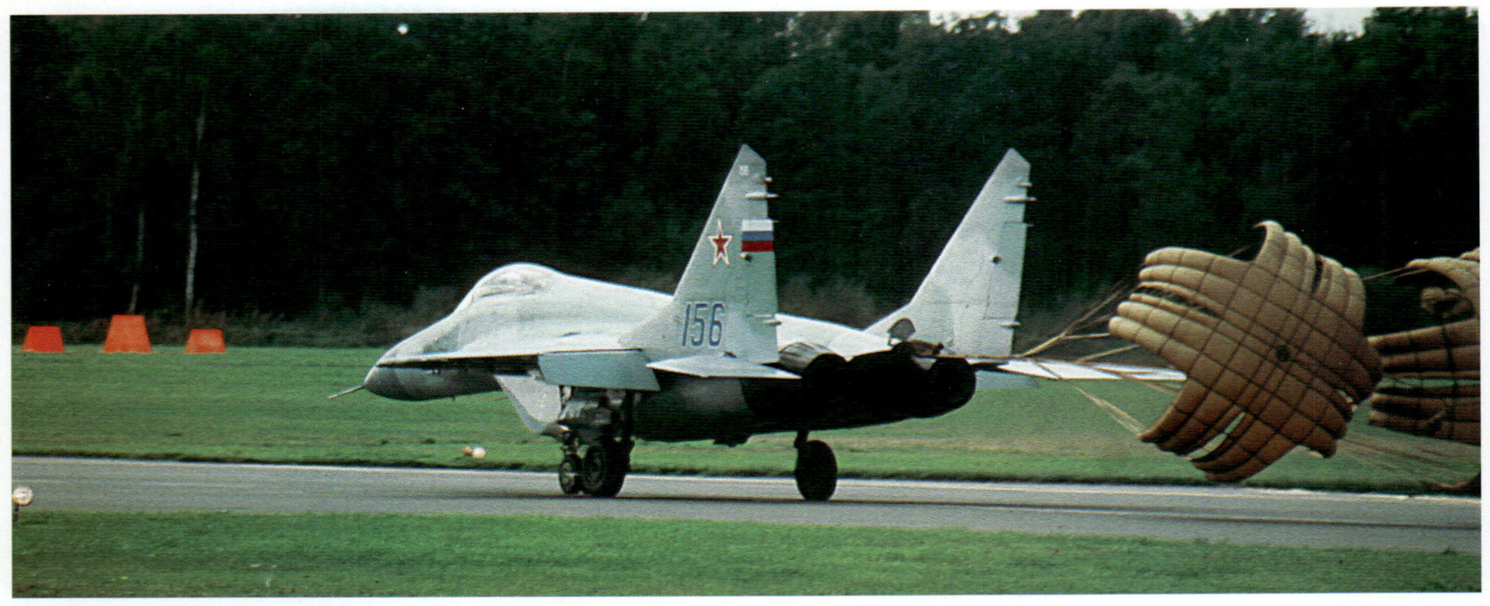

The MiG-33's beaver tail still contains the usual pair of braking parachutes, but the cover is faired into the tail shape. In this rear view, the small doors at the rear tip of the beaver tail are seen open. The MiG-33 uses two braking chutes instead of one as on the earlier versions.

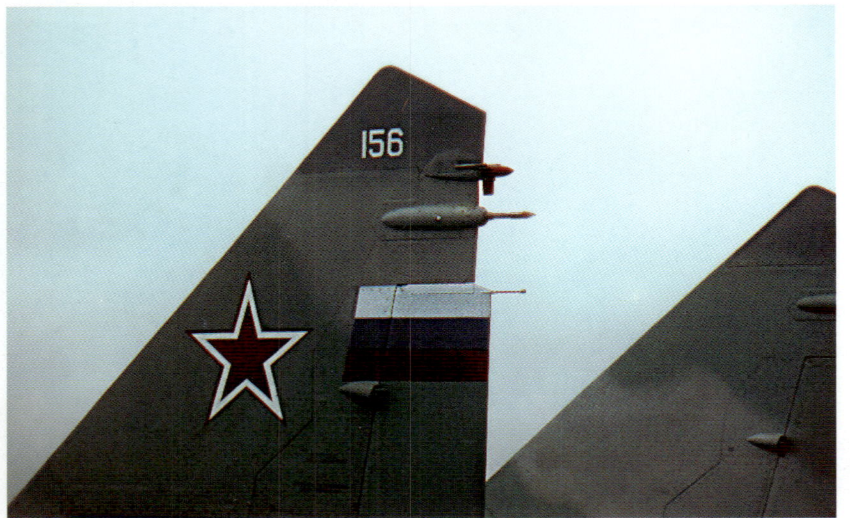

A close-up of the rudder shows several changes on the MiG-33, including a new rear-pointing RWR antenna. On this particular aircraft, the Russian Federation colors are painted in a more abbreviated form than those seen on the MiG-29S at Farnborough.

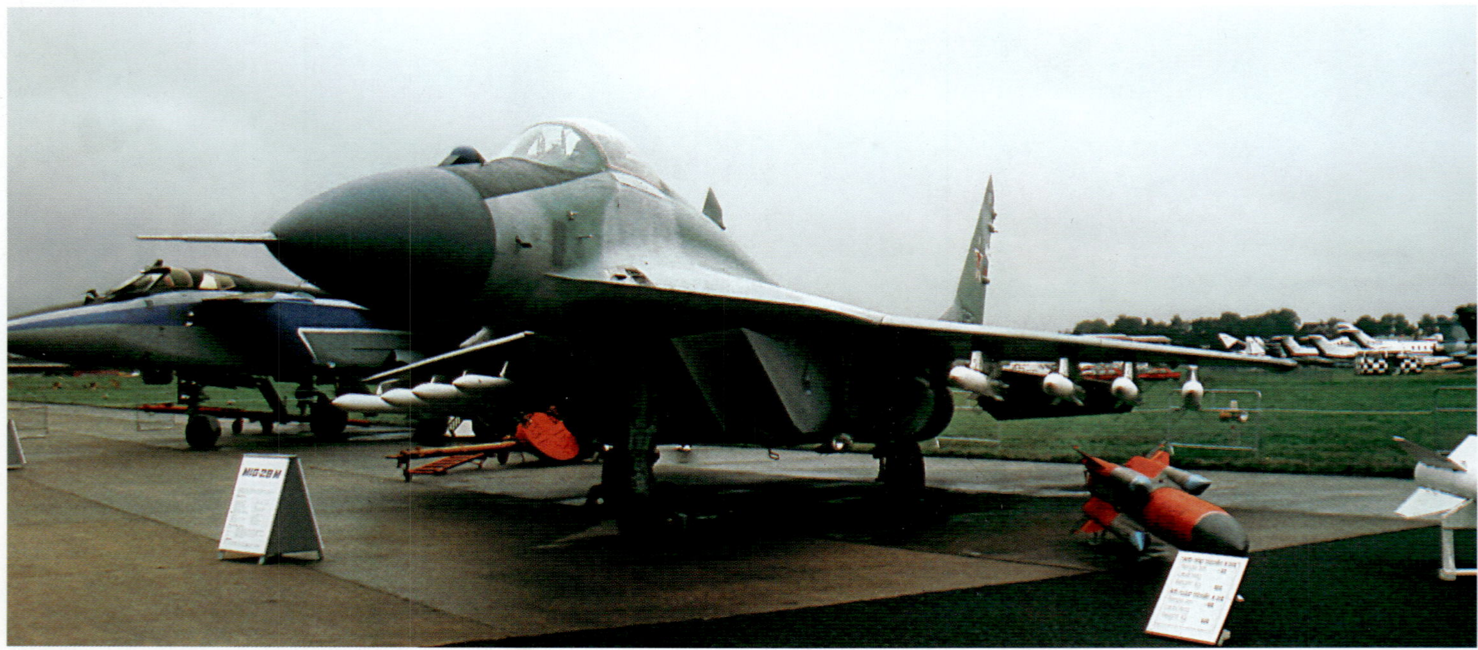

One of the most significant tactical changes between the MiG-33 and earlier models is the provision of new wing hardpoints to permit carriage of a wider range of new weapons. In this case, the MiG-33 is carrying eight R-77 (AA-12) active radar AAMs.

Mikoyan MiG-31 Foxhound

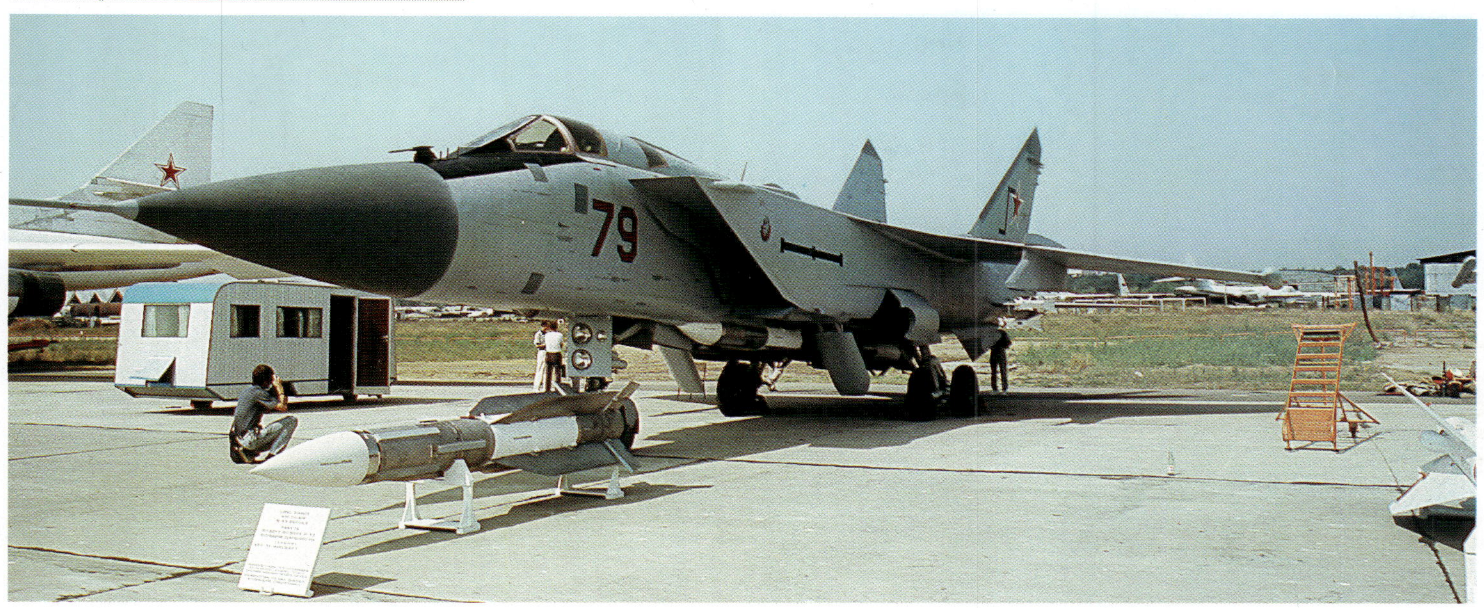

A Mikoyan MiG-31 Foxhound of the LII Flight Test Center displayed at Zhukovskiy in August 1992 in the normal tactical scheme of pale grey. This aircraft has several black band insignia applied which are used to measure aircraft angles during assessments from telemetry footage.

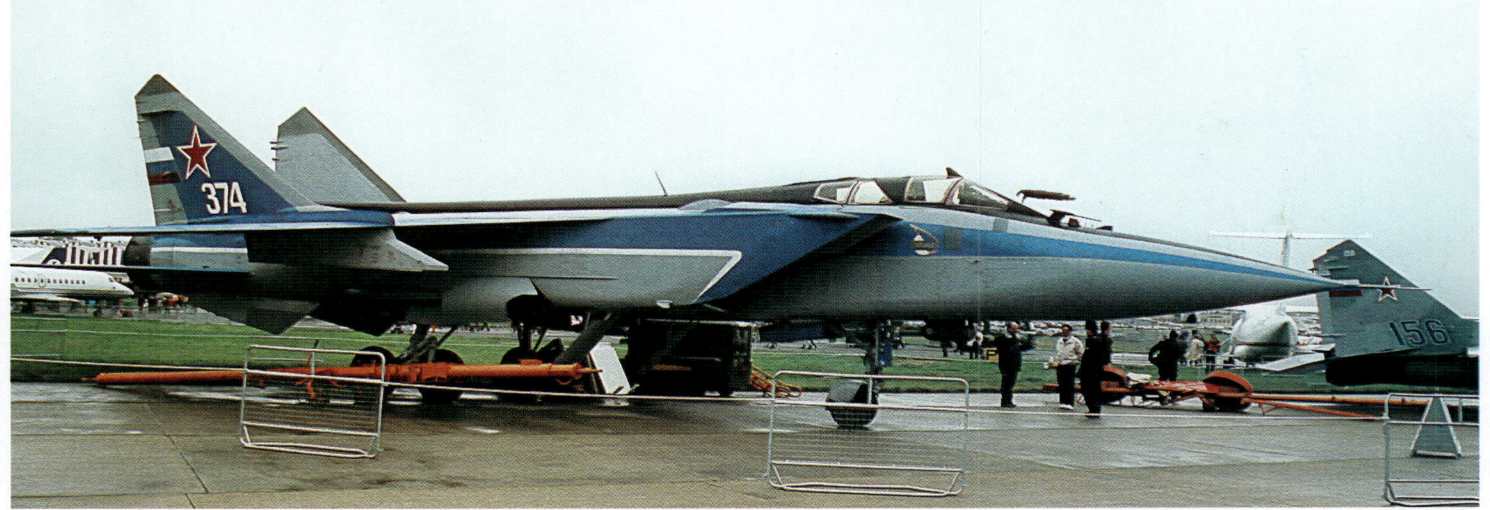

The MiG-31 was first displayed at the 1991 Paris Air Salon at Le Bourget, and the same aircraft in a special blue display scheme returned to Farnborough in 1992.

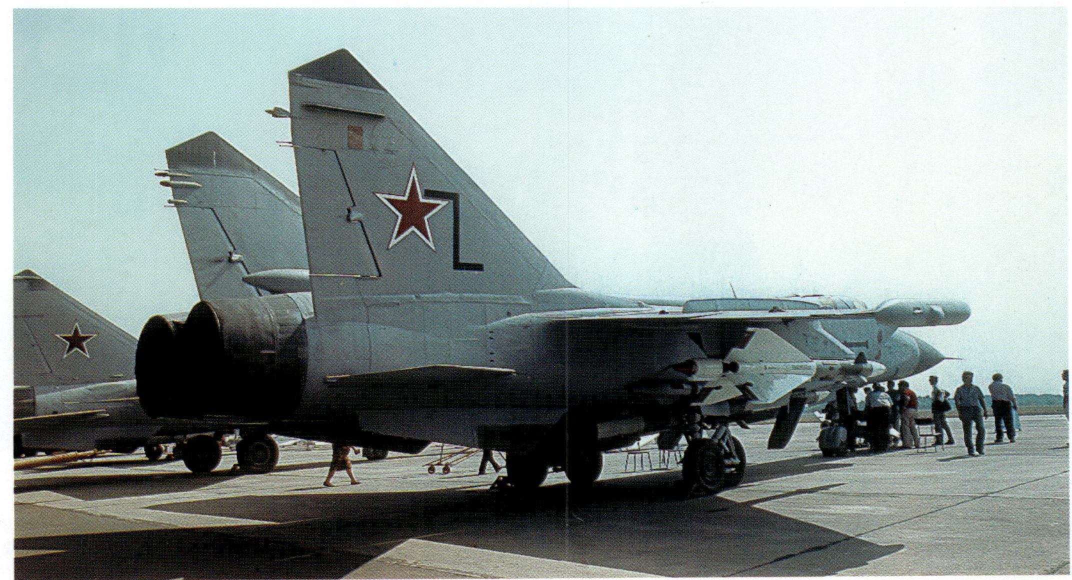

A rear view of the LII aircraft at Zhukovskiy, with the telemetry markings evident on the tail. This aircraft is fitted with a new wingtip pod which may be an electronic warfare system similar to the Sorbtsiya system on the Su-27M.

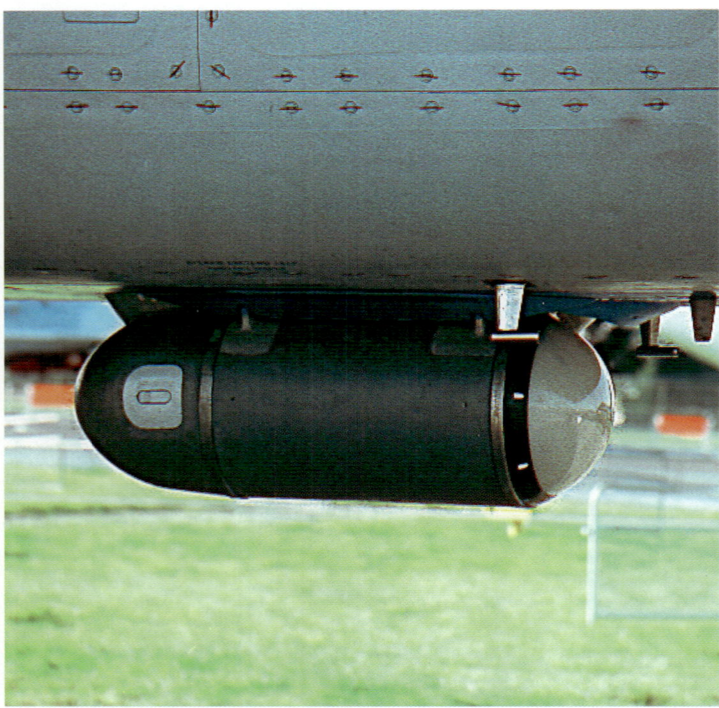

The MiG-31 is fitted with a retractable 8TP infrared tracker under the nose, used under circumstances where the normal radar might give away the interceptor's location or presence.

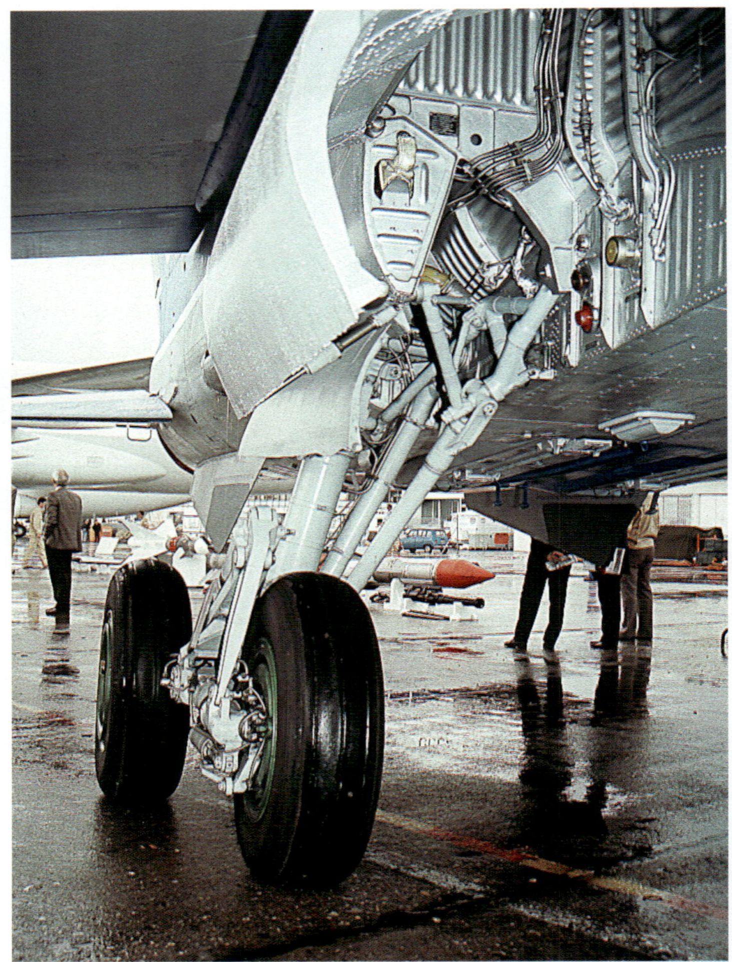

Another view of the complicated starboard undercarriage of the MiG-31 from a forward angle.

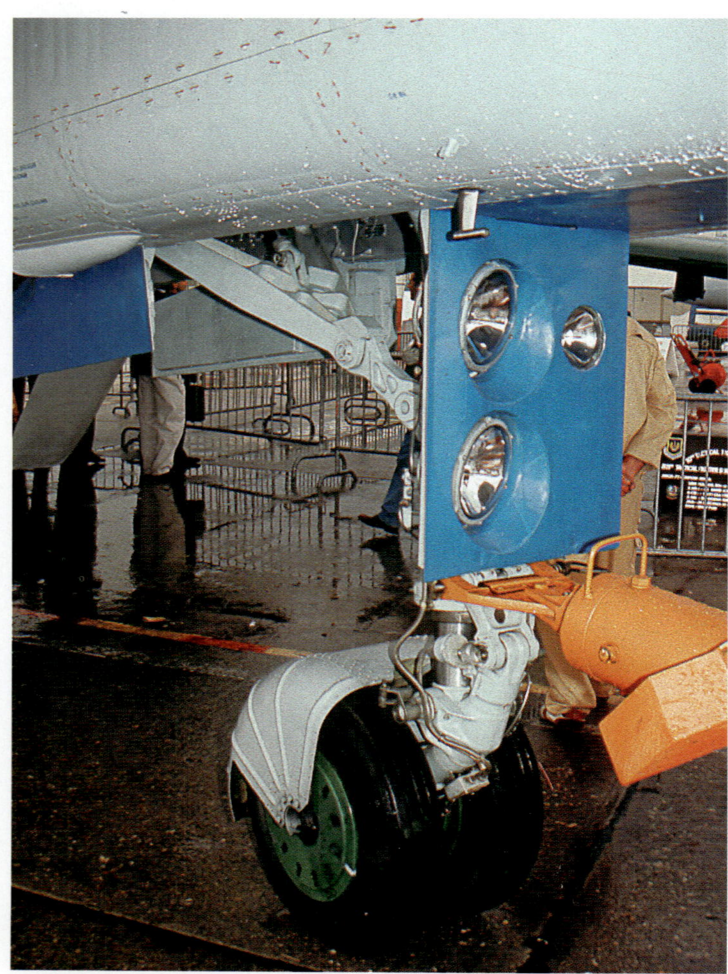

Like its smaller cousin the MiG-29, the MiG-31's nose landing gear is fitted with an anti-FOD cover to prevent pebbles and other debris from being tossed up by the wheels into the jet intake.

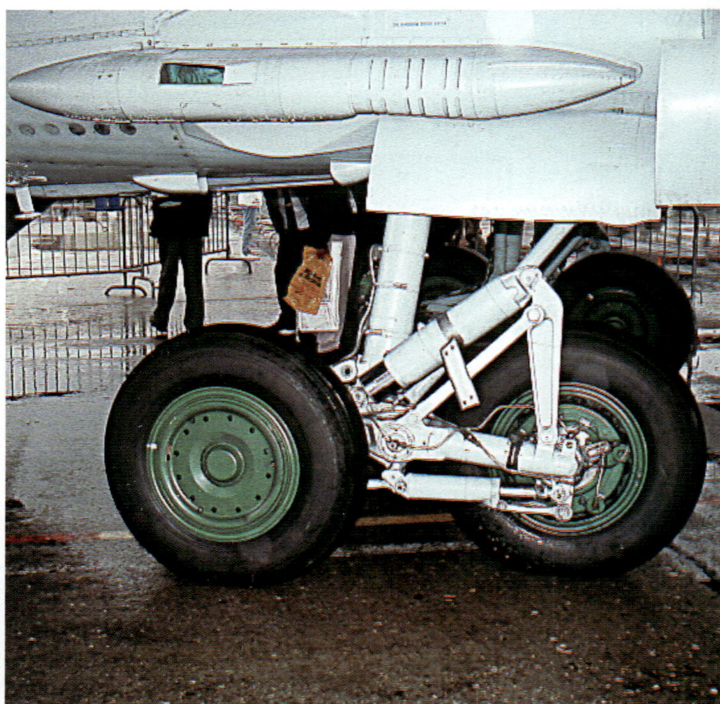

A detail view of the starboard landing gear on the MiG-31. This unusual staggered landing gear was intended to assist the heavy MiG-31 on the type of poor runways often found at the sub-arctic bases where these interceptors are deployed. Above the landing gear is the fairing for the AO-9 gun system, including its six barreled GSh-6-23 revolver cannon.

A weapon seldom seen on the MiG-31 in peacetime is the R-40T (AA-6 Acrid) long-range missile.

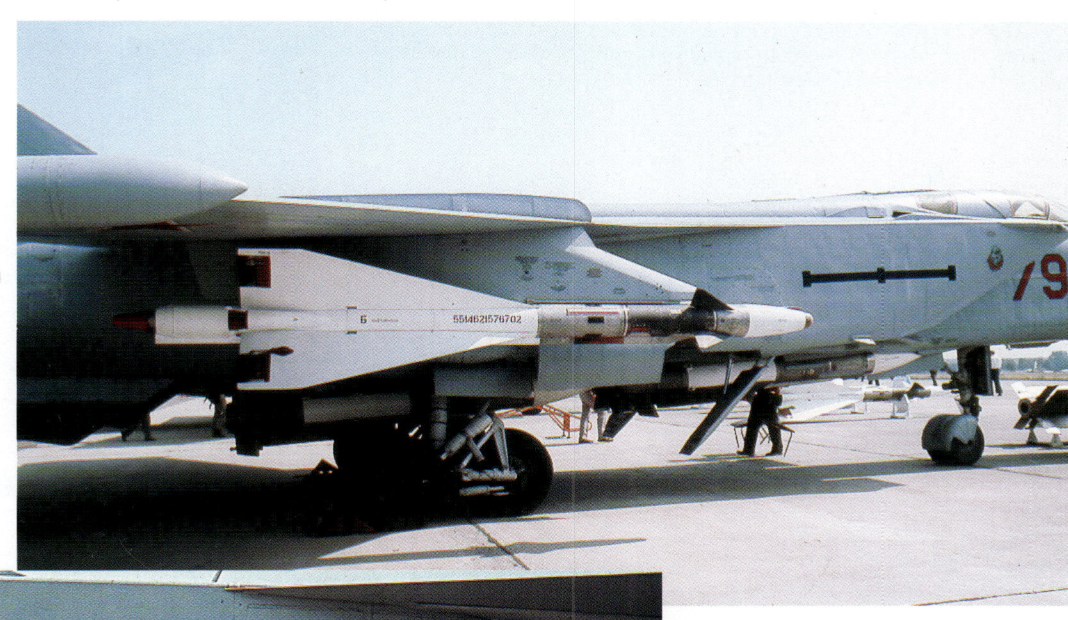

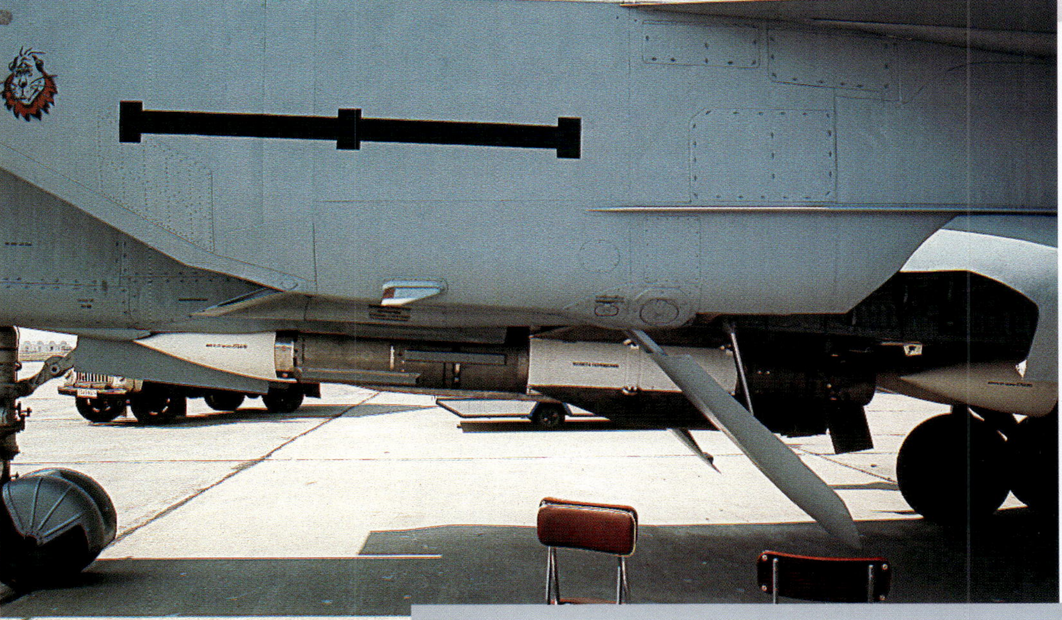

The main armament of the MiG-31 interceptor is four R-33 (AA-9 Amos) missiles, partially recessed under the belly of the aircraft as seen here.

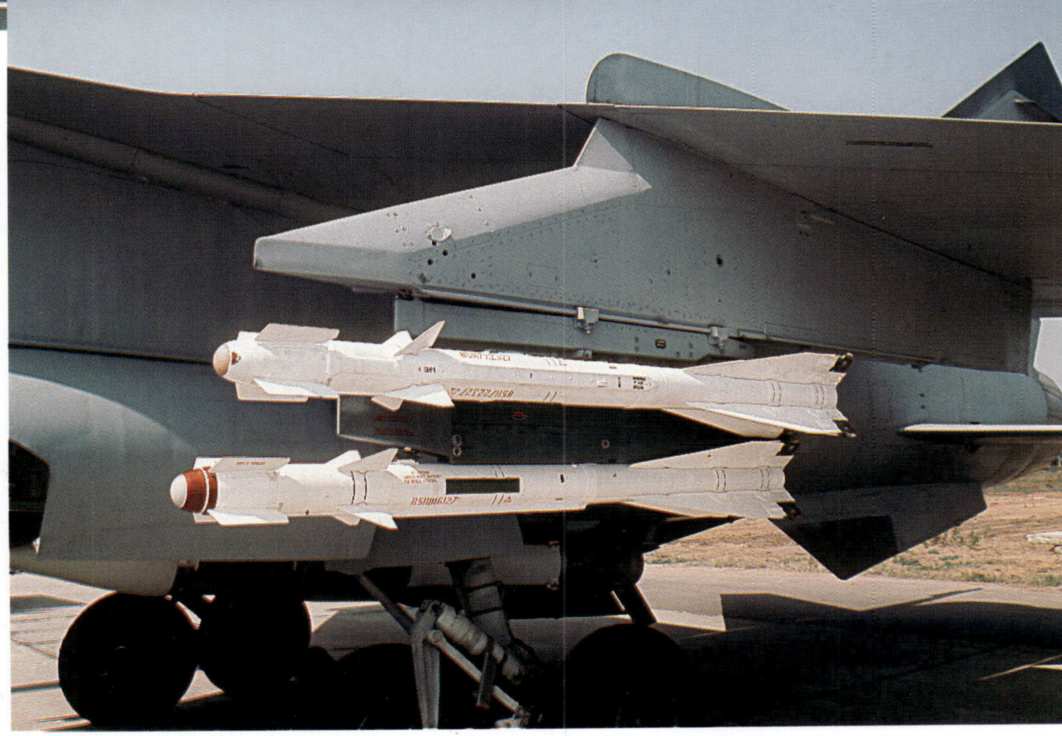

A common supplementary armament on the MiG-31 for self-defense is a pair of R-60MK (AA-8 Aphid) missiles on twin launchers.

The relaxation of tensions between East and West has had its light-hearted consequences. Russian aircraft are now showing up more often with cartoon insignia like this lion on the LII MiG-31.

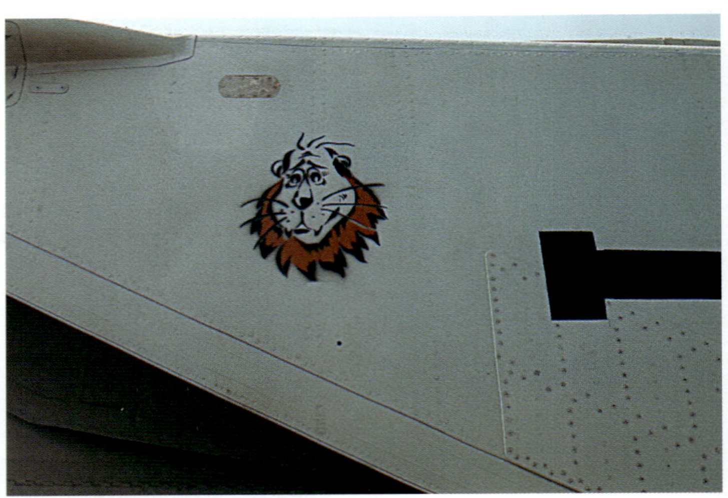

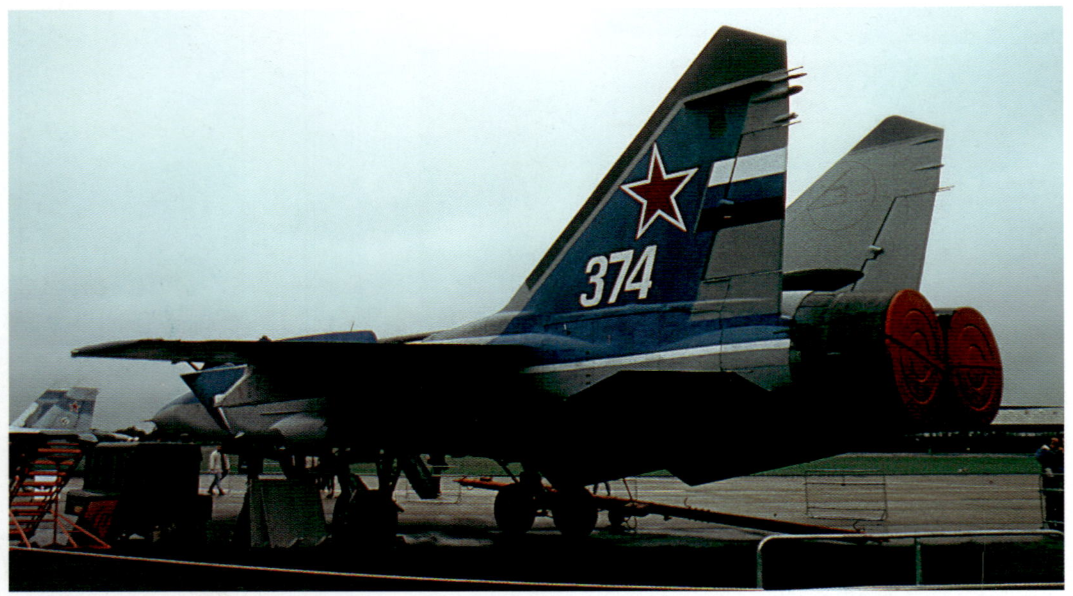

One of the few changes on the MiG-31 displayed at Zhukpovskiy was the change in markings. Note that the display aircraft now carries the Russian Federation flag on the tail.

Mikoyan MiG-31M Foxhound B

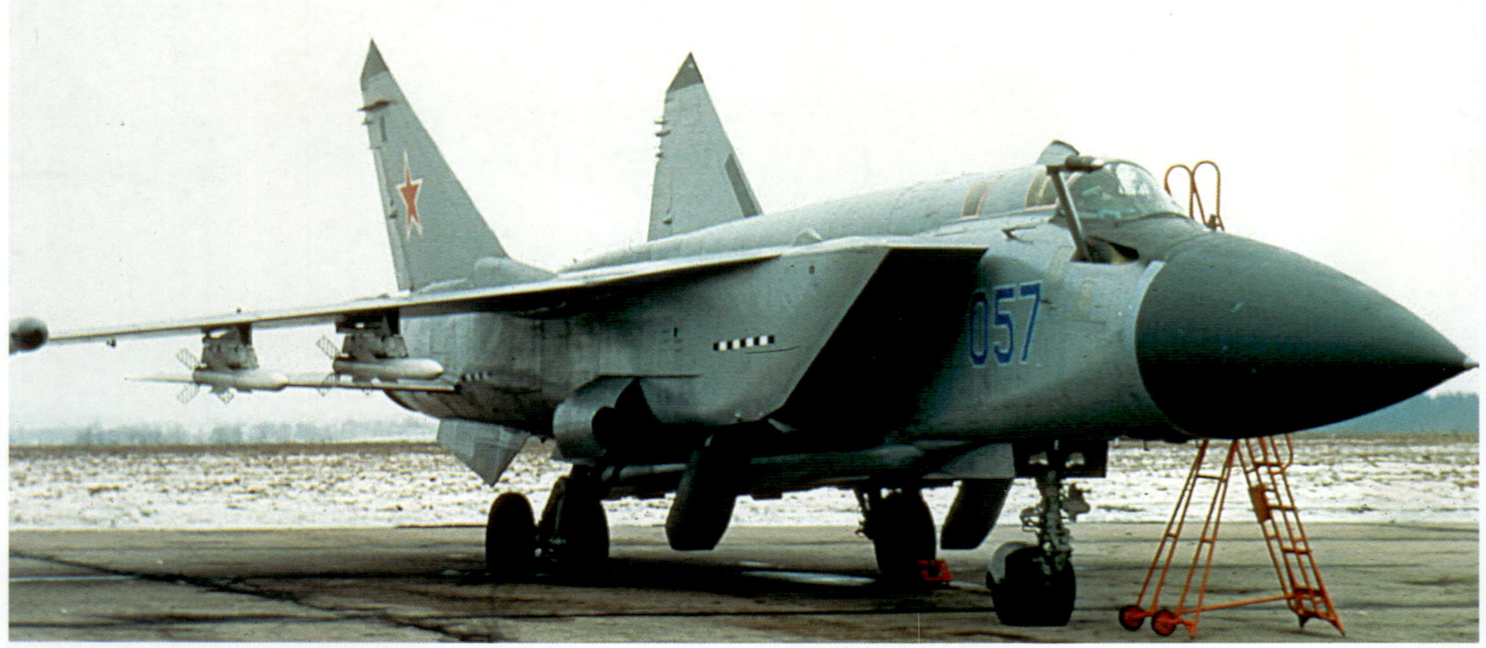

One of the most secretive Russian aircraft is the MiG-31M Foxhound B, one of the few types not publicly displayed at the August 1992 show. It has a whole new armament package, including a new active-homing radar guided missile seen here under the belly to replace the R-33. Under the wing are the new R-77 medium range missiles. (Sovfoto)

Sukhoi Su-24MR Fencer

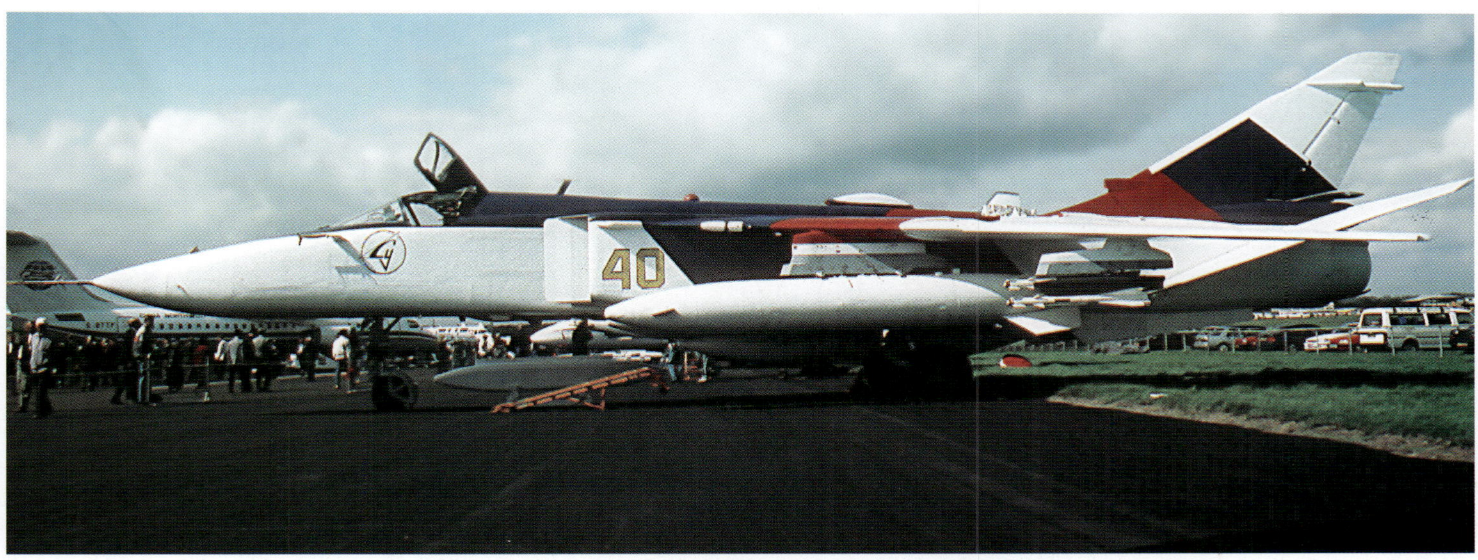

For many years, the Sukhoi Su-24M Fencer was barred from overseas exhibit. In 1992, the Su-24 was finally permitted at foreign exhibits, first at Dubai, then Berlin and Farnborough. The version displayed at Farnborough is the Su-24MR Fencer E reconnaissance version.

Although the nose of the Su-24MR resembles that of the basic Su-24M strike aircraft, in fact it is significantly different. The basic Su-24M contains the Zazorin PNS-24M navigation/attack radar system, similar to the AN/APQ-113 in the F-111 series. In the Su-24MR, the nose contains a pair of side-looking SLAR radars used in its reconnaissance role. The shape of the conformal SLAR panel can be barely seen in front of the Sukhoi emblem on the nose. In the very tip of the nose is a small navigation radar. There is another specialized version of the Su-24M family, the Su-24MP which is an electronic warfare version similar in roles to the EF-111 Raven.

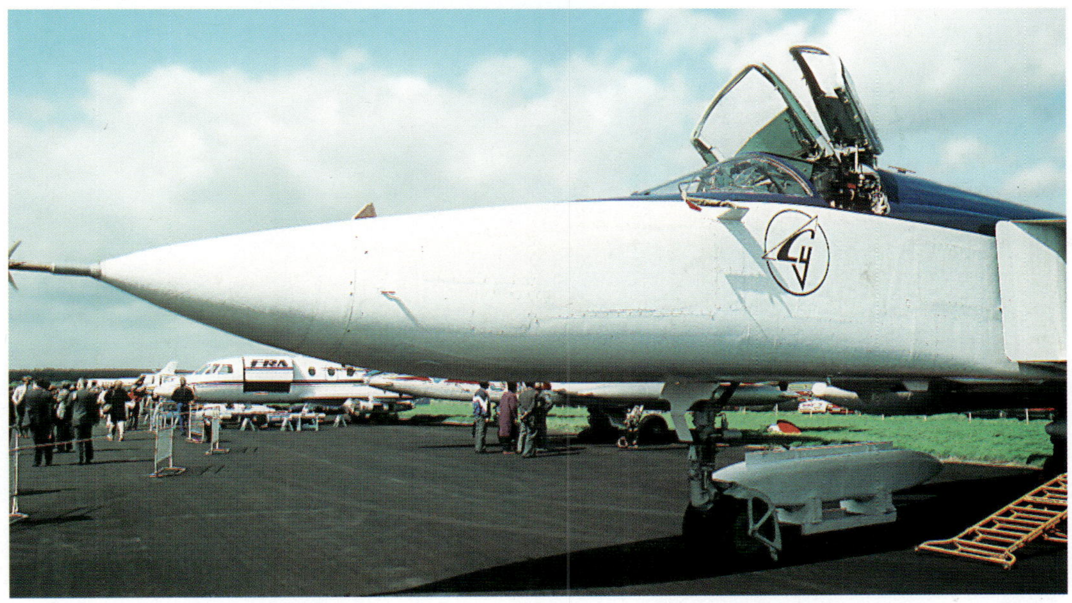

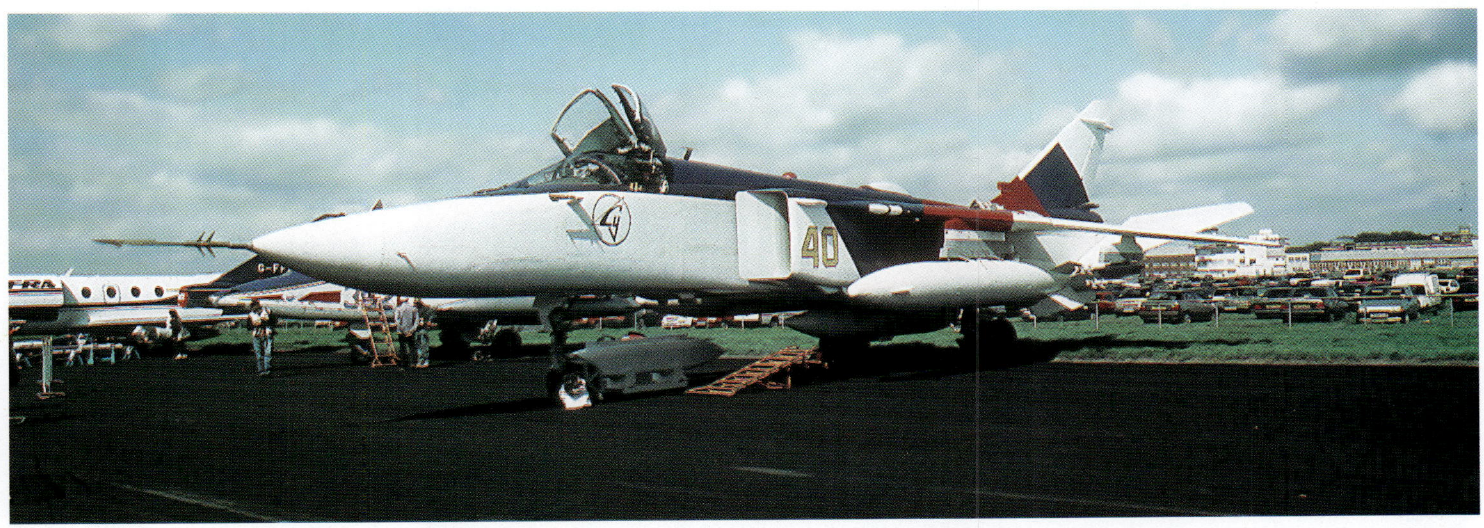

In keeping with recent Russian practices, the Su-24MR was painted up in a special display scheme rather than its traditional pale-grey and white tactical scheme. The Su-24MR bears more than passing resemblance to the General Dynamics F-111 family which was probably its inspiration.

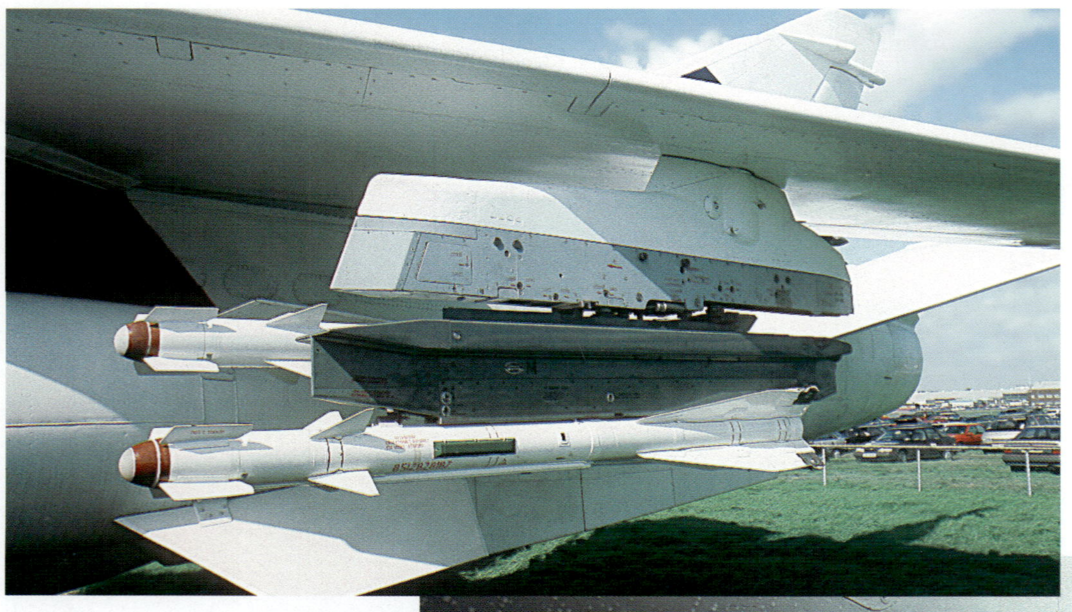

When employed in the reconnaissance role, the Su-24MR is usually armed with a pair of R-60MK missiles for self-defense on an APU-62-2 twin-rail launcher. This missile is often erroneously compared to the Sidewinder, when in fact it is considerably smaller, shorter ranged, and less-potent.

Another significant difference between the Su-24MR and the basic Su-24M is the provision of a ventral camera pack under the belly which replaces the AO-19 23mm cannon pack and the Kaira electro-optical attack system.

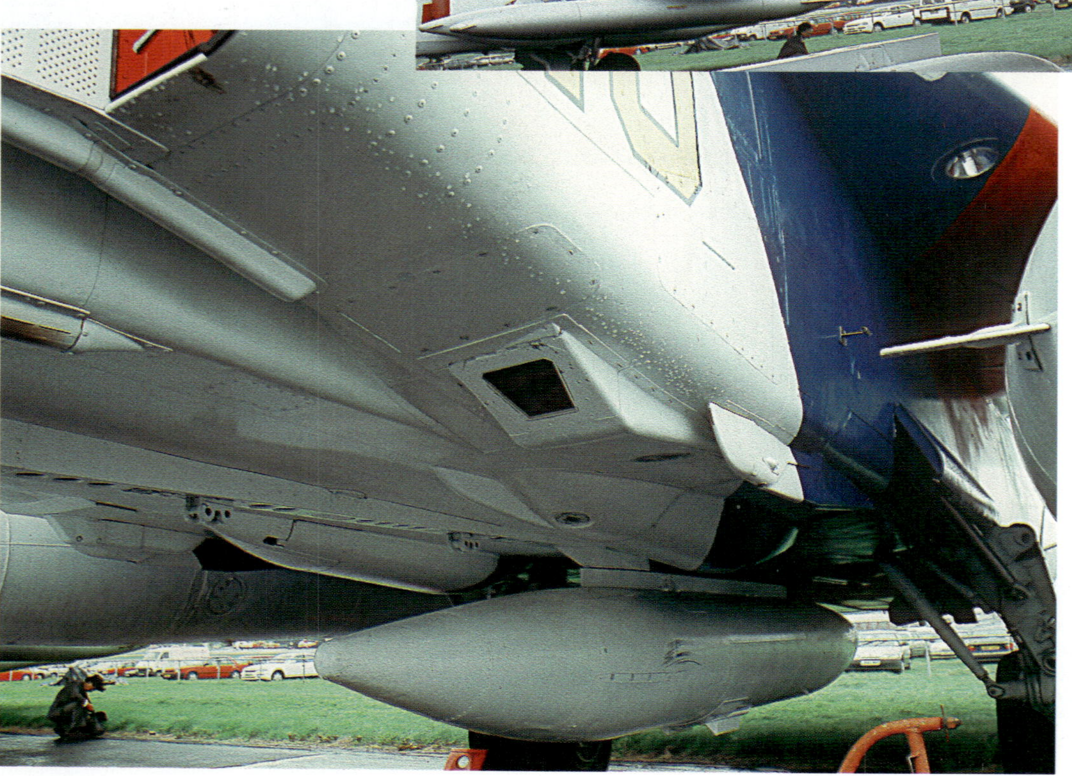

Another difference on the Su-24MR is the provision of a small forward pointing camera aperture on the port air intake. This is probably used by the crew to accurately line up the aircraft for their camera passes over the target area.

A detail view of the port air intake showing the forward pointing RWR antenna from the Bereza electronic countermeasures suite.

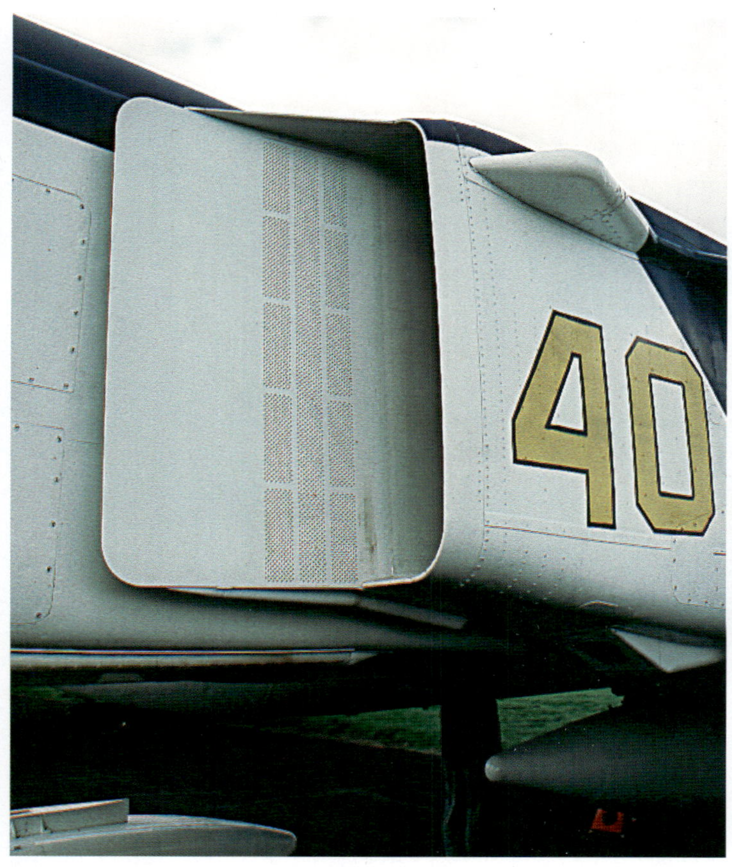

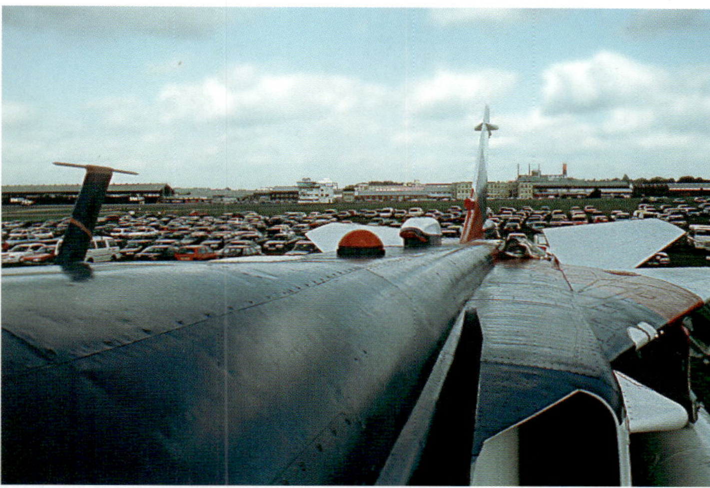

An overhead view down the spine of the Su-24MR. Two characteristic details of this version are the domed missile warning receiver, and behind it, the enlarged dorsal heat exchanger.

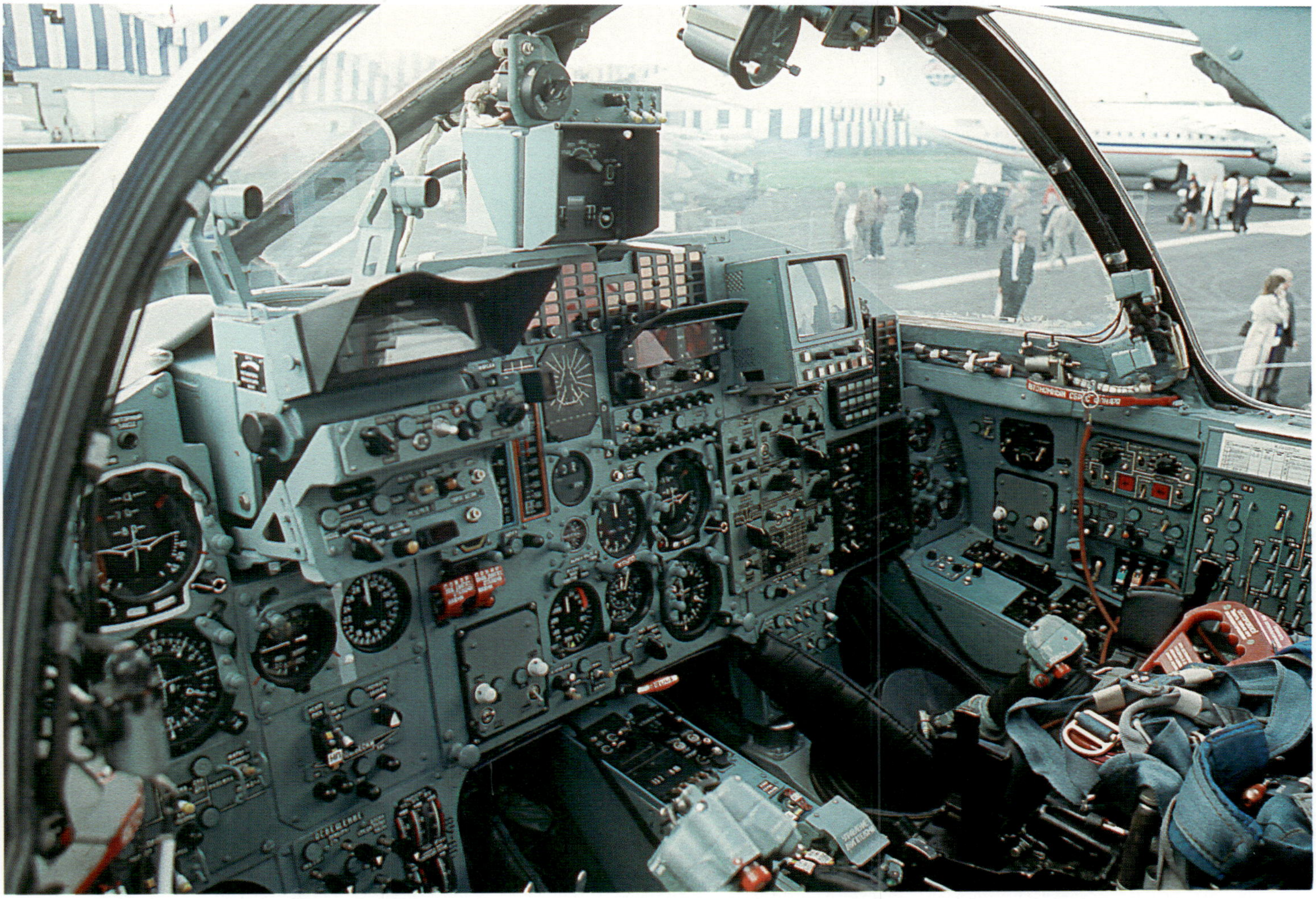

An interior view of the Su-24MR cockpit. The pilot is seated on the left, the *shturman* electronics officer on the right.

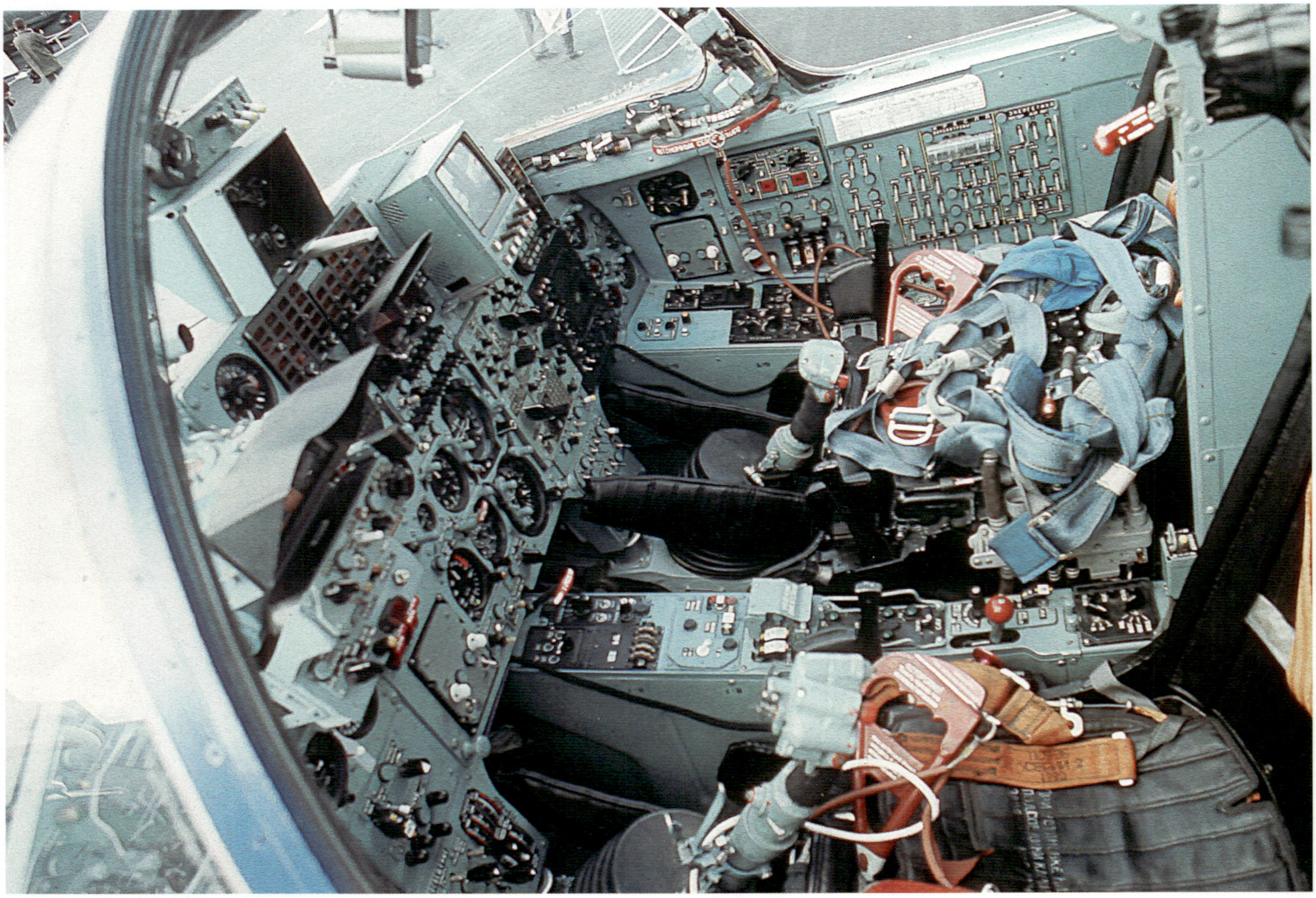

Another view into the cockpit providing a better view of the seating and central console The interior of the Su-24M is narrower and less spacious than the F-111. Also, the Su-24M uses Severin K-36D ejection seats instead of the encapsulated cockpit used on the F-111 family.

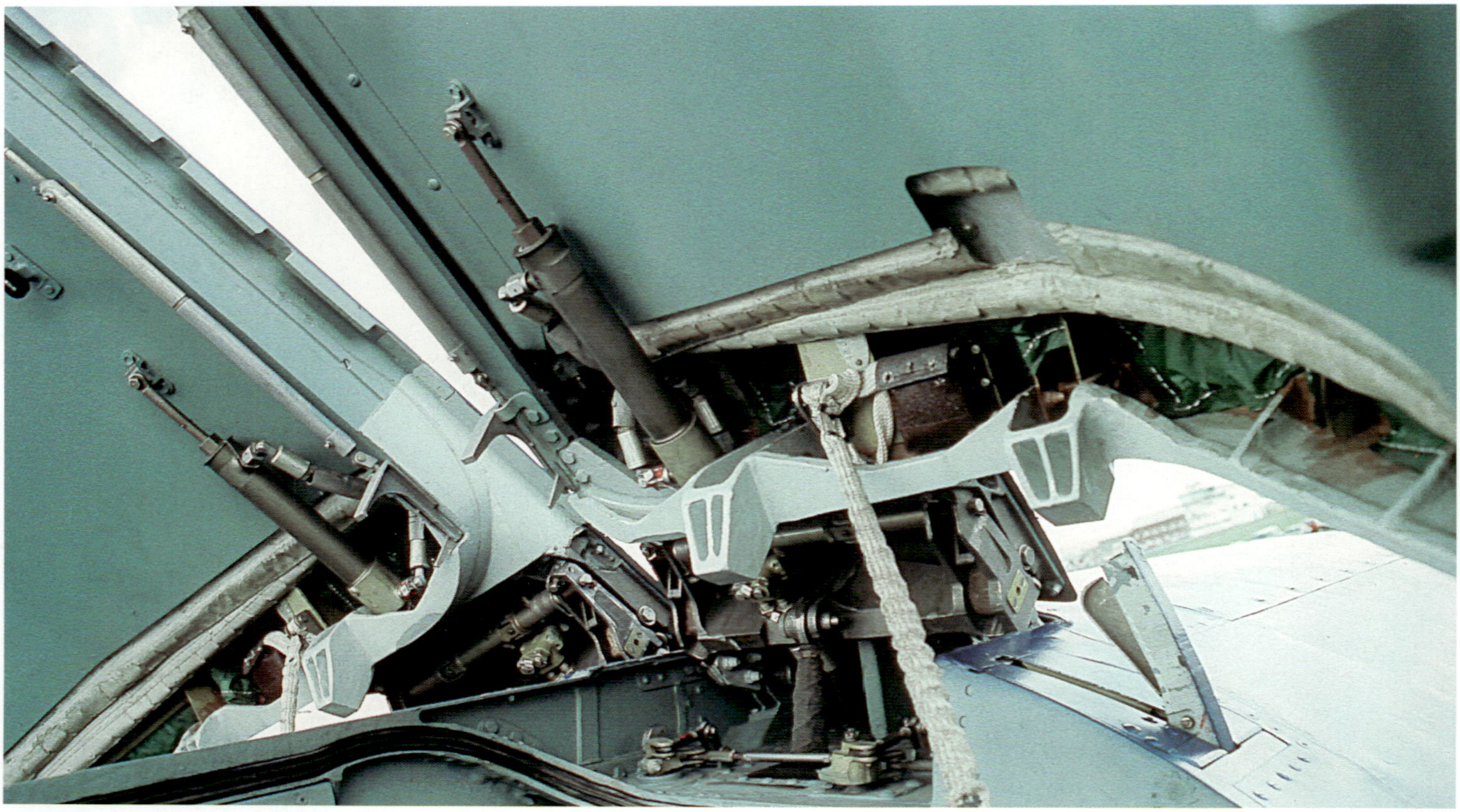

A view towards the upper rear of the cockpit canopy, showing the elaborate hinge assembly for the two split canopy halves.

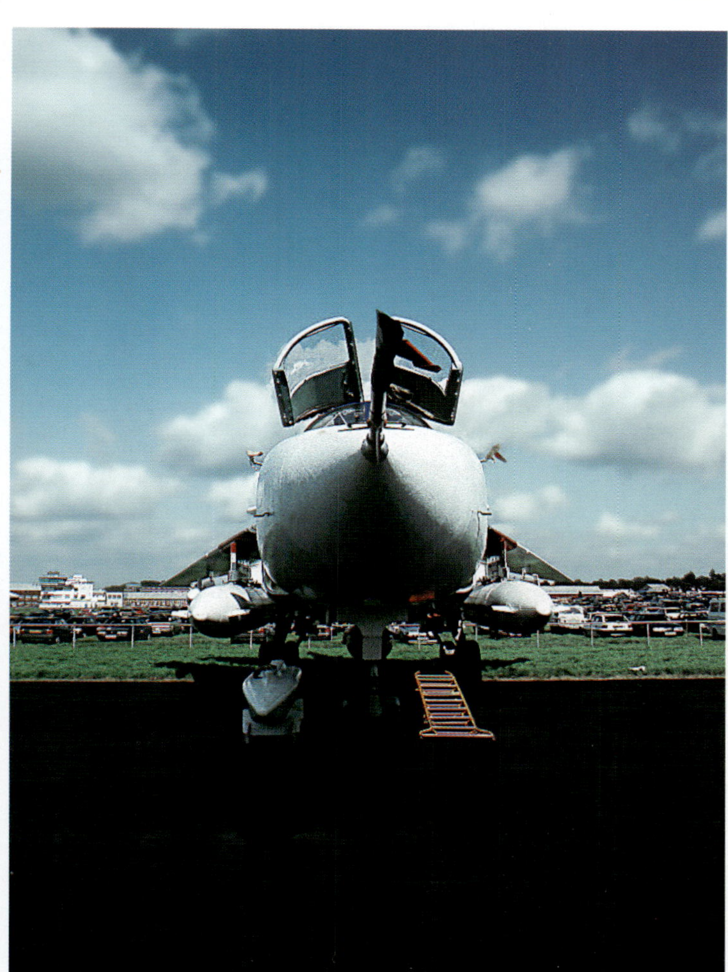

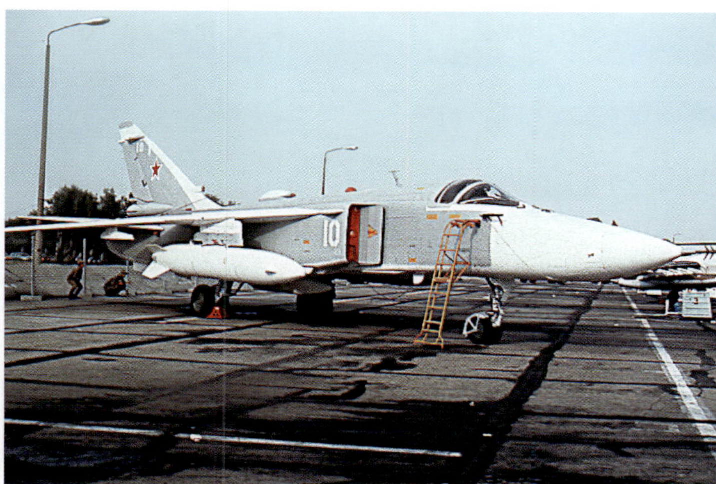

A head-on view of the Su-24MR at Farnborough. This view highlights the substantially different fuselage shape of the Su-24 compared to its American counterpart, the F-111 Aardvark.

In tactical service, the Su-24MR wears the plainer colors typical of the whole Fencer family. This Su-24MR of the 11th Separate Air Reconnaissance Regiment was displayed at Damgarten in 1992. The belly pod is either the Tangazh or Shpil-2M system. (Michael Jerchel)

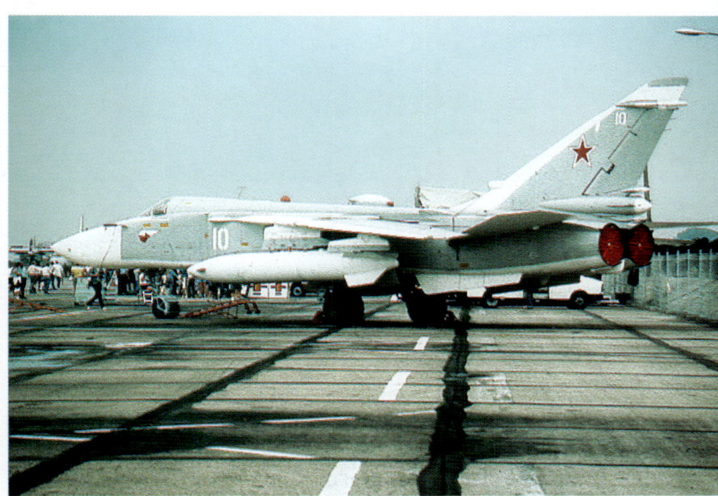

A Su-24MR of the 11th Sep. Air Recce Regt. In this view, the large heat exhanger on the fuselage spine characteristic of this variant is very evident. (Michael Jerchel)

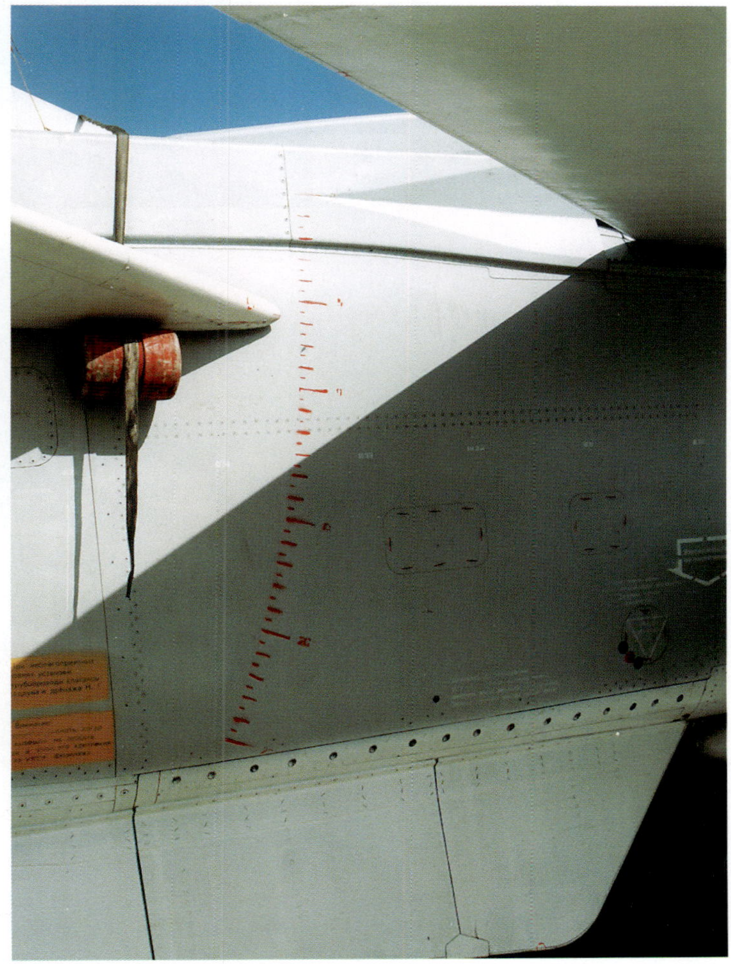

A detail view of the markings forward of the tail on the Su-24MR. The red markings show the depression and elevation of the tail surface. (Michael Jerchel)

Sukhoi Su-25T Frogfoot

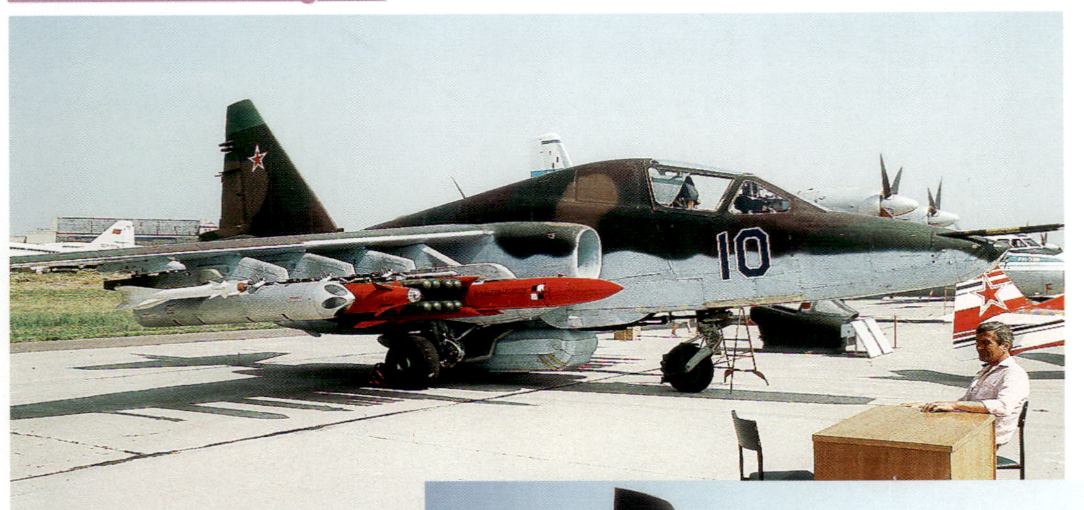

The Su-25T is a new all-weather attack version of the Su-25 Frogfoot family. Although based on the lengthened fuselage of the Su-25UB trainer, the aircraft has only a single crewman. The Su-25T is based on the lessons of the Afghanistan War where Soviet pilots demanded more sophisticated target attack avionics than were fitted to the basic Su-25. The Su-25T may be redesignated Su-34 if production begins and the export version is called Su-25TK or Su-34K.

Besides the extensive reworking of the nose, the Su-25T also has significant changes in the rear fuselage, notably a large fairing at the base of the tail containing an infrared jamming system to decoy man-portable anti-aircraft missiles such as Stinger and SA-7.

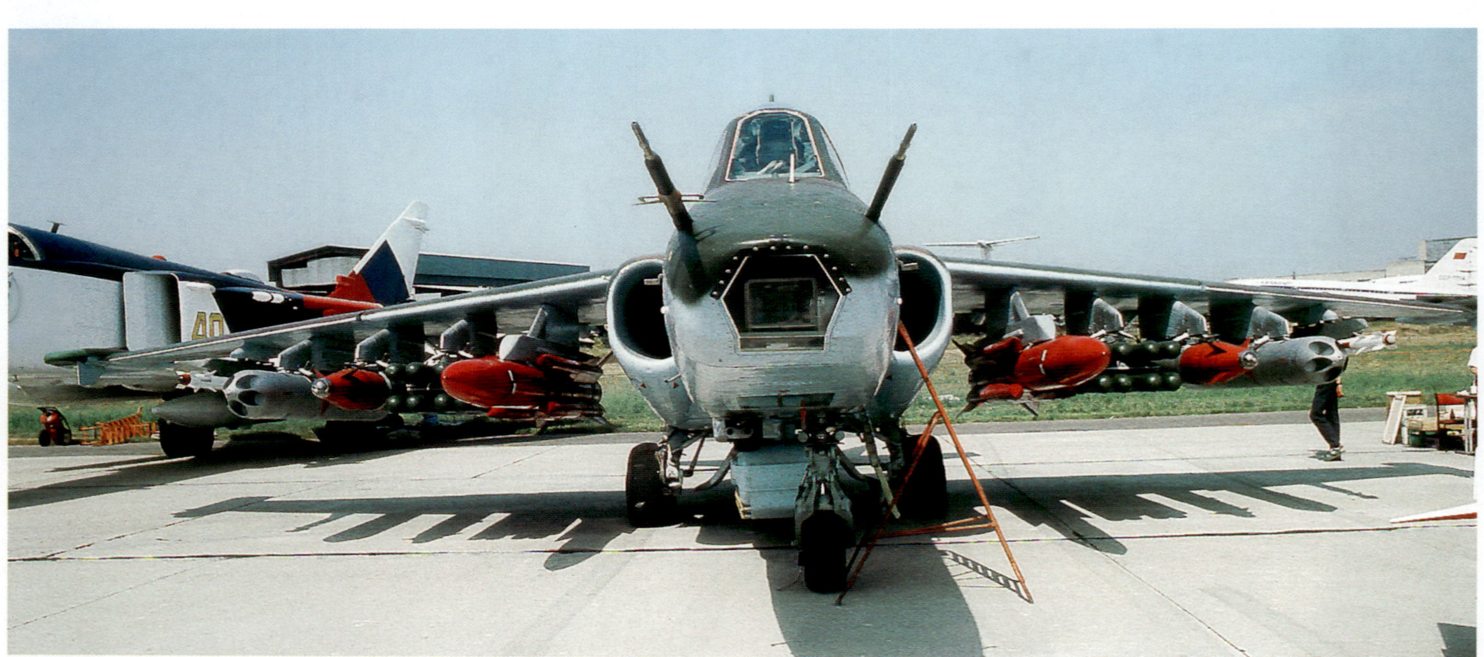

In the nose of the aircraft is a new stabilized laser rangefinder and target designator system and *I-251 Shchval* electro-optical sight, part of the new *Voshod* navigation attack package, which replace the simpler *Klon* laser-rangefinder found in the basic Su-25. The electro-optical system was developed by the Zenit NPO.

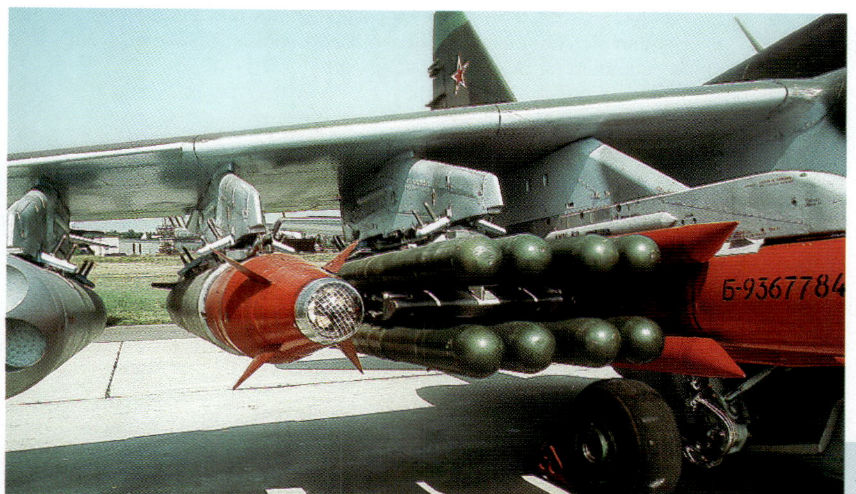

The armament package of the Su-25T can include laser designated weapons, including laser guided bombs and the new *Vikhr* (Whirlwind) long range anti-tank missile, seen here in the eight round APU-8 launch rack. The inboard most pylon is fitted with a Kh-31 anti-radar missile, evident in other pictures here , and outboard the green Vikhr missiles is a S-25L laser guided rocket.

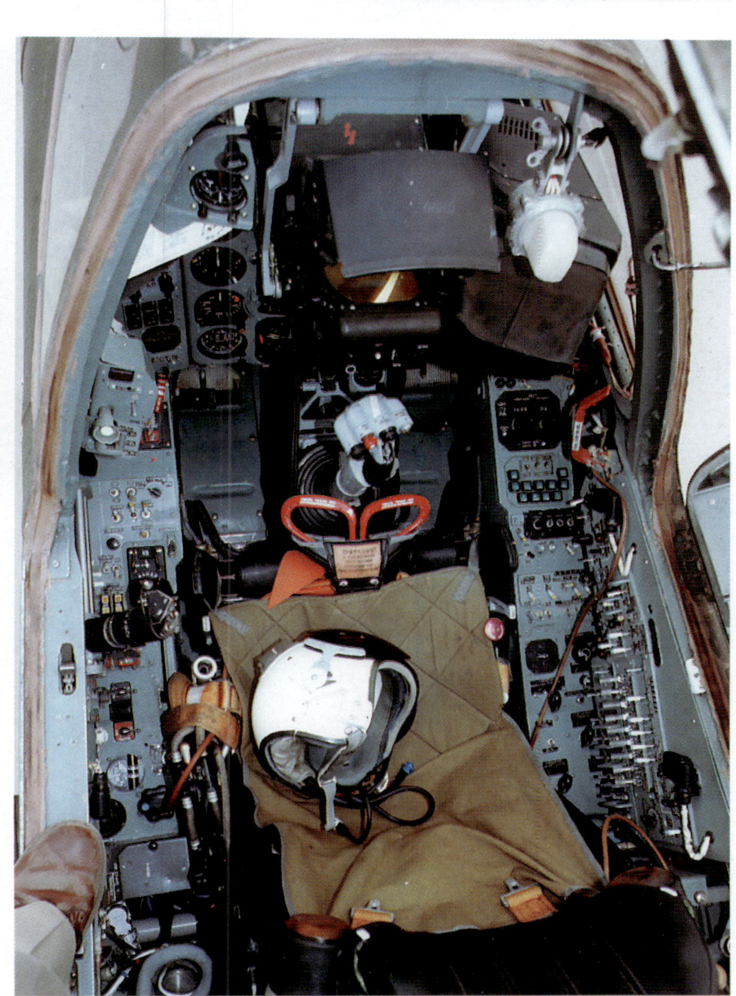

Under the Su-25T are two important new additions. The aircraft cannon has been moved to the belly to increase the space in the nose for avionics. In addition, a large thermal imaging night target pod, code-named *Merkuriy,* has been added. Merkuriy is the first Russian thermal imaging pod for strike aircraft, and gives the Frogfoot night attack capability for the first time.

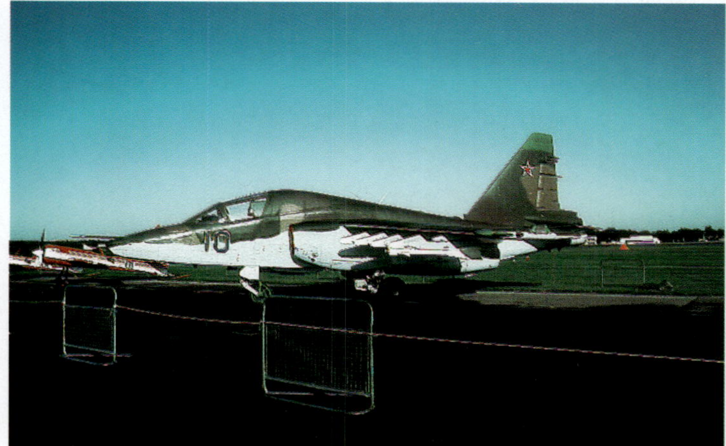

Su-25T number 01 resurfaced in Farnborough in September 1992, minus most of its extensive armament array. This aircraft is being heavily marketed in the Mid-East as an ideal platform for the type of precision guided munitions attack that was so successful in Operation Desert Storm. The Su-25T at Farnborough was armed only with a pair of R-60MK (AA-8 Aphid) self-defense missiles. A small production batch of these aircraft have been in trials with the Russian Air Force for several years, but there is still no firm commitment for production.

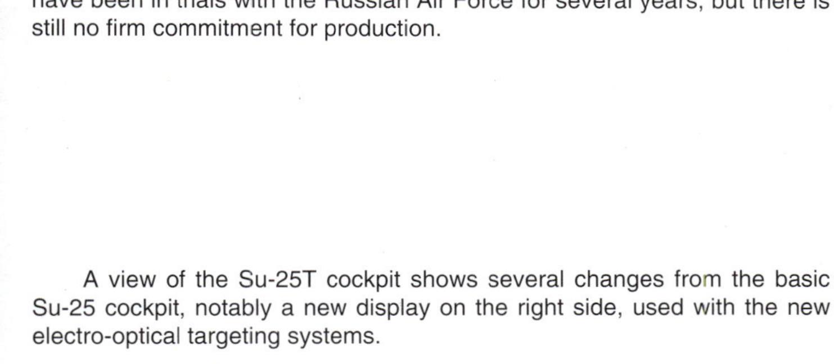

A view of the Su-25T cockpit shows several changes from the basic Su-25 cockpit, notably a new display on the right side, used with the new electro-optical targeting systems.

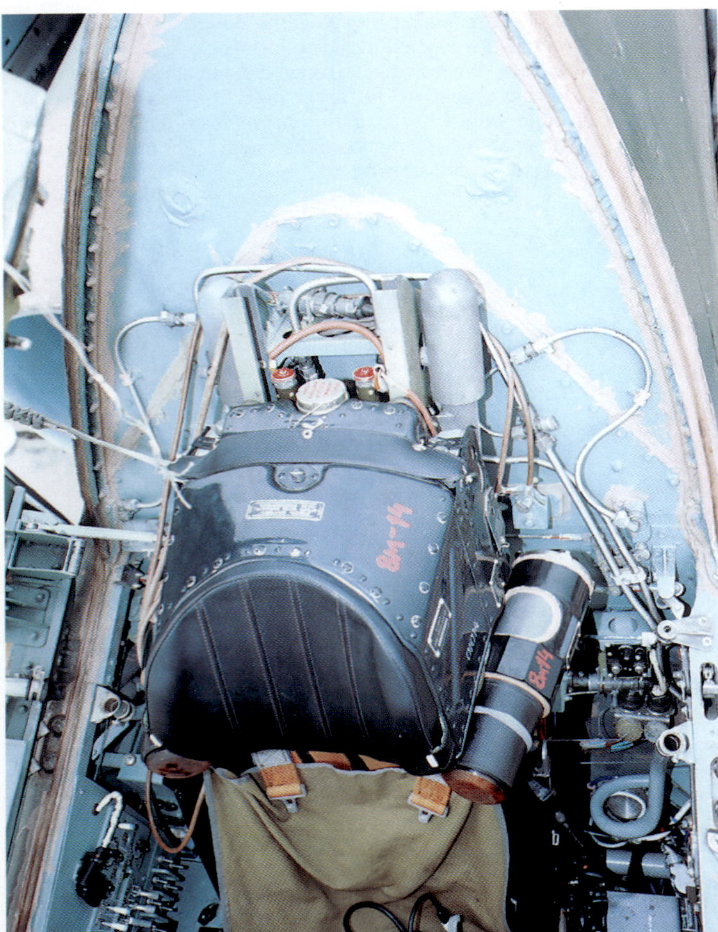

A view towards the rear of the cockpit shows how the area behind the pilot is completely sealed off. The ejection seat is a Severin K-36D, the current standard for Soviet combat aircraft.

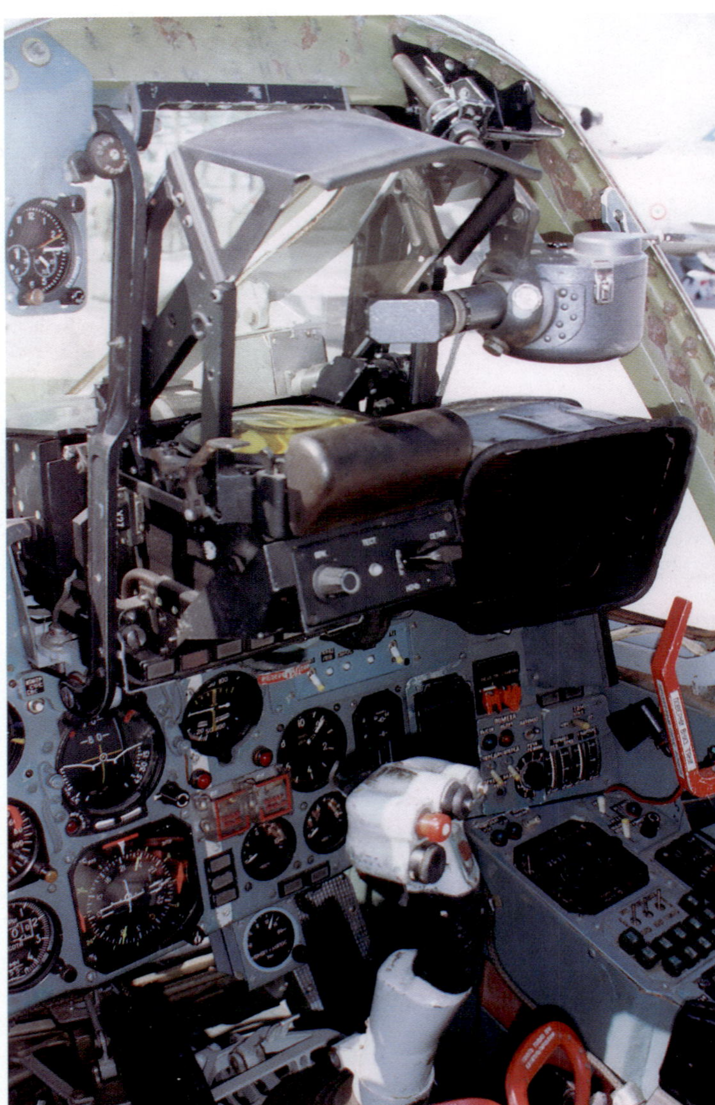

A close-up of the heads-up-display and new video display in the Su-25T. (Nick Cook)

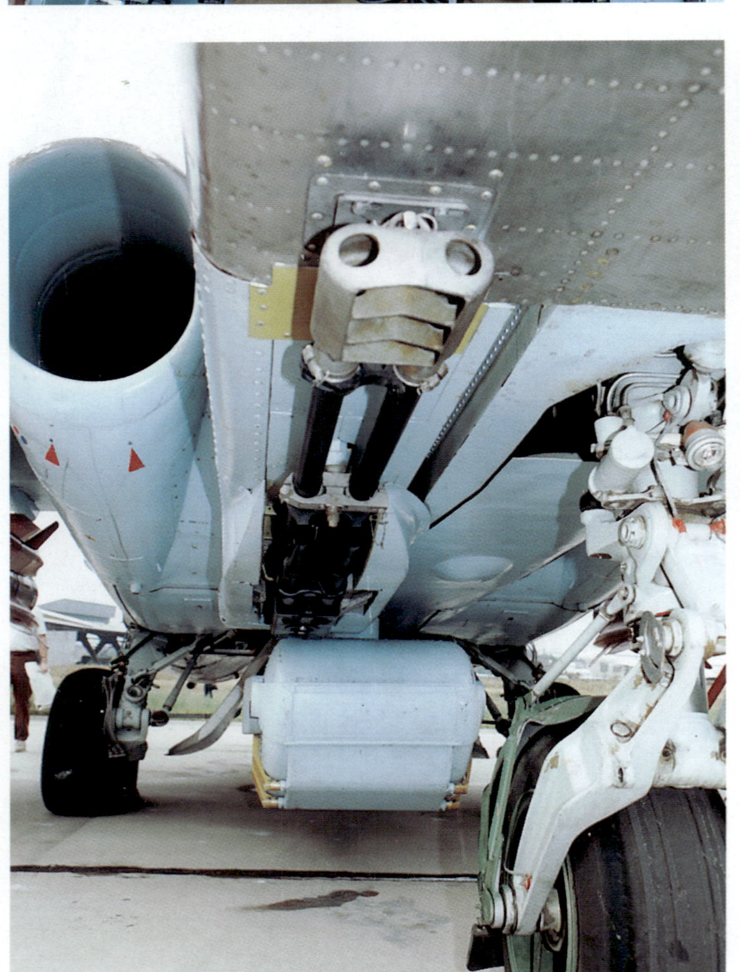

Another detail view of the belly, showing the belly mounting of the twin-barreled 30mm cannon. This is the same weapon as used in the AO-17A mounting in the basic Su-25.

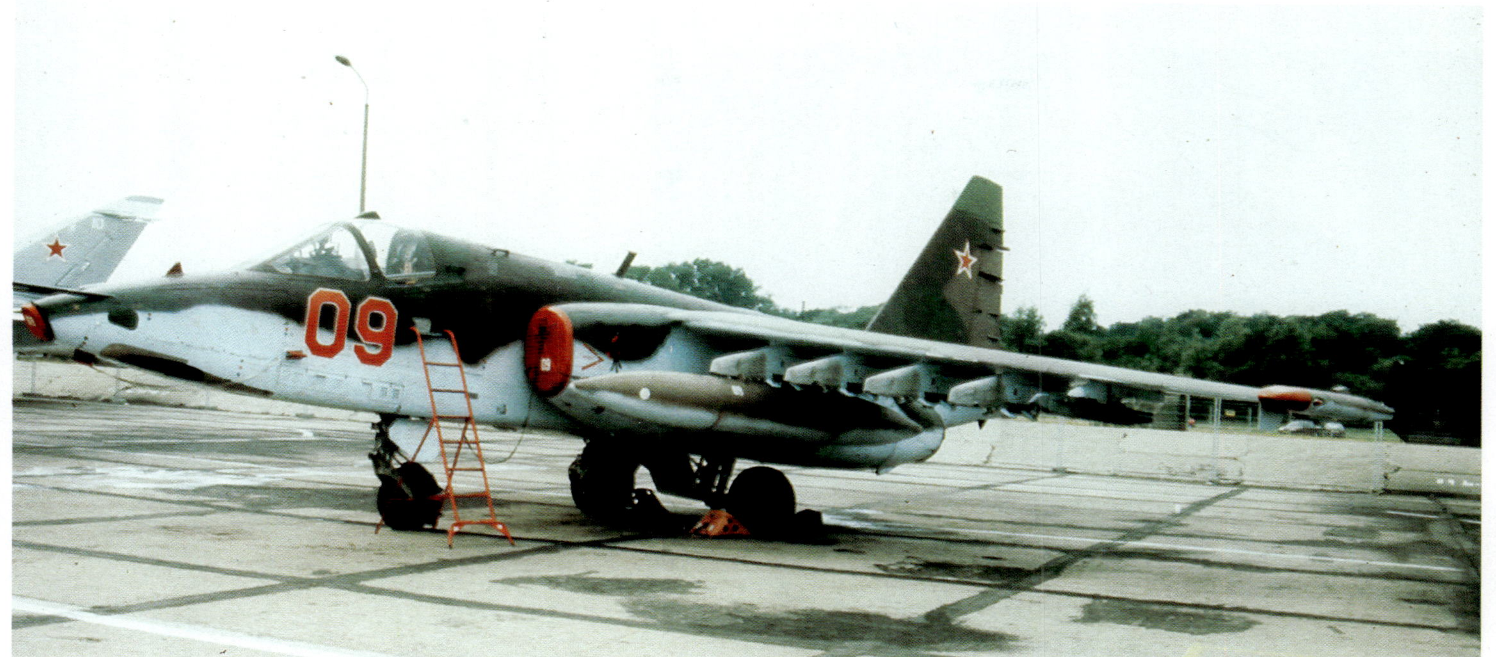

Russian ground attack regiment still rely on the earlier versions of the Su-25 Grach. Two regiments of Su-25 have served in Germany until recently, the 357th Sep. Ground Attack Air Regiment at Brandis and the 368th at Demmin. This aircraft was displayed at Grossenhain in the summer of 1992. Notice that it carries a Rook (European Crow) cartoon on the air intake, a reflection of the popular Russian name for this aircraft. Grach means rook in Russian. (Michael Jerchel)

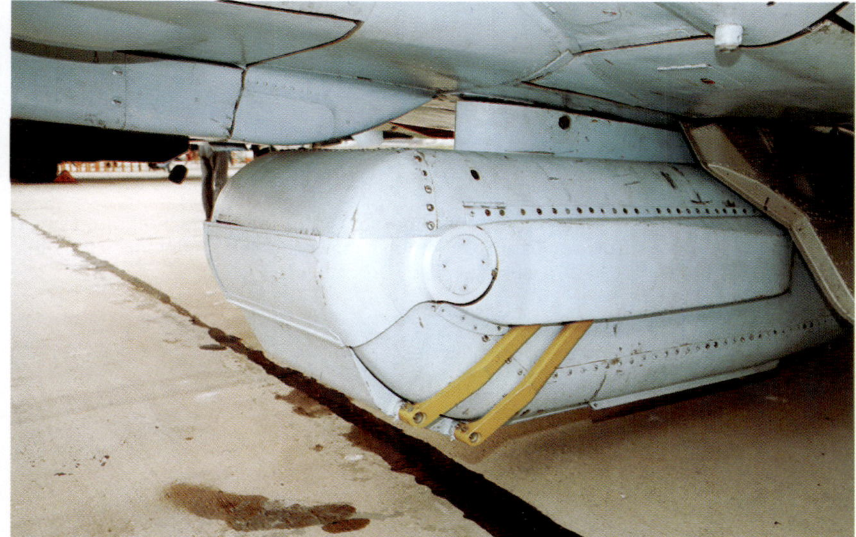

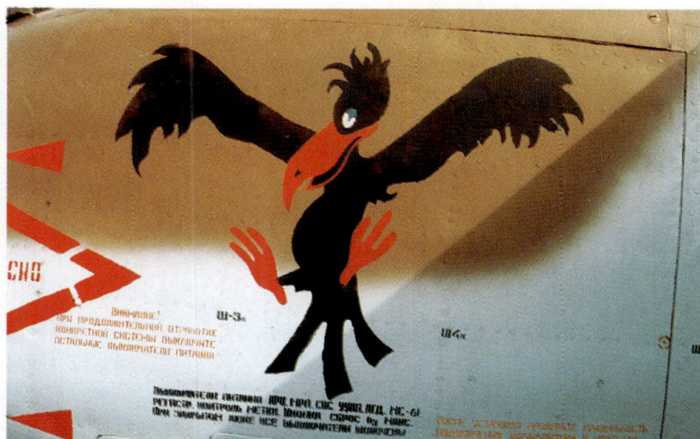

A close-up detail of the Rook insignia on the Russian Su-25 Grach. (Michael Jerchel)

A detail view of the new Merkuriy thermal imaging night attack pod under the belly of the Su-25T. This will give the Su-25T night attack capability for the first time.

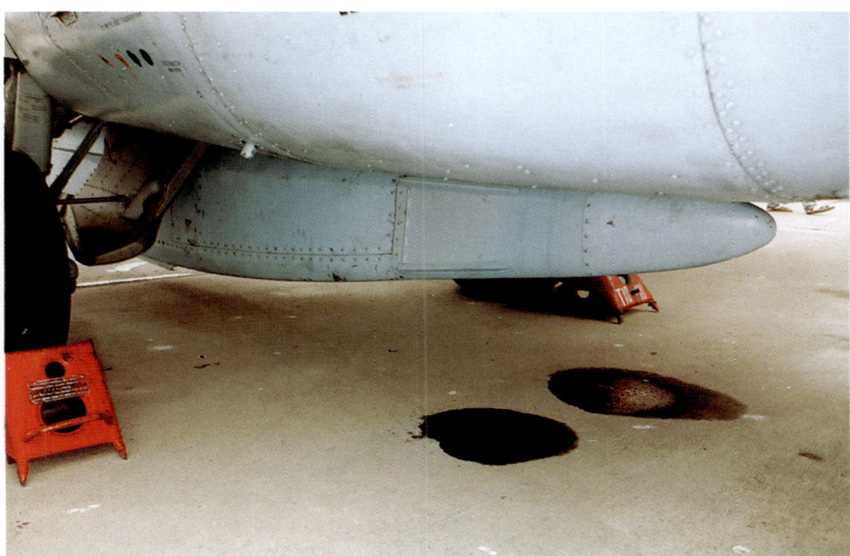

A rear view of the Merkuriy pod under the belly of the Su-25T.

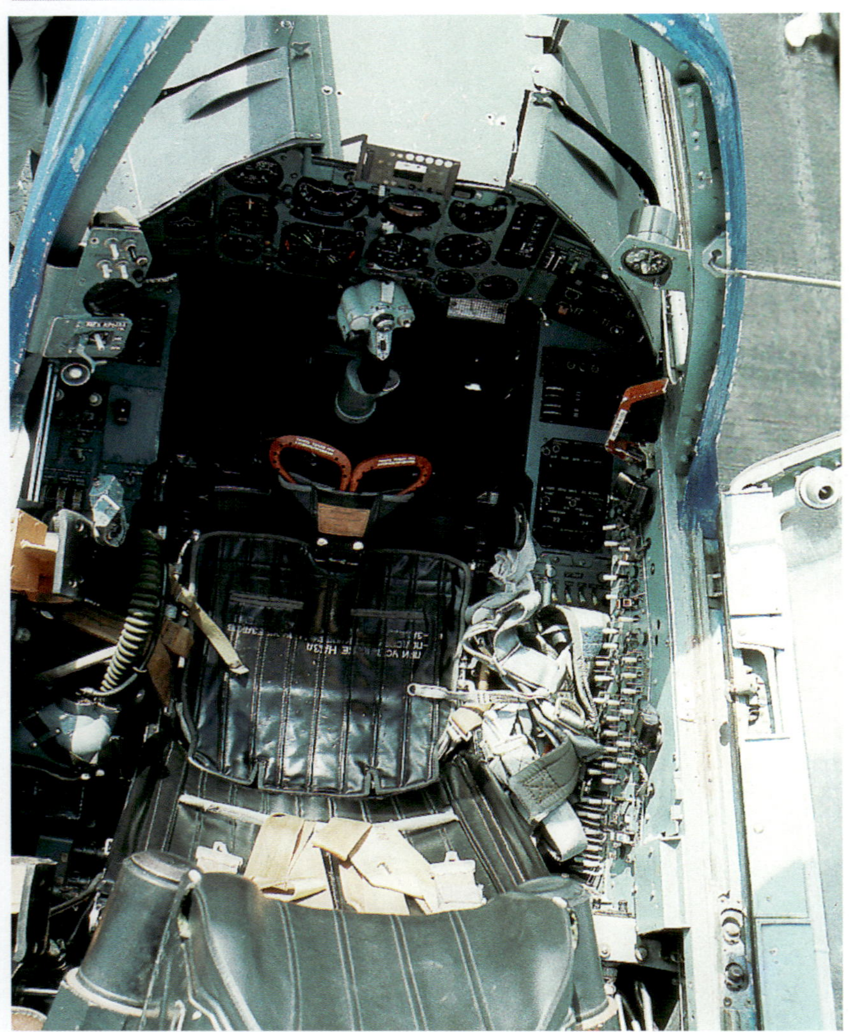

This view into the cockpit of the Su-28 Frogfoot trainer displayed at Farnborough shows the detail differences from the Su-25T strike version.

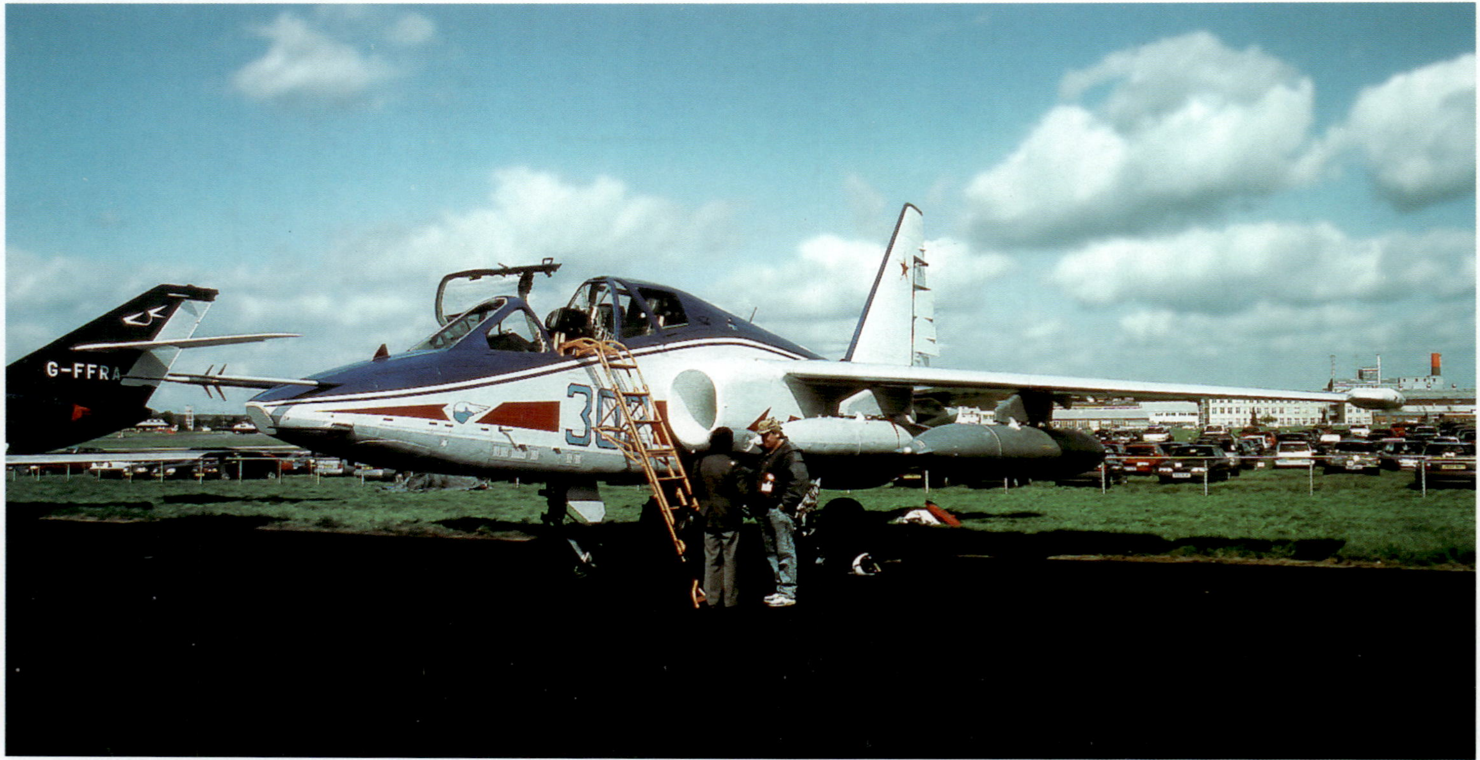

The Su-28 Frogfoot trainer was first displayed in 1989 at the Paris Air Salon, but then disappeared from Western demonstrations for several years. It reappeared at Farnborough in 1992 as part of a campaign to reopen the Frogfoot production line for foreign export.

SUKHOI Su-27/35 FLANKER

Su-27 Flanker

A perennial favorite at the international airshows is Su-27 number 388, and the flying display at Farnborough in 1992 was up to the usual high standards of the Sukhoi test pilot. Here the aircraft is landing with its speed brake open.

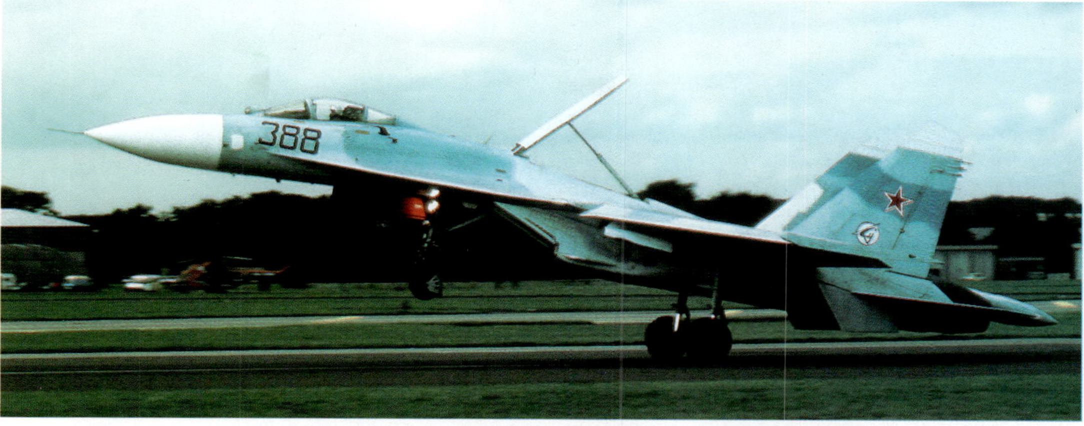

Su-27UB Flanker

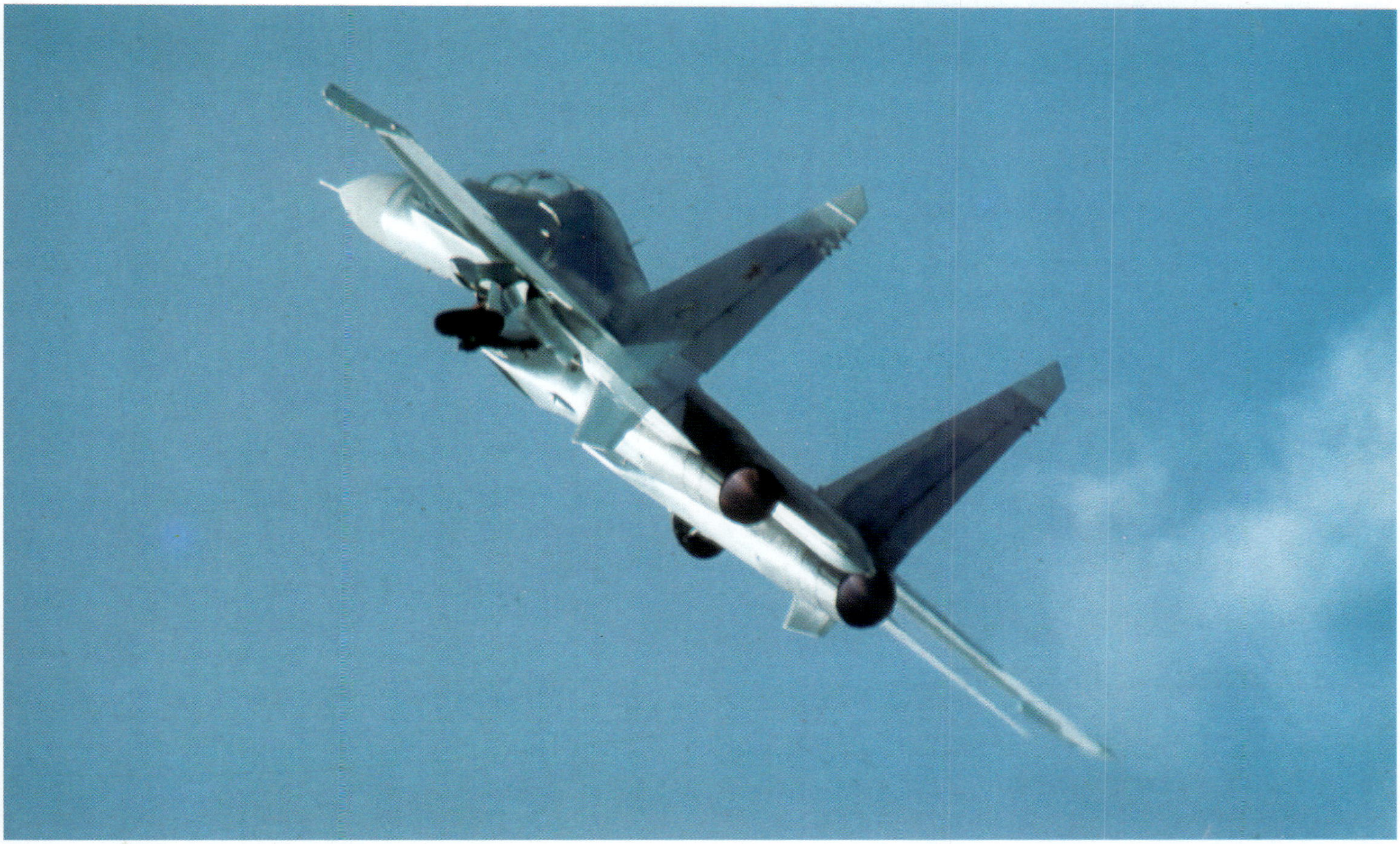

The Sukhoi test-pilots traditionally put the Su-27UB trainer through the same unbelievable maneuvers as its fighter ancestor, seen here in a steep climb moments after take-off.

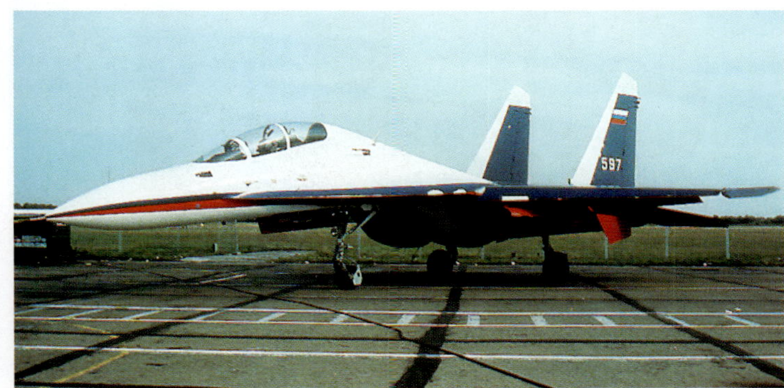

A popular new flying team is the Test Pilot team, seen here in Germany in 1992. This team uses pilots of the LII Experimental Flight Institute at Zhukovskiy. (Michael Jerchel)

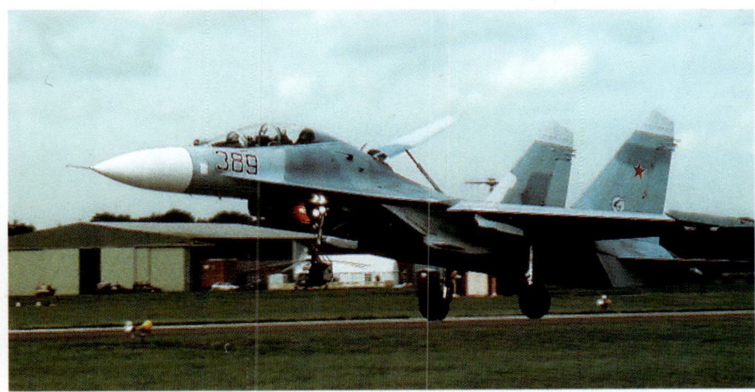

Another steady performer at the international air show circuit is Su-27UB number 389, seen here in the final landing stages at Farnborough.

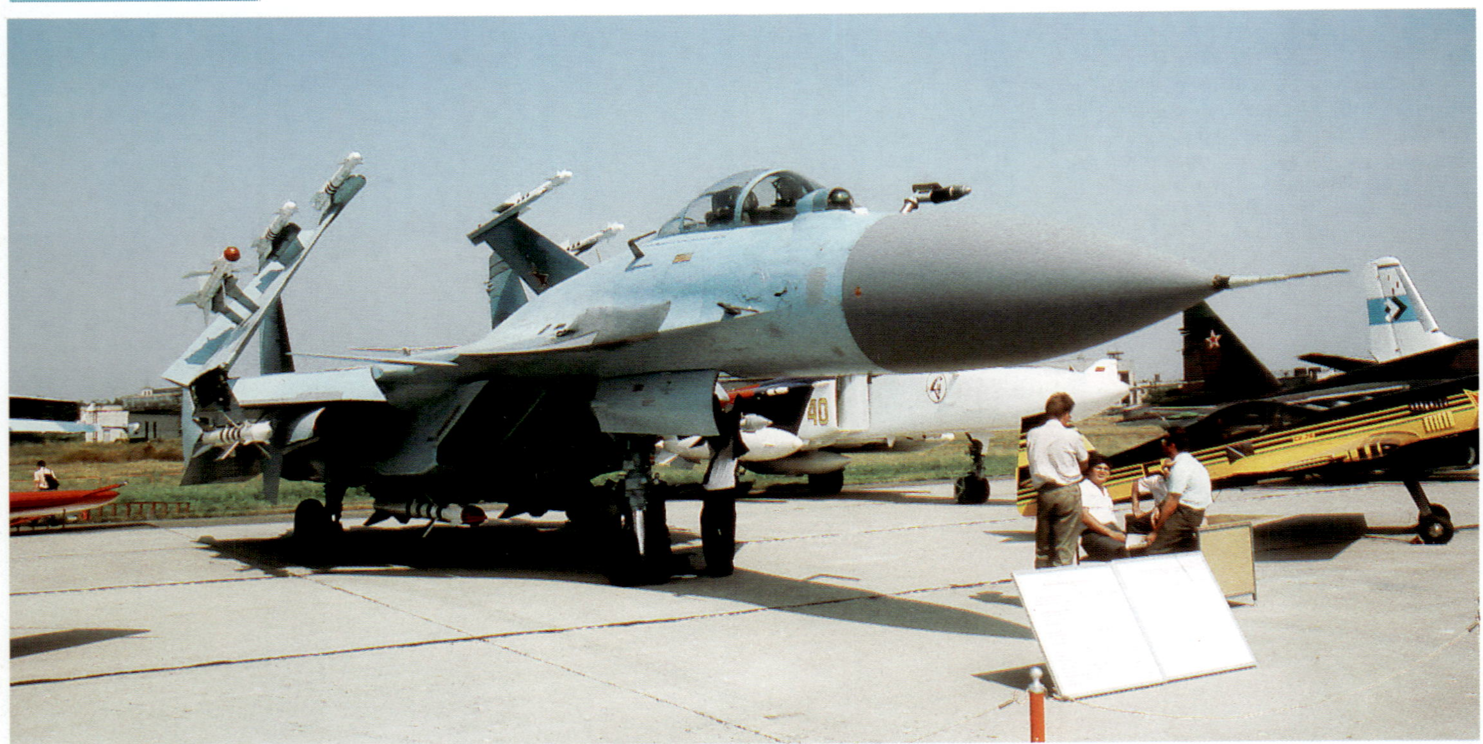

The Su-27K is a navalized version of the Flanker intended for the new full-deck carriers of the Project 1153.5 (Adm. Kuznetsov) class. One of the most obvious changes is the folding wing arrangement and the forward canards.

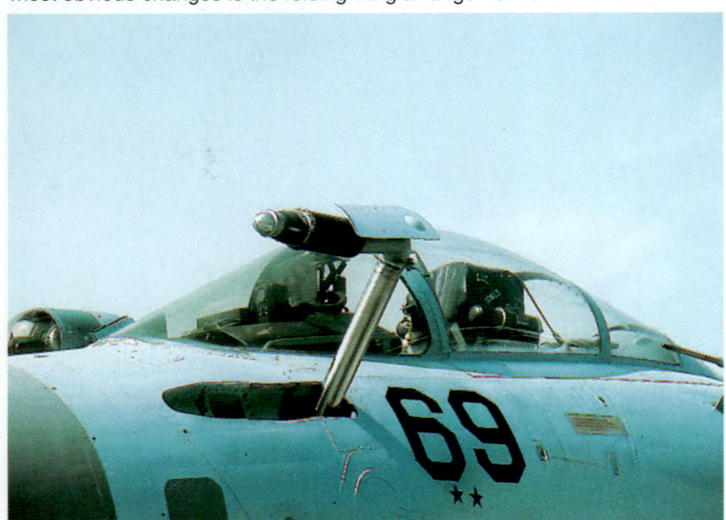

The Su-27K is also fitted with a retractable refueling probe on the port side of the cockpit.

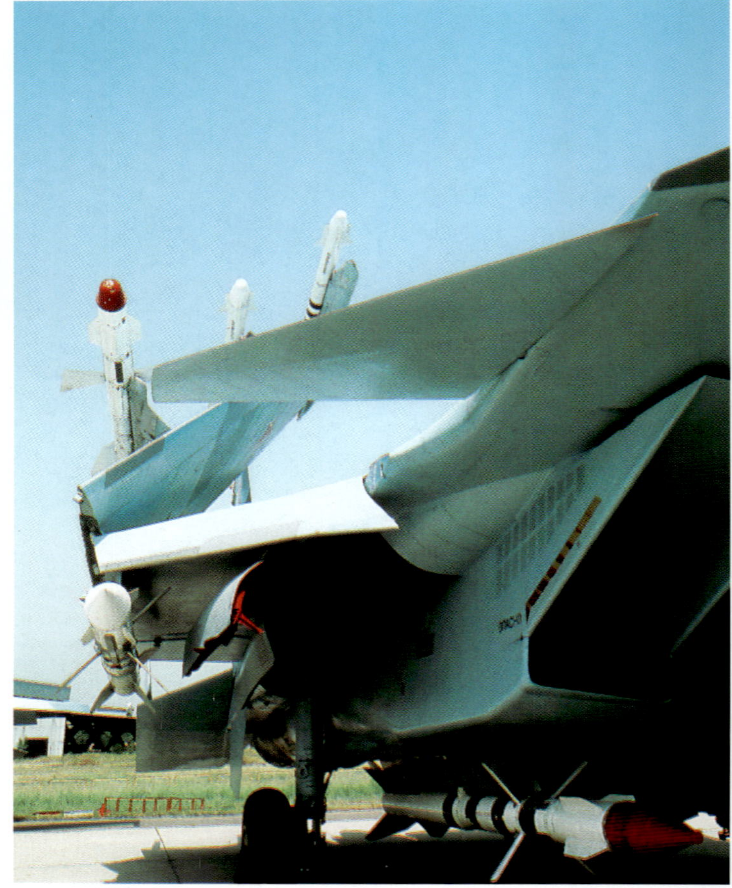

This detail view of the inner wing shows the large canard fitted immediately forward of the wing, as well as the large leading edge slat.

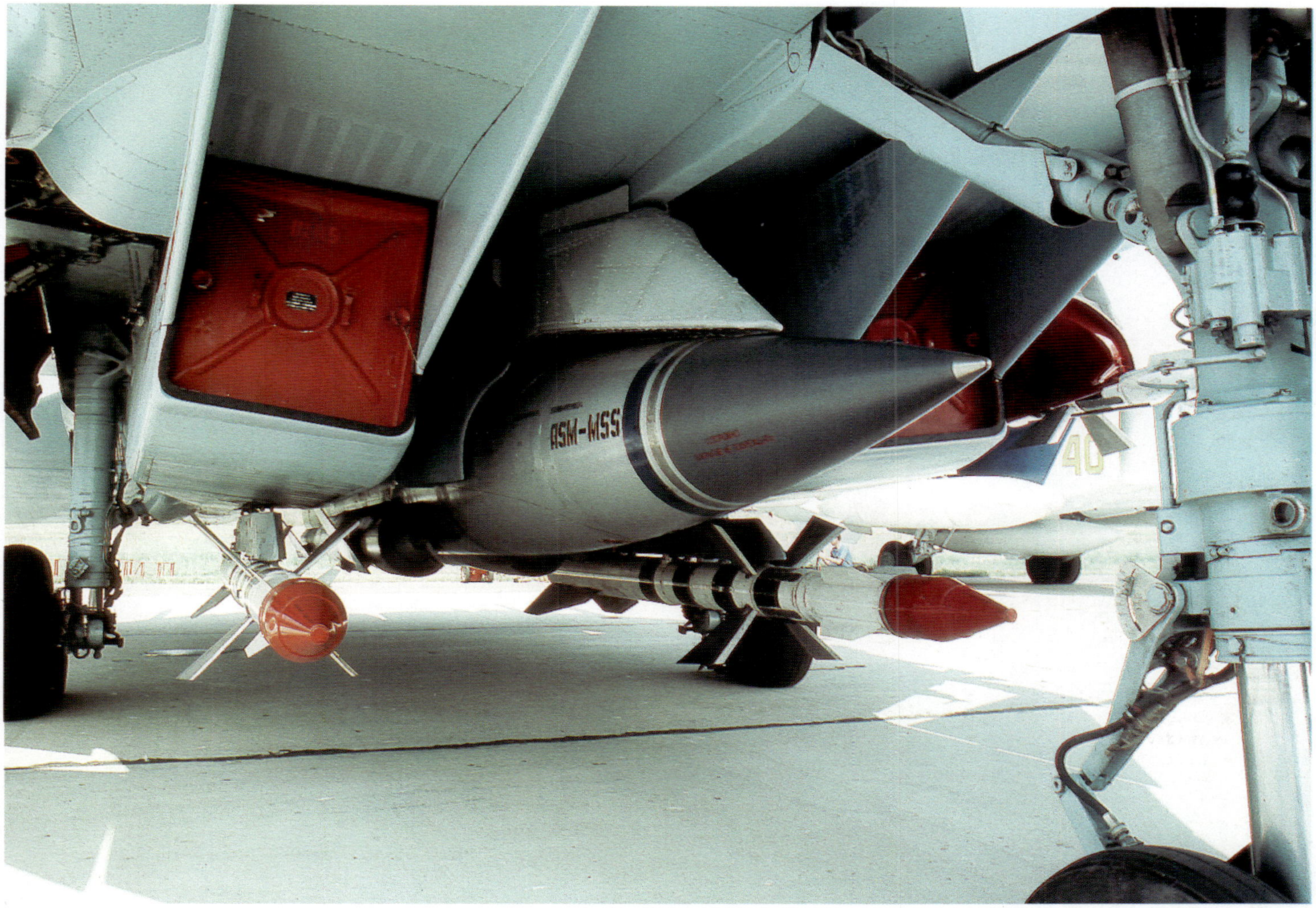

Although the Su-27K is intended primarily as a fighter, it has been modified to permit its use in the naval strike role. Under the belly is the Raduga *Moskit* (Mosquito), a large, 4.5 ton anti-ship missile which strikes its target at Mach 2 with a 350kg warhead.

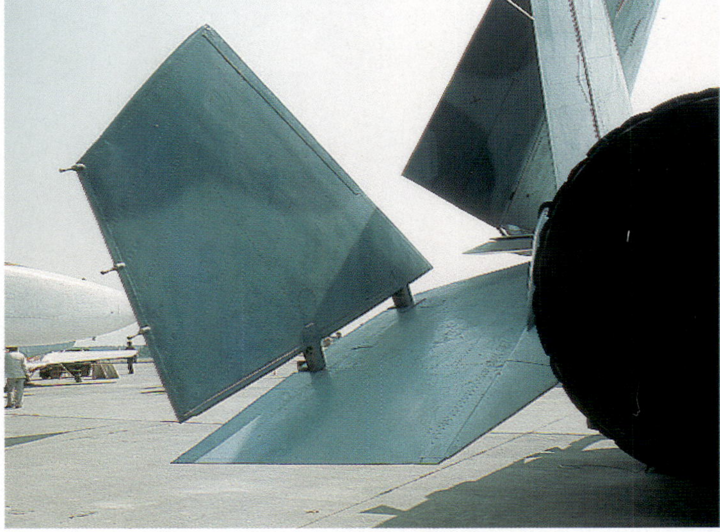

A detail view of the folding rear tail on the Su-27K.

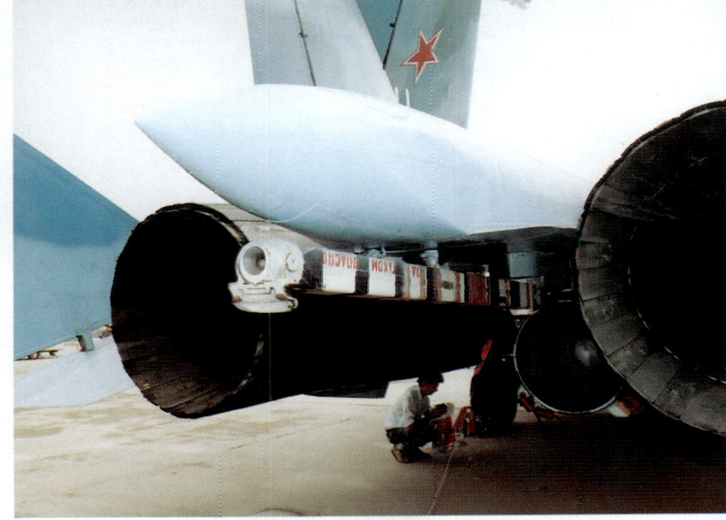

A detail view of the rear arrestor hook assembly on the Su-27K.

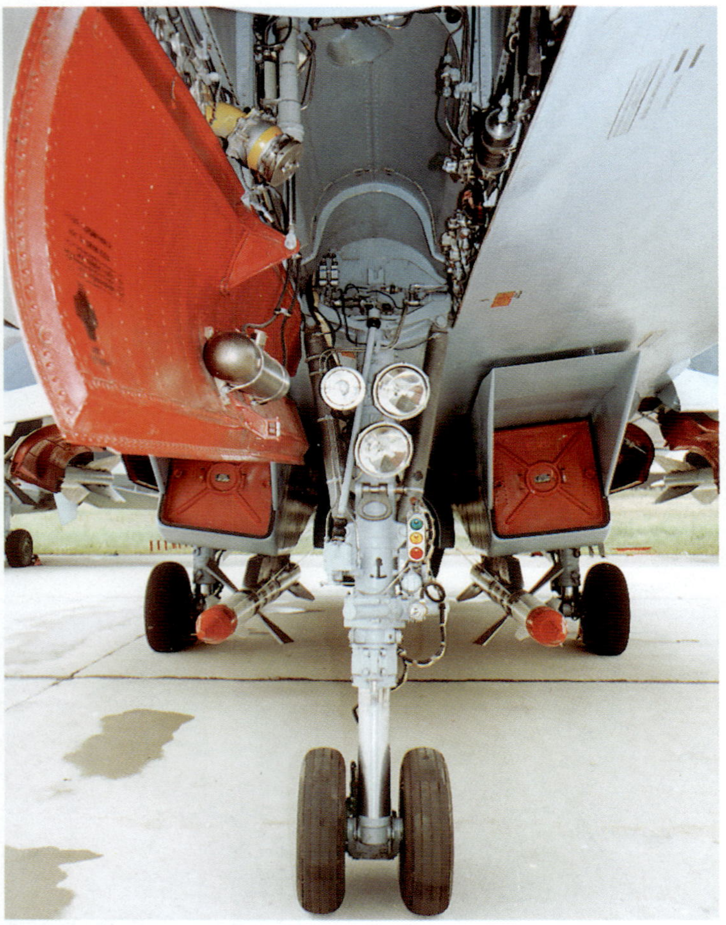

A detail view of the reinforced nose landing gear on the Su-27K.

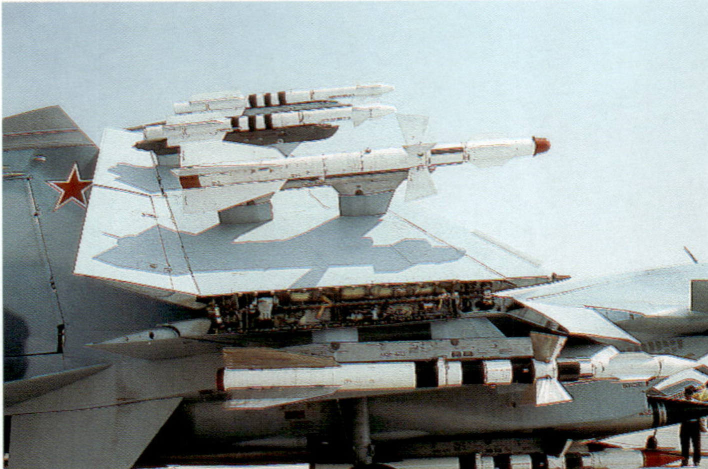

A detail view of the starboard side showing the wing in the folded position. The missiles under the belly and under the inner wing section are R-27ER; the black bands indicate they are UZR-27 training rounds, not live missiles. On the folded portion of the wing is an R-27T IR guided AAM and two R-73 IR guided short range AAMs.

Su-27IB Flanker

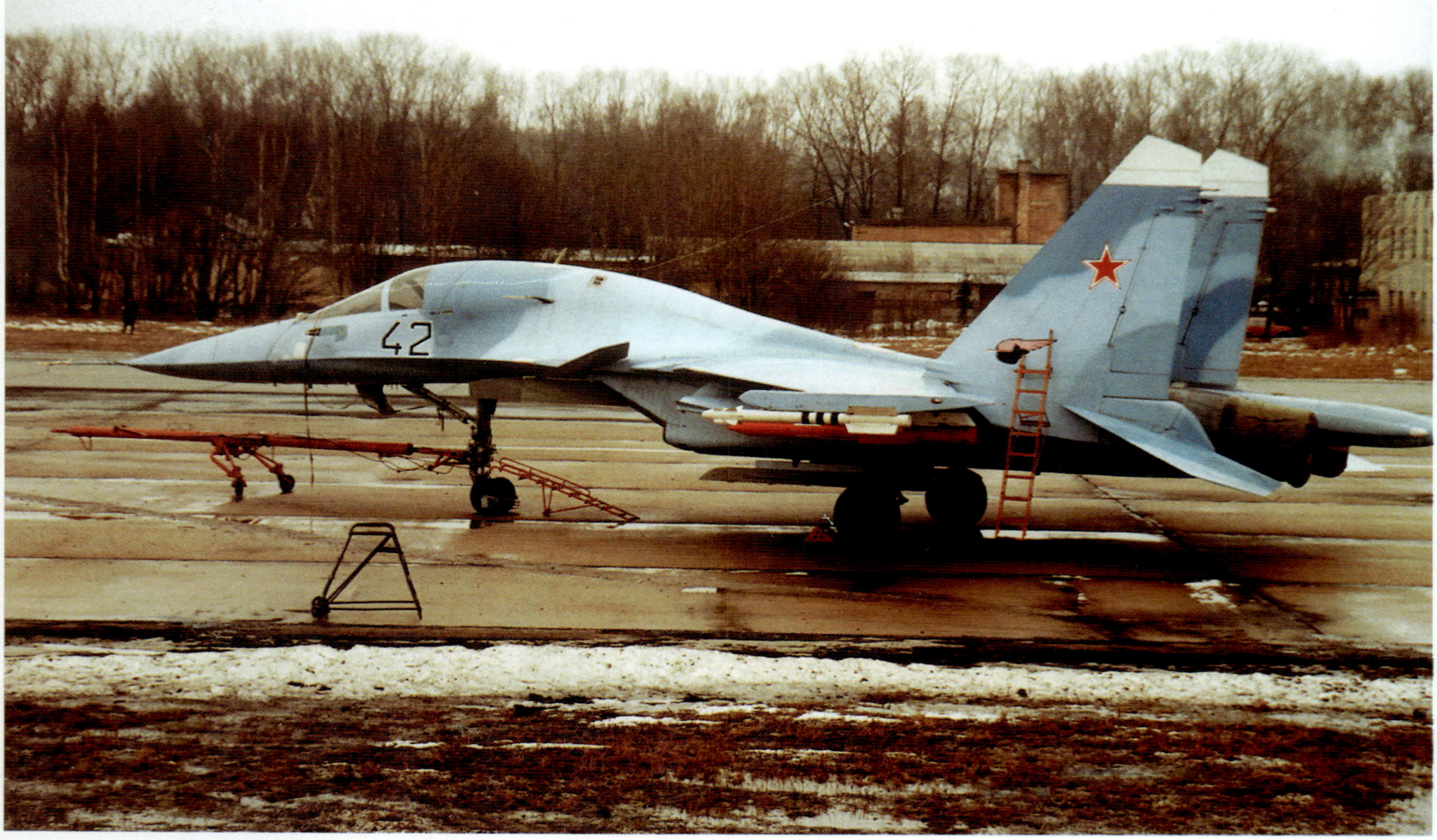

One aircraft which did not play a prominent role at either Zhukovskiy or Farnborough was the new Su-27IB strike aircraft. This aircraft was first displayed at a closed gathering of CIS leaders outside Minsk in February 1992 where these photos were taken. At Zhukovskiy, the aircraft took part in the flying display, but it was never placed in the static exhibits.

A port view of the Su-27IB. This aircraft is part of a Sukhoi effort to interest the new Russian Air Force in standardizing on a common airframe for both the fighter and strike aircraft role. This version would be used to replace the earlier Su-24M strike aircraft, and could also be adapted to the carrier role if needed.

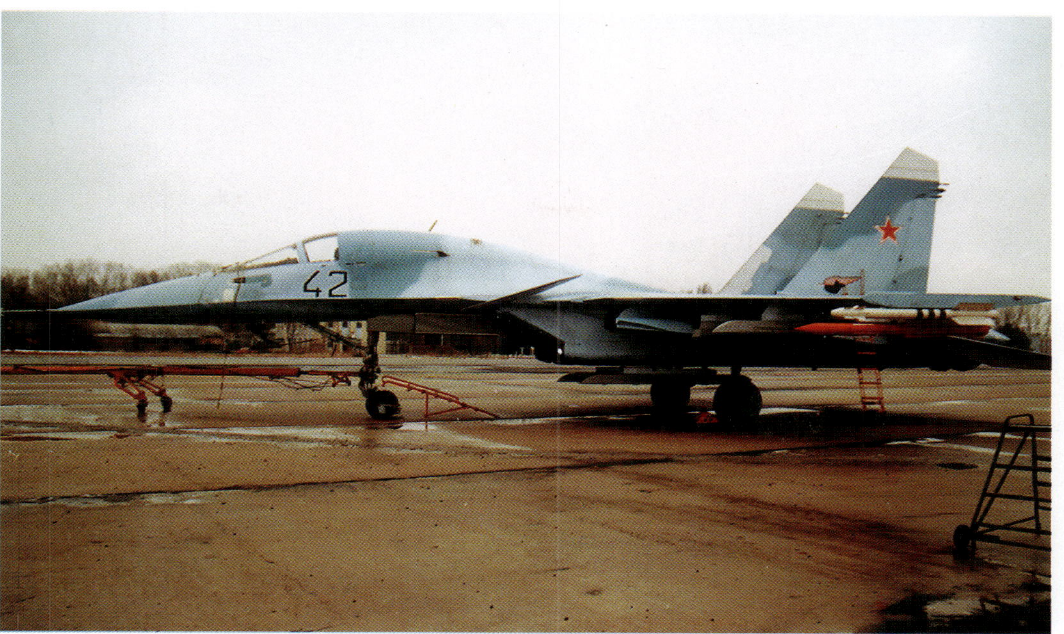

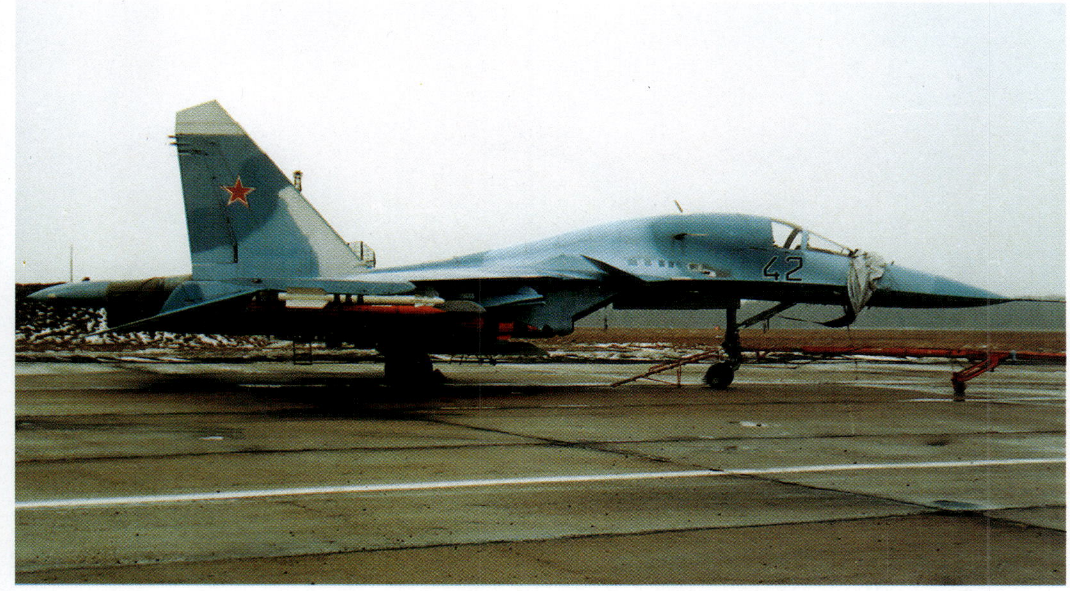

A starboard side view of the Su-27IB. The most obvious change on the aircraft is the reconfiguration of the cockpit for side-by-side seating. This arrangement is generally preferred in the low altitude strike role. The Su-27IB shares some features in common with the new Su-27K such as the canard wings. However, it lacks many of the improvements incorporated into the more advanced Su-27M/Su-35.

Although it was widely reported that the Su-27IB was planned for carrier use, this rear view makes it quite clear that the aircraft is not fitted with an arrestor hook. In fact, the photos showing the Su-27IB trials on the carrier Kuznetsov were taken during approach trials, not actual landings.

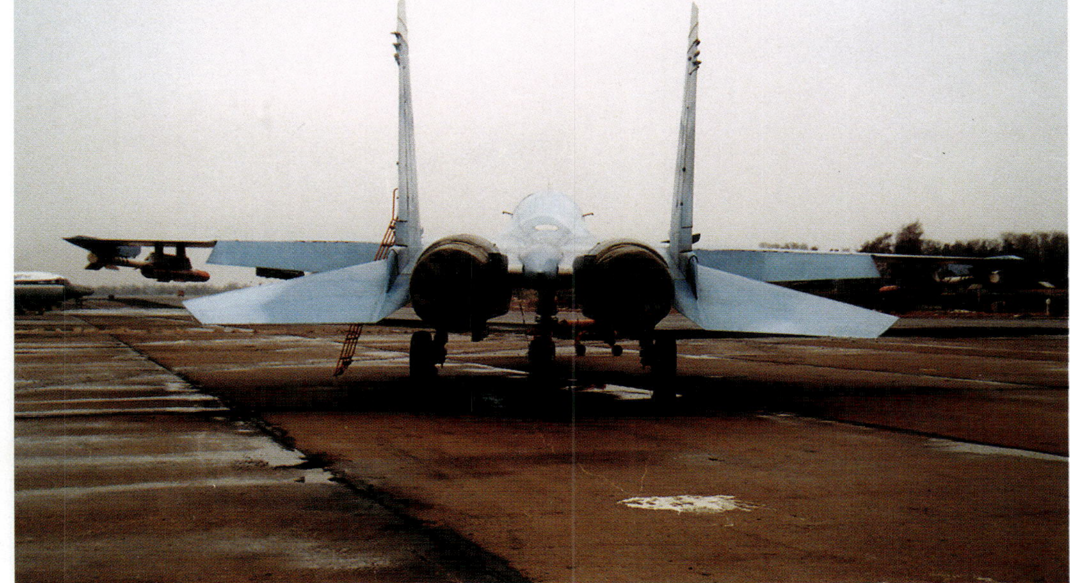

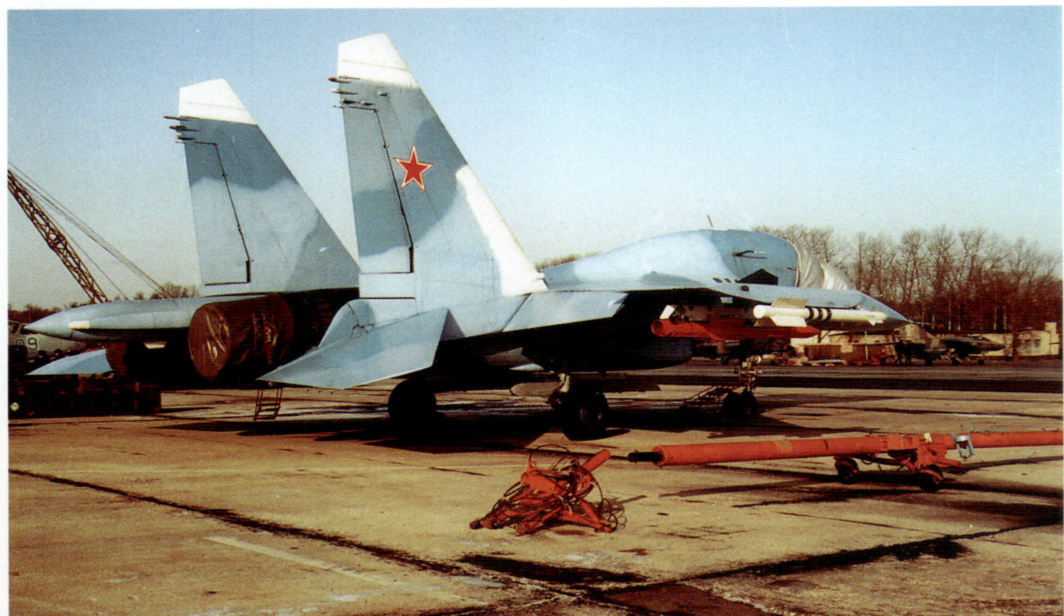

A rear view of Su-27IB shows an R-72 missile fitted to the outer wing rail launcher, a feature not often seen. The three black bands on the missile indicate it is a training round.

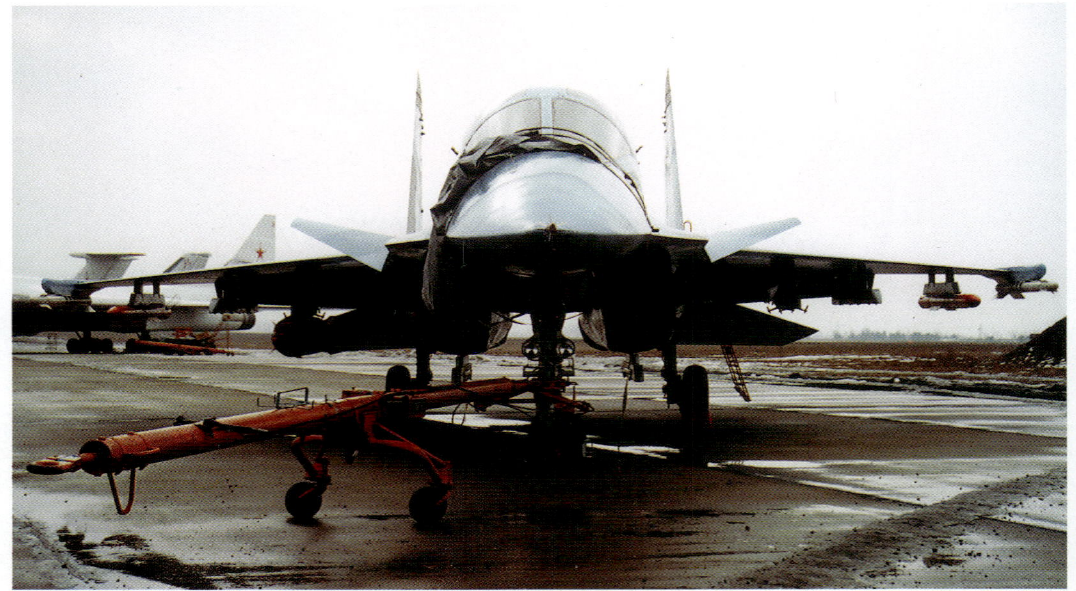

There is some question whether the Su-27IB configuration is an actual production configuration for a strike aircraft, or merely a test bed. The forward flattened "platypus" nose has led to some question whether the aircraft is fitted with an actual navigation/attack radar.

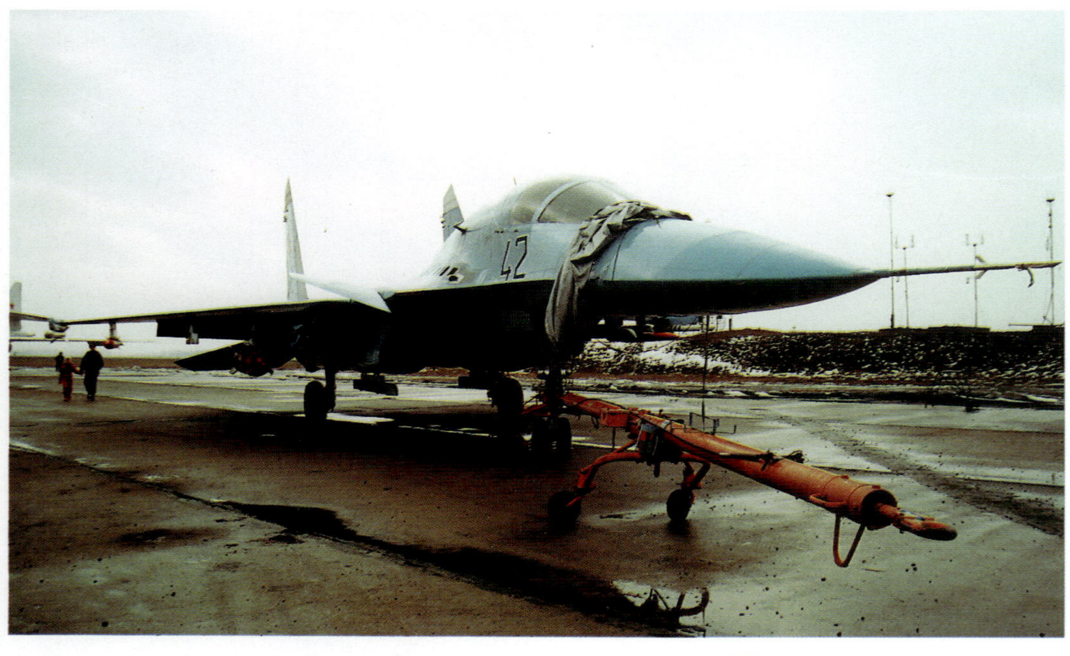

A nose view of the Su-27IB prototype. The aircraft number, 42, stems from the project number: T-10-42 (T-10 being the Sukhoi bureau designation for the Su-27 family).

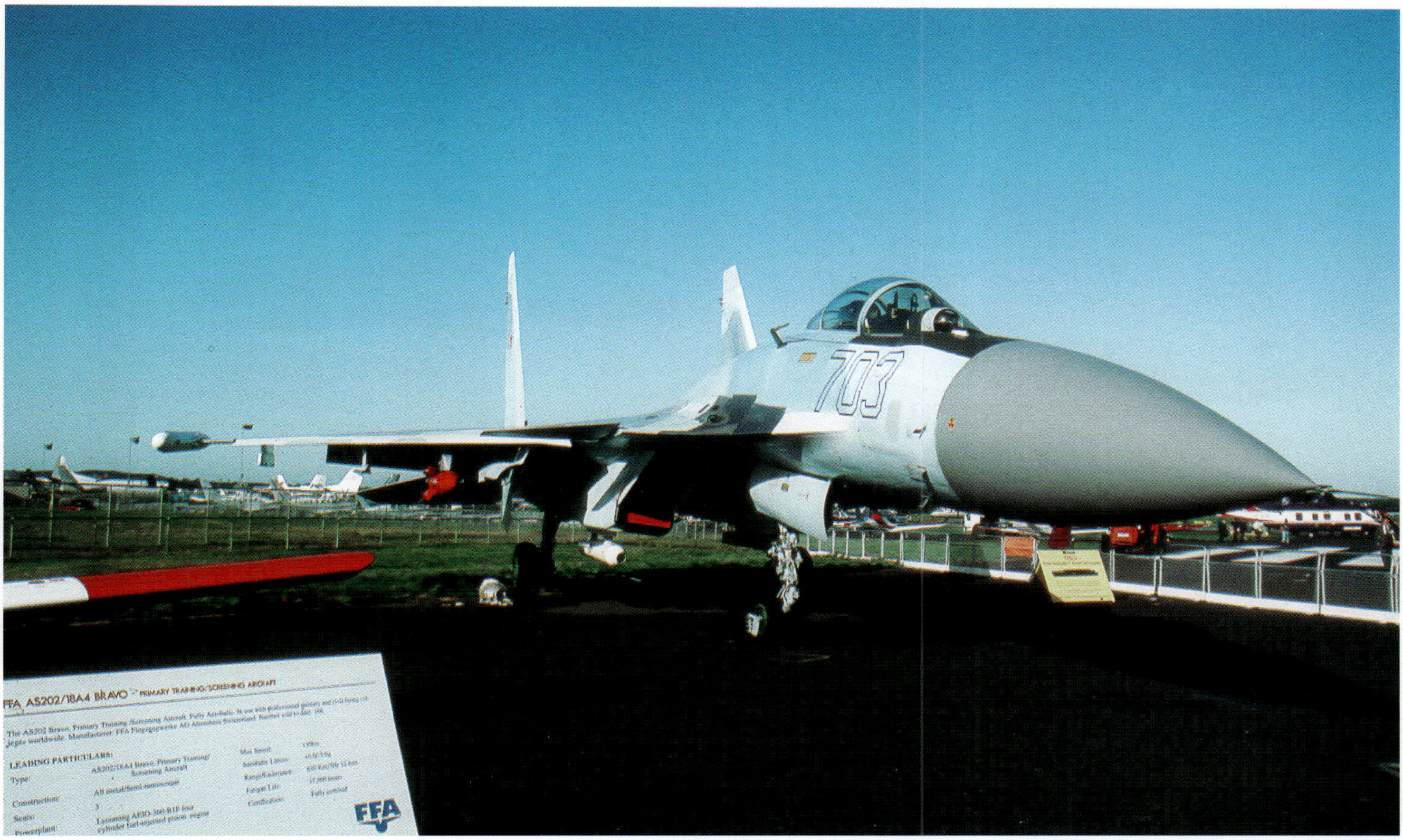

The Sukhoi Su-35, originally known as the Su-27M, is a heavily modernized version of this popular Russian interceptor. The RLPK-27 radar found in the basic Su-27 has been replaced by a new radar with a larger dish.

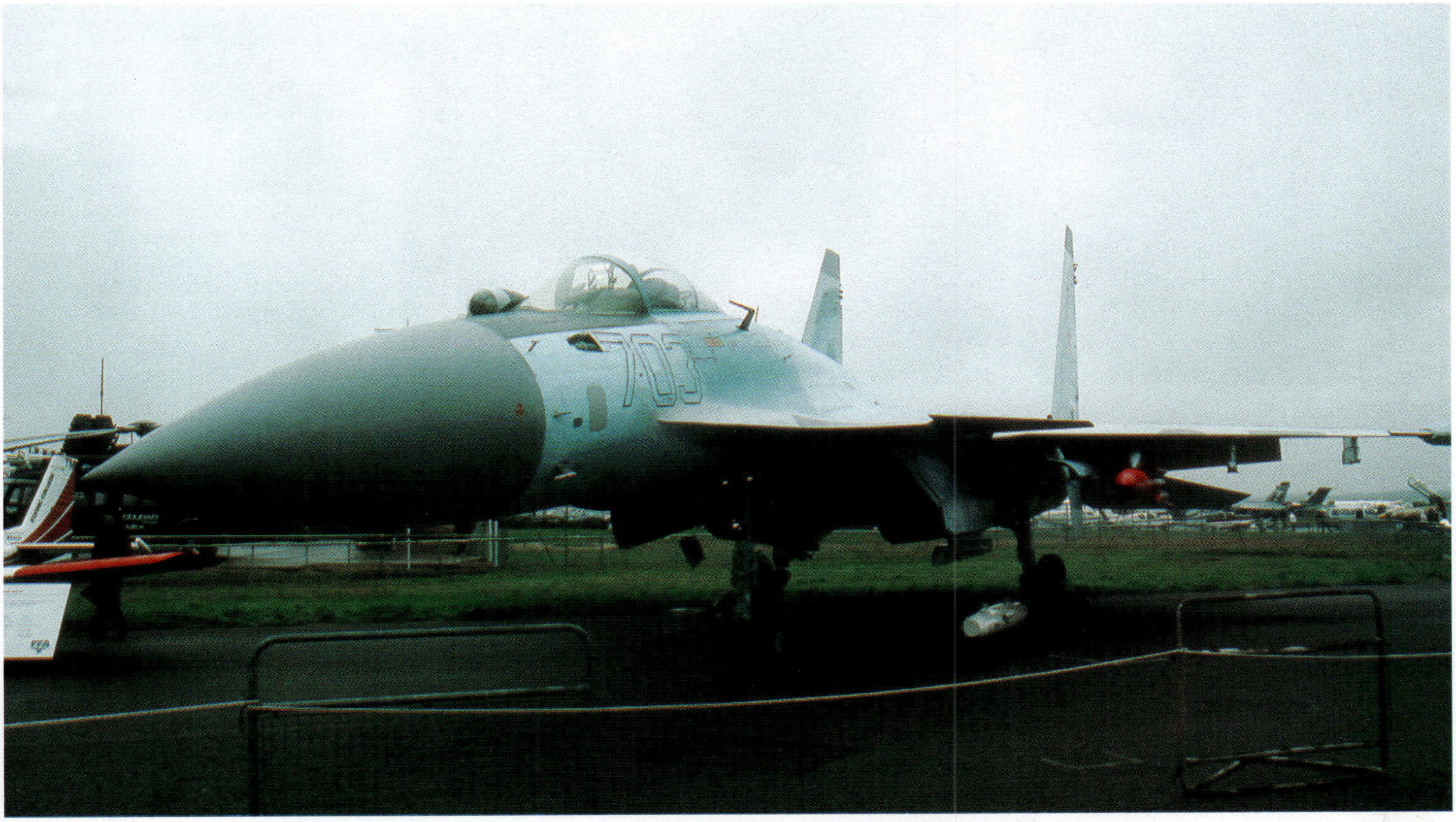

Other changes on the Su-35 include a new IRST sensor in front of the pilot, canard wings like those on the Su-27K carrier fighter, and substantially improved avionics. Unlike the Su-27 which was configured solely as an interceptor, the Su-35 can be used in the ground attack role as is evidenced by the Kh-31 missiles under the wing.

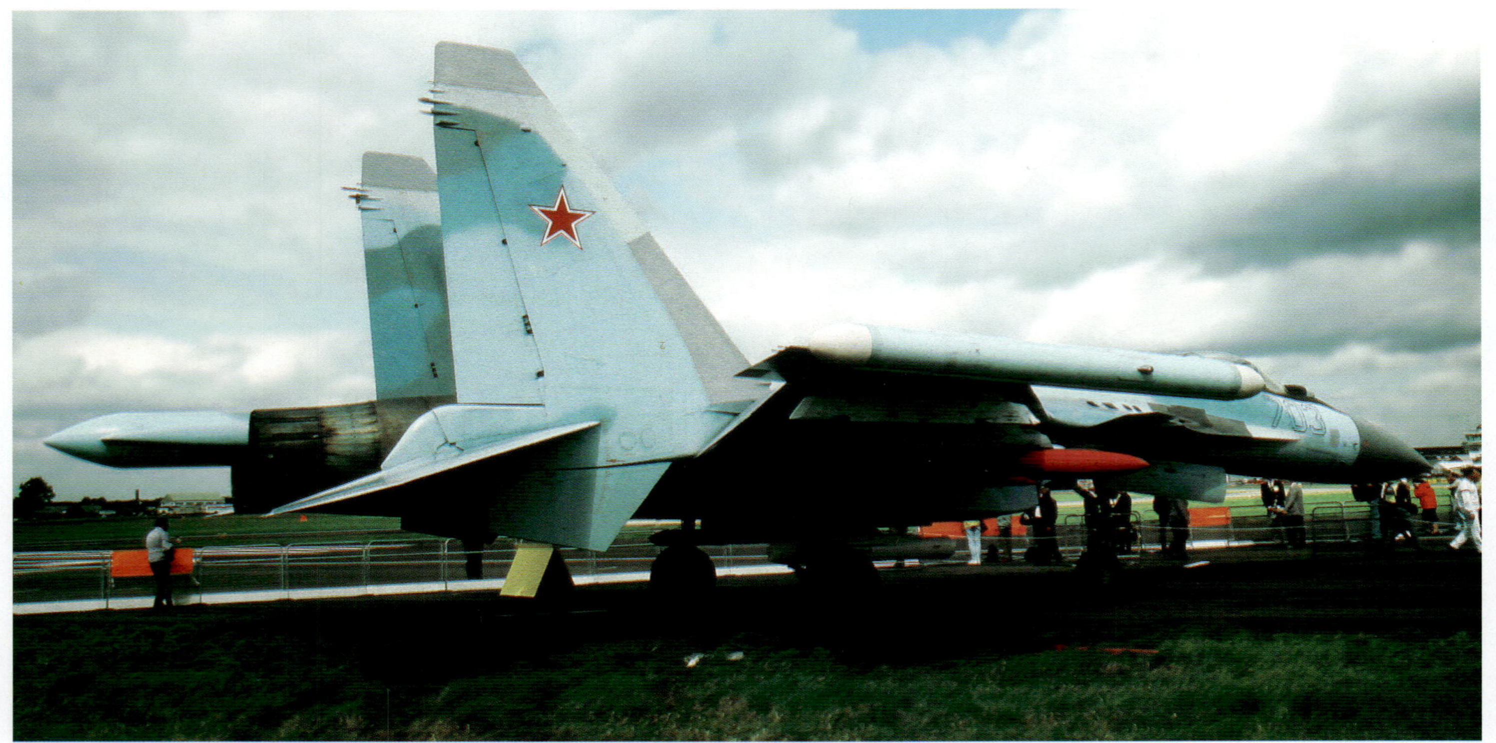

Another view of the modified tail area. The tail is higher, as on the Su-27UB trainer, but the tips of the rudder are squared off. The tail stinger is longer and thicker than on the earlier Su-27 family.

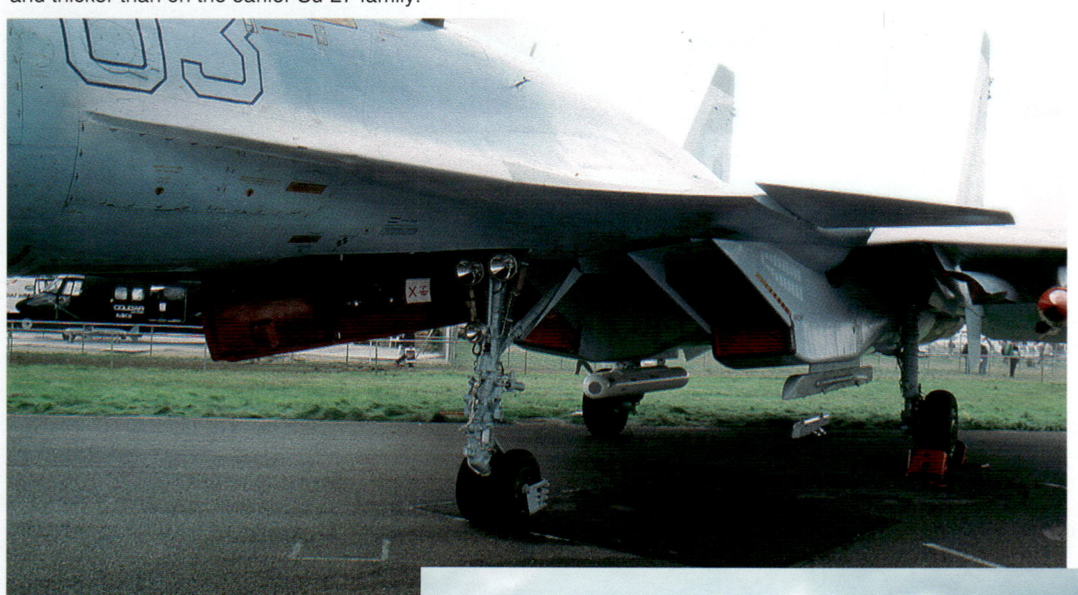

One of the more novel features seen on the Su-35 at Farnborough was GEC TIALD laser designator pod under the starboard engine pod. This is the same system used by the Tornados for guiding laser guided bombs during Operation Desert Storm, and is part of a cooperative British-Russian aviation electronics project announced at Farnborough. TIALD is intended for exported Su-35, not for Russian aircraft.

The large pod on the wing tips of the Su-35 replaces a missile launch rail. The pod is part of the *Sorbtsiya* electronic warfare suite.

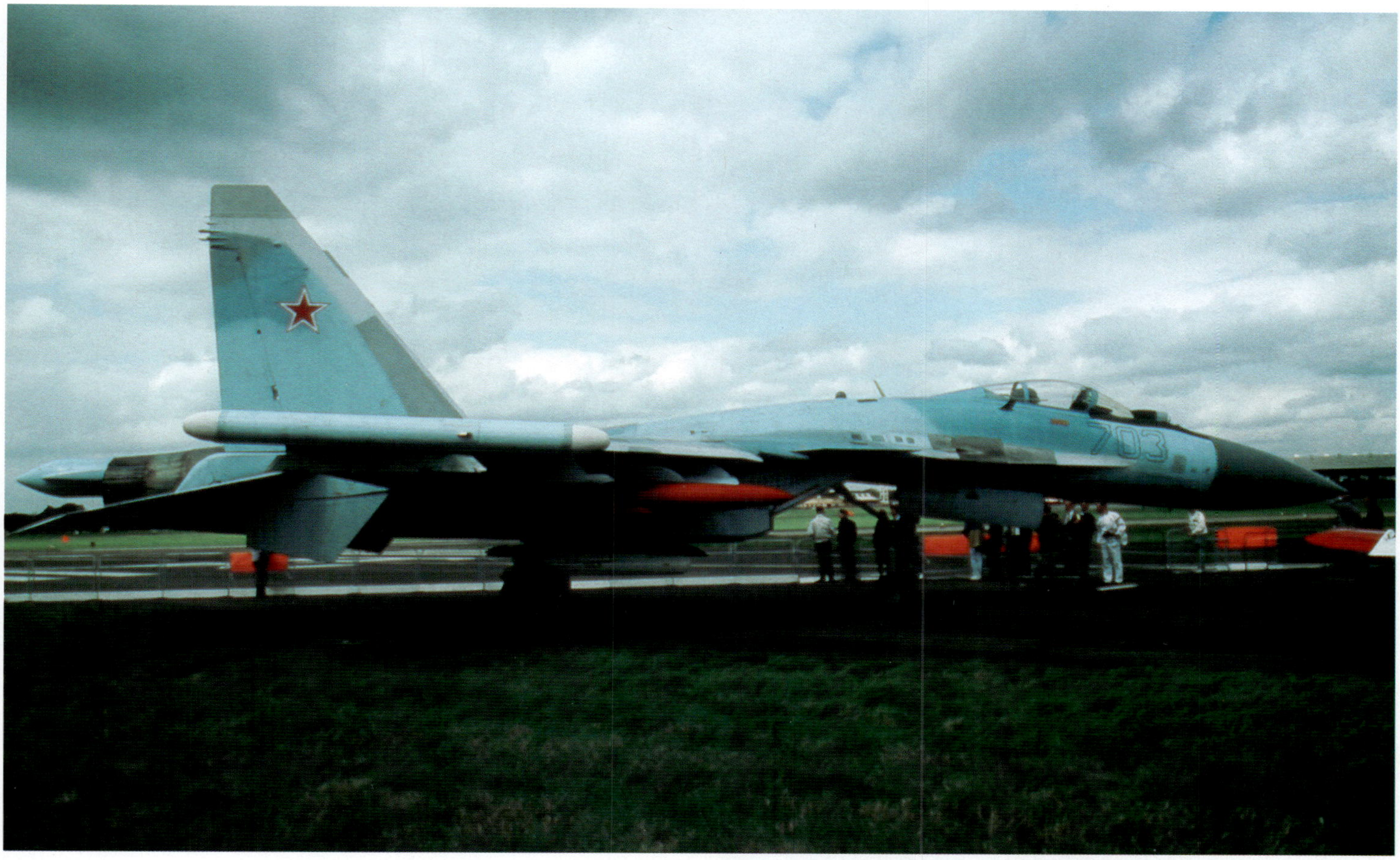

The large nose has forced several changes on the design, including a new higher tail. The tail "stinger" is also modified from the Su-27.

A rear view of the Su-35 showing the thickened tail stinger on the Su-35. The change in this tail was probably another aerodynamic off-shoot of the enlarged nose from the new radar.

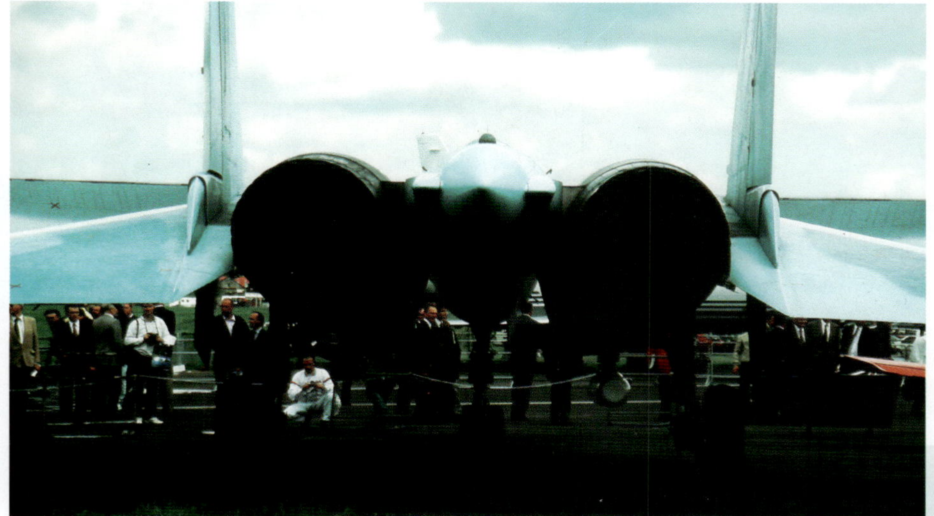

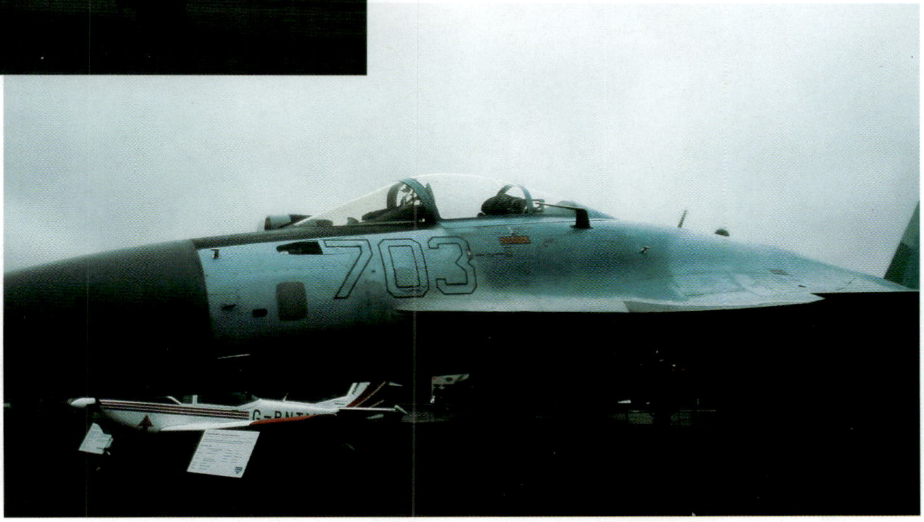

Like the Su-27K, the Su-35 is also fitted with a retractable nose probe for aerial refueling. It is contained in the recess immediately in front of the *bort* number 703.

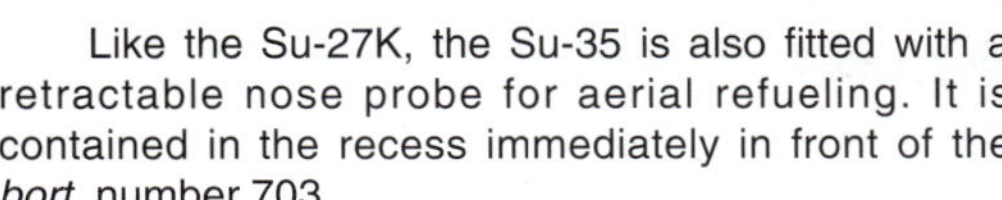

Another view of the redesigned tail area, clearly showing its increased height and modified shape.

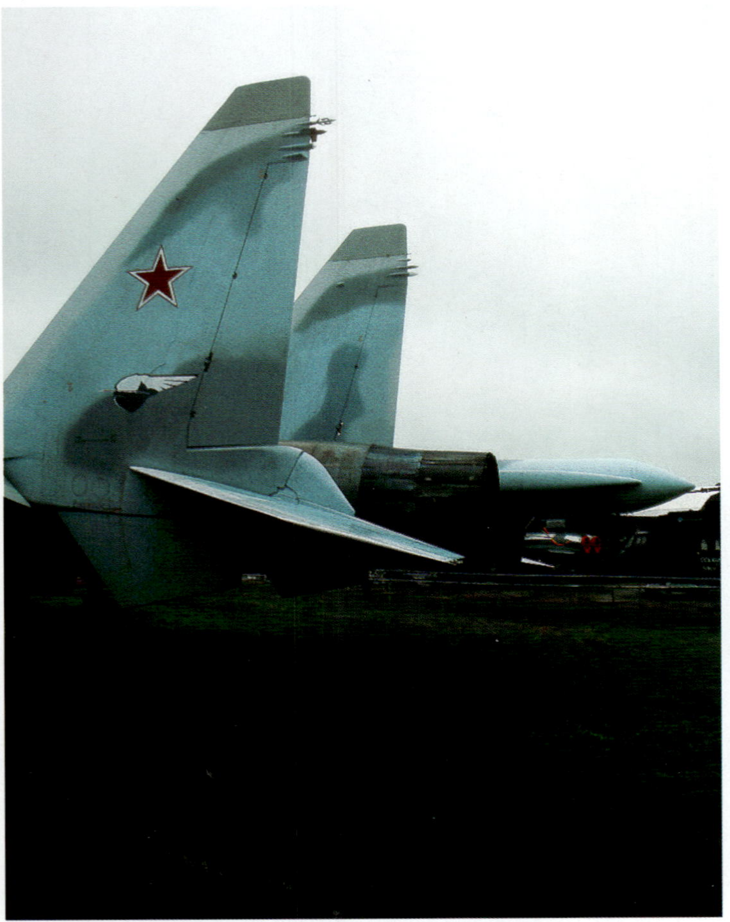

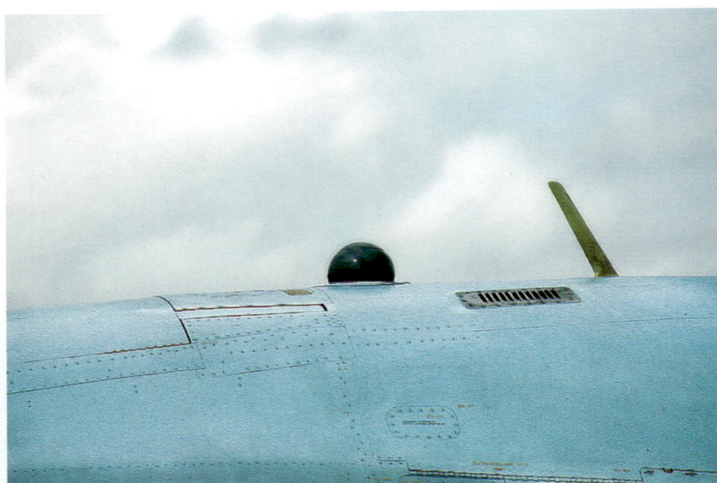

A small change on the Su-35 has been the addition of a missile warning receiver on the fuselage spine. This sensor picks up the hot exhaust gas of an enemy air-to-air missile, warning the pilot of the angle of the missile attack.

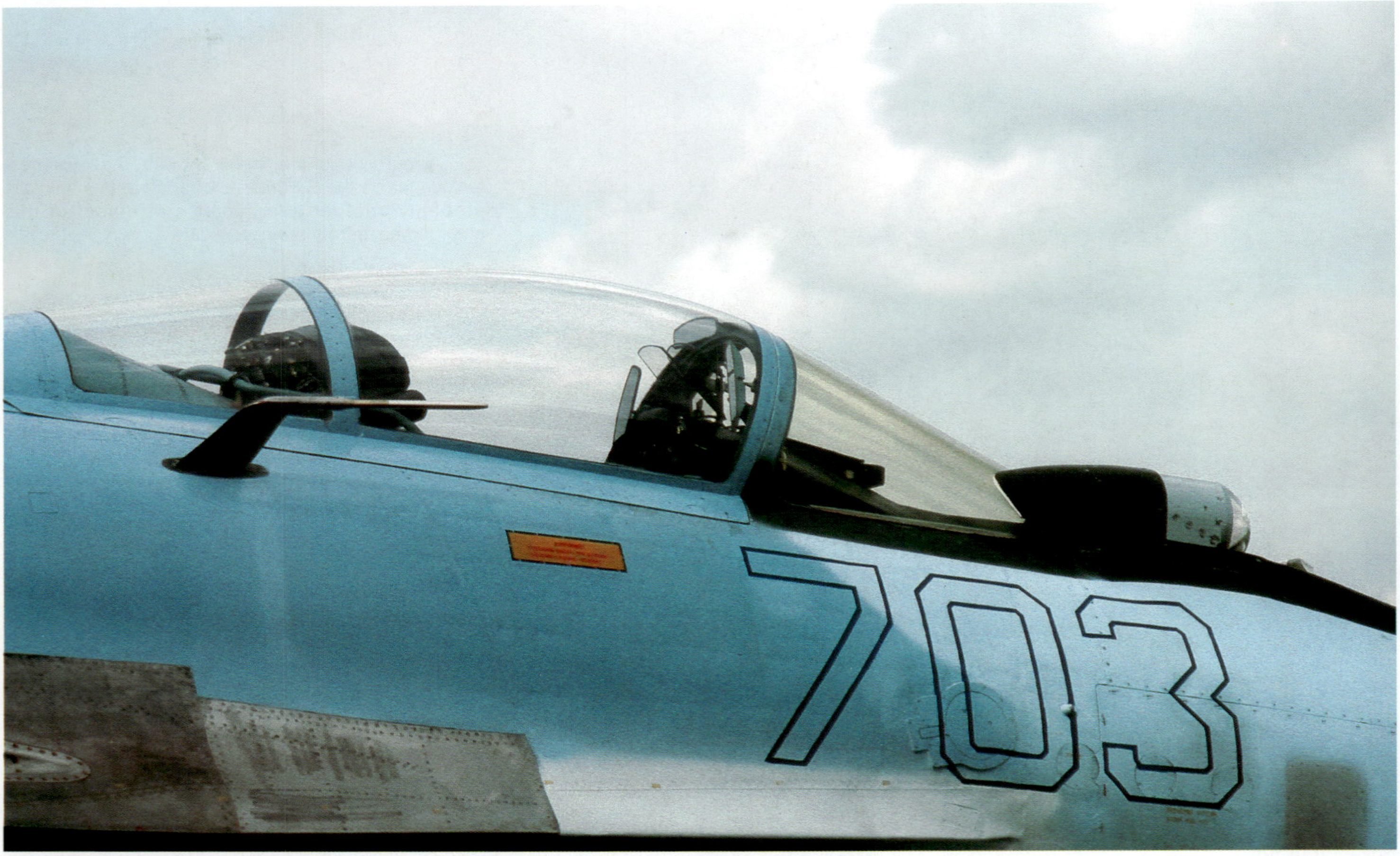

A detail view of the Su-35 cockpit. This aircraft has an enlarged and improved infra-red search and track (IRST) ball in front of the cockpit which is used to track enemy fighters in lieu of the radar at close ranges.

YAKOVLEV Yak-38 FORGER

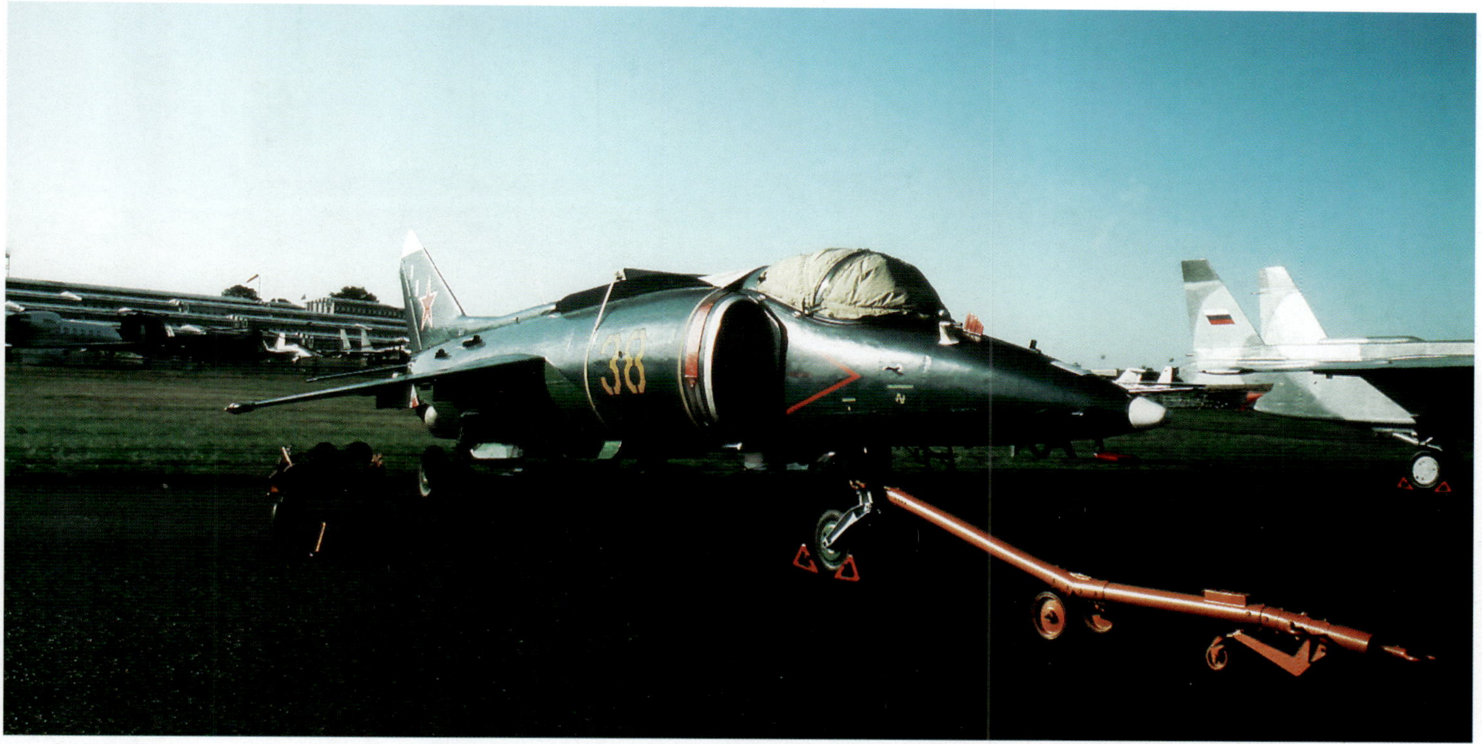

A strange visitor to Farnborough, the Yak-38 Forger. The Forger was retired from Russian Navy service use in 1992, after a long but troubled career. A total of 36 of the 90 aircraft built were lost in crashes, and the aircraft had developed a very poor reputation amongst its pilots by the end of its career. The Farnborough display was the first foreign visit of the Yak-38, in this case a later production Yak-38M.

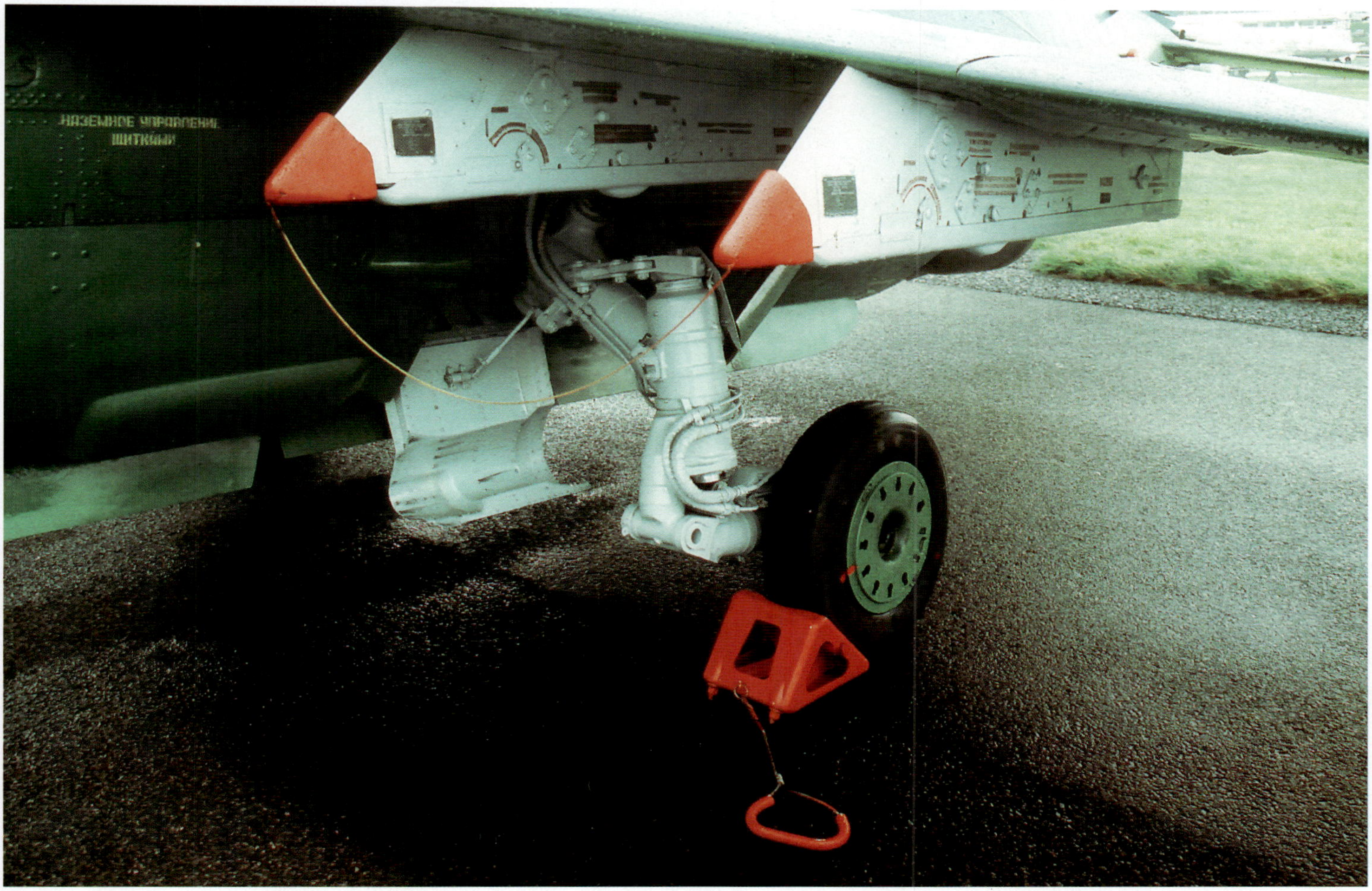

A detail view of the landing gear of the Yak-38M fighter at Farnborough.

YAKOVLEV Yak-141 FREESTYLE

Yakovlev Yak-141 Freestyle

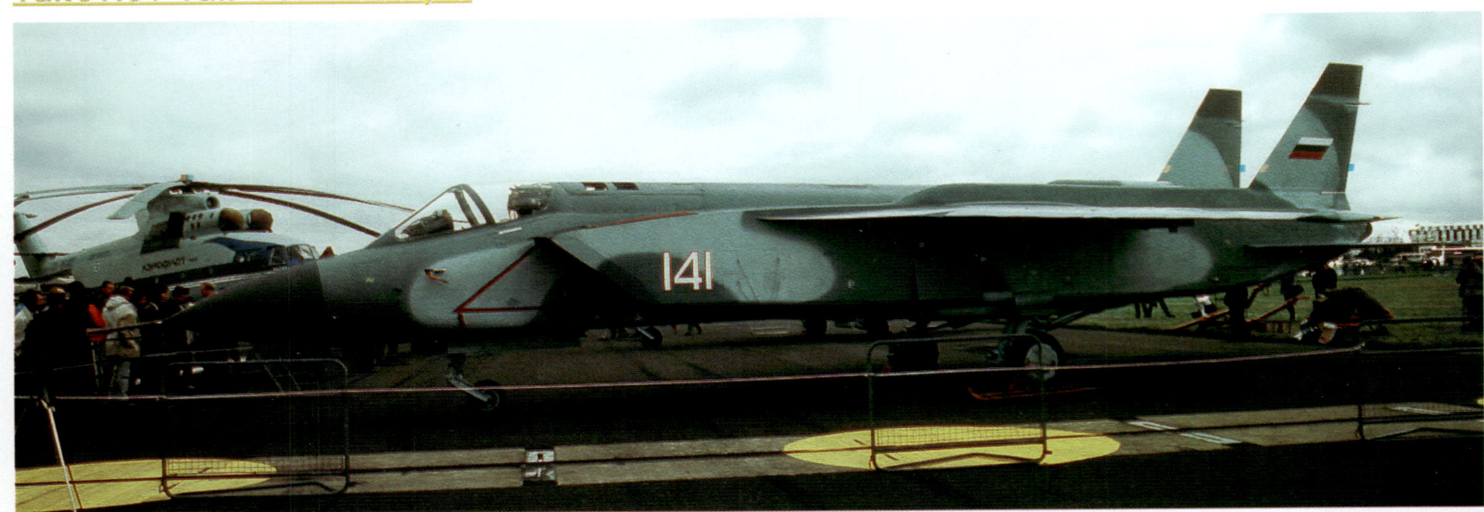

The intended successor of the Yak-38 is the Yakovlev Yak-141 supersonic V/STOL aircraft. This aircraft has had a troubled history, suffering from serious funding problems in the wake of heavy defense budget cuts in the 1990s. These problems were compounded by the loss of one of the two flying prototypes during trials in 1991 due to a hard landing on the carrier deck. Two other prototypes have been used for ground testing.

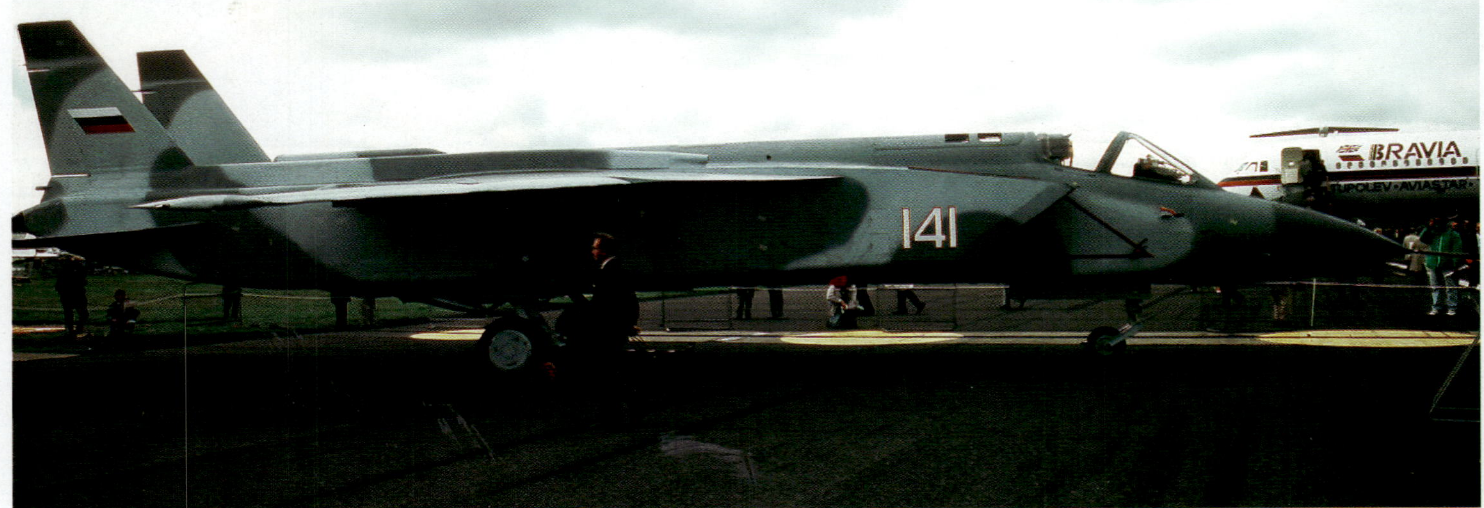

A starboard side view of the remaining prototype of the Yak-141. A two seat training version reached the nose mock-up stage in 1991, but was not completed. The second seat is located forward of the pilot in place of the Zhuk radar.

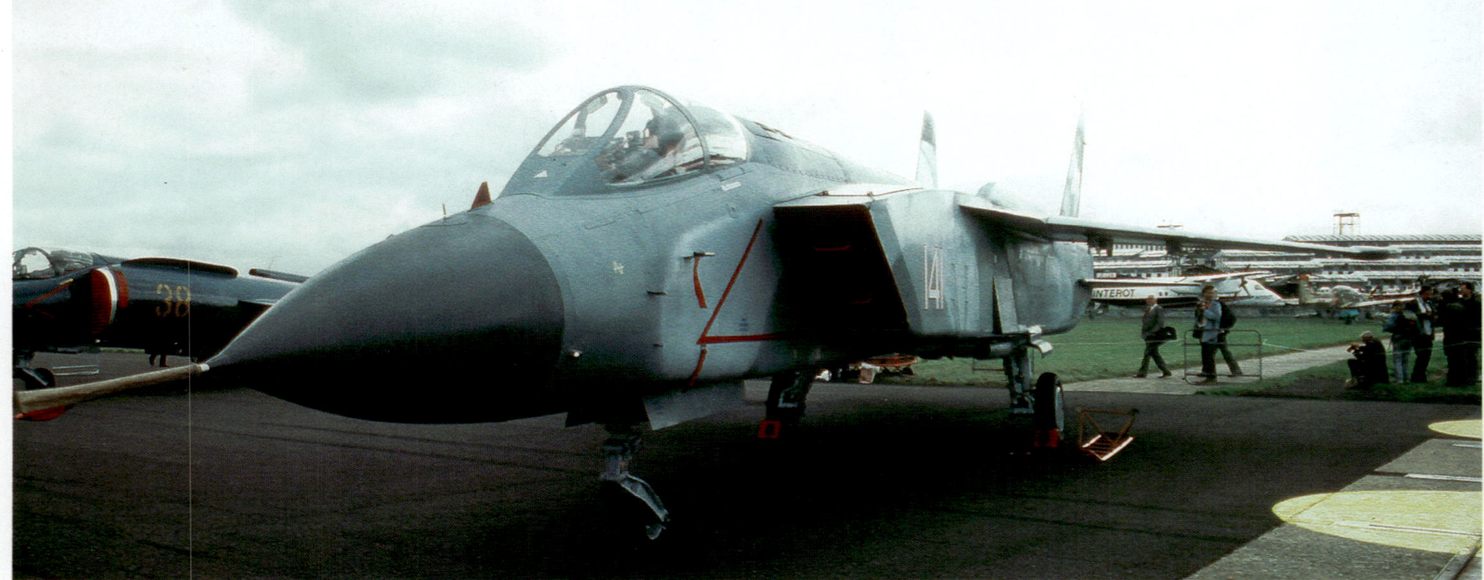

The Yak-141 has drastically improved performance compared to the Yak-38. It is fitted with a full radar system, essentially similar to that on the MiG-29 but with a smaller diameter dish.

The new grey air superiority scheme on the Freestyle displayed at Farnborough differs from previous photos of the aircraft during trials.

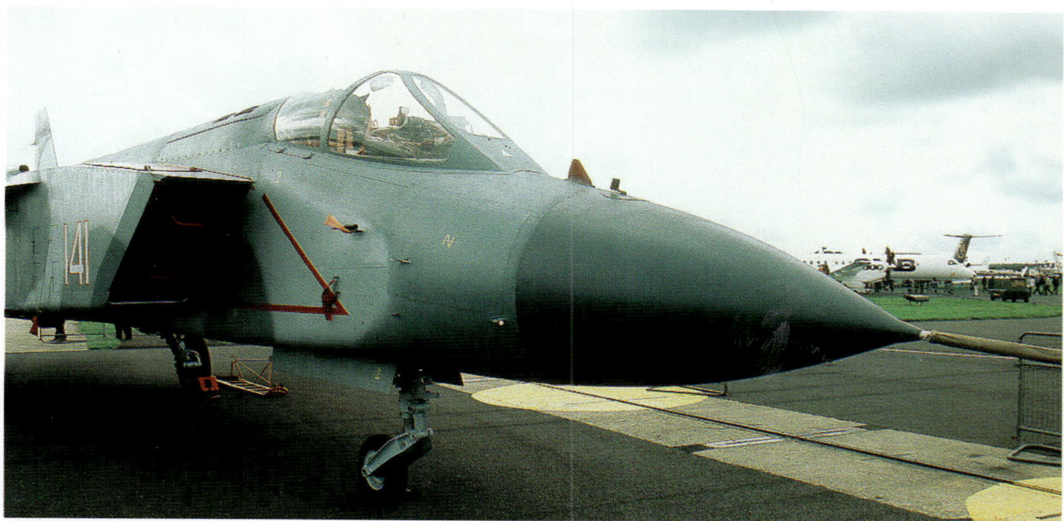

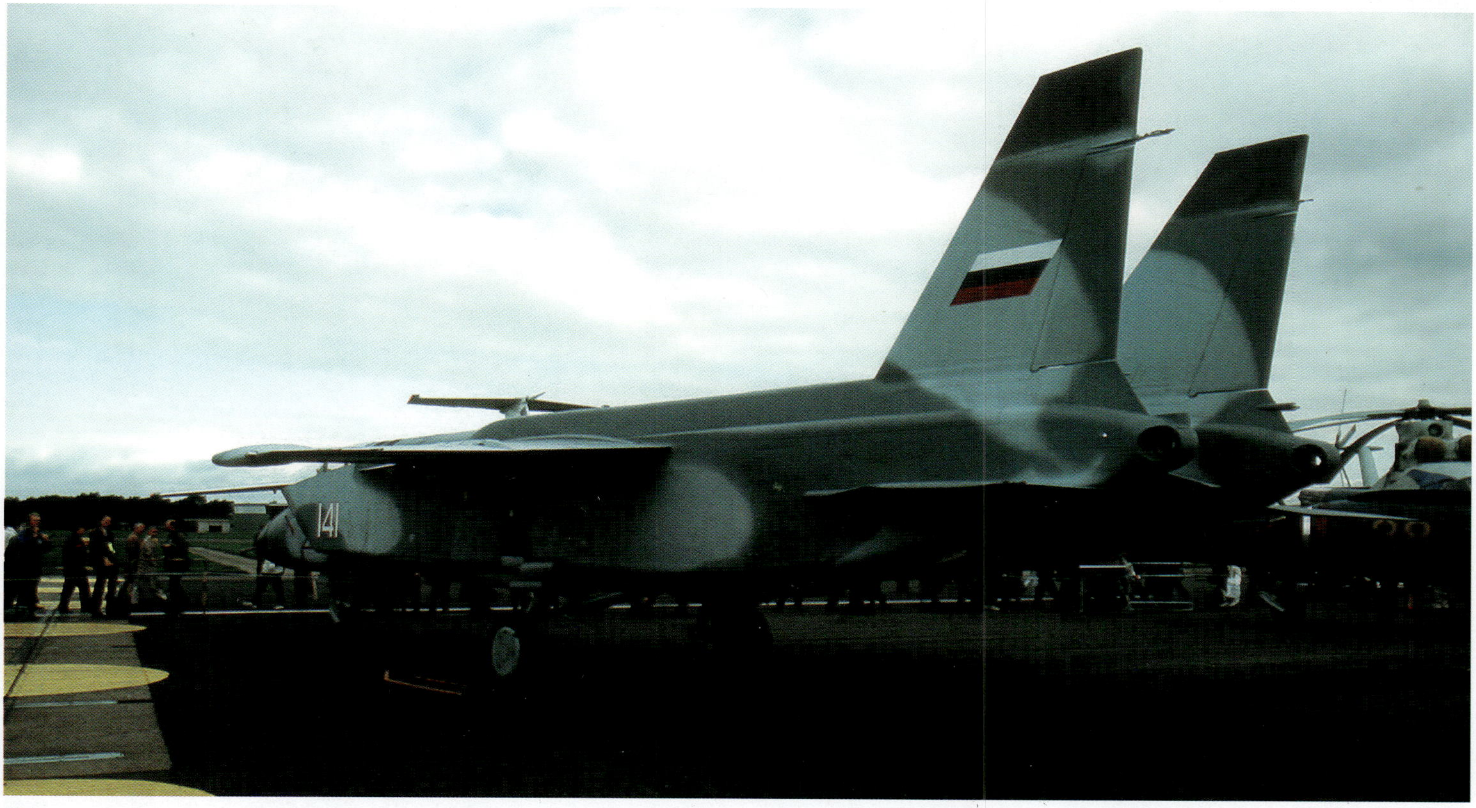

This rear shot accents the slab-sided appearance of the design. The twin boom configuration permits the installation of the unique R-79 powerplant.

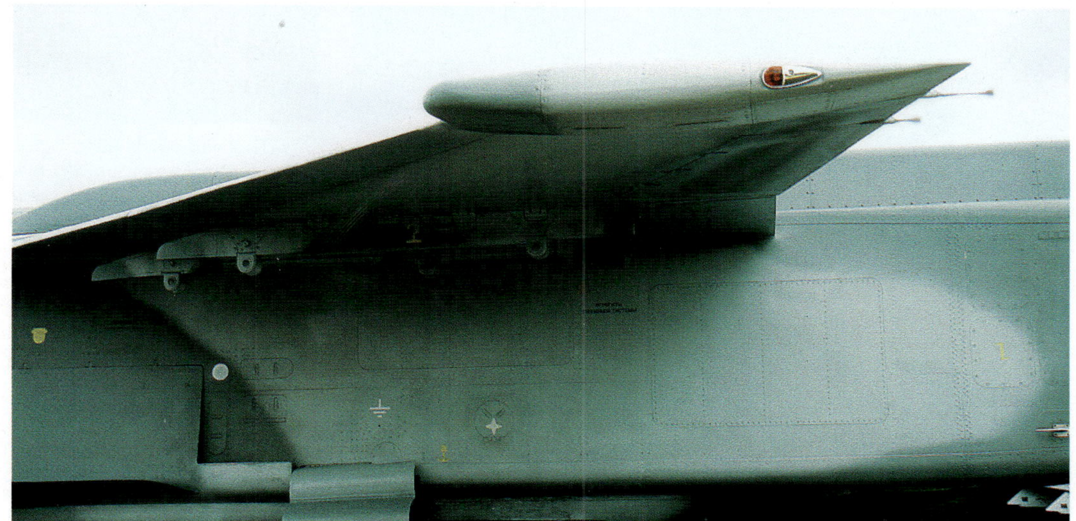

A detail view under the port wing showing the RWR antenna pod on the wing tip and the hardpoints under the wing.

A rear view looking at the Yak-141's Soyuz R-79V-300 lift/cruise engine. This turbofan engine has an unusual configuration permitting the thrust to be ducted downward 95 degrees. The thrust from this engine is supplemented by two RD-41 lift jets on the centerline behind the pilot.

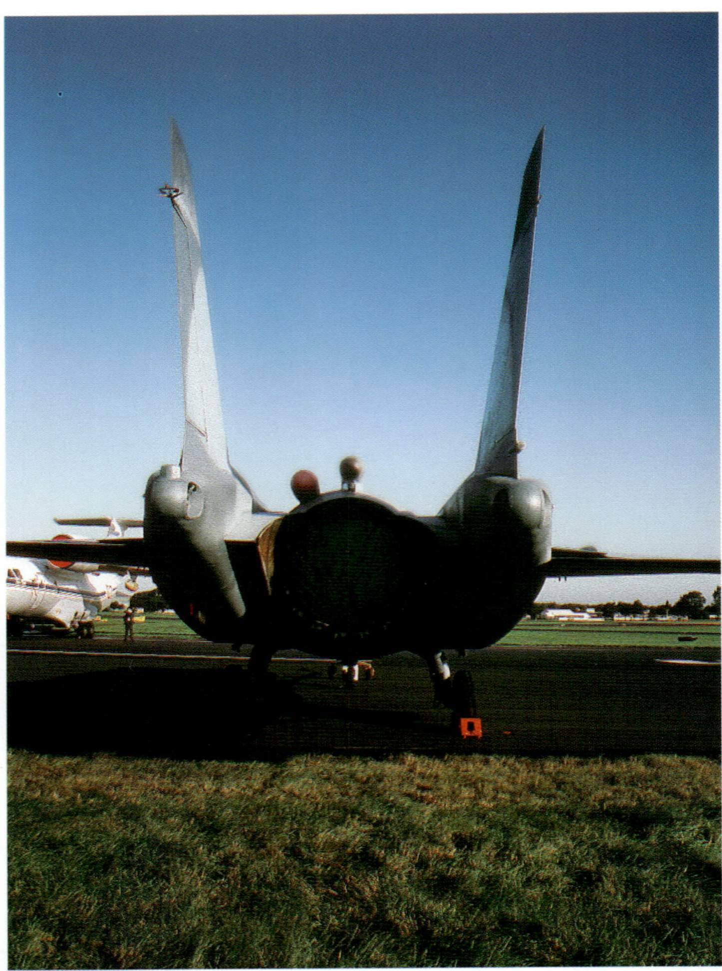

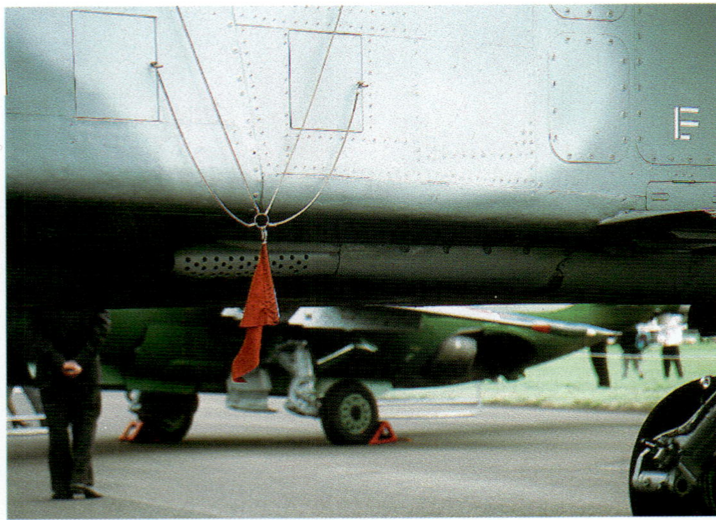

The Yak-141 Freestyle is armed with a single 30mm cannon under the port center section of the fuselage, the perforated muzzle brake of which is evident here.

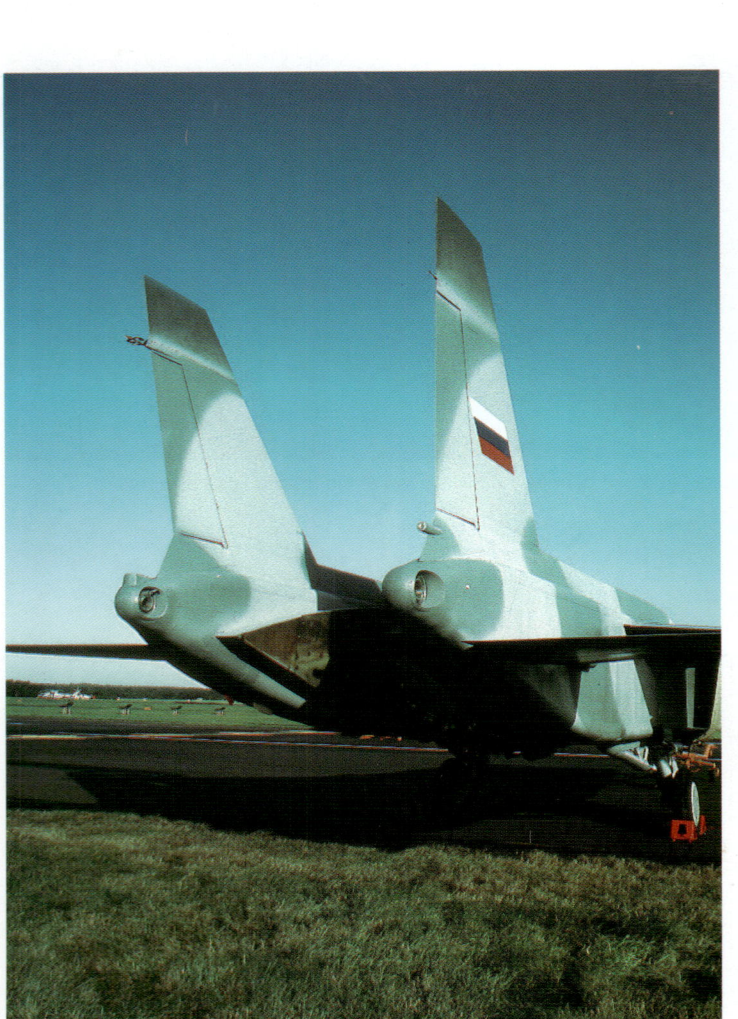

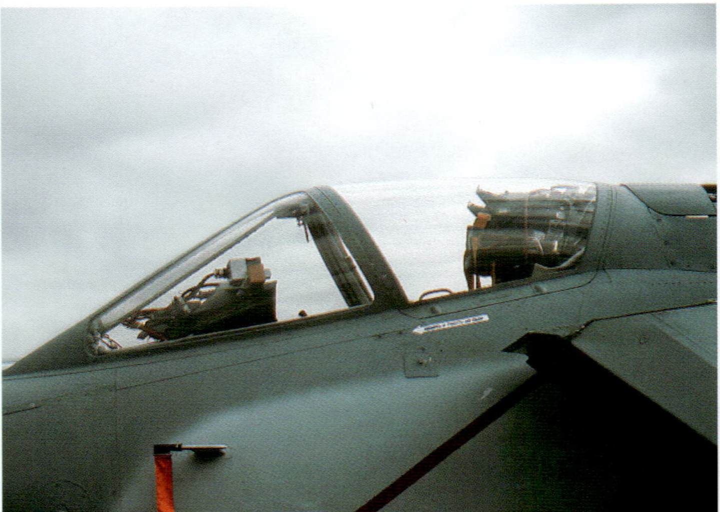

The Yak-141 is fitted with a modified version of the K-36 ejection seat incorporating an automatic ejection sequence if the aircraft roll exceeds prescribed limits. This close-up of the cockpit canopy shows the upper element of the seat as well as the HUD.

A view of the unusual rear configuration from the right side. Note that the aircraft is marked in Russian Federation markings and does not appear to carry the Soviet red stars at all. Note the titanium shields on the side of the fuselage booms to protect the airframe from the exhaust heat.

At the tip of the rear fuselage strakes are a pair of small ducted fans, presumably used for lateral control of the aircraft during hover.

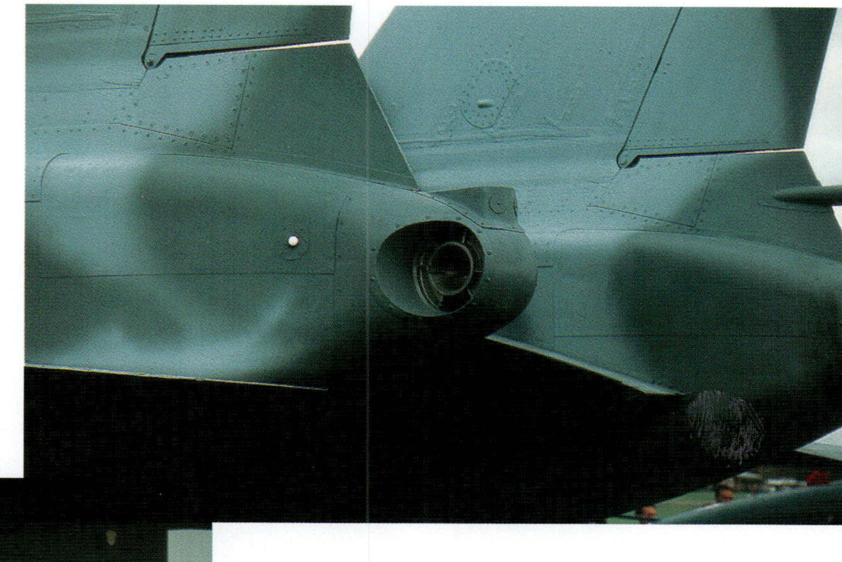

A detail view of the right main landing gear leg.

A detail view showing the inner detail of the landing gear leg.

A detail view showing the landing leg from the forward quarter.

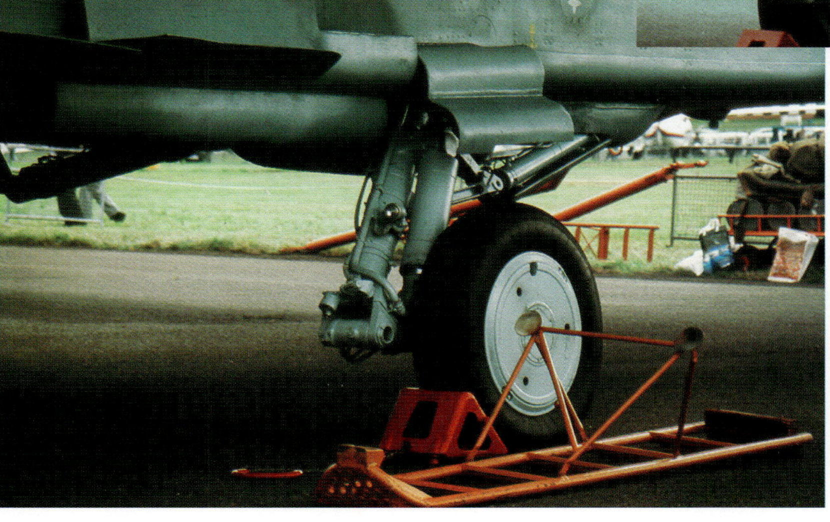

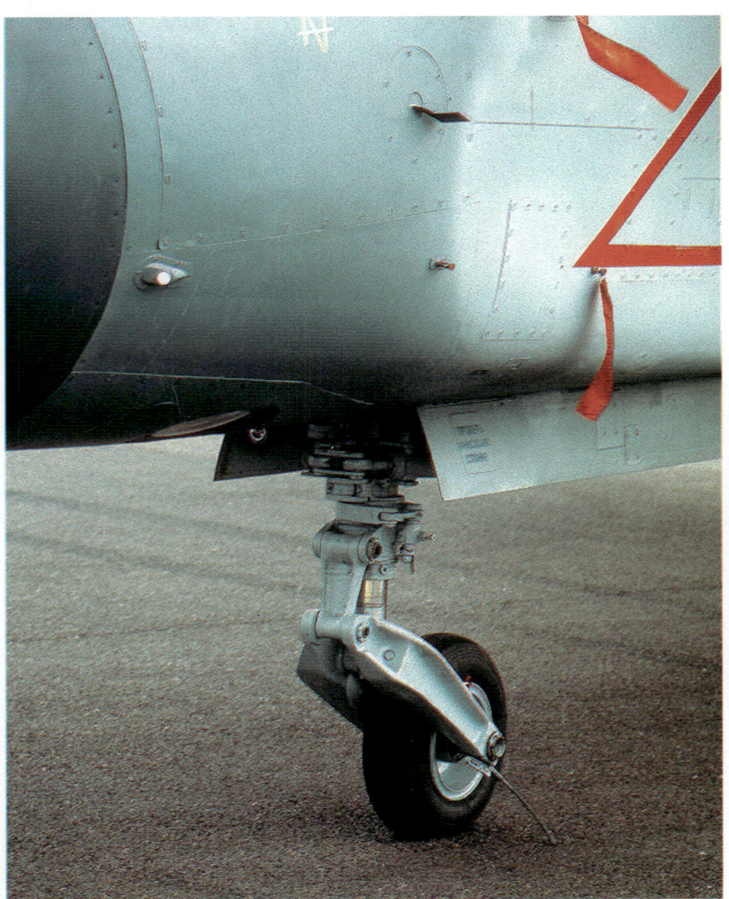

A detail view of the nose landing gear leg.

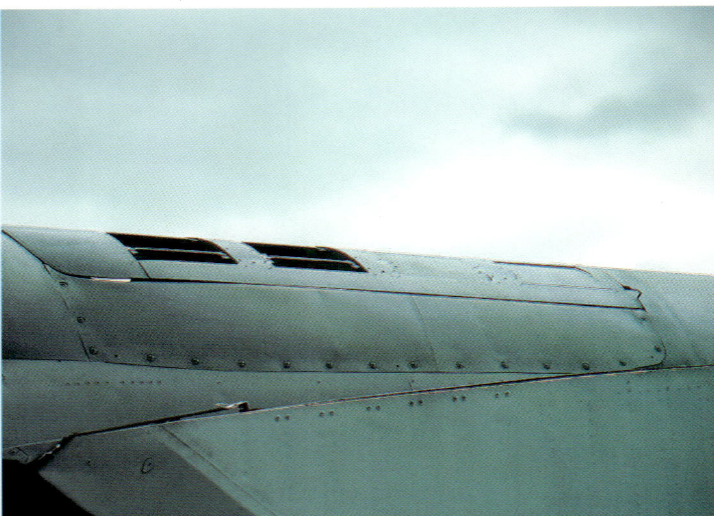

This detail view of the fuselage spine aft the cockpit shows the air intake doors for the Rybinsk RD-41 auxiliary lift engines.

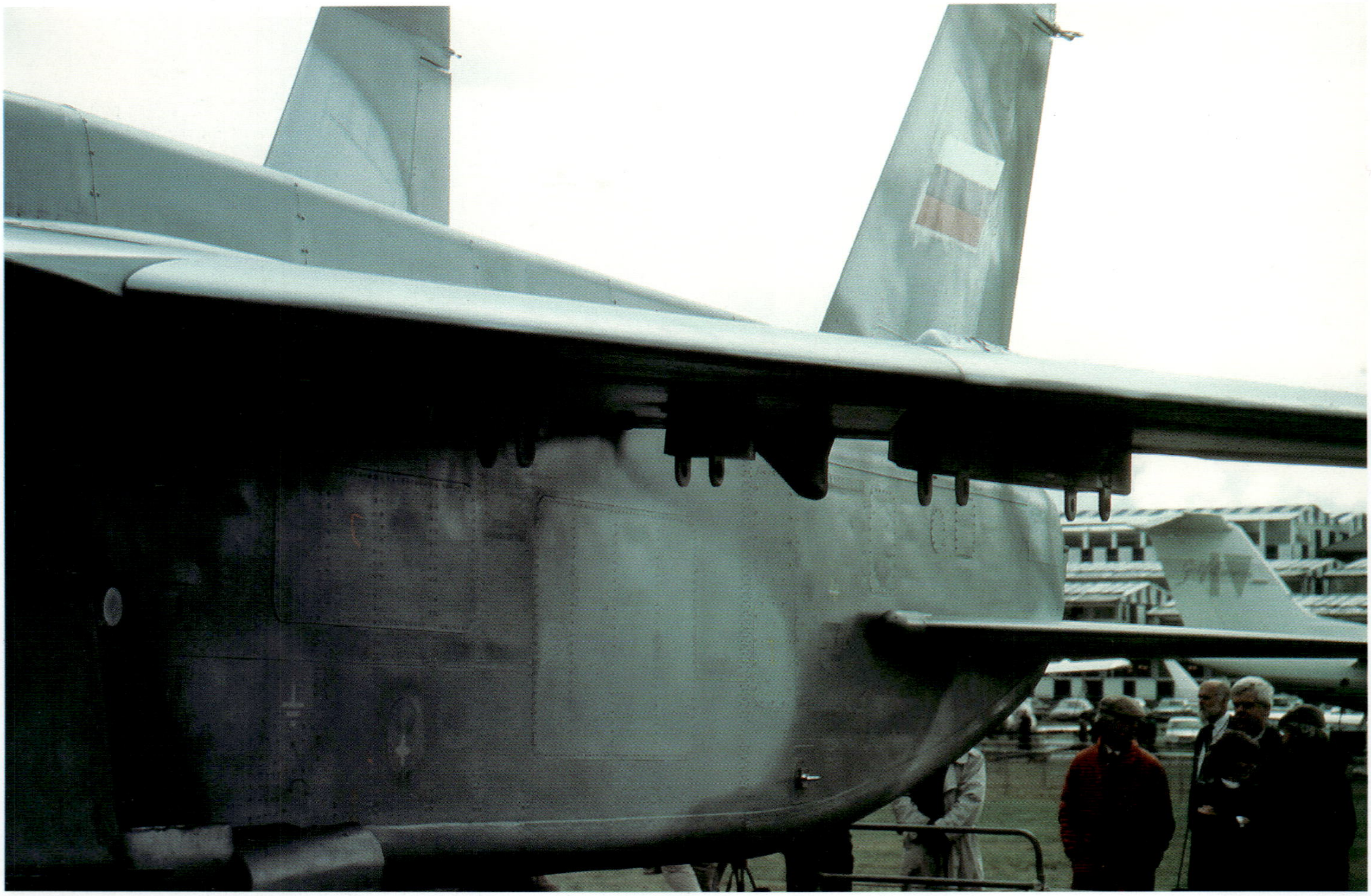

A detail view under the wing of the Yak-141 showing the three wing hard-points.

TUPOLEV Tu-95/Tu-142 BEAR

Tu-95MS Bear H

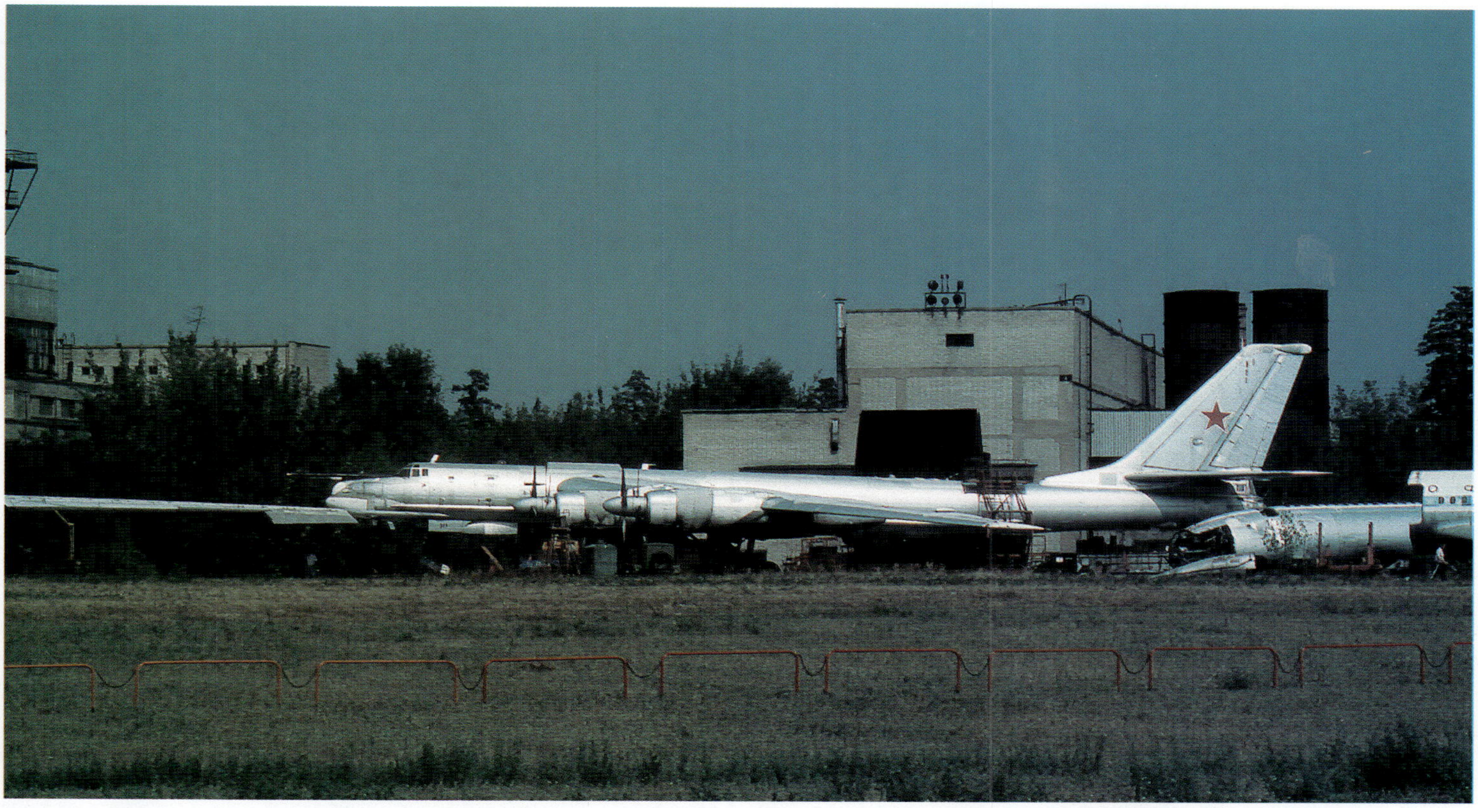

The ultimate strategic bomber version of the Tu-95 Bear family is the Tu-95MS Bear H. This version is used as a cruise missile carrier, the Tu-95MS6 carrying 6 RKV-500 (AS-15 Kent) cruise missile, and the improved Tu-95MS16 carrying 16. This Tu-95MS is under repair at Zhukovskiy.

Tu-142M3 Bear F

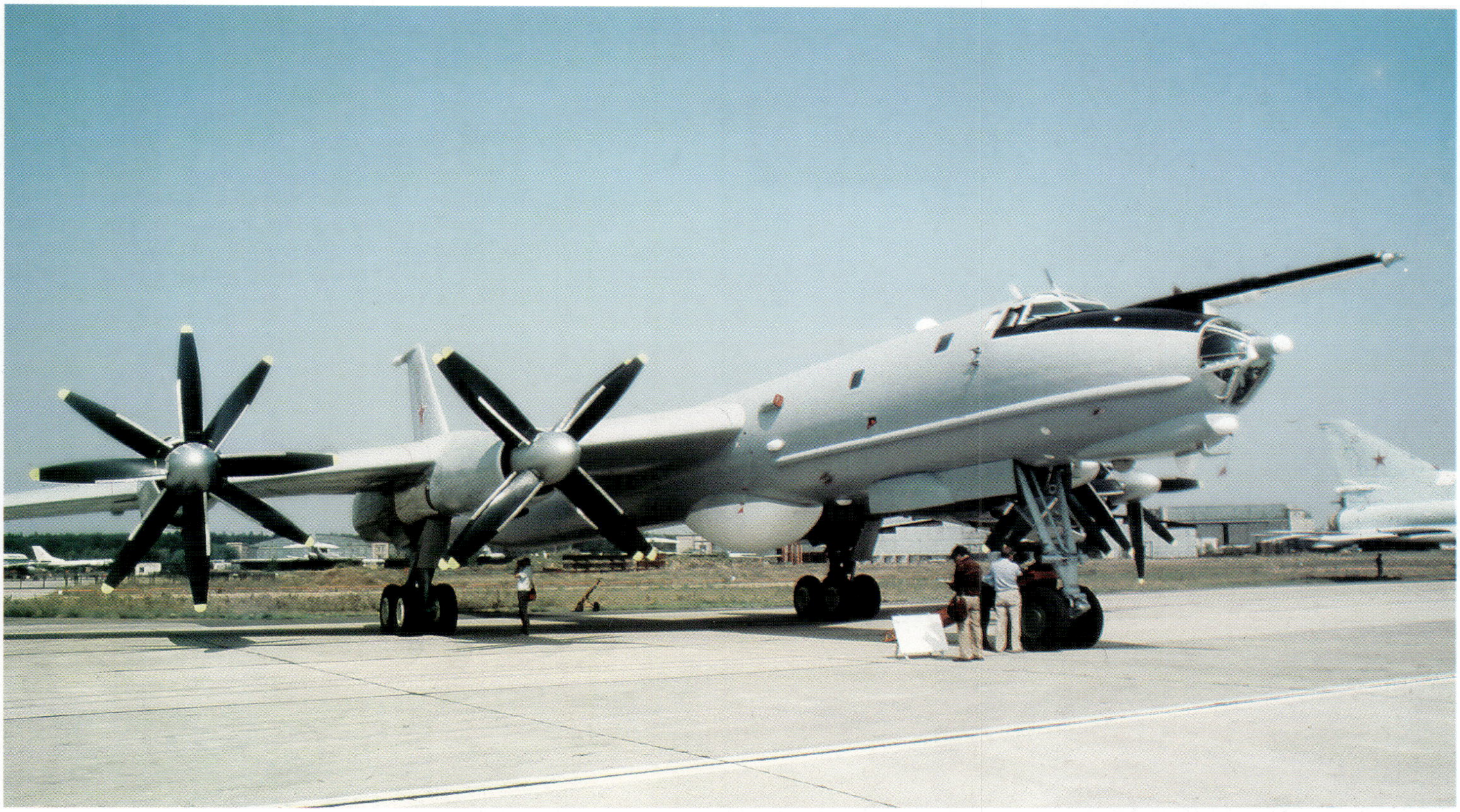

Still in production over forty years since its introduction into service, the Bear has been the most successful of the post-war Russian heavy bombers. This is a Russian Navy Tu-142M3 Bear F Mod 3, the final production model of the aircraft used for maritime roles. This version of the aircraft was first spotted in 1986. About 55 Tu-142Ms are in service with Russian Navy anti-submarine squadrons.

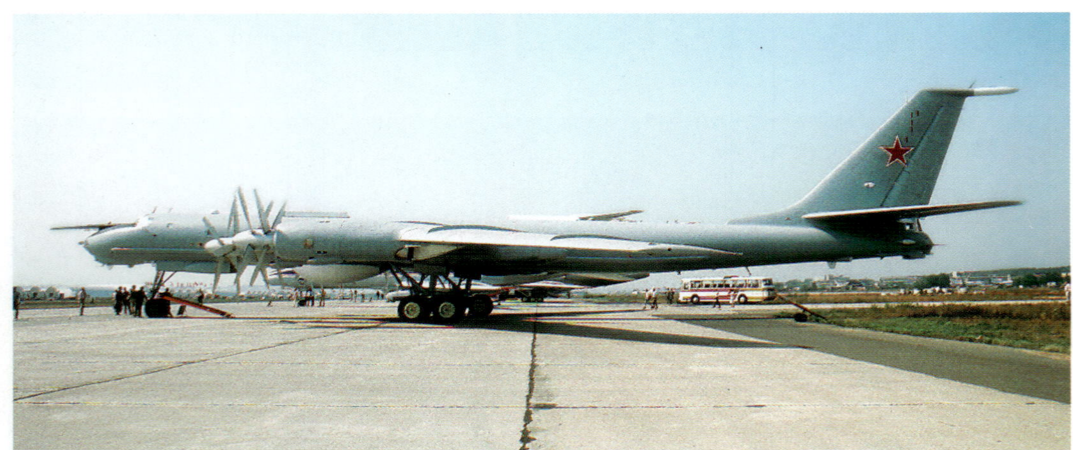

A side view of the Tu-142M3. The large projection off the tail is a magnetic anomoly detector for use in submarine detection.

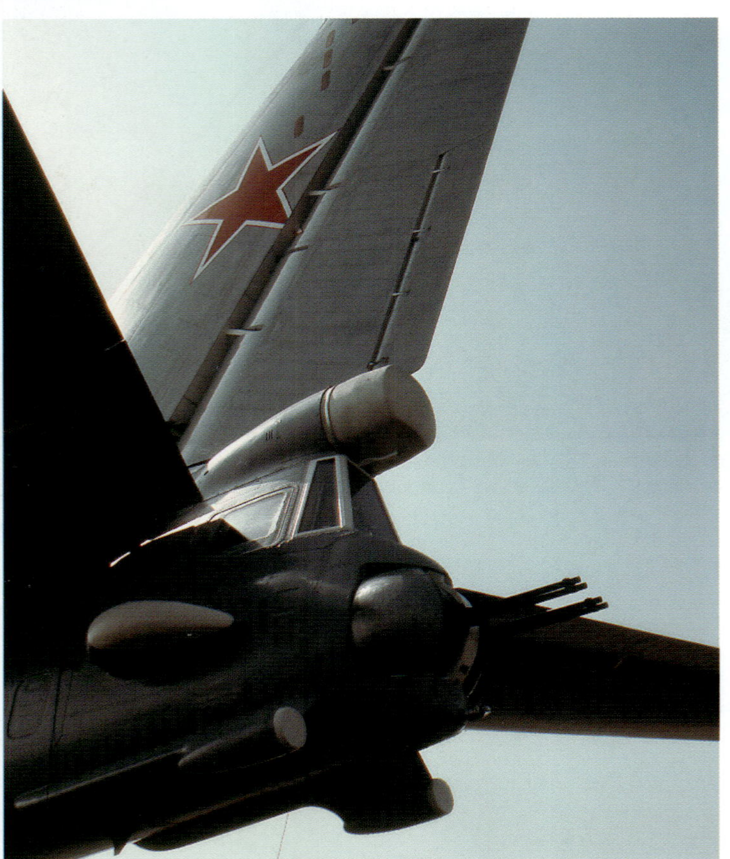

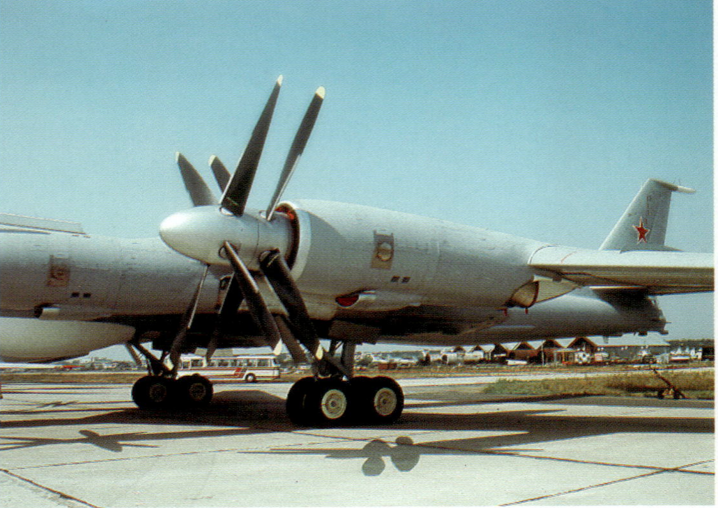

The Tu-142M3 is powered by the Kuznetsov NK-12MV turboprop engines with contra-rotating propeller blades.

A close-up view of the rear gun position on the Tu-142M3. Above the gun position is a small Box Tail radar used for acquiring and tracking rear approaching targets. The other antennas are presumably RWR sensors which pick up the radar emissions from enemy aircraft tailing the Tu-142M3 and warn the crew of their approach.

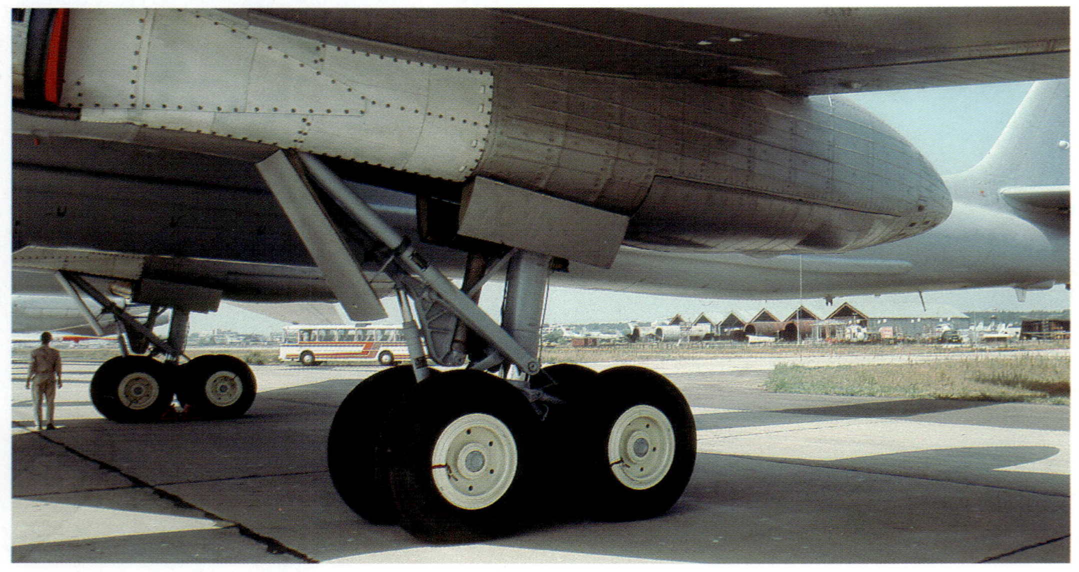

A detail view of the massive main undercarriage of the Tu-142M3.

Another nose view of the Tu-142M3 showing the substantial forward landing gear.

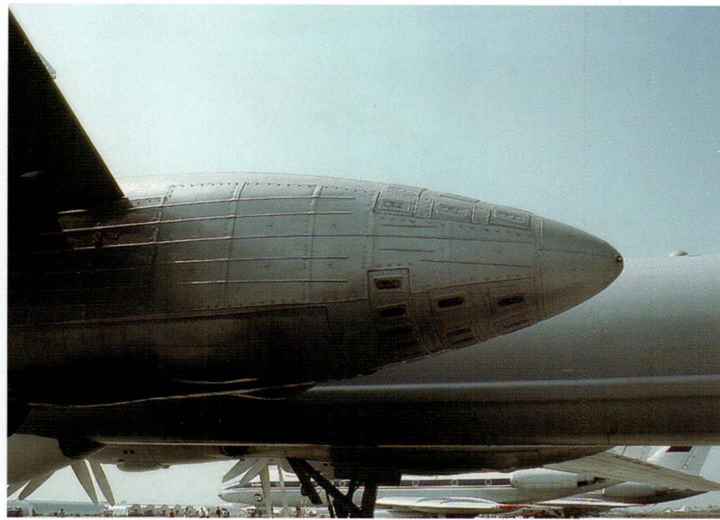

A detail view of the rear engine pod of the Tu-142M3 showing the many small ejector ports for ASO IR flare and chaff launchers.

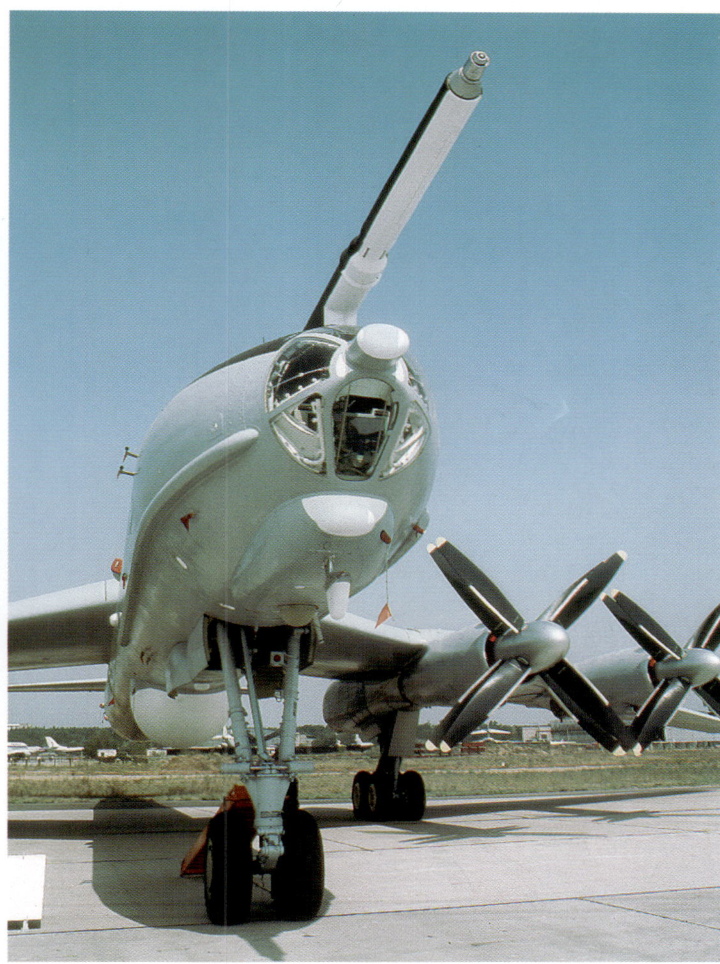

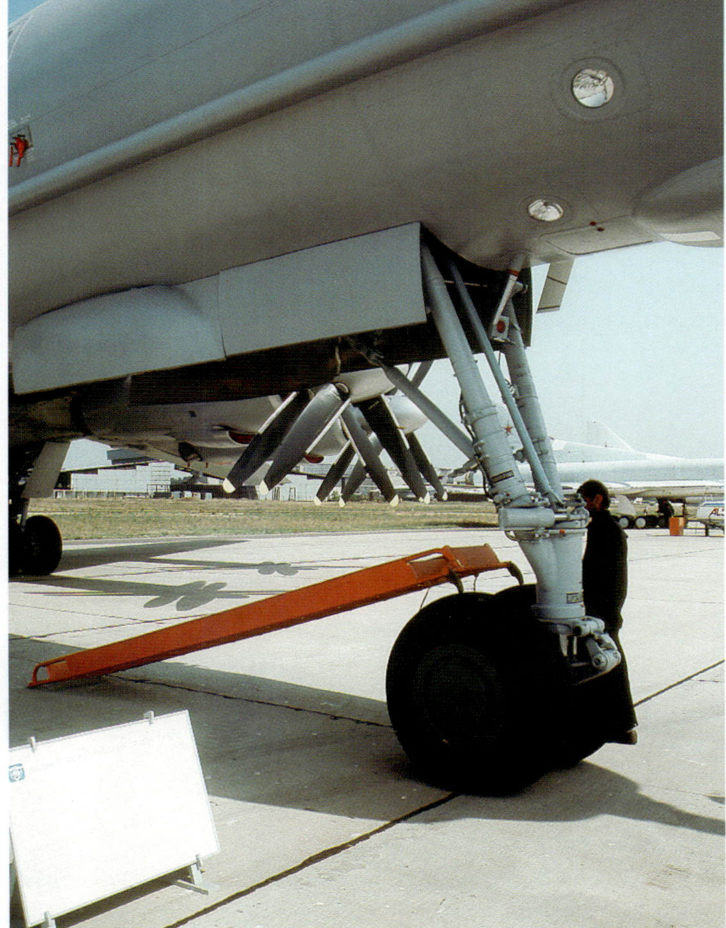

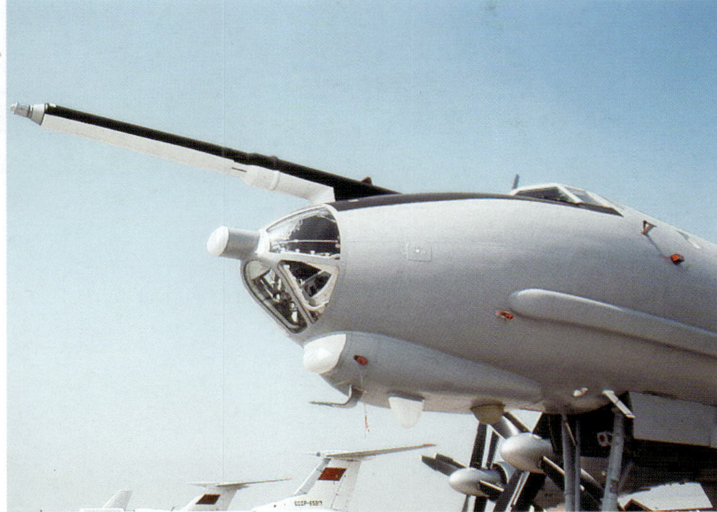

A detail view of the nose of the Tu-142M3 showing the refueling probe above the nose the ESM and radar sensors, and the long side communications antenna housing along the side of the fuselage.

A detail view of the nose landing gear of the Tu-142M3.

TUPOLEV Tu-22M BACKFIRE

Tupolev Tu-22M3 Backfire C

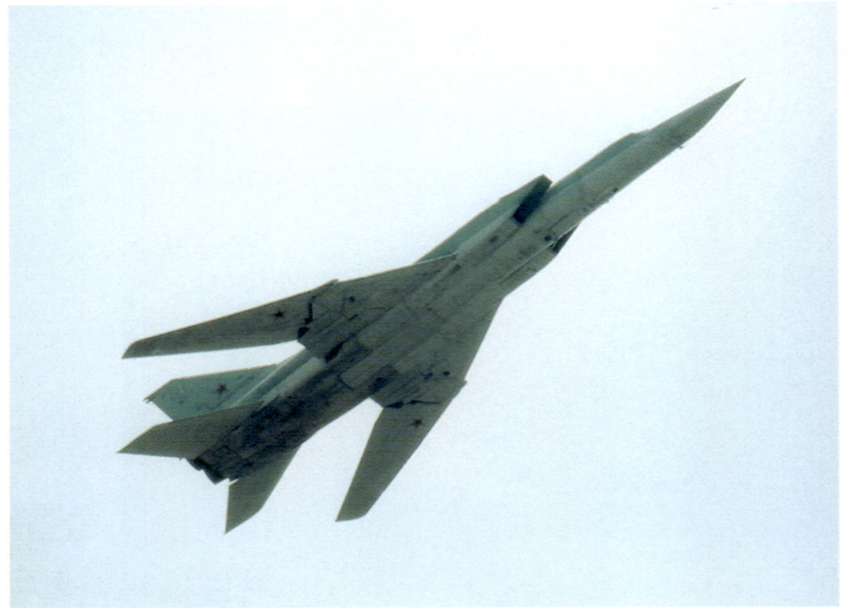

The Tu-22M3 Backfire C is the most advanced version of this long-range strike bomber. This view during the Mosaeroshow aerial demonstration shows the aircraft with its wing swept back.

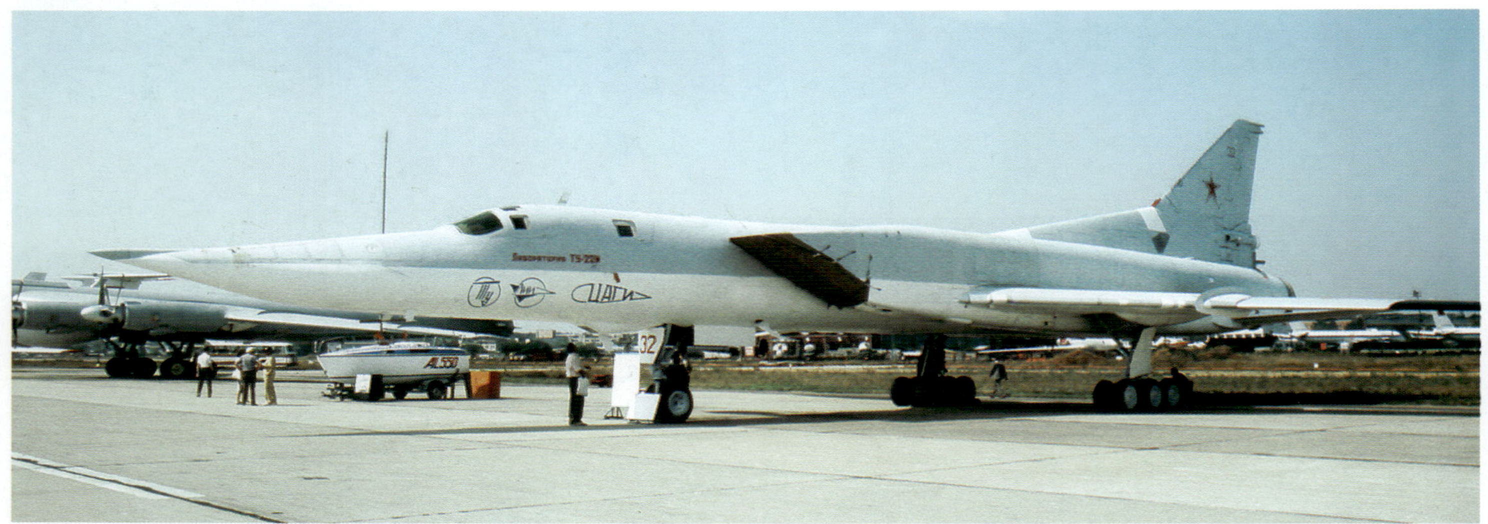

The Tu-22M3 displayed at Zhukovskiy airfield in August 1991. This particular aircraft is used at Zhukovskiy as a "flying laboratory" as is indicated by the red inscription under the cockpit.

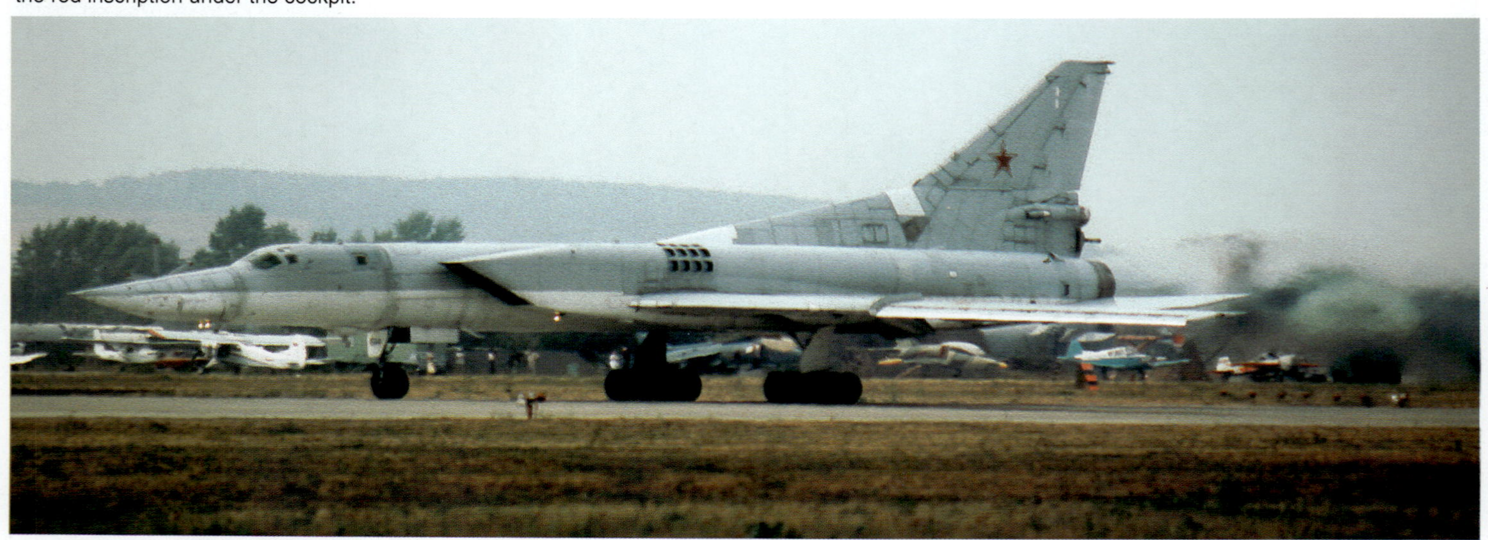

During the air display at Zhukovskiy, this well-weathered veteran was used for the flying displays. Notice that during take-off, a series of additional air intake doors are opened on the central portion of the air intake trunk.

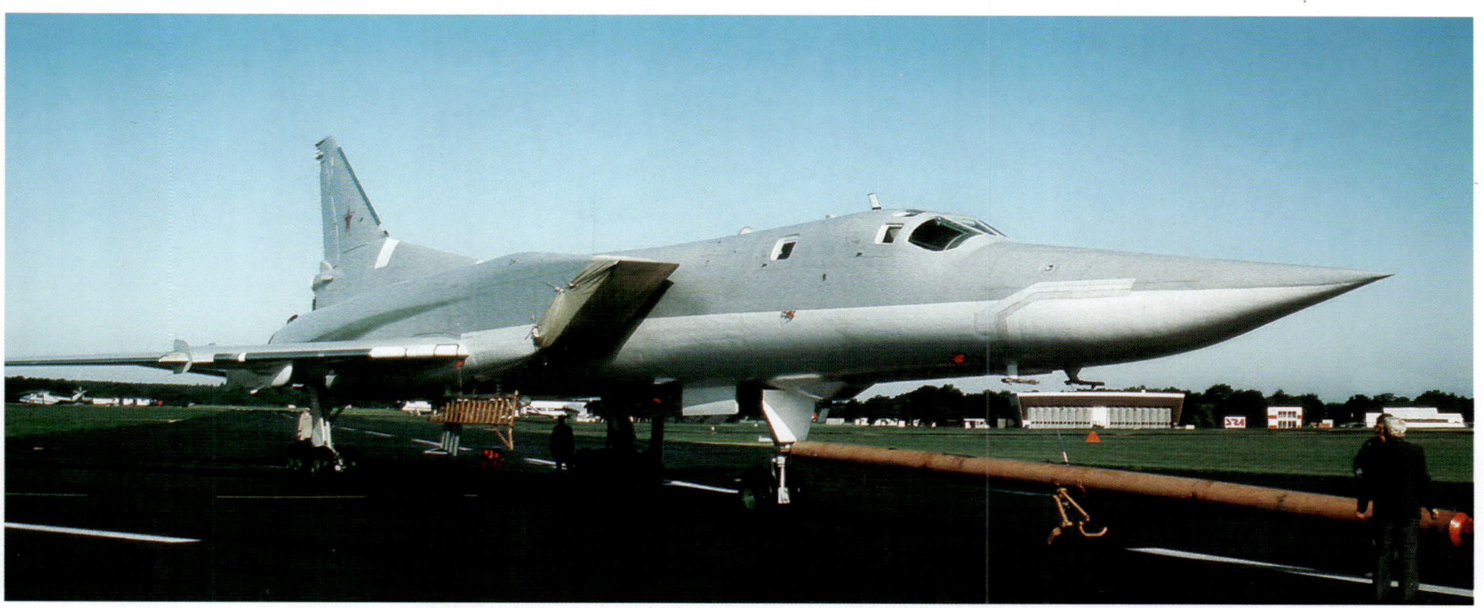

The Tu-22M3 displayed at Farnborough was freshly finished in its normal tactical pattern of pale grey and white. The Tu-22M3 differs from the earlier Tu-22M2 in its reconfigured air intakes and in a new navigation and attack radar with a new nose.

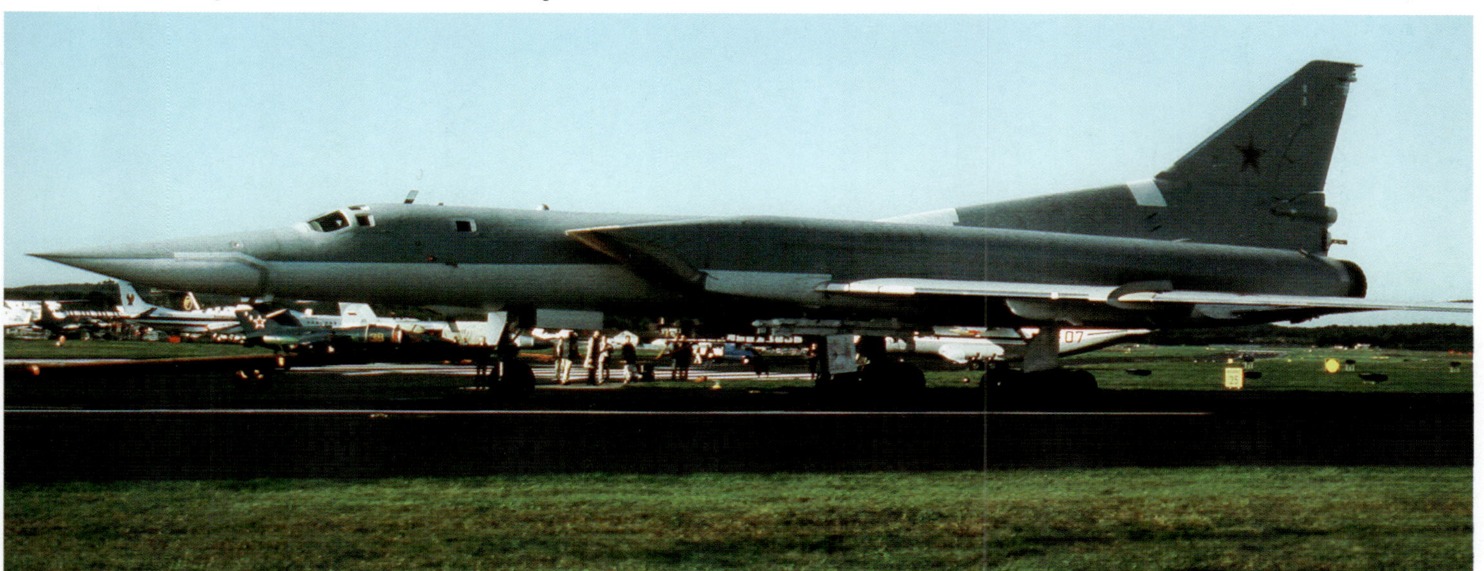

The Tu-22M3 being towed out for display at Farnborough. This was the first time that the Backfire was publicly displayed outside of the former Soviet Union.

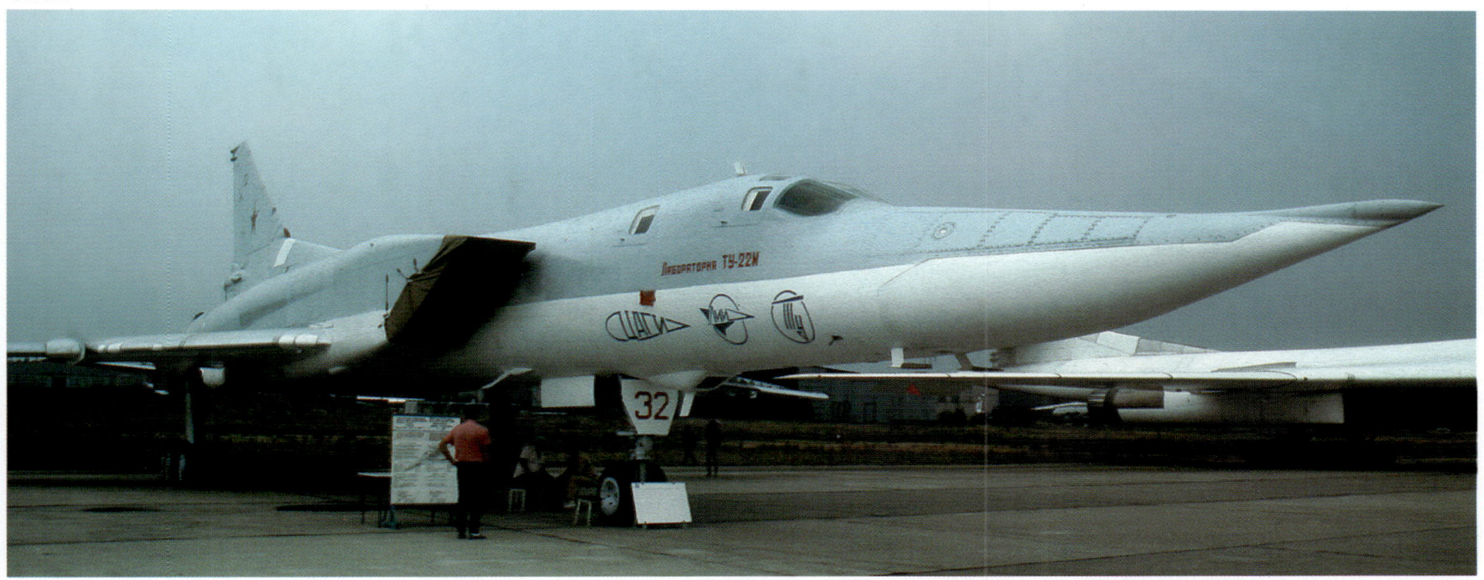

A detail view of the nose of the aircraft displayed at Zhukovskiy. The insignia on the nose (right to left) are those of the TsAGI (Central Aerodynamics Institute at Zhukovskiy), the LII (Experimental Flying Institute, at Ramenskoye/Zhukovskiy) and the Tupolev OKB-116 design bureau.

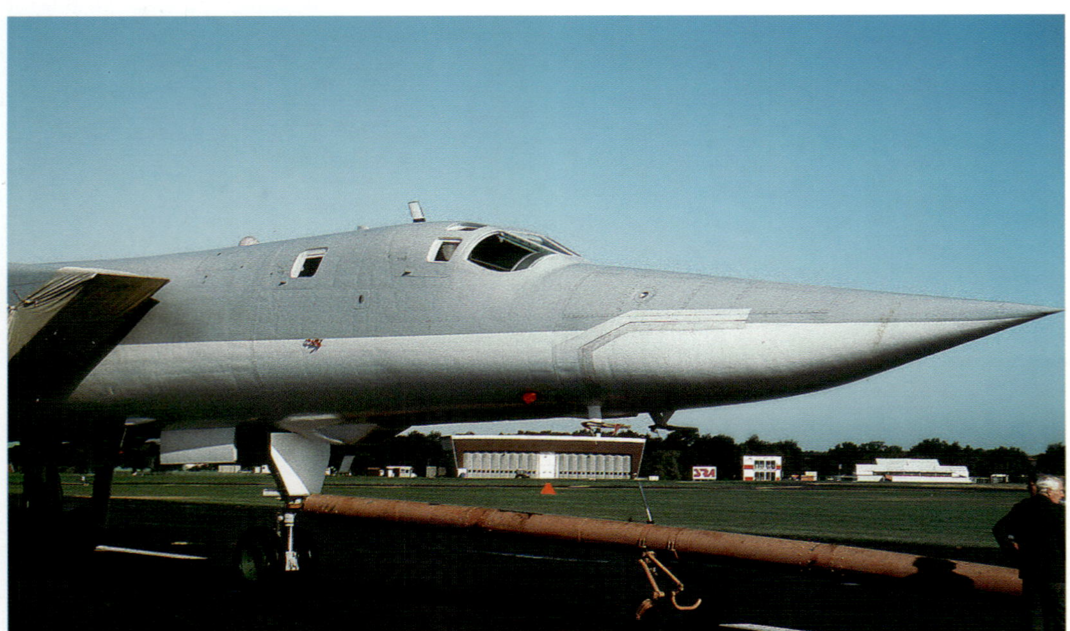

A detail view of the nose of the Tu-22M3. The nose houses a new navigation/attack radar system, probably designated PNS-22M3.

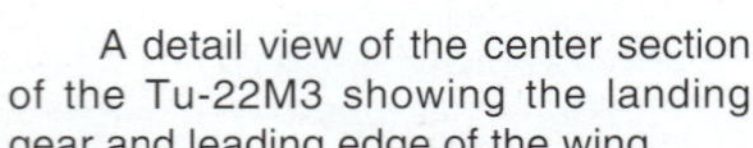

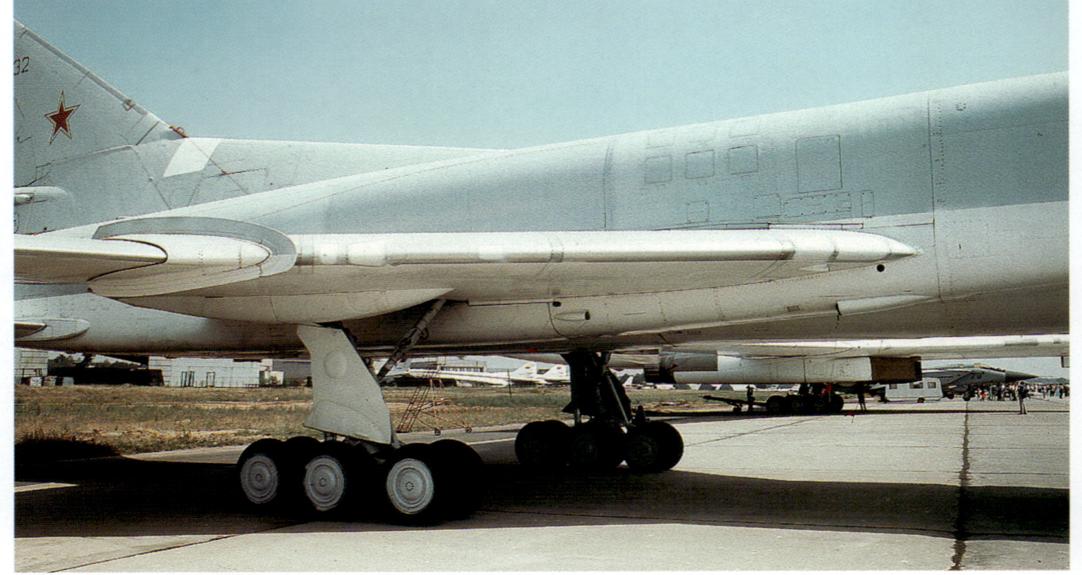

A detail view of the center section of the Tu-22M3 showing the landing gear and leading edge of the wing.

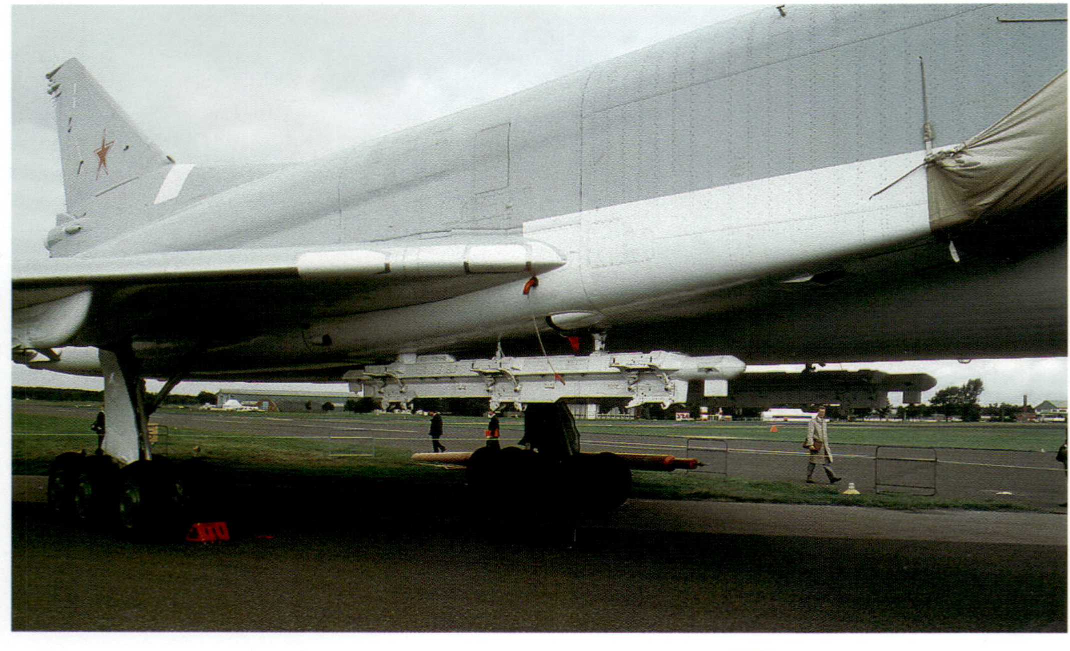

An interesting comparison between the Zhukovskiy and Farnborough Tu-22M3. The Farnborough aircraft was fitted with this MBDZ-U9M multiple ejector bomb rack.

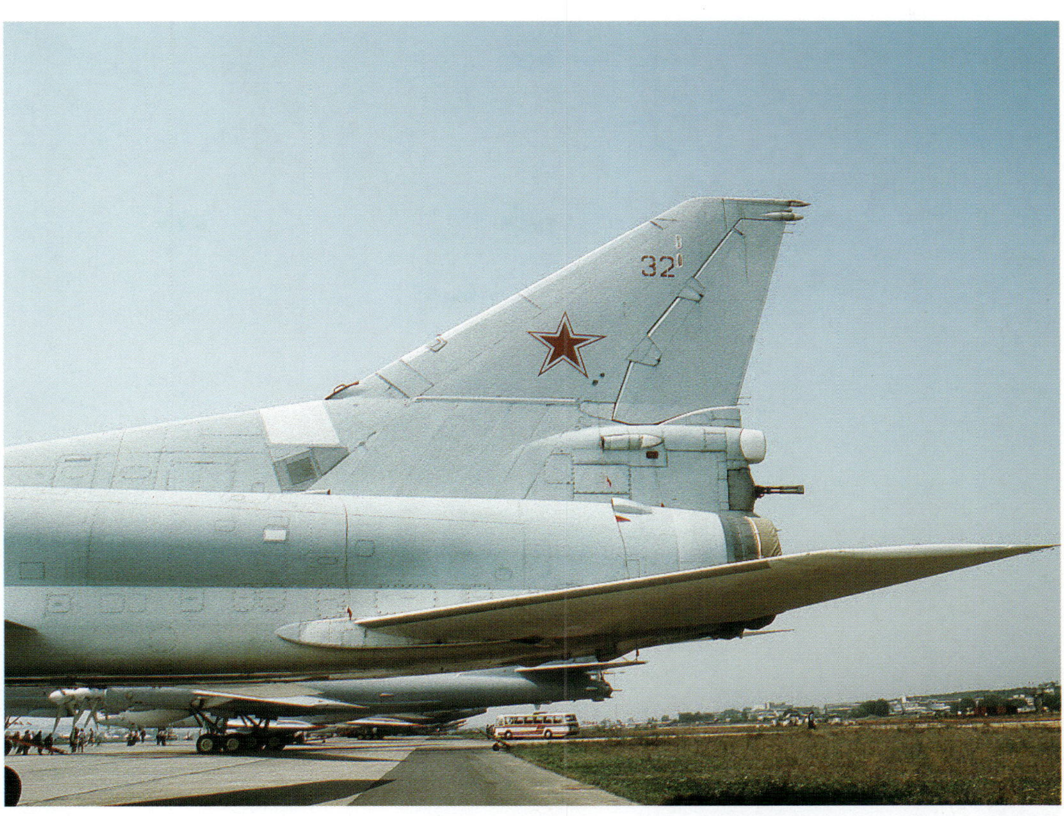

A detail view of the tail area on the Tu-22M3.

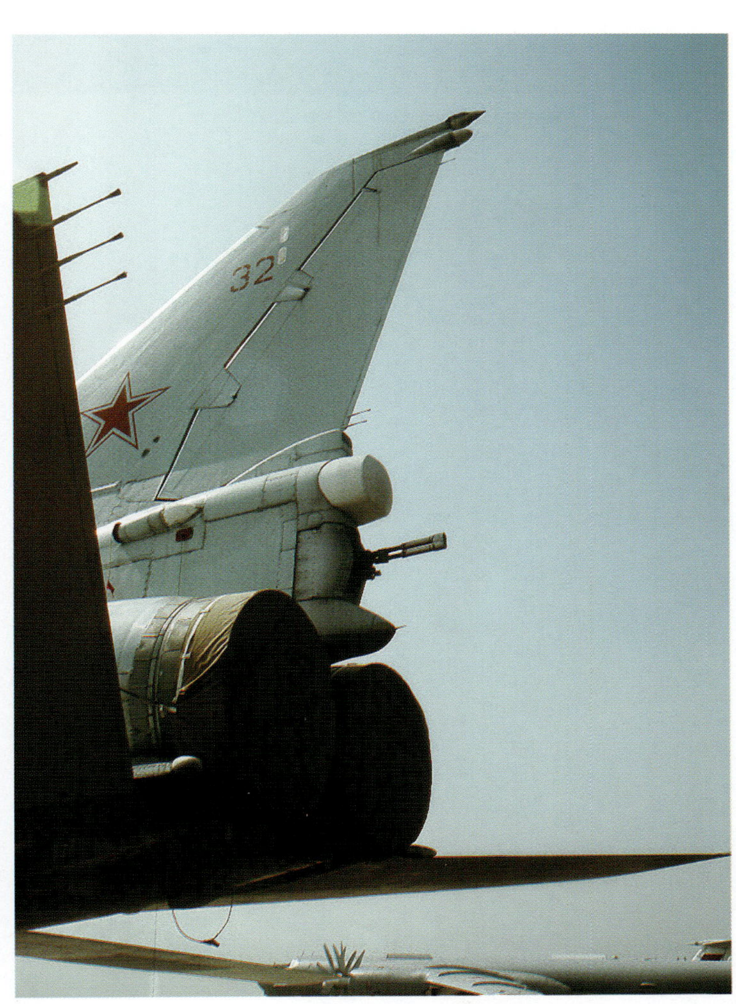

A close-up of the tail of the Tu-22M3. The Backfire C uses the same Kuznetsov engines as the Tu-160 Blackjack, but two rather than four.

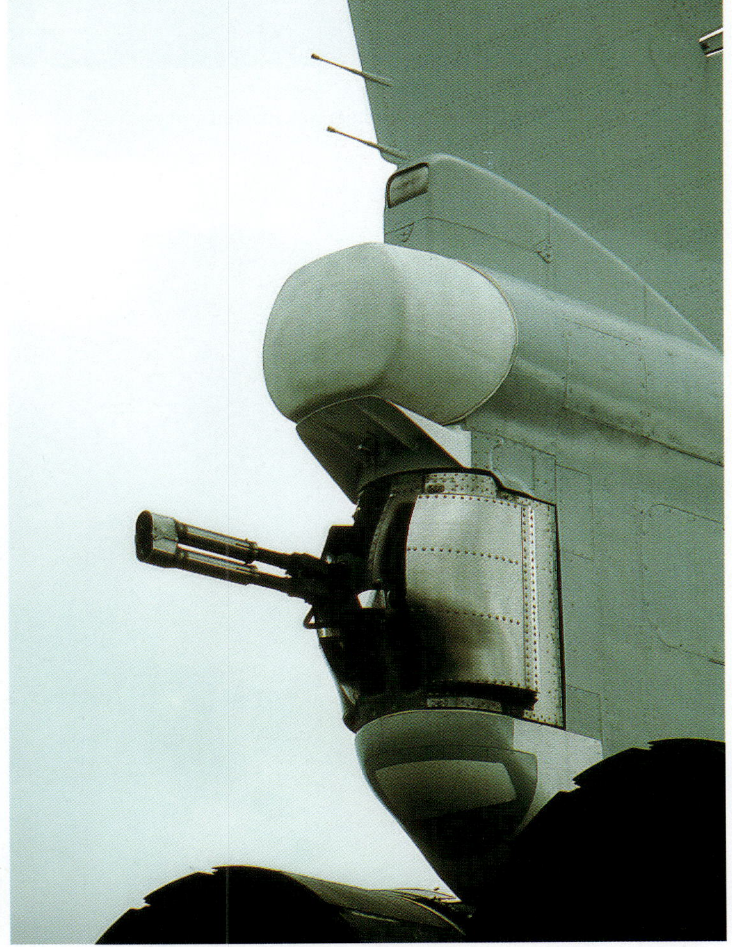

A detail view of the twin 23mm cannons at the tail of the Tu-22M3. The configuration of the tail mount shifted between the Tu-22M2 and the Tu-22M3. As is evident from this view, the rear gun is remotely radar directed, with the Fan Tail radar antenna being located immediately above the gun package.

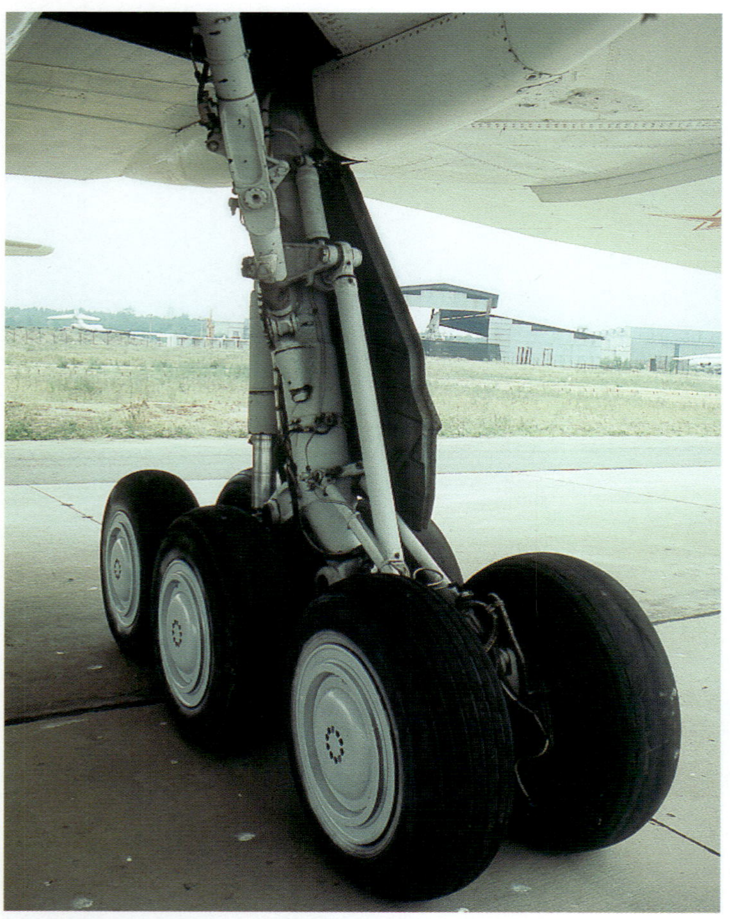

A detail view of the landing gear of the Tu-22M3. On the earlier versions of the Tu-22M, the middle wheel was located outboard of the other two wheels.

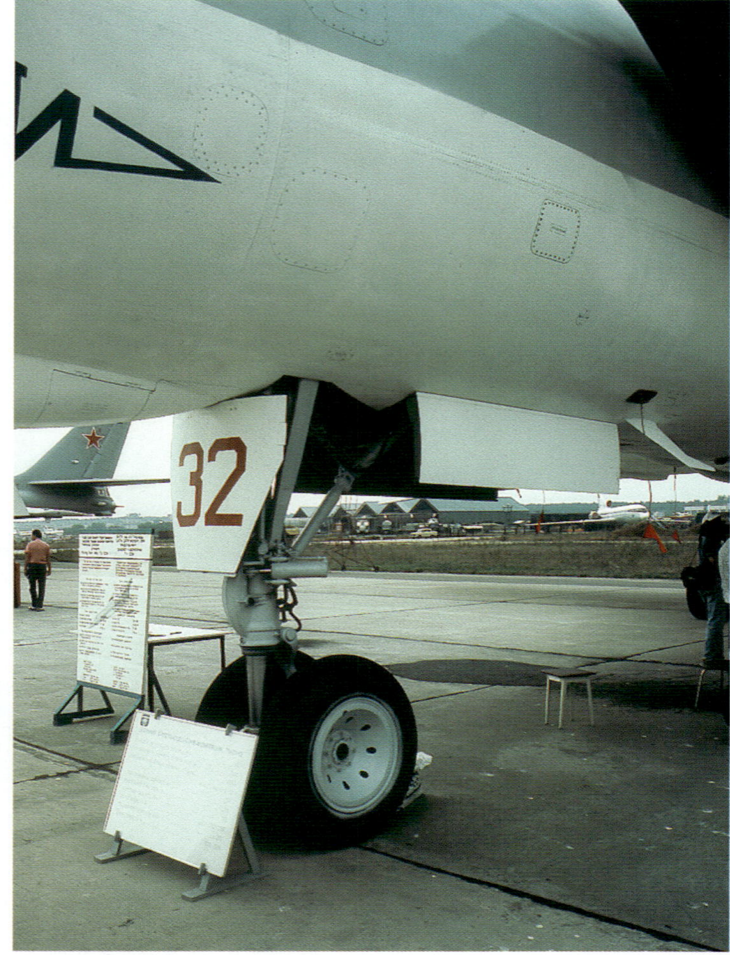

A detail view of the nose-landing gear on the Tu-22M3.

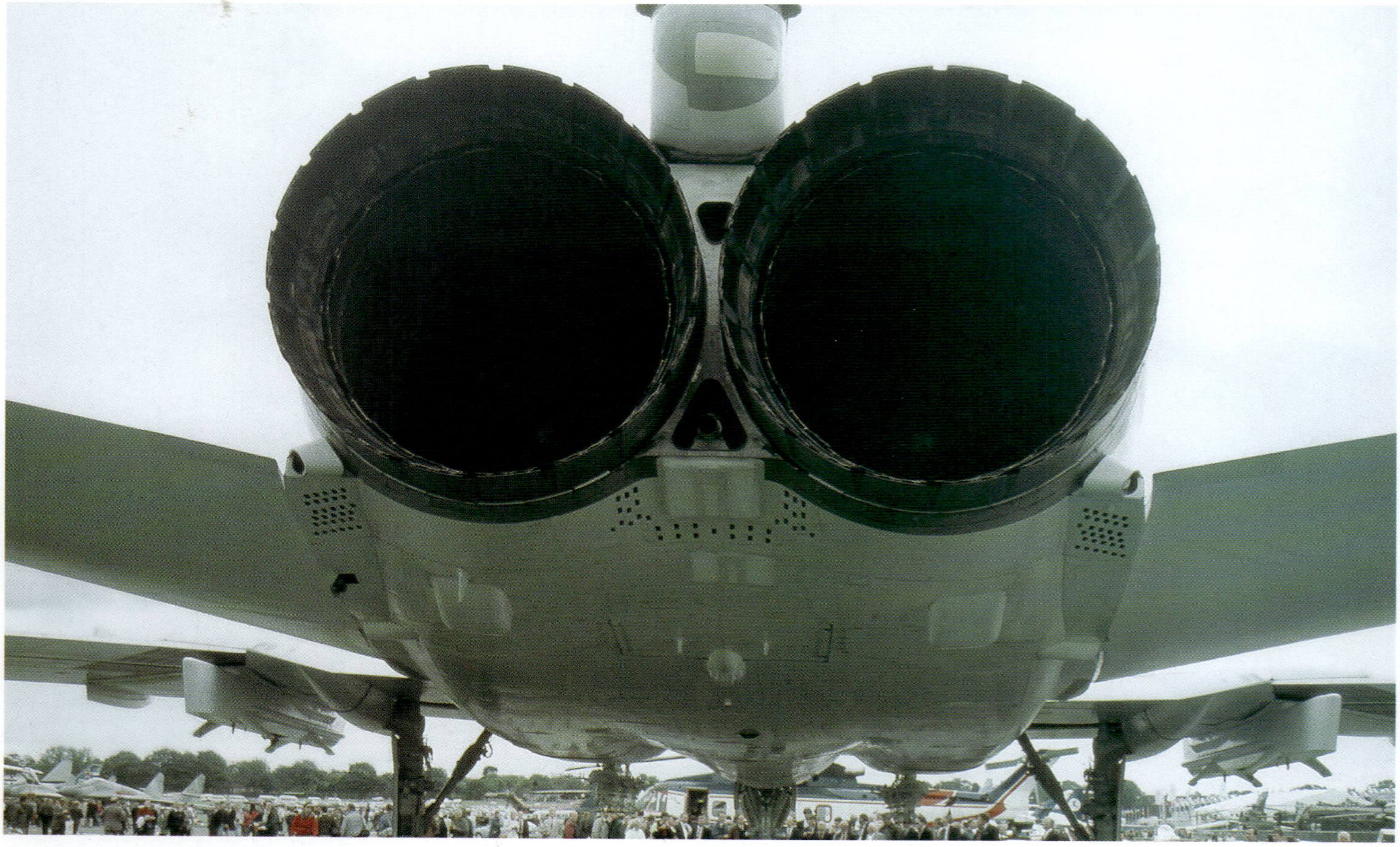

A rear view of the Tu-22M3 showing the engine exhaust as well as the underside details of the aircraft.

Surprisingly, the Tu-22M1 did not have the rear defensive gun position, which was added on the Tu-22M2.

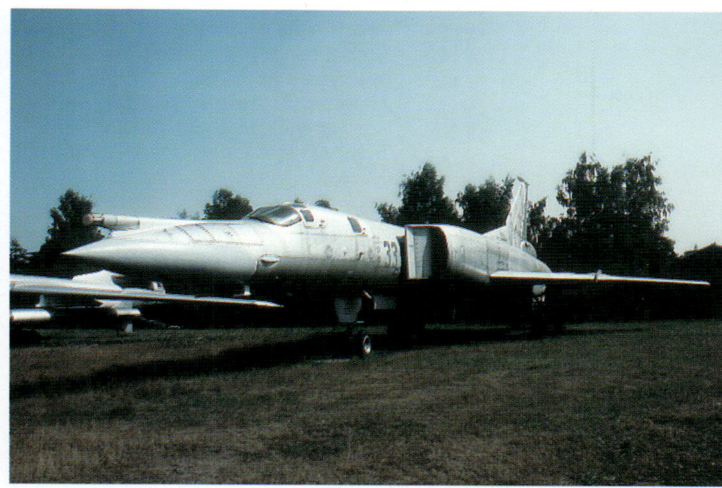

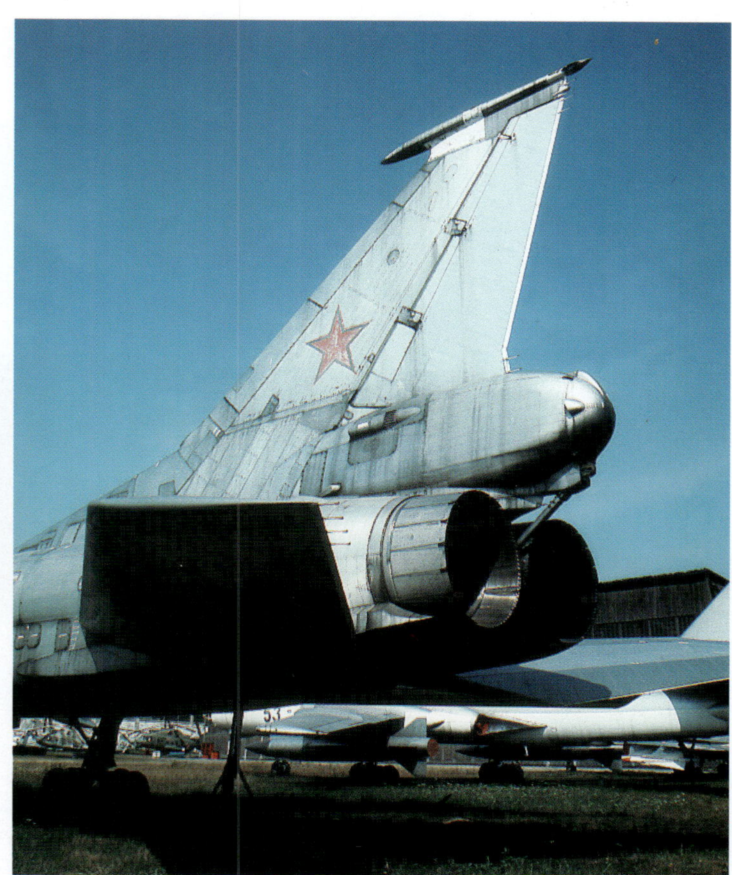

A recent addition to the VVS museum at Monino outside Moscow is the Tu-126 prototype Backfire A which was later designated Tu-22M1. This provides an interesting contrast with the Tu-22M3. It has the early style nose with the Down Beat radar as well as the early refueling probe which was deleted from later aircraft due to the SALT treaty. The air intakes on this aircraft are essentially similar to those on the Tu-22M2 Backfire B bomber.

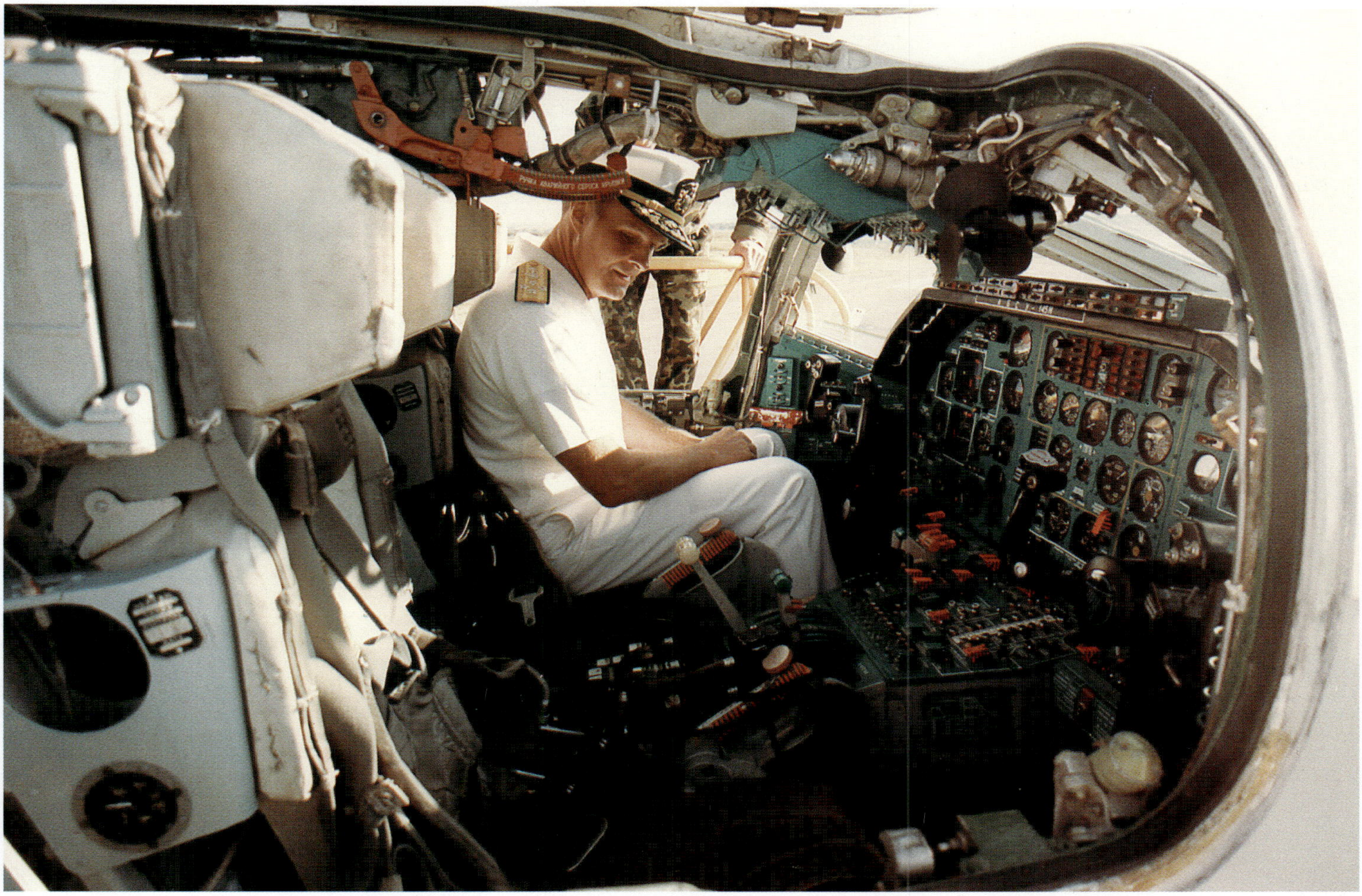

A view of the cockpit interior of a Tu-22M3 of the Russian Pacific Fleet with Adm. Charles Lawson of the US Navy inspecting the controls during a goodwill visit to Vladivostok in September 1990.

TUPOLEV Tu-160 BLACKJACK

Tupolev Tu-160 Blackjack A

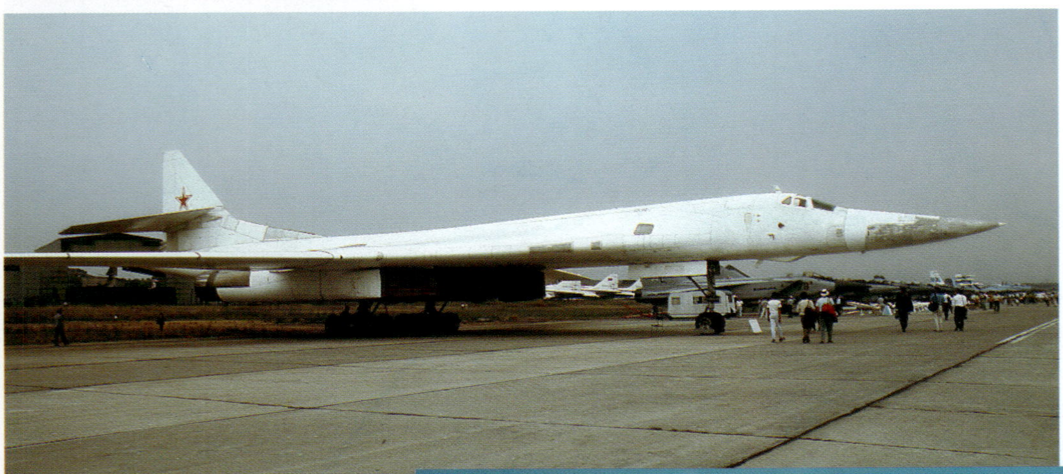

The Tu-160 Blackjack is the final heavy strategic bomber of the Russian and Ukrainian Air Forces. Production of the type has ended in 1992 due to recent strategic arms control agreements. Most operational Tu-160 bombers are located in Ukraine, not Russia.

Although resembling the American B-1B Lancer bomber, the Tu-160 is in fact a substantially larger and heavier aircraft than its American counterpart.

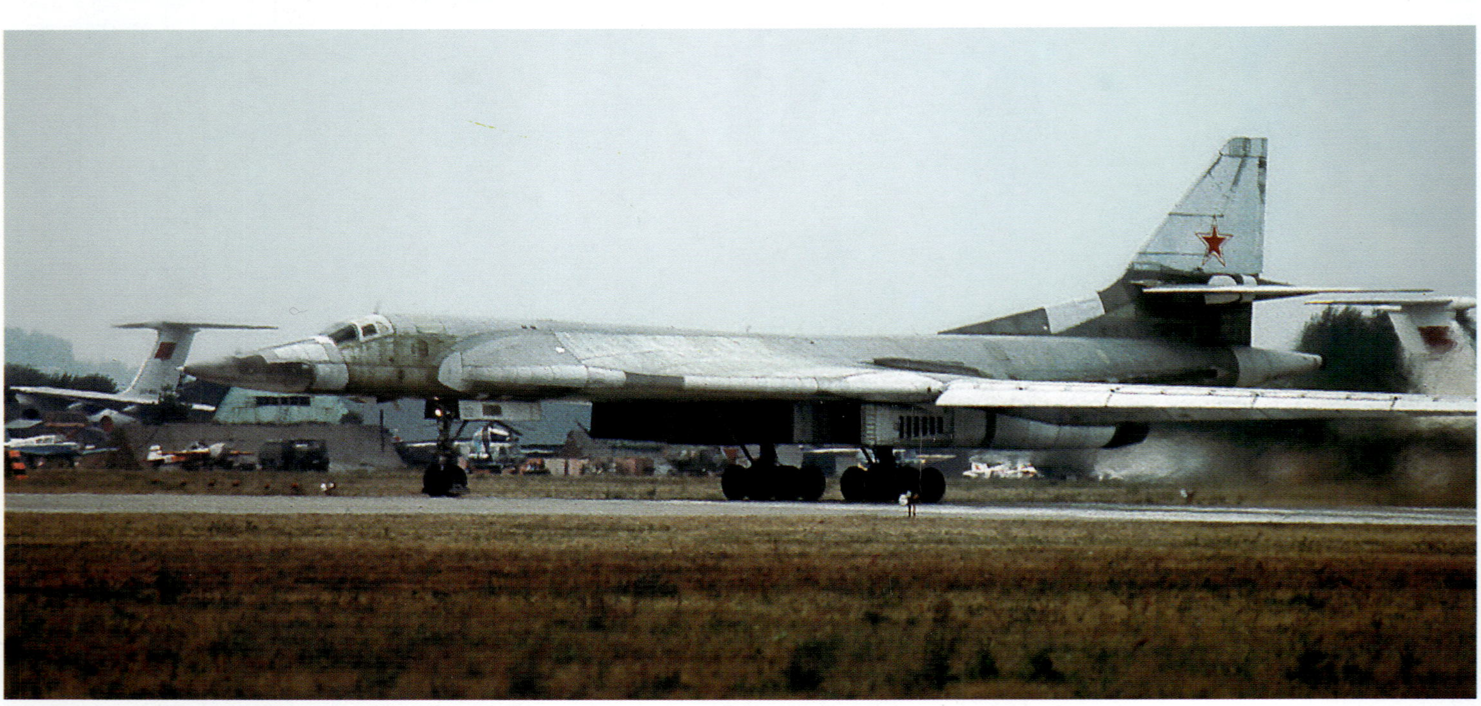

The Tu-160 used in the aerial displays at Zhukovskiy was this partially unpainted aircraft which gives a somewhat better view of the structural details than the white service aircraft.

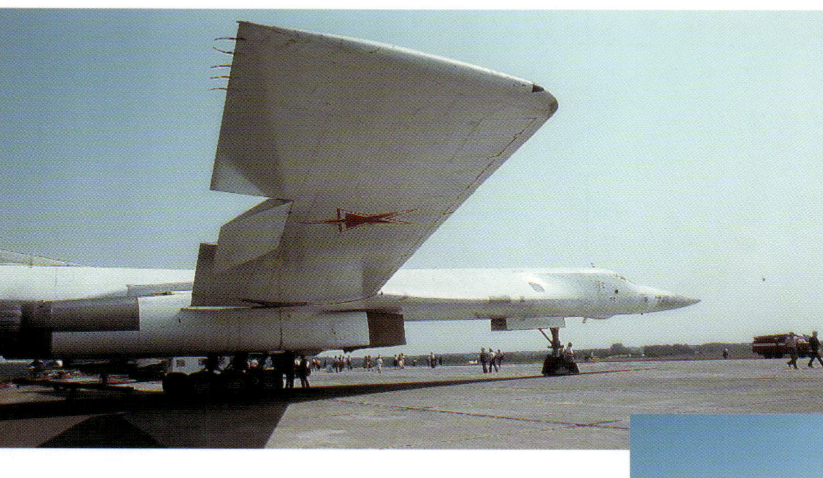

A view under the starboard wing of the Tu-160 bomber.

A continuation of the previous photo, providing a better view of the tail configuration.

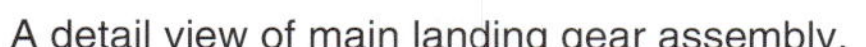

A detail view of main landing gear assembly.

An additional landing gear detail view, also showing the large engine housings.

Mil Mi-24 Hind

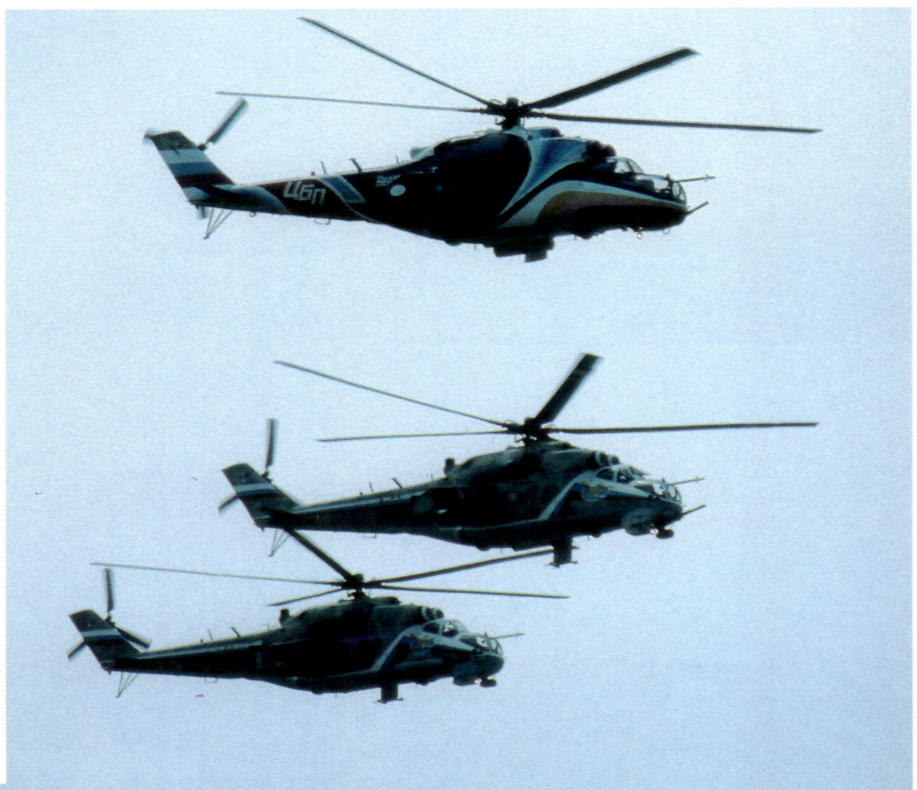

One of the surprises at the Zhukovskiy display was an exhibition by the *Berkuty* (Eagles), a new helicopter demonstration team from the Torzhak Assault Helicopter Regiment. The team consists of five Mi-24P Hind Es in a normal camouflage finish with decorative markings, plus a sixth Mi-24V Hind named *Vertikal-T* in a garish paint scheme. Vertikal-T, seen here at the top has the acronym *TsBP* in a red band around the tail.

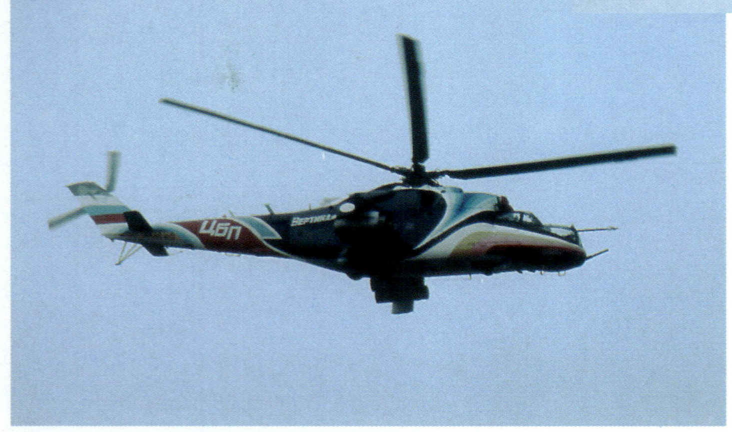

A single view of Vertikal-T flight. The helicopter is overall matt black with a pale blue undersides and colorful trim.

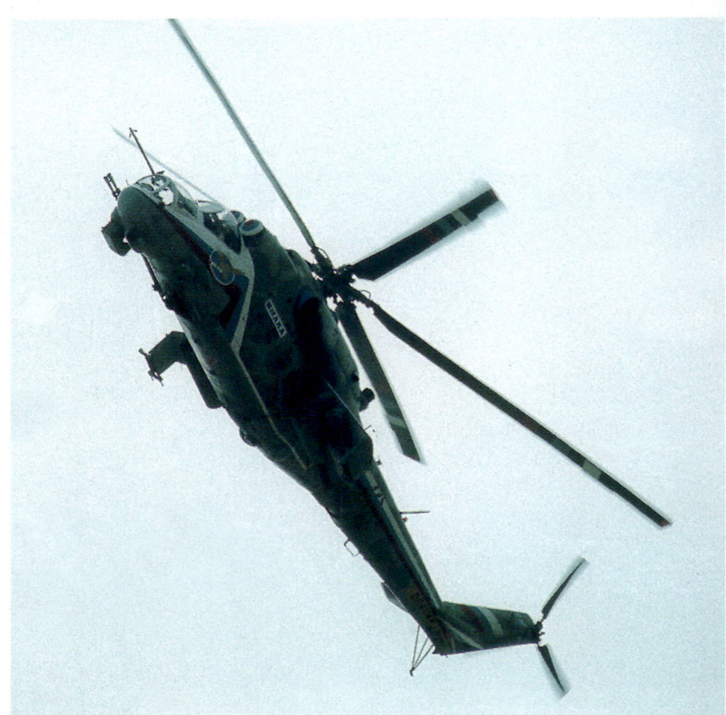

Another view of one of the Berkuty, giving a better view of the markings added over the basic tactical camouflage scheme.

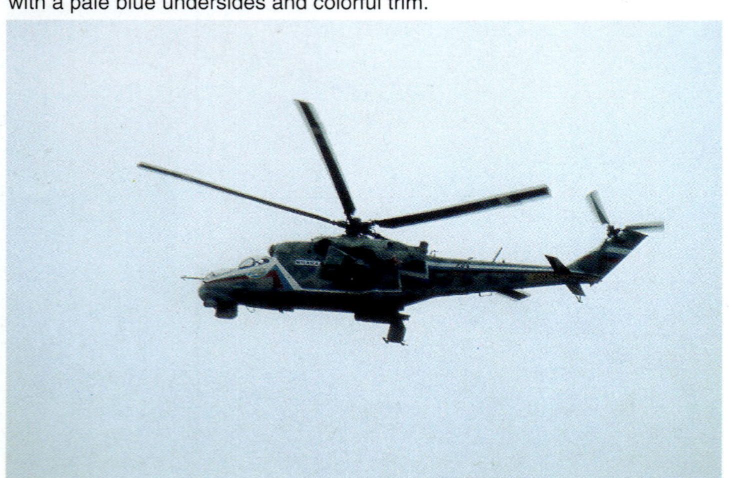

An overhead pass by one of the Mi-24Vs of the Berkuty.

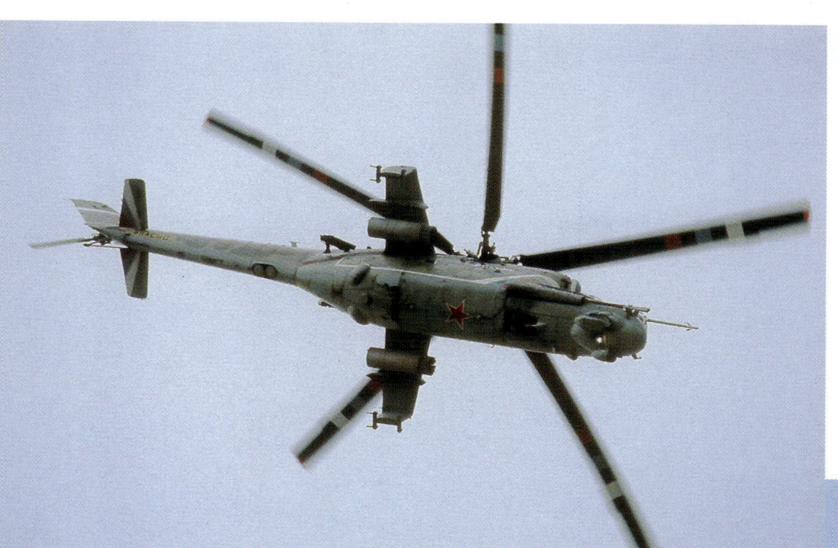

An interesting undersides view of a Mi-24P Hind. As is evident from this view, these helicopters are still fitted with their ASO flare dispensers on the rear fuselage sides.

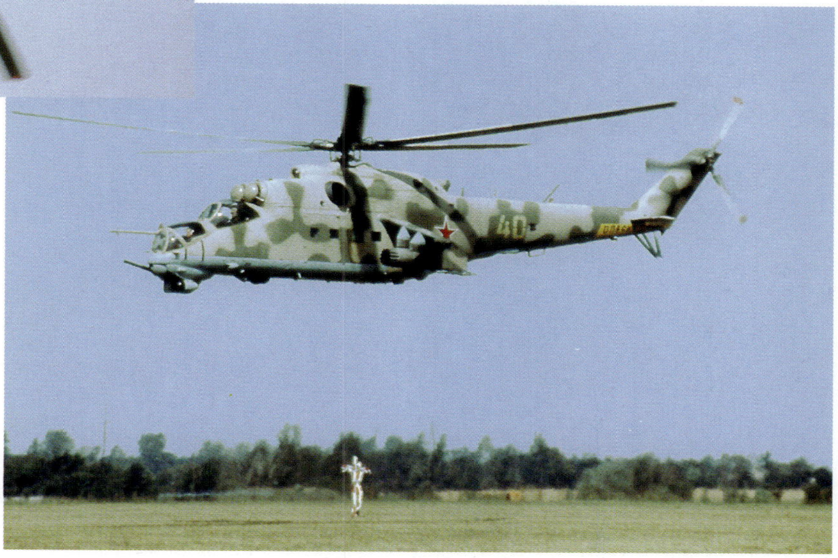

The classic version of the Mi-24, the Mi-24V, is seen here near Grossenhein, Germany in the summer of 1992 prior to the withdrawal of Russian units from Germany. Russia has laid claim to all former Soviet units in Germany. (Michael Jerchel)

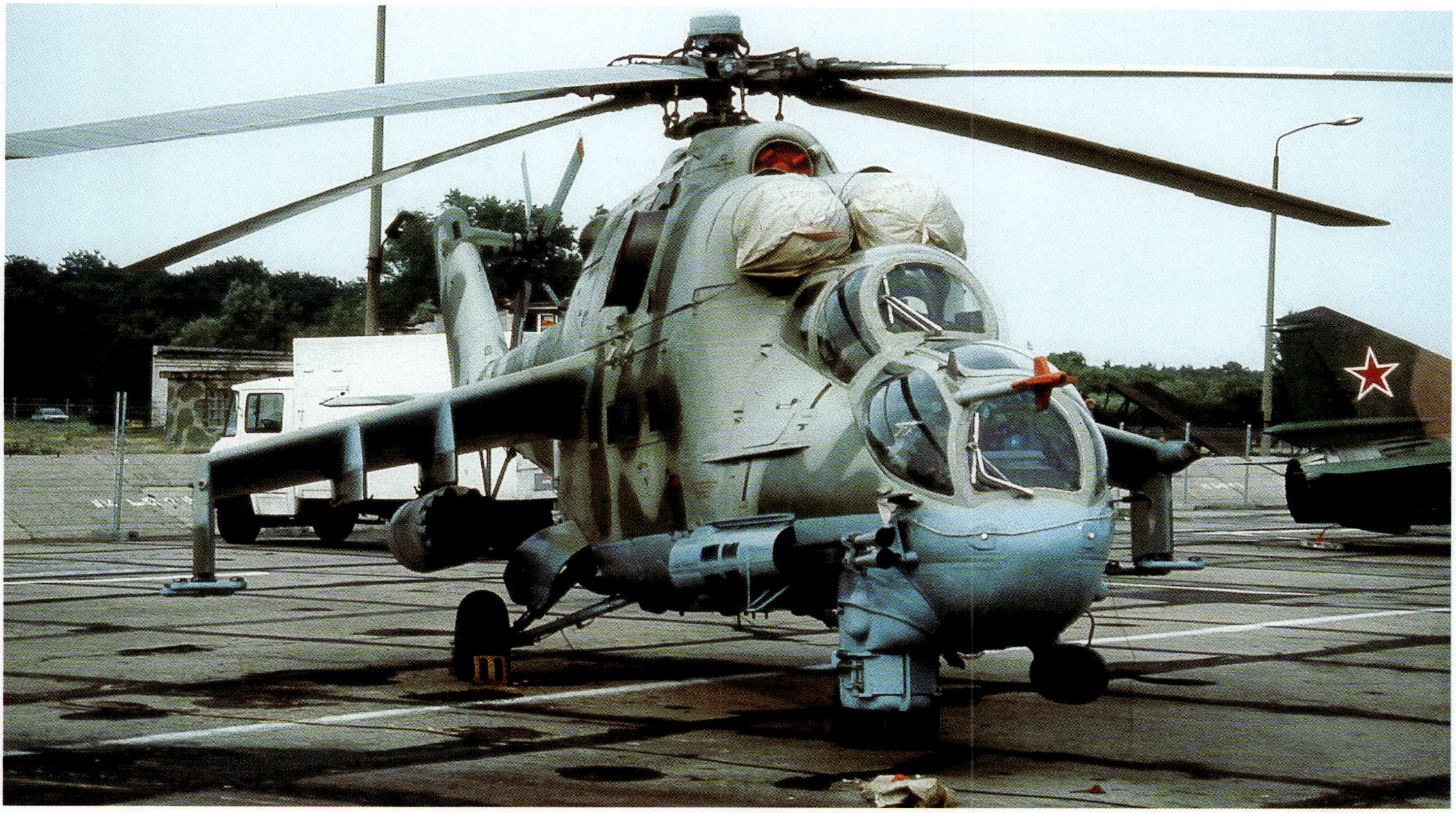

The Mi-24P Hinds in service have less garish finishes. This is a cannon armed Mi-24P displayed at Damgarten, Germany in July 1992. (Michael Jerchel)

Mil Mi-26 Halo

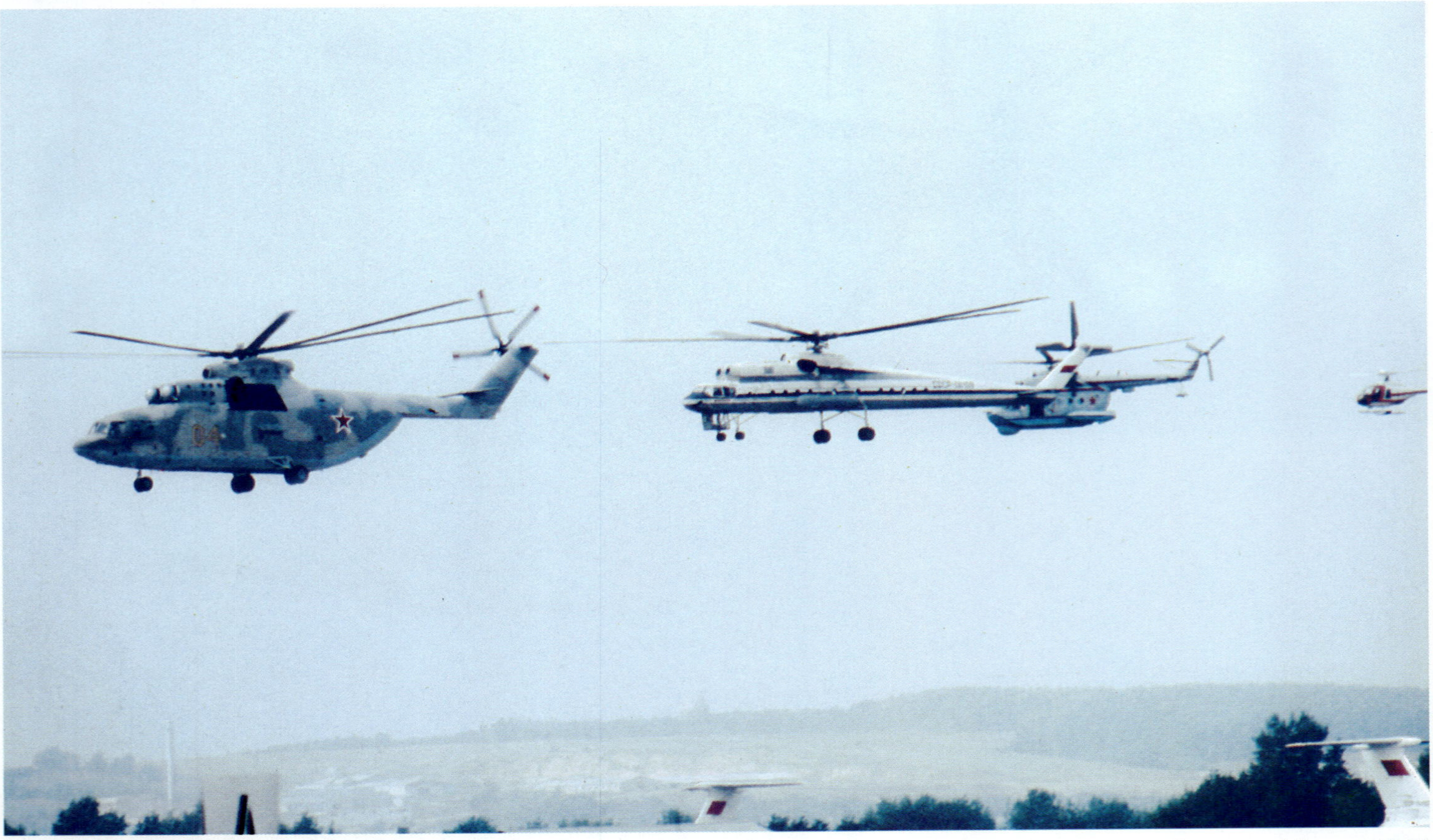

A rare sight: a display of Mil helicopters with an Mi-26 in the lead, followed by an Mi-10 flying crane, an Mi-14 naval helicopter, and the new Mi-34 trailing in the rear.

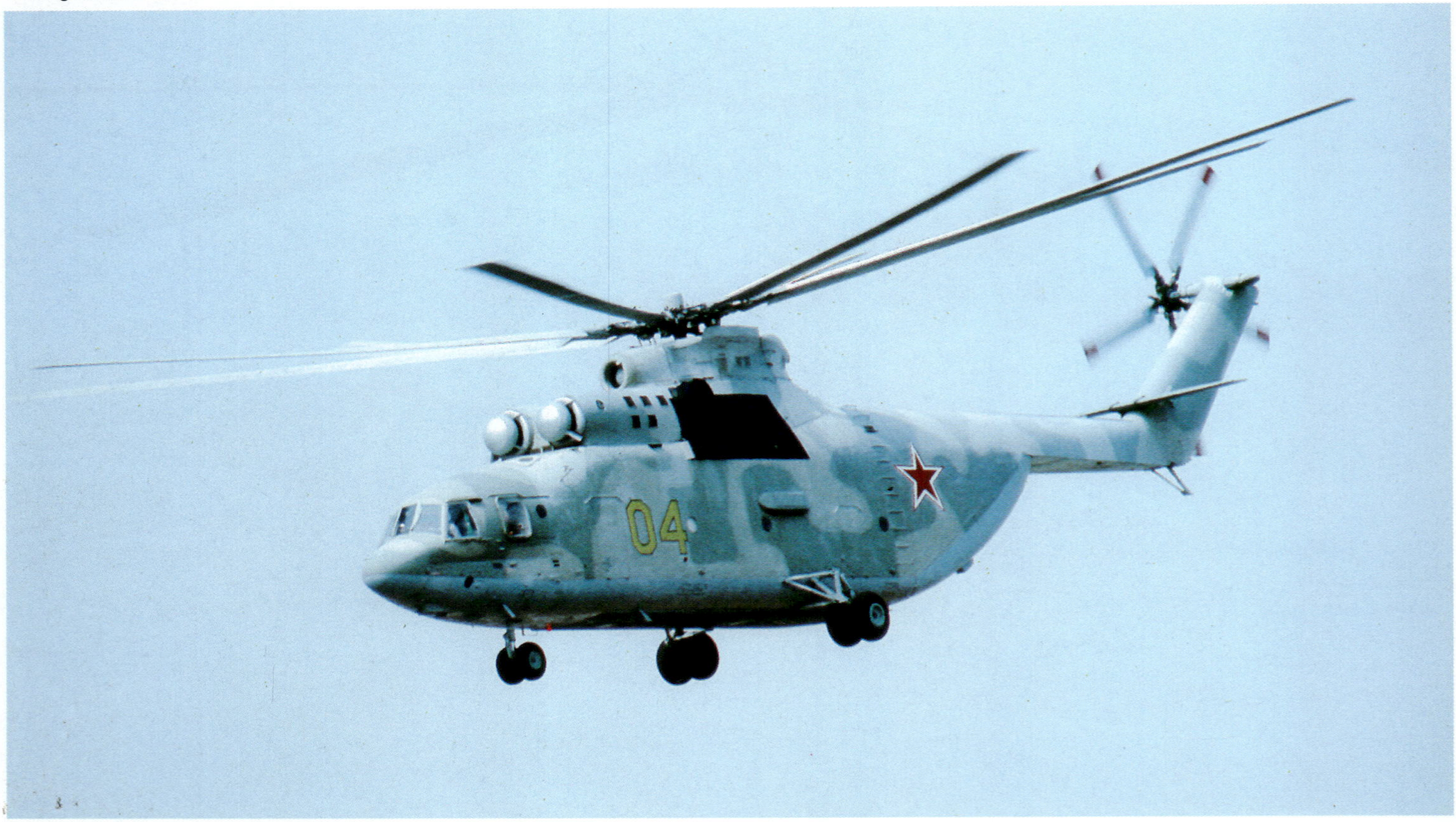

In the former Soviet Union, the Mi-26 heavy lift helicopter is best known for its role in the Chernobyl accident where several crews bravely flew over the reactor dumping boron, lead and sand onto the reactor to prevent further radioactive activity.

Mil Mi-28 Havoc

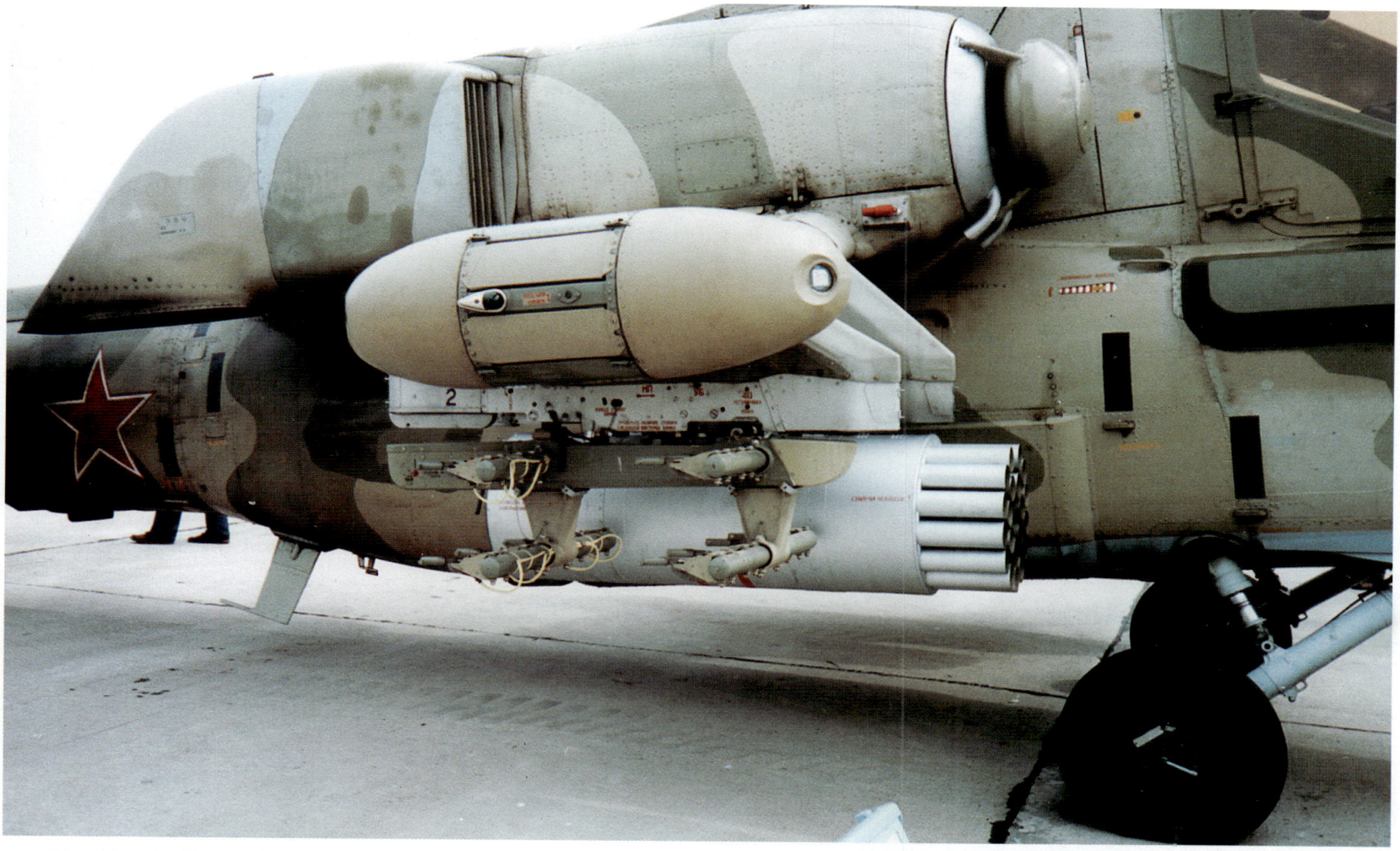

26a. Since its first appearance at the Paris Air Salon in 1989, the Mi-28 Havoc has undergone some modest changes. This view shows a new electronic warfare pod mounted on the stub winglet.

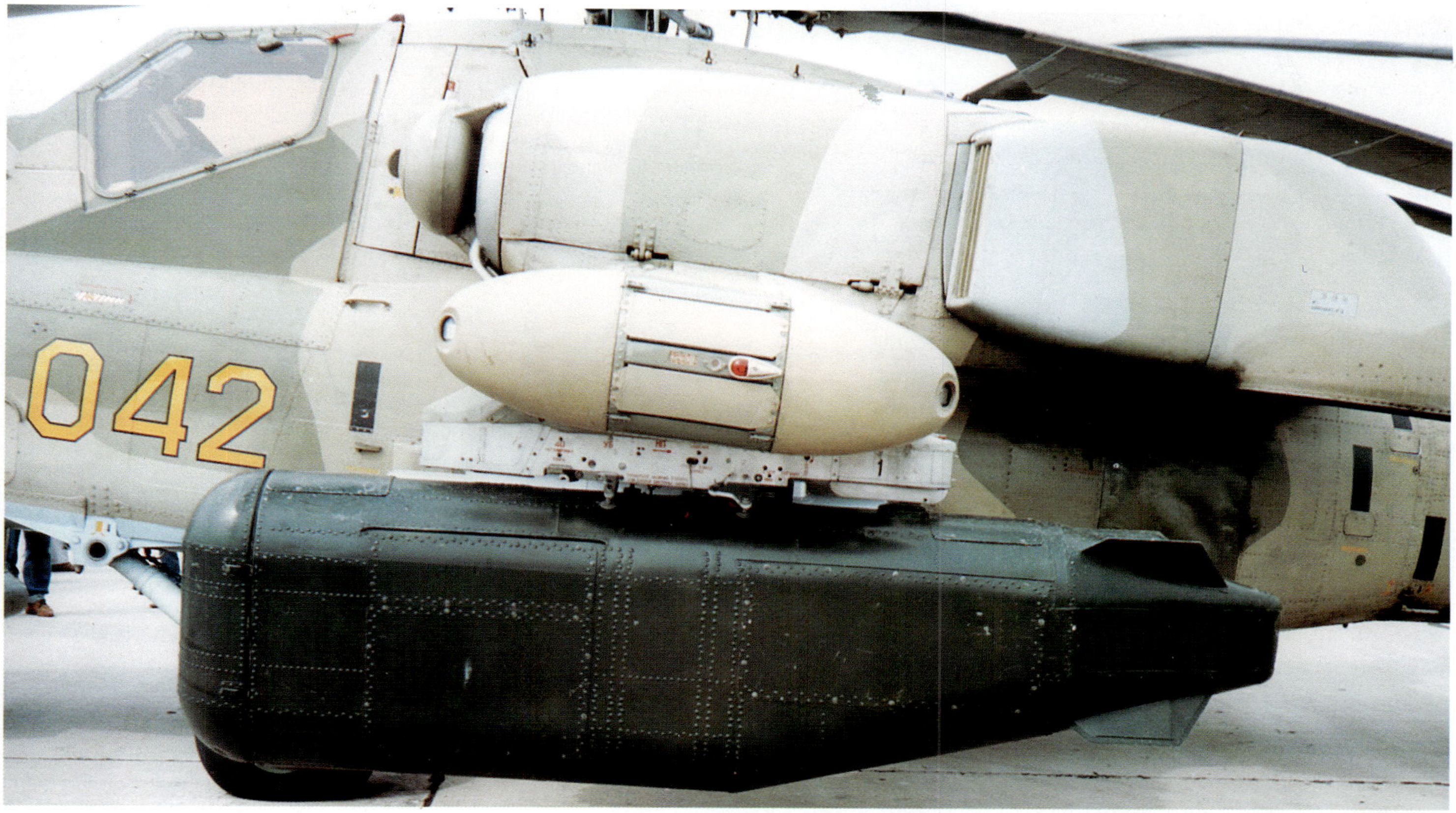

26b. Another change noted on the Mi-28 Havoc at Zhukovskiy was this unusual load, probably a transport container for carrying crew equipment.

Kamov Ka-27

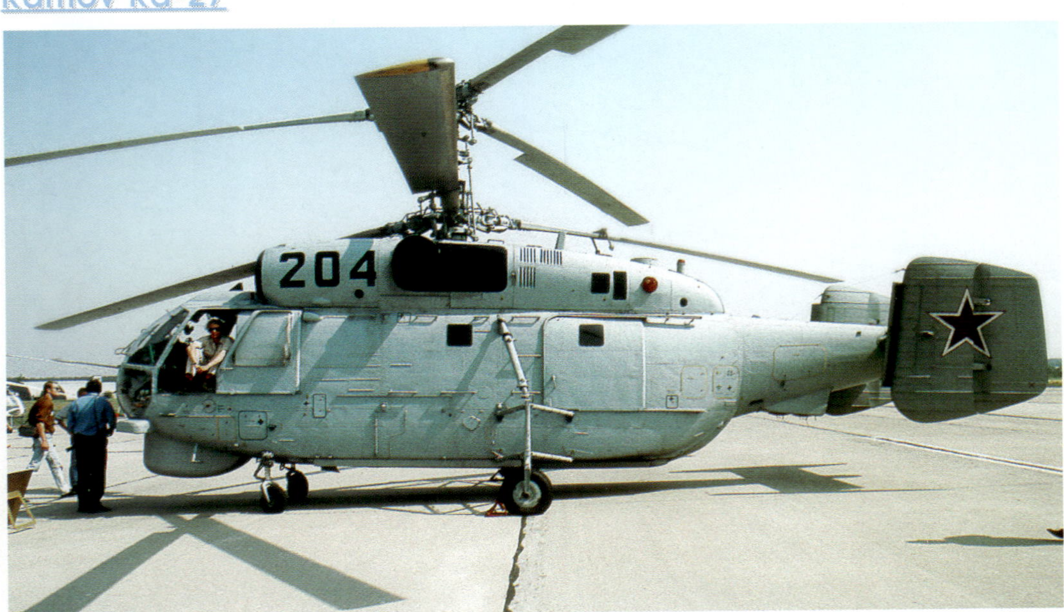

The basic anti-submarine variant of the Helix family is the Kamov Ka-27PL Helix A, seen here at Zhukovskiy.

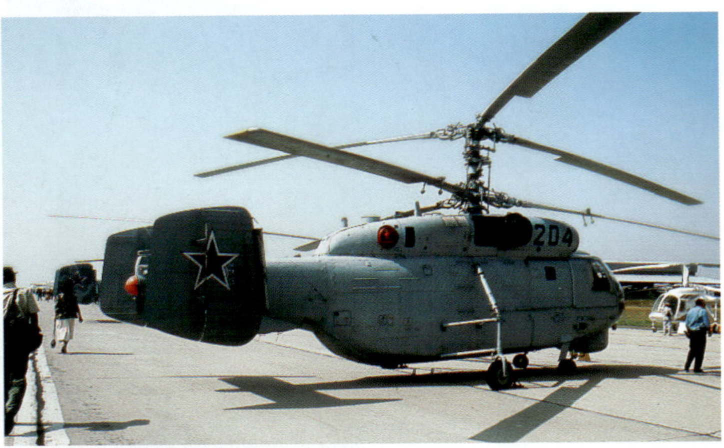

The Ka-27PL is one of the most common types of helicopters now used aboard Soviet warships for anti-submarine patrol as well as general logistics work.

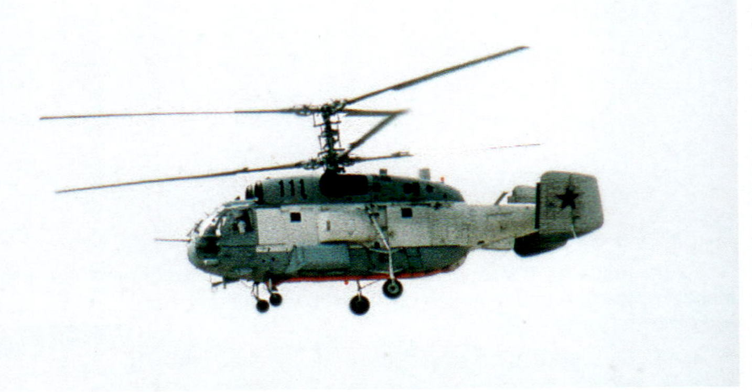

Another common shipboard variant is the Ka-27PS seen here during the air display. The Ka-27PS is a search and rescue variant of the Helix family, and is usually finished in this scheme of grey and white with the under-fuselage tray painted red.

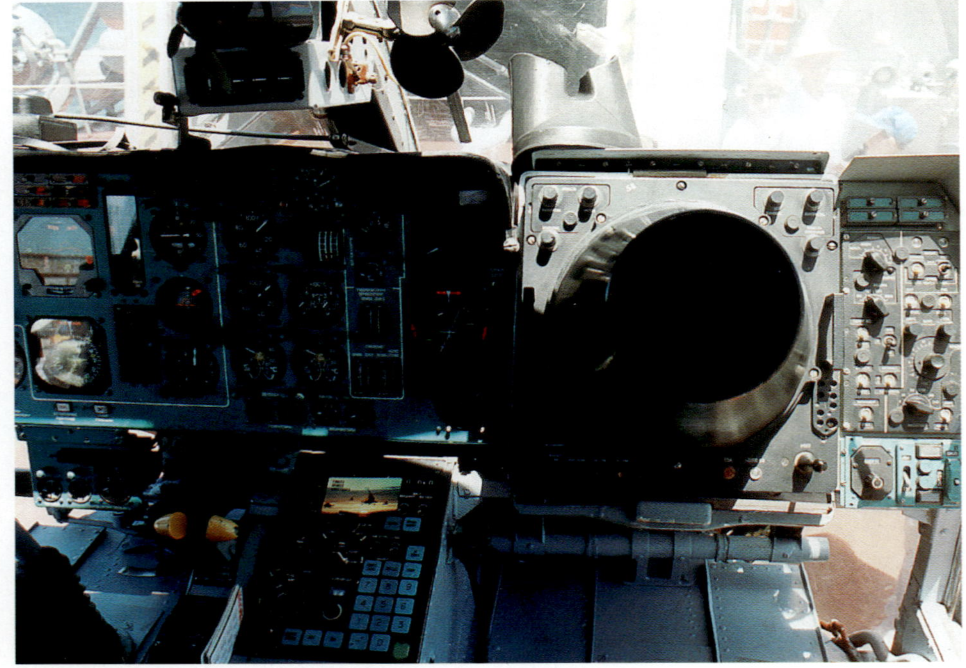

An interior view of the starboard station in the Ka-27PL occupied by the radar search operator. The third crew member, the sonar operator, is behind him.

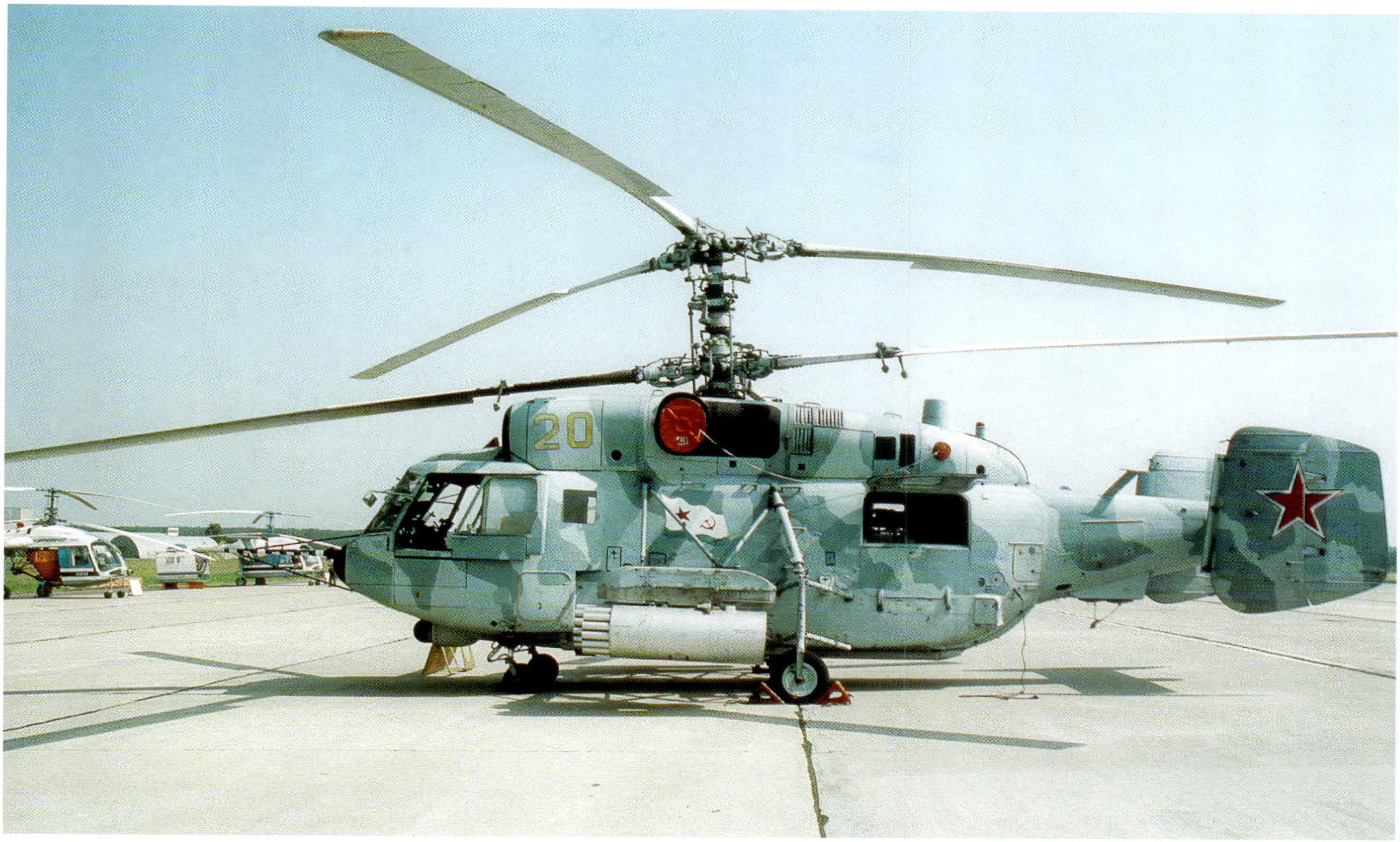

The Ka-29TB Helix-B is an air assault version of the Helix family, used on Soviet amphibious assault ships to support heliborne landings by the Naval Infantry. Although closely resembling the basic Ka-27, it has a wider forward cabin.

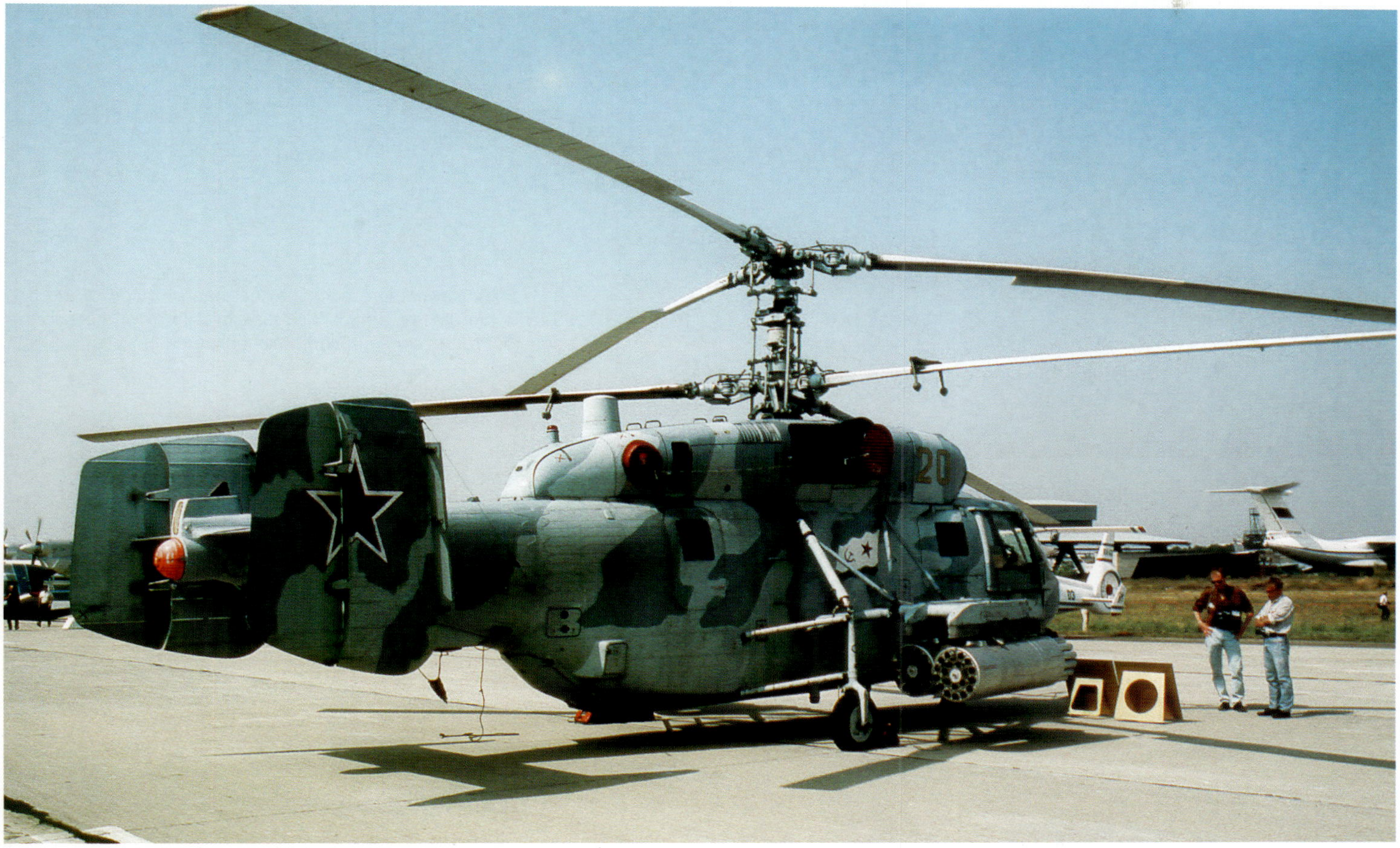

The Ka-29TB is the only member of the Helix family regularly equipped with air-to-surface weapons, in this case, 80mm rocket pods.

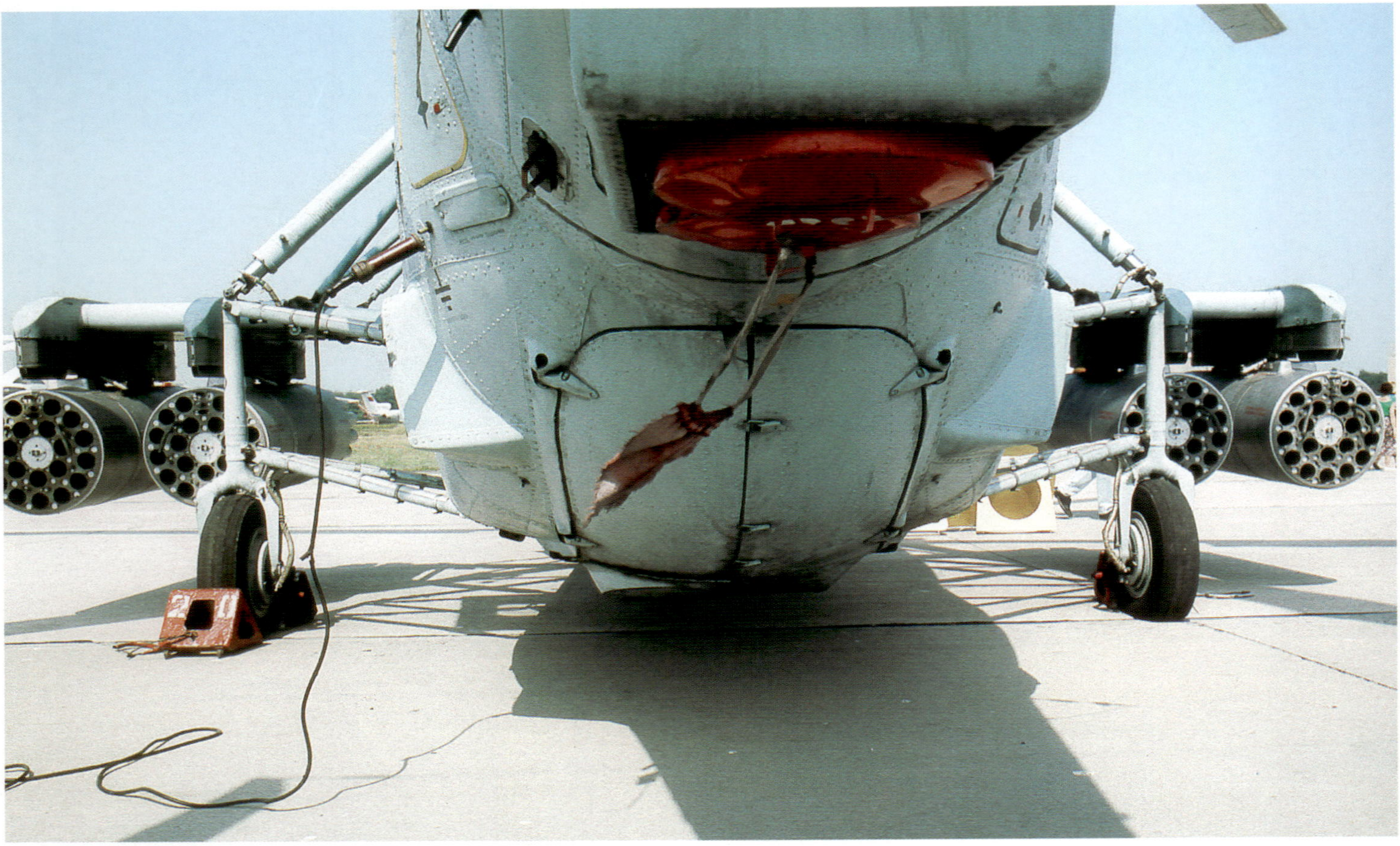

A detail view of the rear fuselage of the Ka-29TB Helix-B. Note that this variant still retains some of the features of the anti-submarine warfare variant, including the aft dipping sonar door and the under-belly weapons tray which is used to drop sonobuoys and torpedoes on the anti-submarine variant.

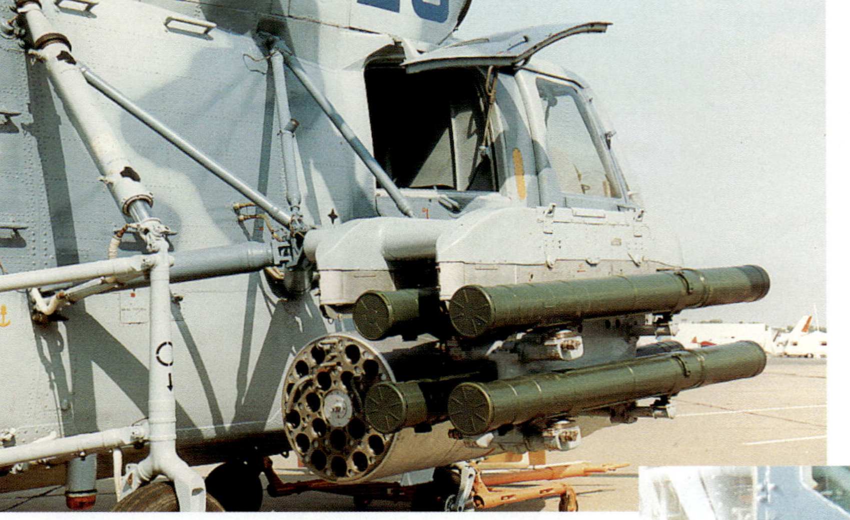

Another armament package that can be fitted to the Ka-29TB is the 9M114 Shturm anti-tank missile, seen here in the usual four round configuration. (Michael Jerchel)

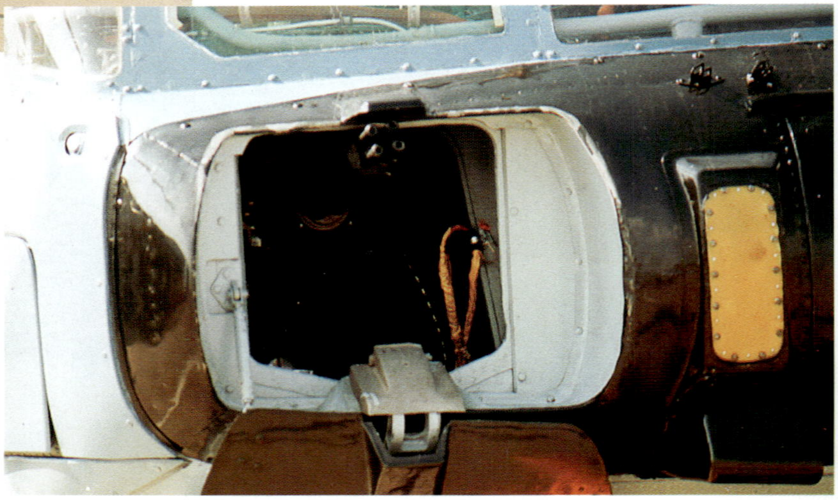

It is often not realized that the Ka-29TB contains its own armament package, a 4 barrel 9A622 7.62mm revolver cannon hidden behind a panel in the right side nose of the aircraft. (Michael Jerchel)

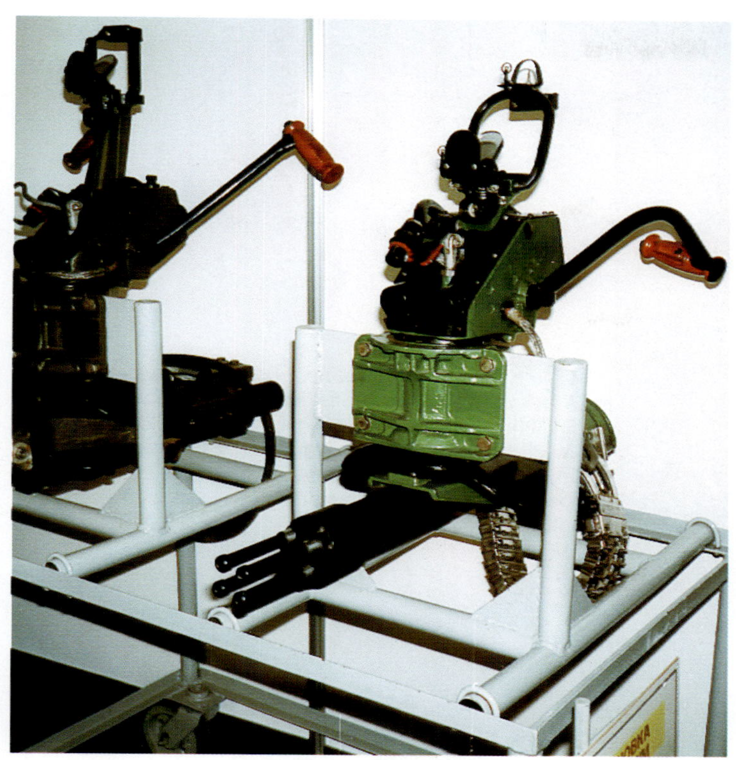

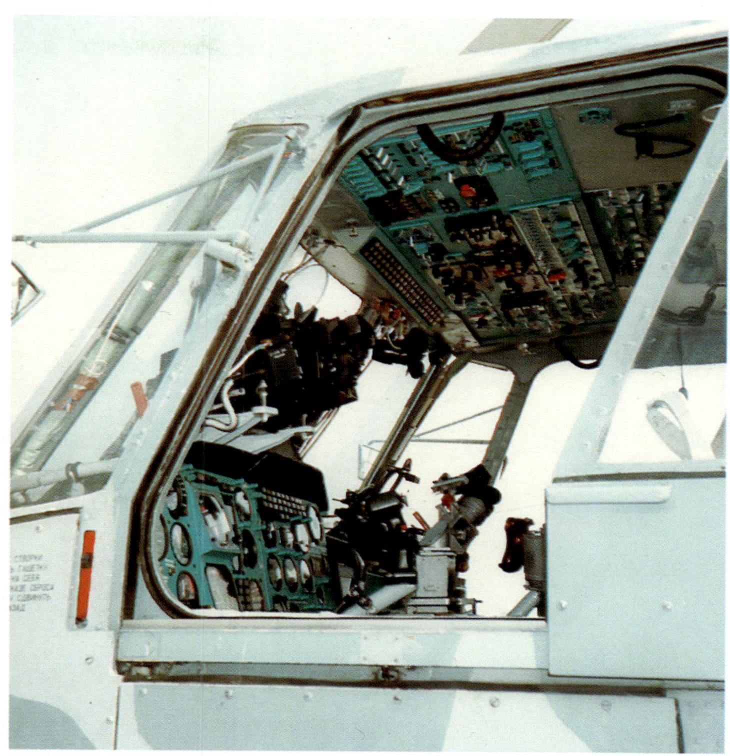

A detail view of the NUB-1UM mounting for the 9A622 7.62mm machine gun from the Ka-29TB built by MMPP Kommunar.

A view of the pilot's station on the Ka-29TB showing the overhead switch panel.

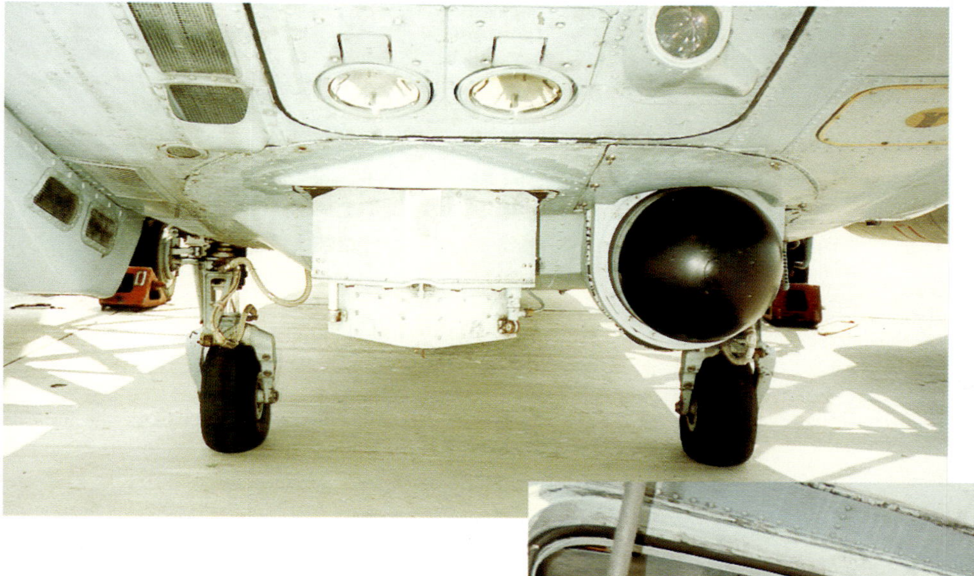

A detail view of the sensor package under the nose of the Ka-29TB showing the guidance antenna for the 9M114 Shturm missiles with its black dielectric cover and the armored box for the electro-optical sighting system in the center.

A view into the center bay of the Ka-29TB showing the electronics array.

Kamov Ka-50 (V-80) Hokum

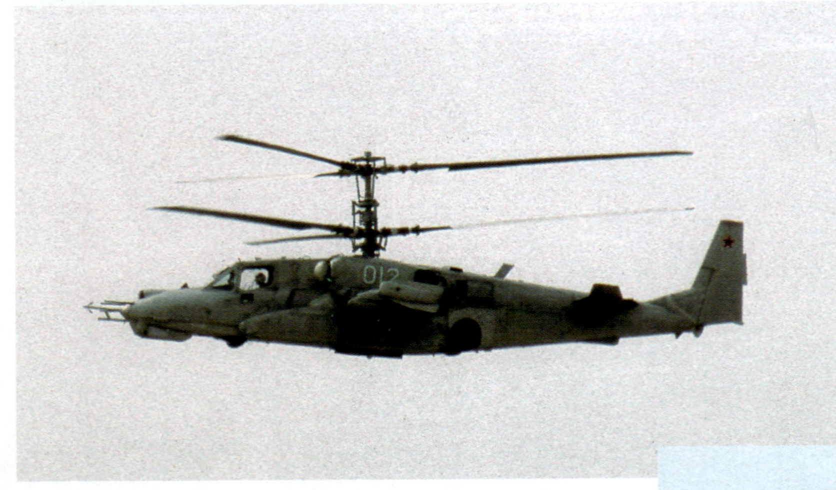

The Kamov Ka-50 *Oboroten* (Werewolf), better known in the West as the Hokum, was announced the winner of the Soviet Army's competition for a new attack helicopter against the Mi-28 Havoc. The helicopter flown at the Mosaeroshow is prototype number 12, which has an early nose configuration compared to the more commonly seen number 14, and the aircraft displayed at Farnborough.

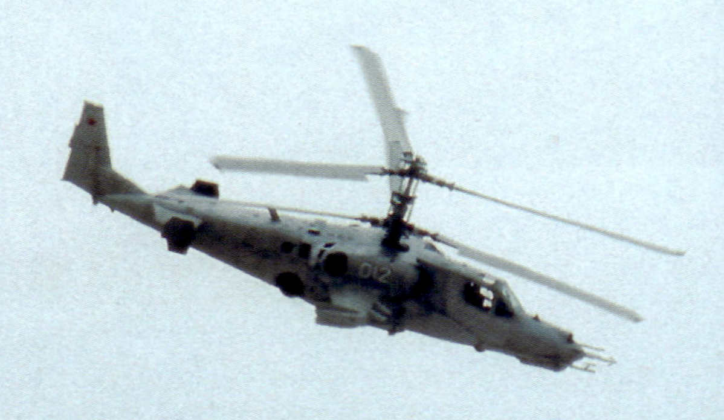

Although originally believed to be an anti-helicopter helicopter, it is now apparent that the Ka-50 Oboroten was developed from the outset for the more conventional attack helicopter role.

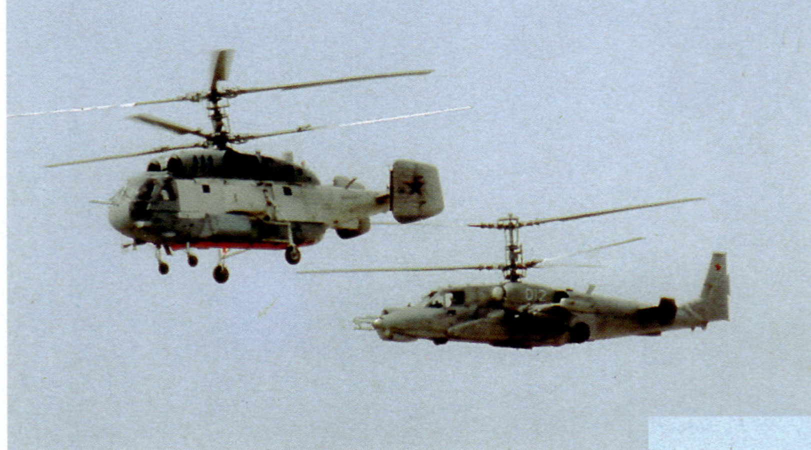

The Ka-50 at the beginning of its air display, with the Ka-27PS alongside.

The Ka-50 Oboroten differs from most of the world's attack helicopters in that it has a single crewman. Kamov representatives explained that this was made possible by greater automation of the aircraft's controls.

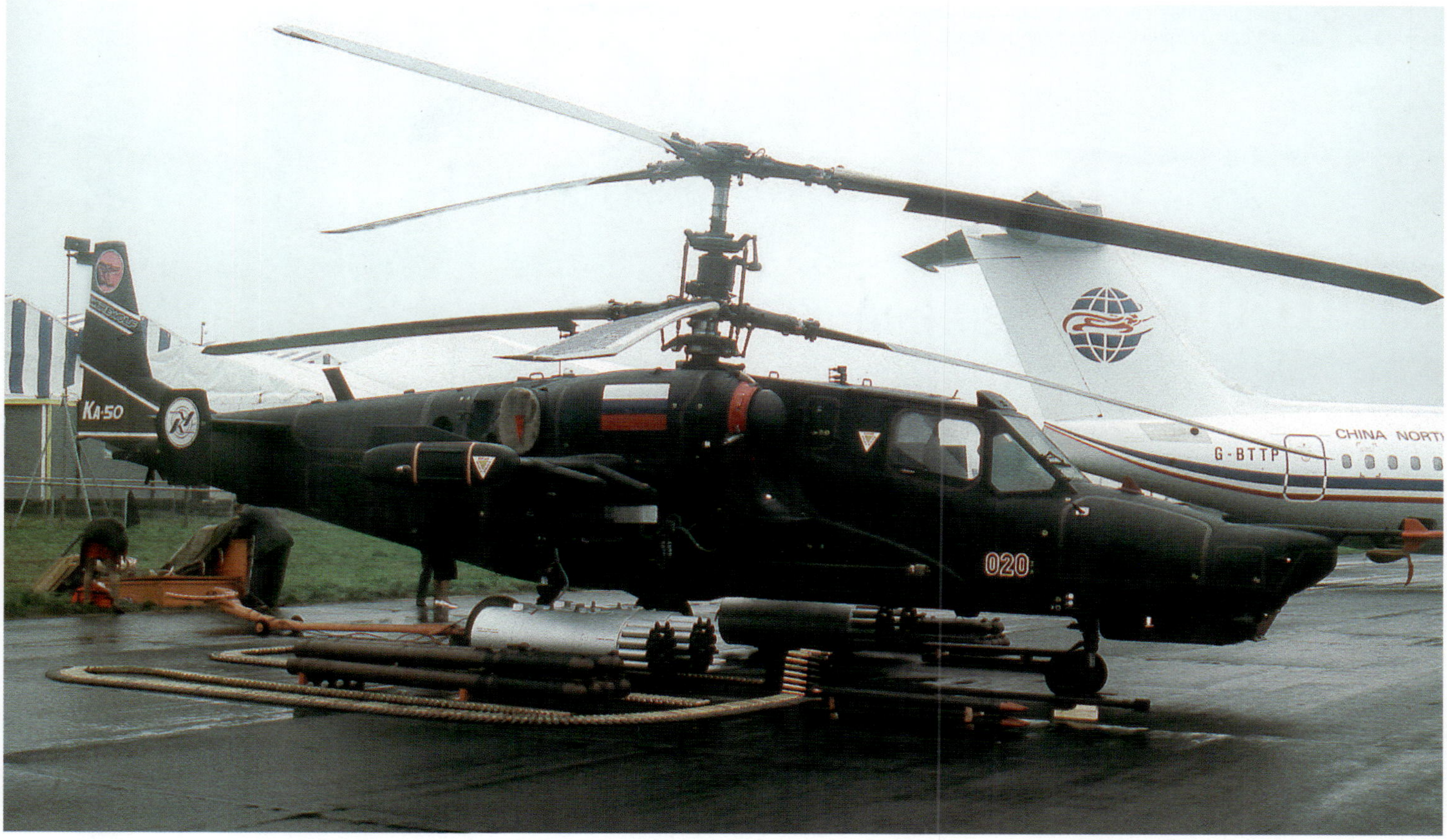

The Ka-50 Werewolf displayed at Farnborough had the lengthened nose seen on prototypes 14 and later. It is finished in a very dark olive drab, similar to that on US Army attack helicopters. It carries only the Russian national flag as it's insignia, aside from special display markings for the air show.

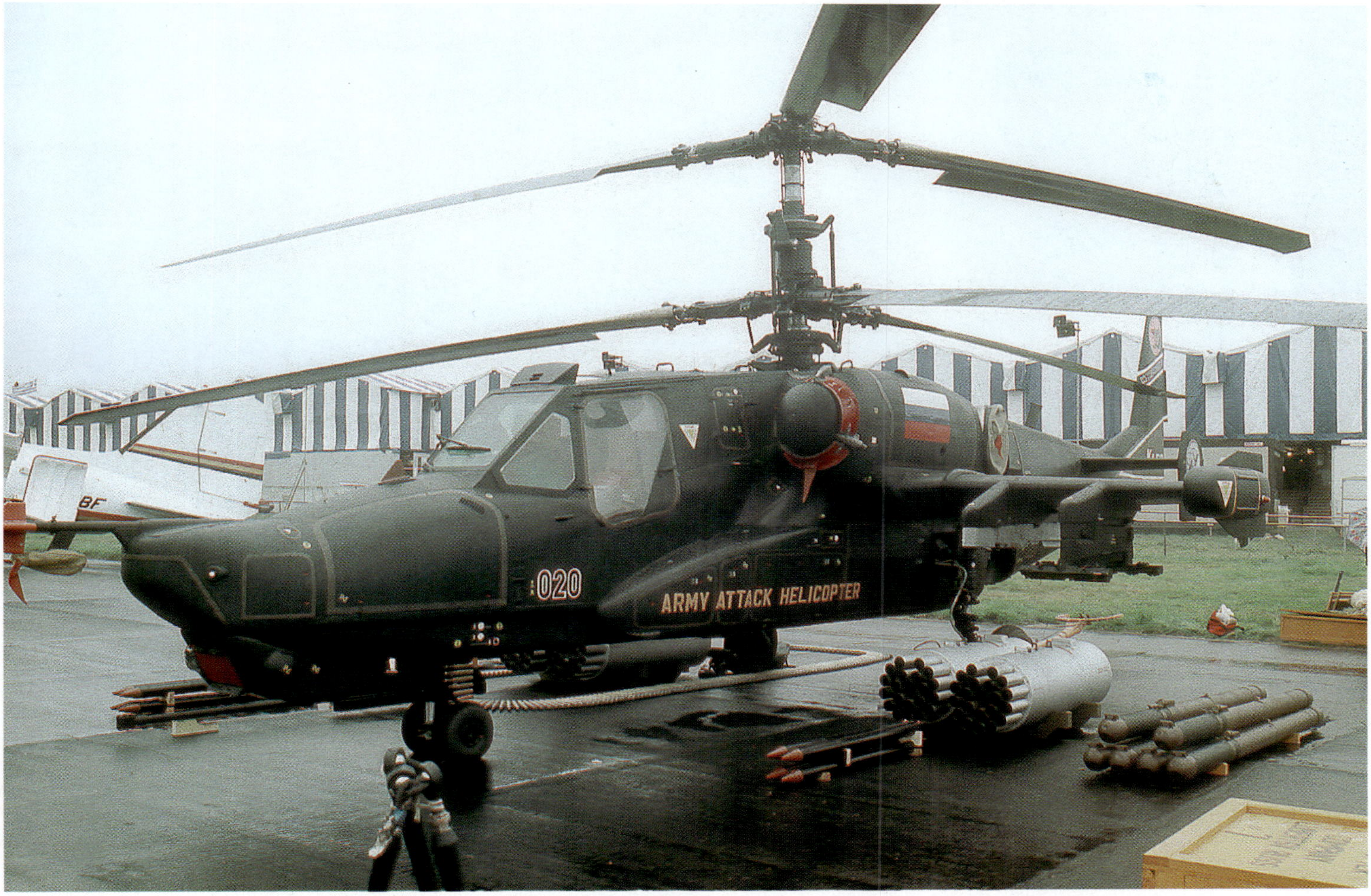

The Ka-50 was originally designated V-80, meaning "Helicopter for the 1980's", but received the Ka-50 designation when accepted for service use.

The bulge under the nose contains a stabilized laser guidance system used to control the *Vikhr* (Whirlwind) long-range anti-tank missiles.

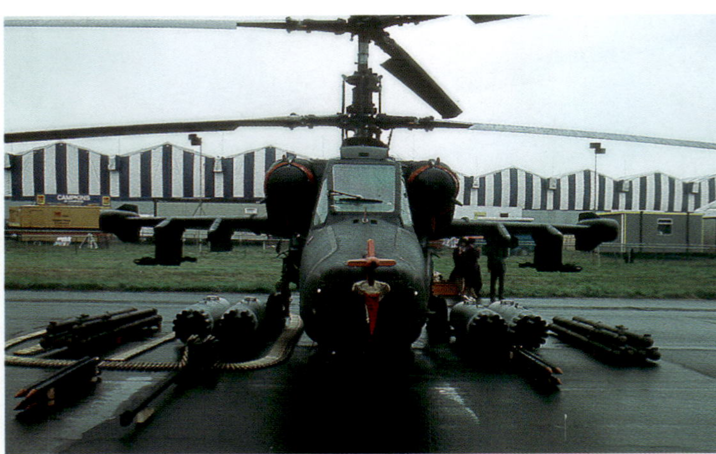

The Ka-50 as currently configured is a day-only attack helicopter. Material released by the Kamov design bureau indicates that other sensor packages are envisioned for the nose of the helicopter to give it night attack capability as well. It seems likely that later versions of the Ka-50 will have a revised nose for thermal imaging sights.

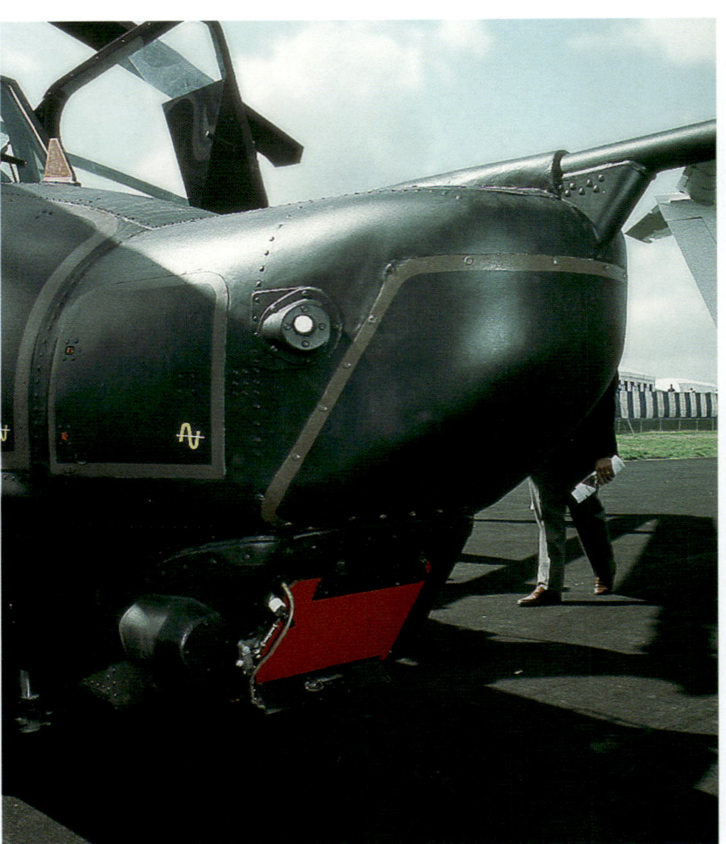

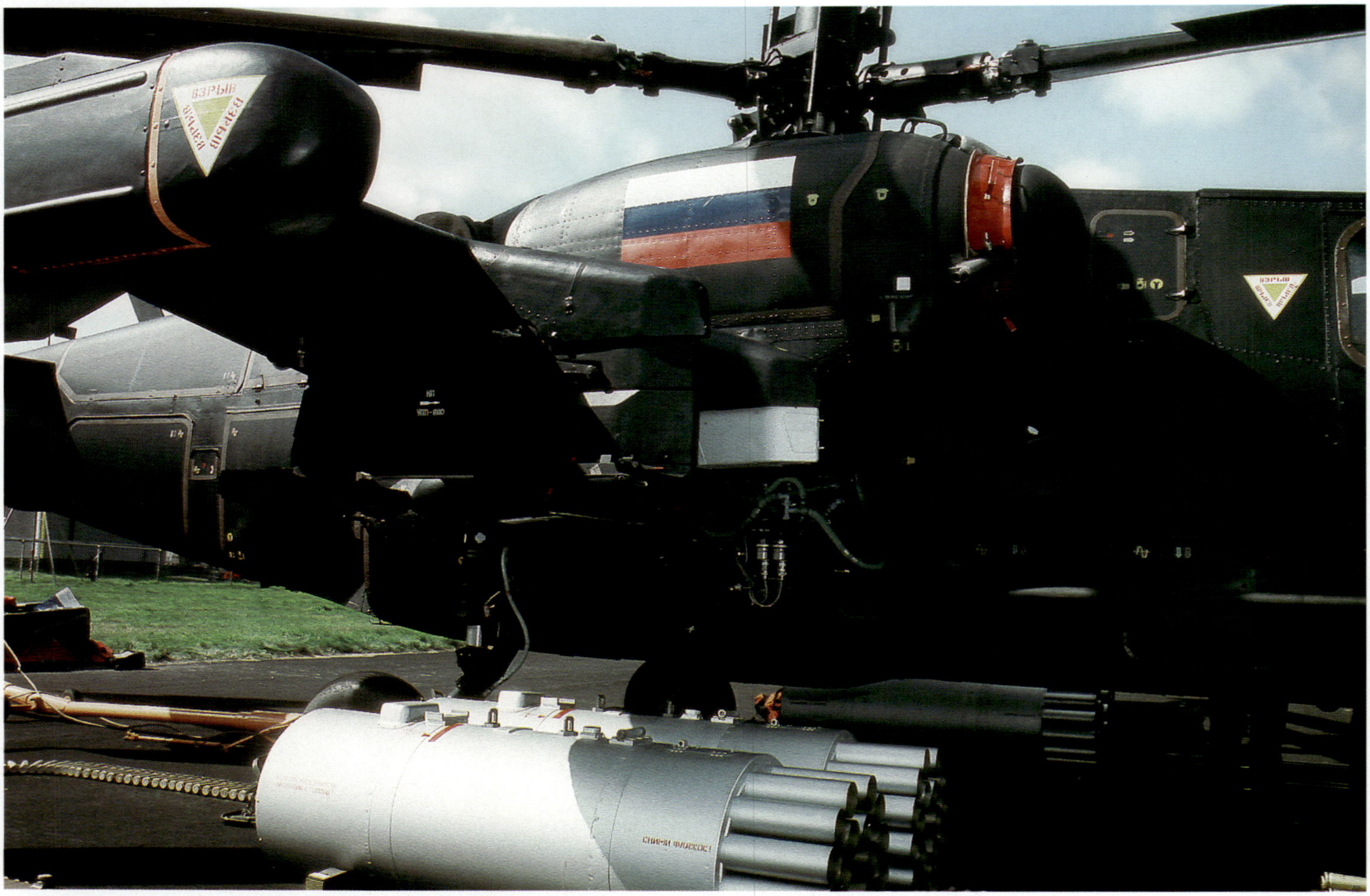

A view under the starboard winglet showing the elaborate hydraulic system around the Werewolf's 2A42 30mm cannon. The cannon can be depressed and traversed. The bright yellow triangle on the winglet pod is a warning that the pod contains explosives, probably referring to the charges used to dispense chaff and IR flares.

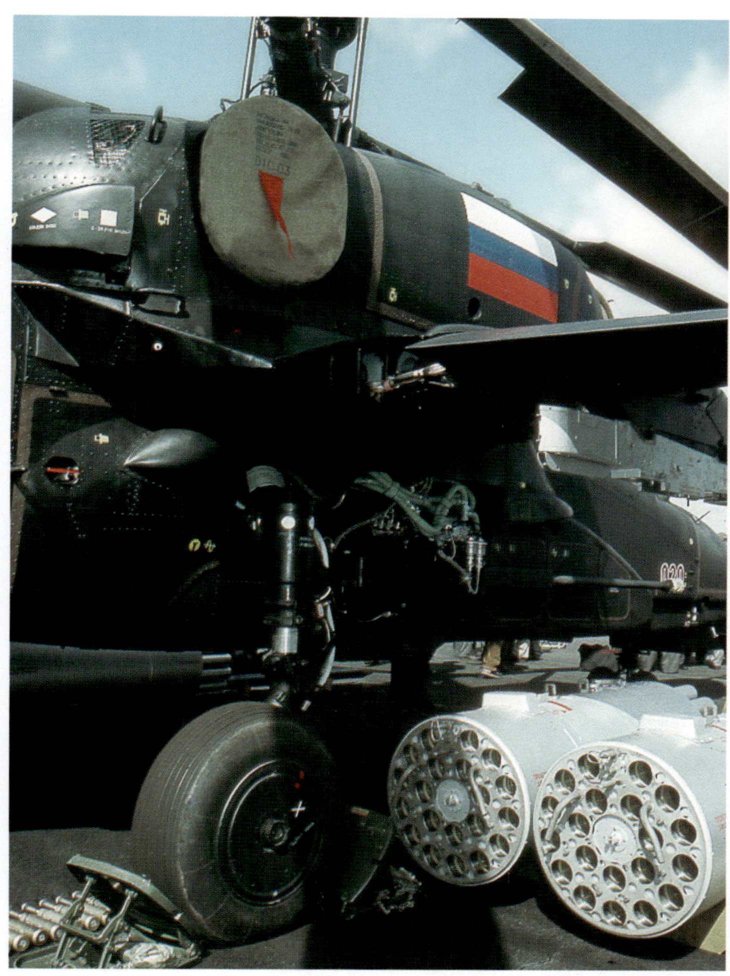

A detail view of the right side showing the retractable landing gear, and giving another view of the gun system.

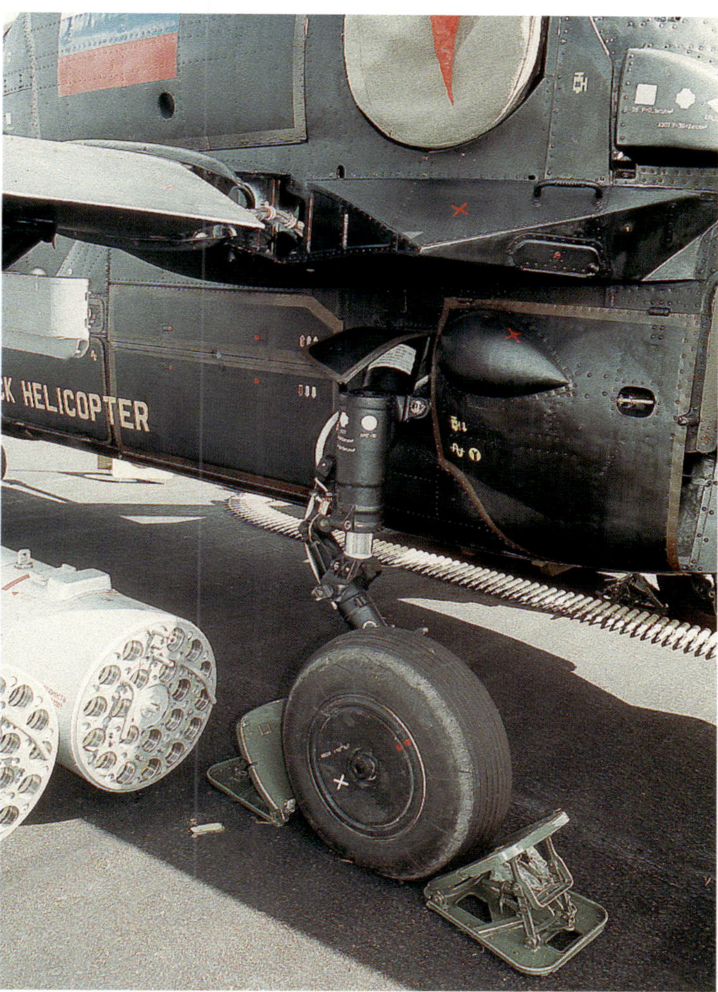

A detail view of the left side undercarriage.

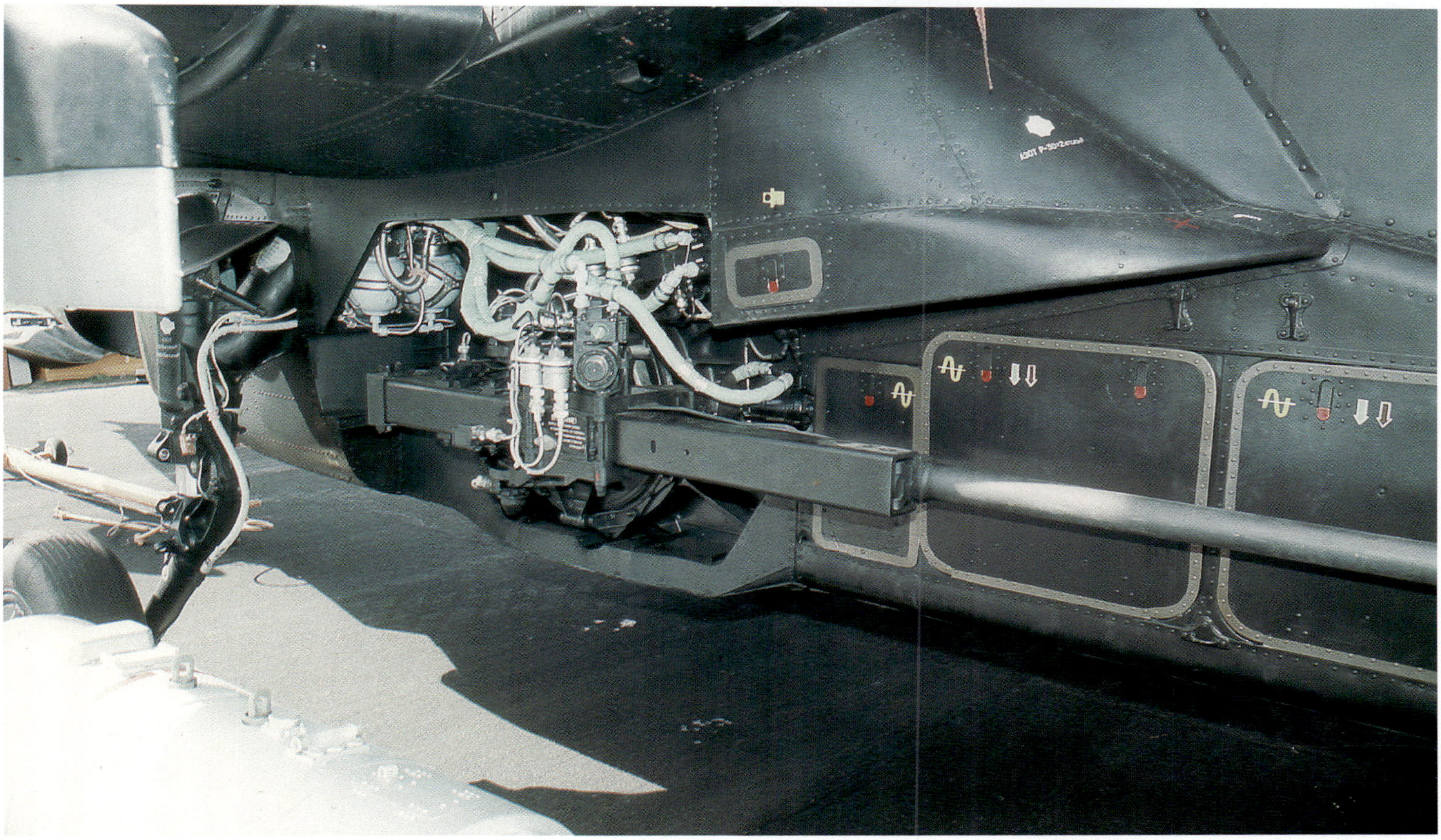

A close-up of the 2A42 30mm cannon on the right side of the Ka-50 fuselage.

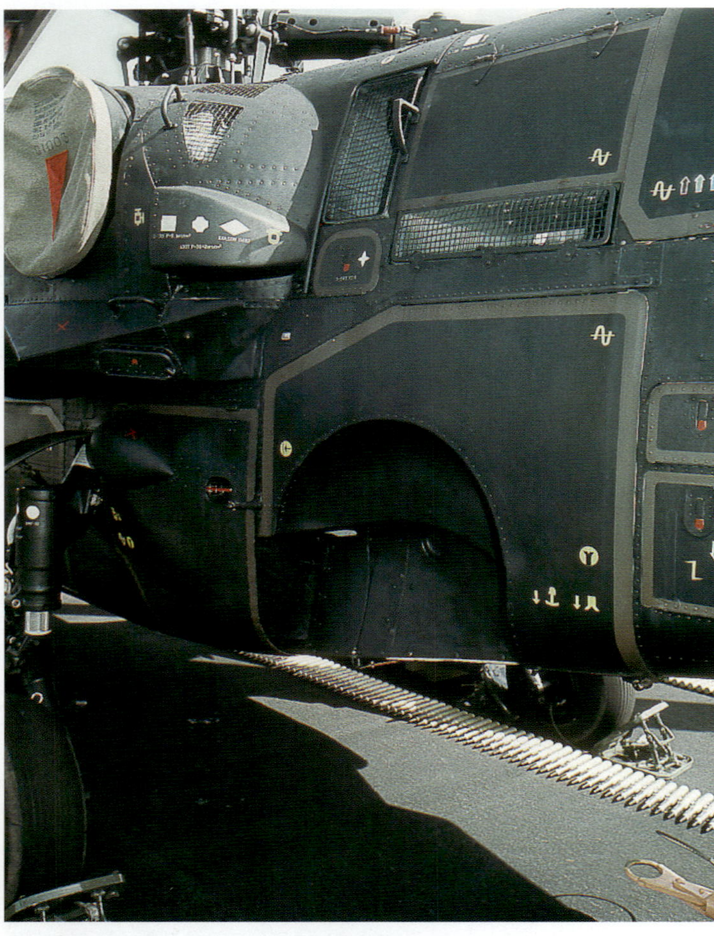

A detail view showing the fuselage recess for the undercarriage.

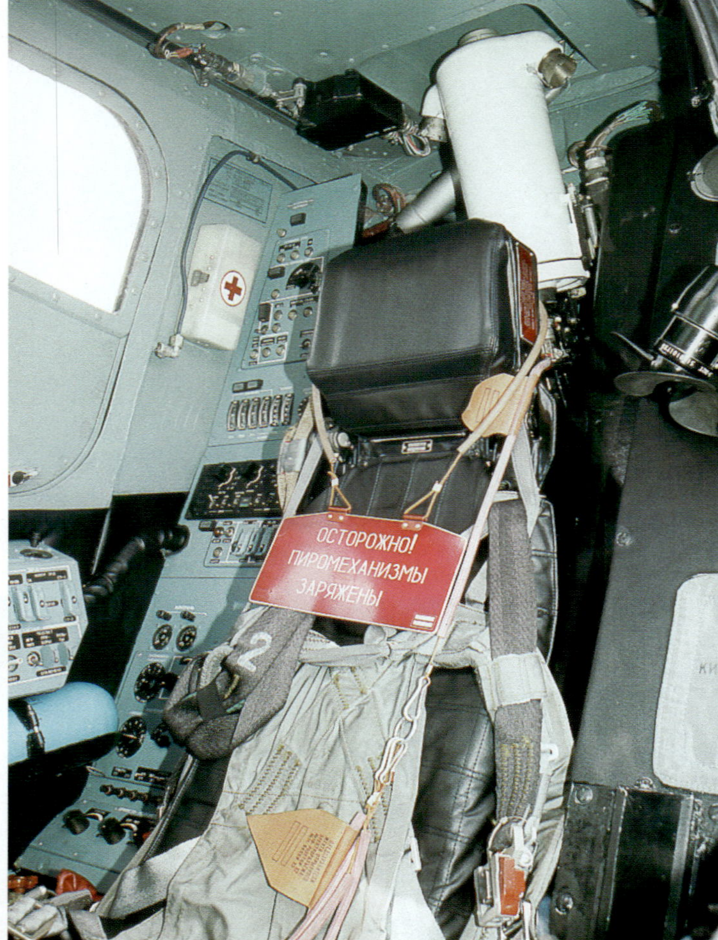

A view of the K-37 ejection seat in the Ka-50 Werewolf. The white container above the pilot's head is the rocket used to extract the pilot during ejection after the rotor blades have been blown off. The Ka-50 is the only helicopter in the world fitted with an ejection seat.

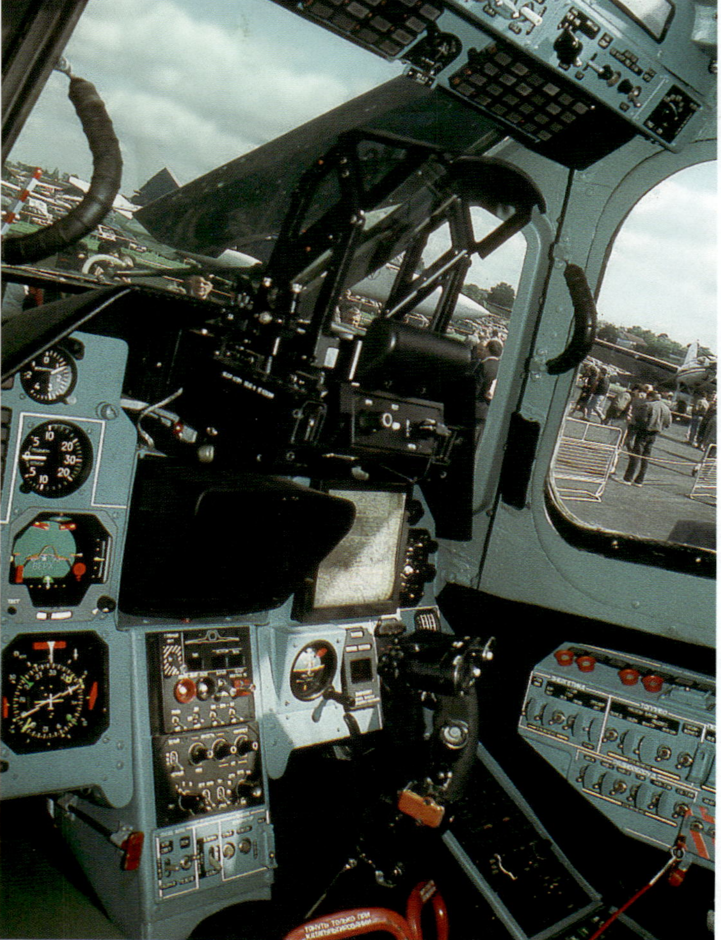

An interior view of the head's-up-display and main instrument panel in the Ka-50 attack helicopter.

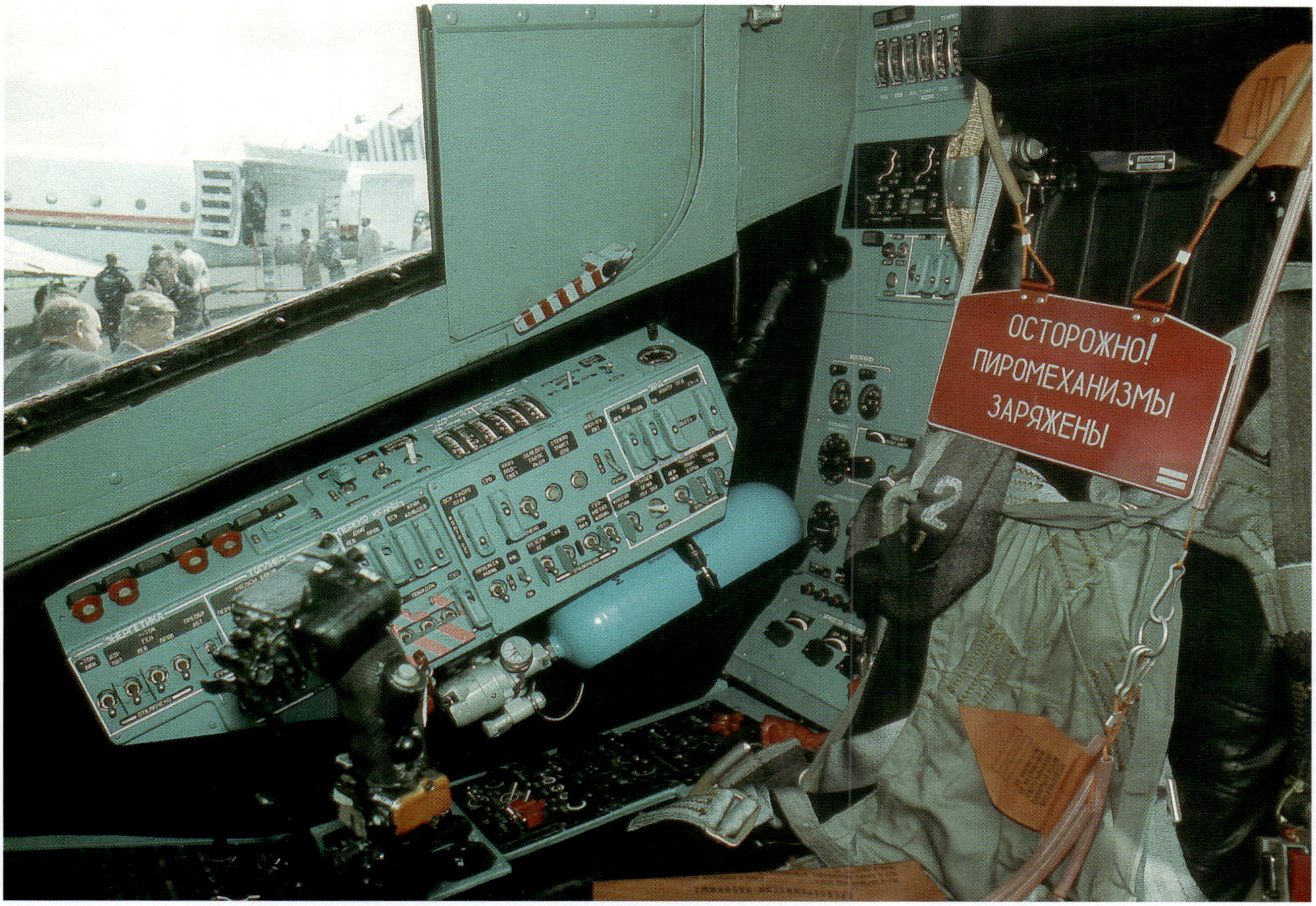

A detail view of the instrument panel on the pilot's left side in the Ka-50 Werewolf attack helicopter.

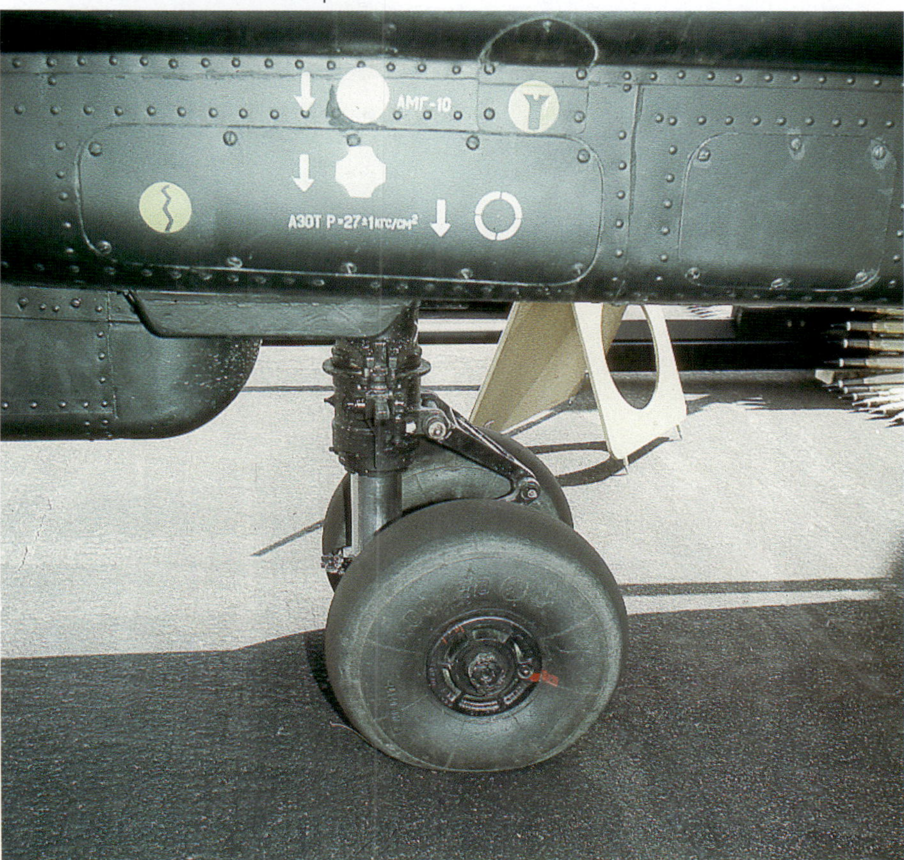

A detail view of the forward landing gear in the Kamov Ka-50 Oboroten.

Antonov An-72P

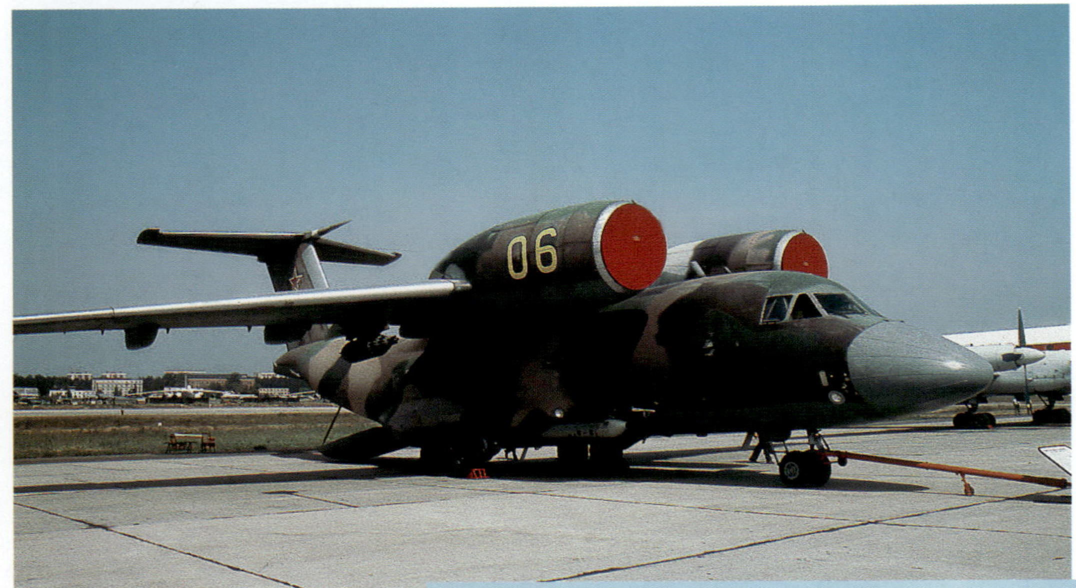

The An-72P is a new maritime surveillance version of the Coaler transport. It is armed for this role, including a 23mm gun pack seen here mounted on the fuselage side forward of the main landing gear.

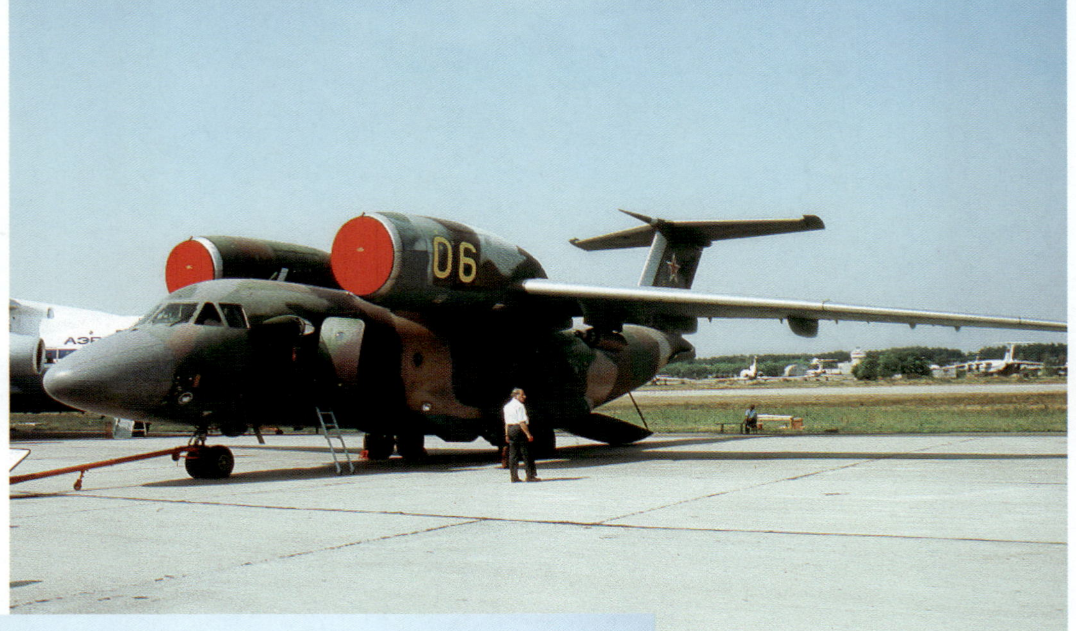

The An-72P displayed at Zhukovskiy differed from the aircraft later displayed at Farnborough. The Zhukovskiy aircraft has a new nose, presumably incorporating a new search radar, while the Farnborough aircraft was configured like the normal Coaler transport.

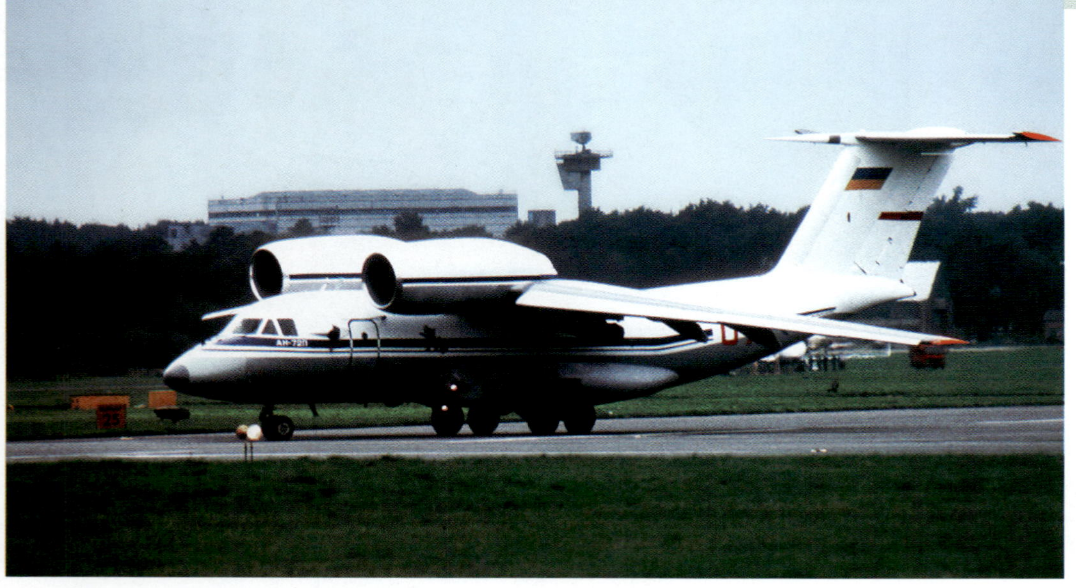

The Antonov An-72P naval patrol aircraft displayed at Farnborough was in civil colors, and carried the blue and yellow Ukrainian flag on the tail since the Antonov design bureau is headquartered in Ukraine rather than Russia.

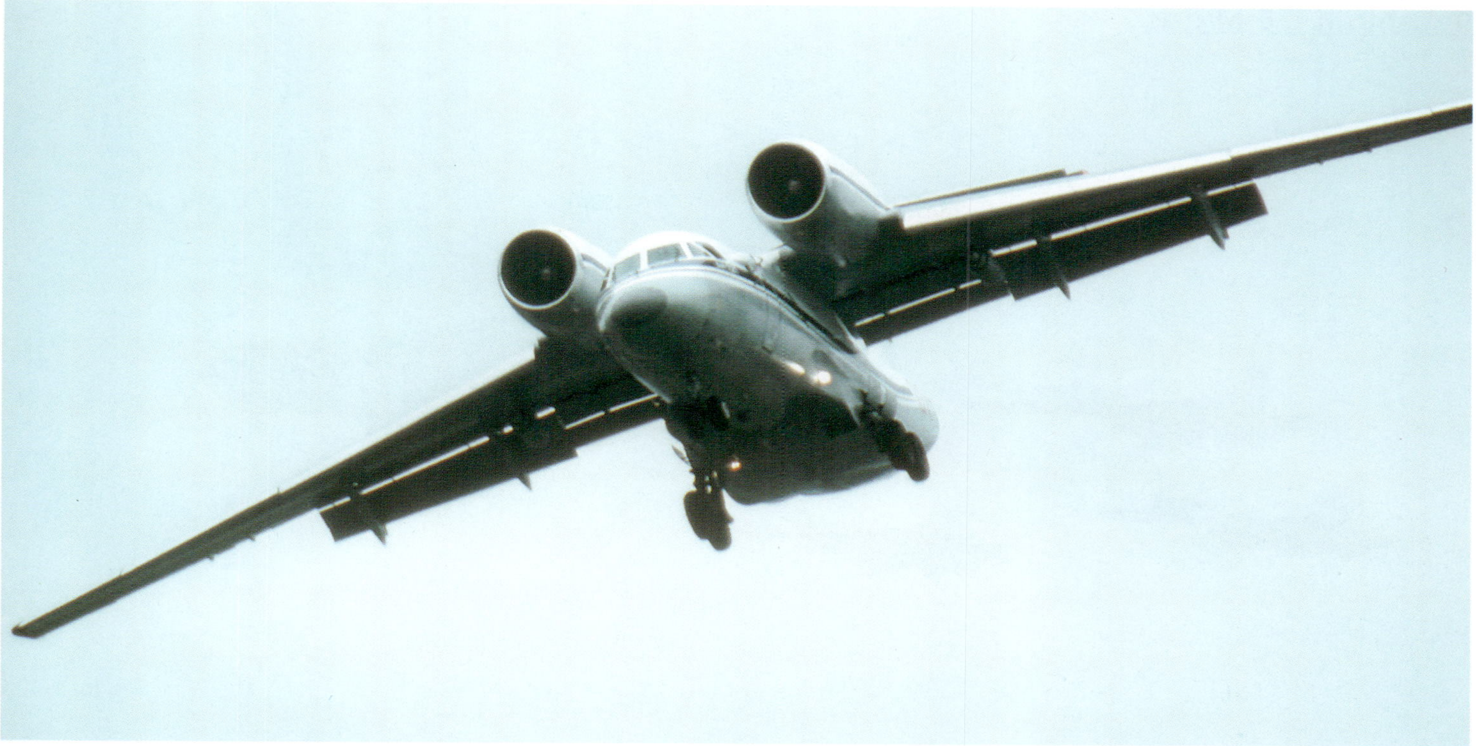

The An-72P comes in for a landing. The overwing engine design was part of the attempt to give the An-72P exceptional short-take-off and landing capability.

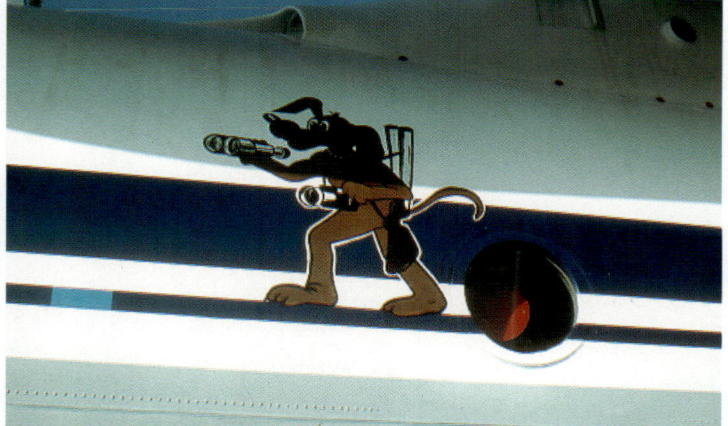

A close-up shot of the cartoon carried by the An-72P at Farnborough.

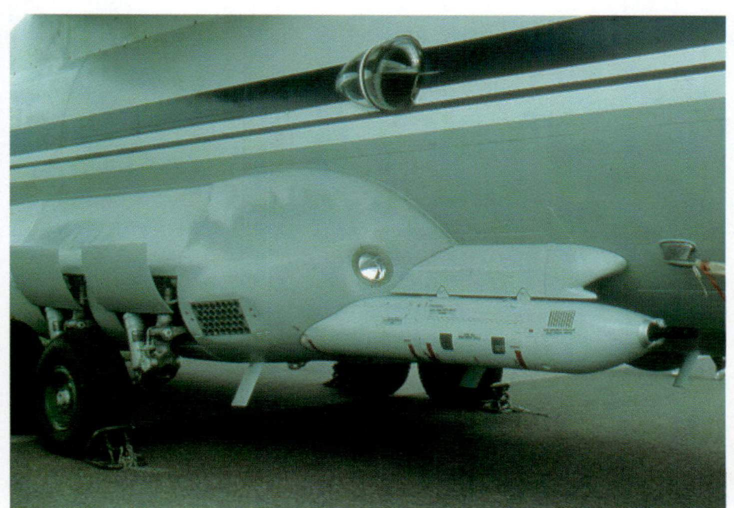

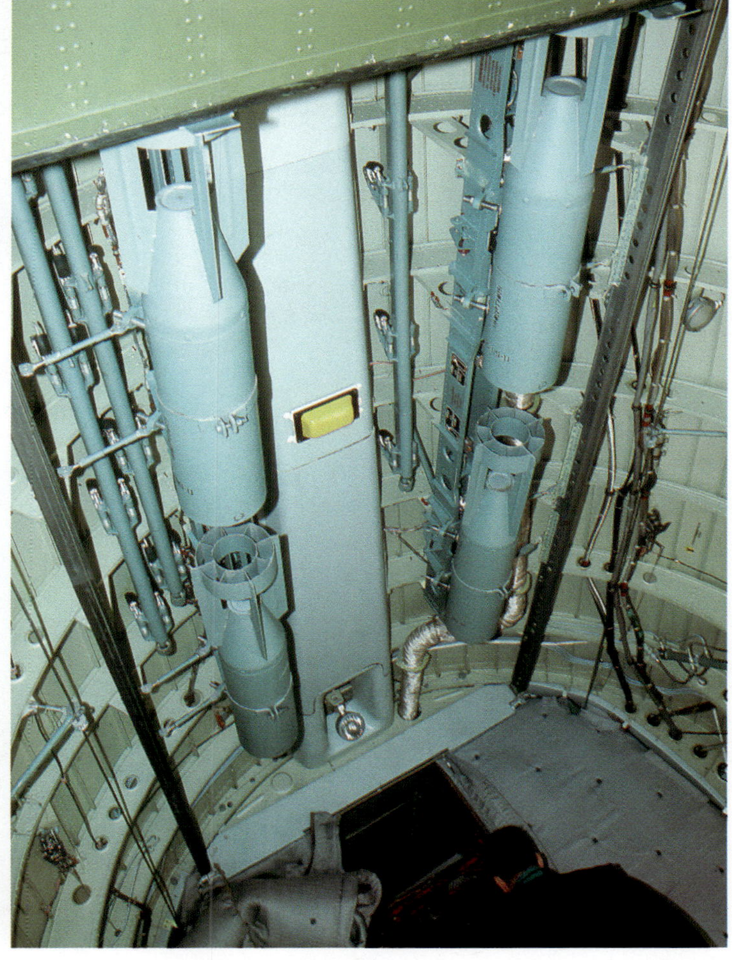

A detail view of the GSh-23-2 gun pack carried on the right side of the An-72P fuselage. This aircraft is intended mainly for border patrol and the armament is incorporated mainly to deal with smugglers, illegal fishing and the like, not serious military opposition.

One of the oddest elements of the An-72P design is that it has bomb racks for four 100kg. bombs in the tail immediately above the rear cargo doors. The cargo doors can be opened and pulled away, allowing the rear opening to be used as an improvised bomb-bay.

Ilyushin IL-78 Midas

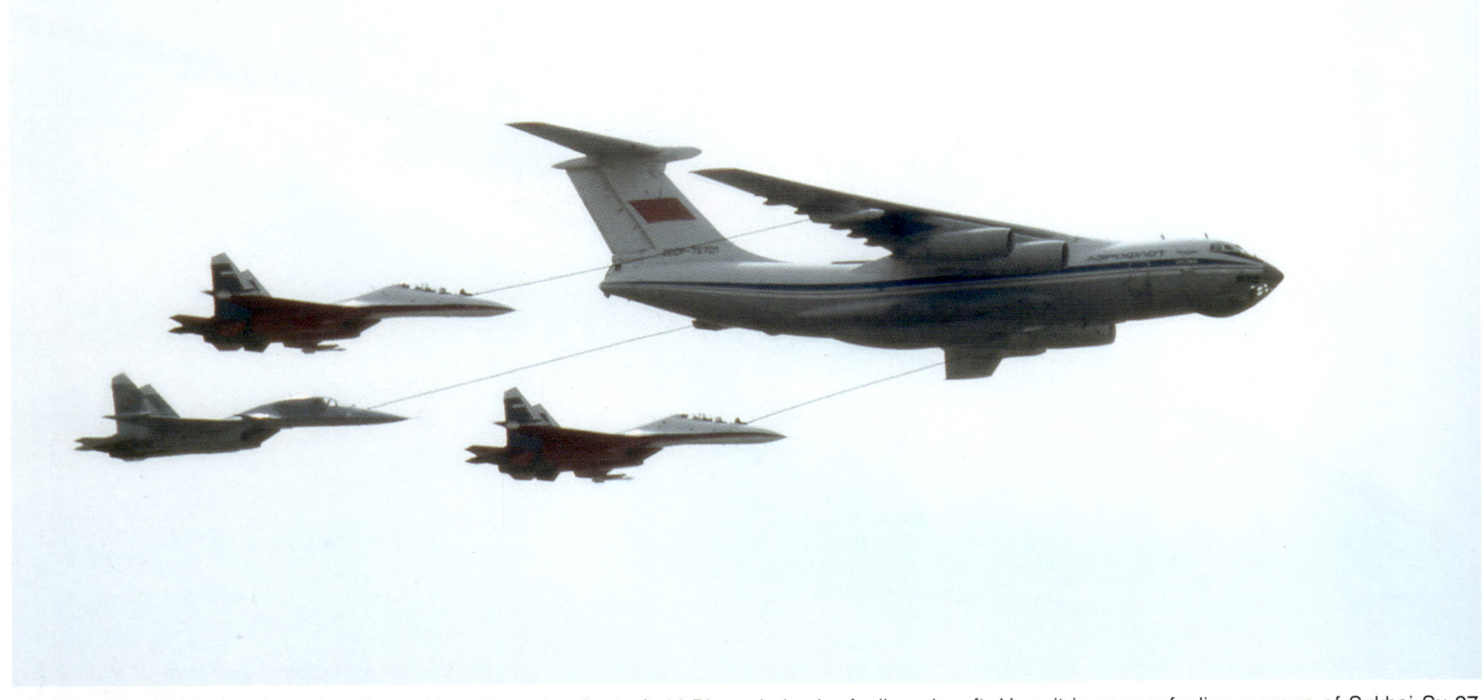

The IL-78 Midas was developed to replace the aging fleet of old Bison-derived refueling aircraft. Here it is seen refueling a group of Sukhoi Su-27 fighters and the Su-27IB prototype.

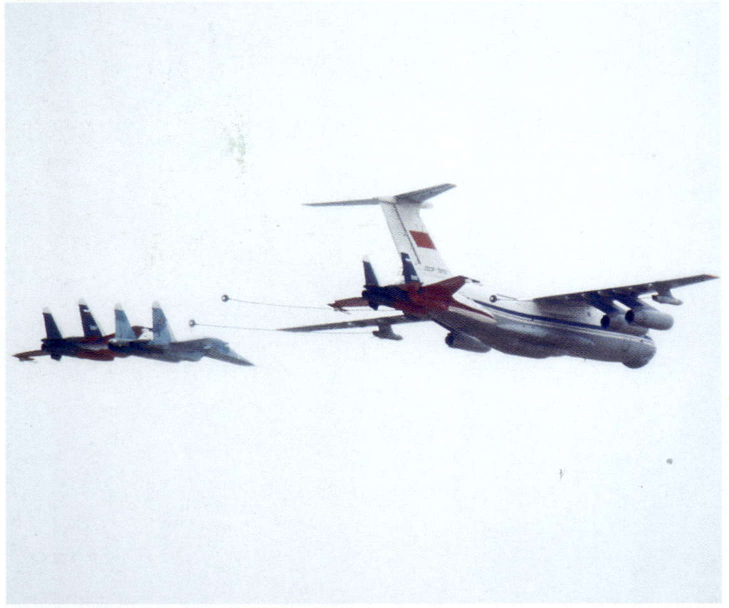

Until recently, the Soviet Air Force did not deploy large numbers of refueling aircraft. Most refueling aircraft were used to support strategic bombers, not tactical aircraft. In recent years, more interest is being shown in the use of refueling aircraft for tactical air operations, hence the continued production of the IL-78 beyond strategic force requirements.

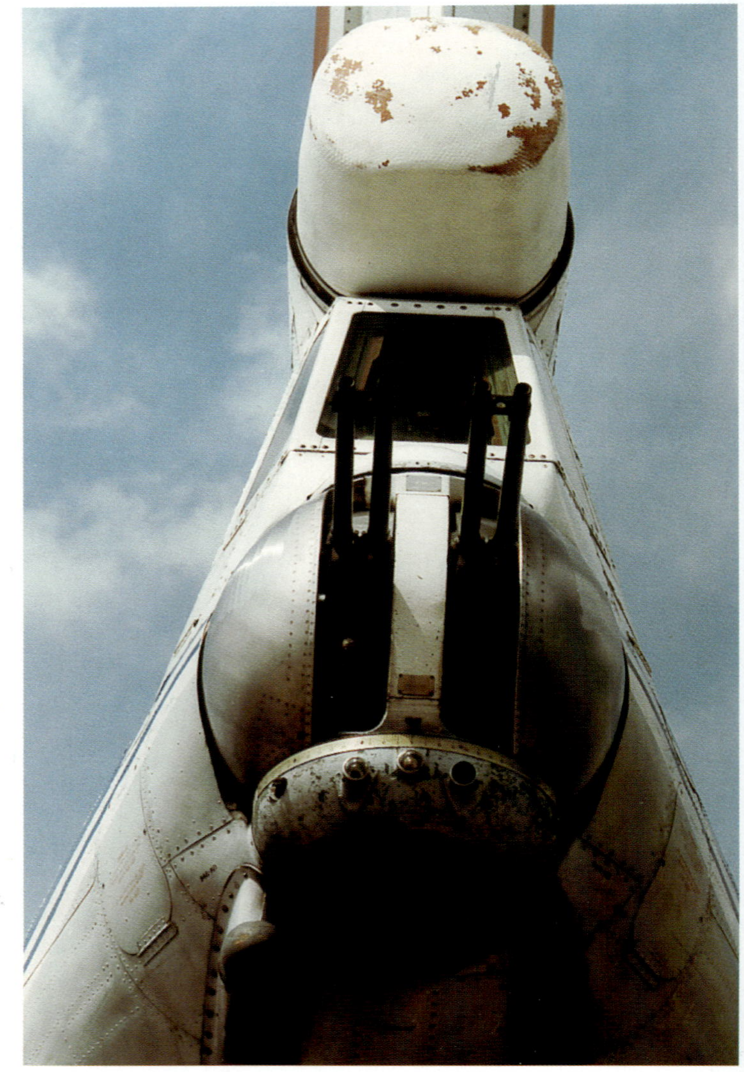

The normal troop transport versions of the IL-76M are fitted with this quadruple radar-directed defensive gun position. (Michael Jerchel)

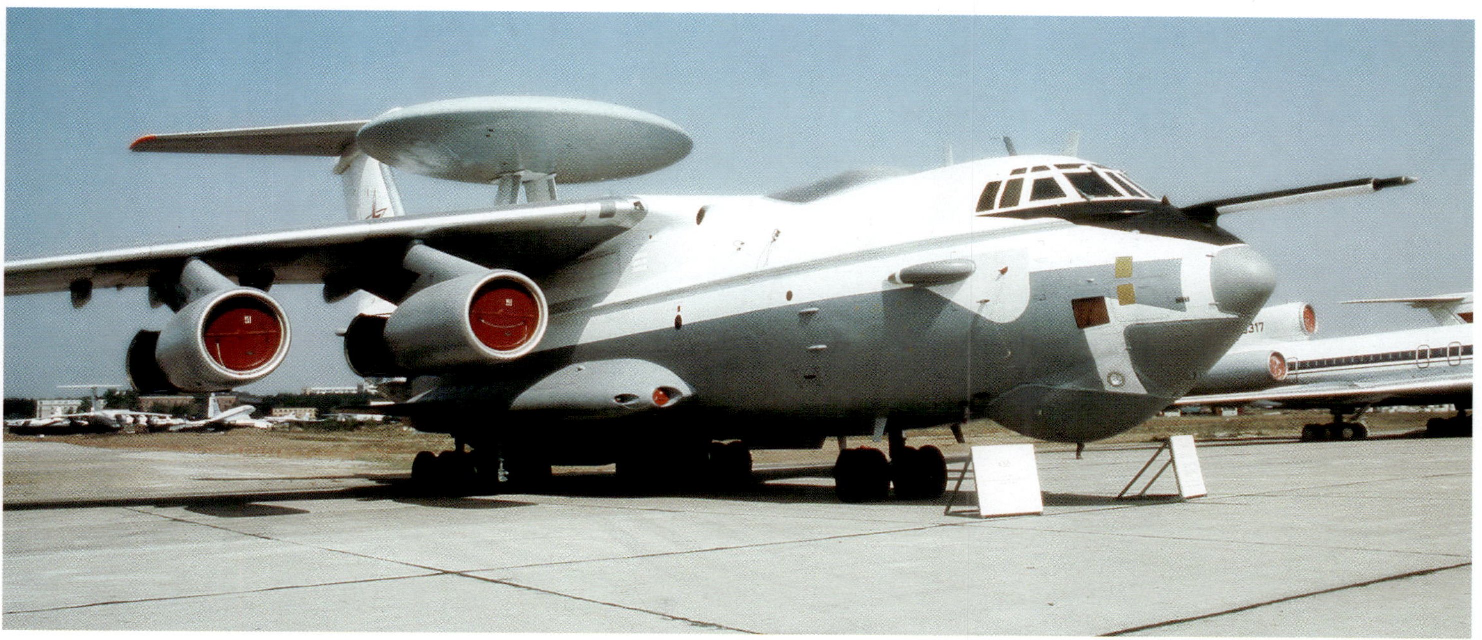

The Ilyushin A-50 Mainstay is the Russian equivalent of the American E-3A Sentry AWACS. Based on the IL-76 transport, the A-50 was used at the time of the Gulf War to monitor air activity, the A-50s performing circuits over the Black Sea.

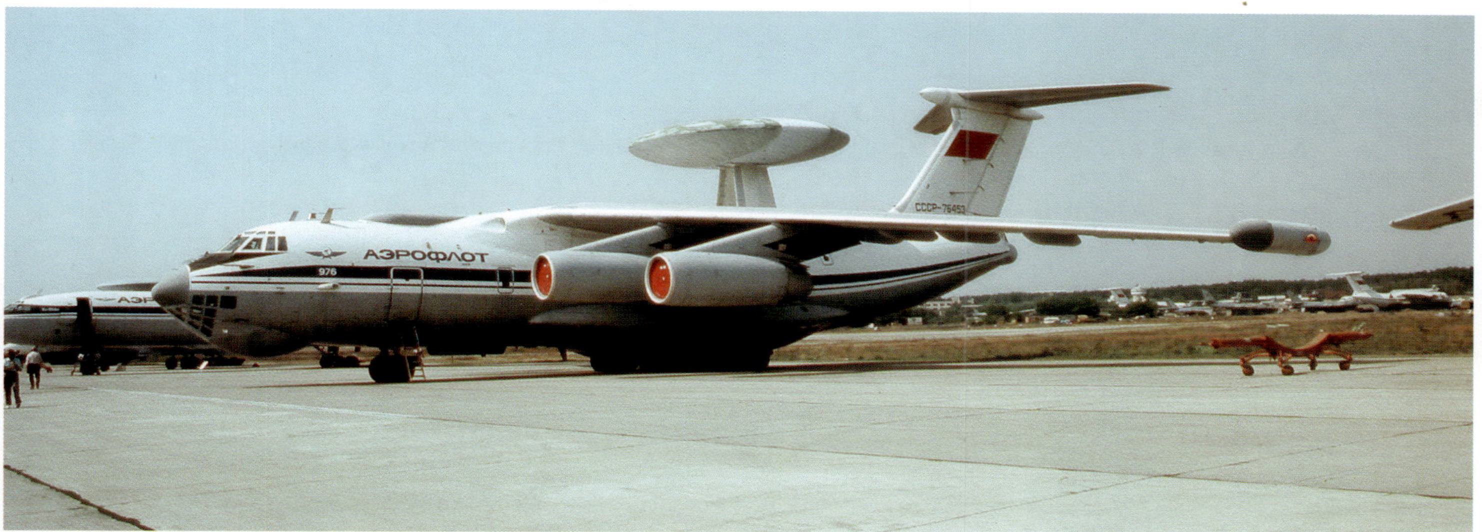

Two A-50s were displayed at Zhukovskiy, one of them in Aeroflot markings which belongs to the LII at Zhukovskiy for testing. Note that this aircraft is still fitted with original transparent nose of the IL-76.

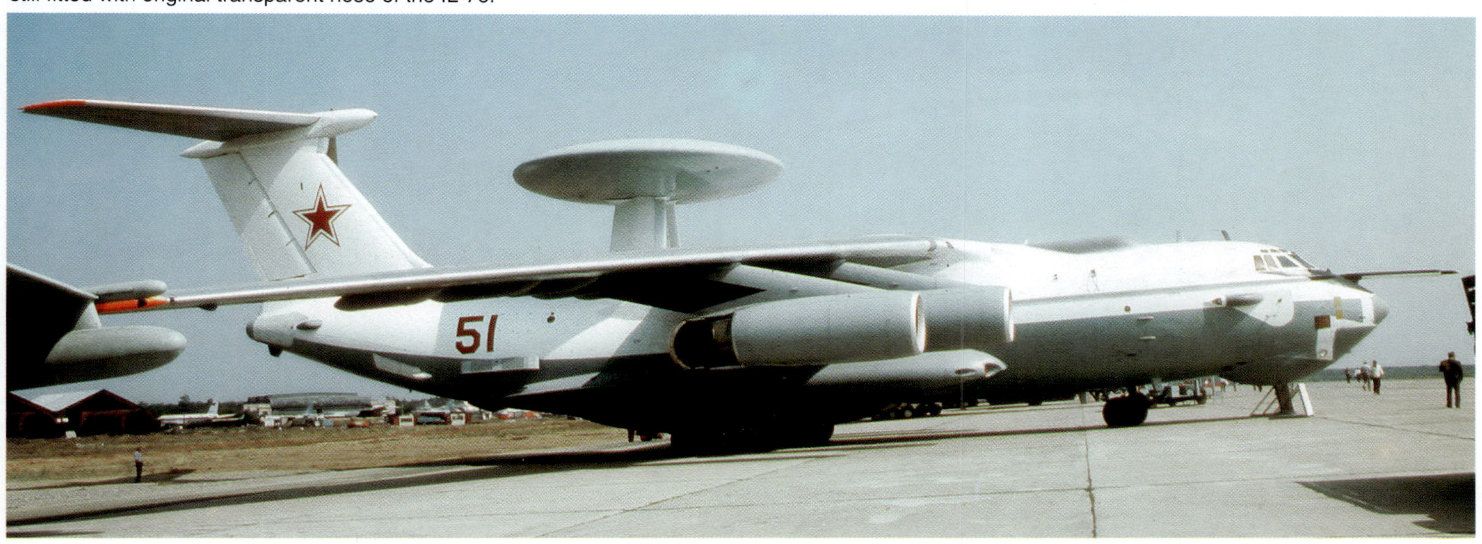

A side view of the later production A-50 with the solid nose. The Russian Air Force is not entirely happy with the performance of the A-50, feeling that the heavier weight of the electronics does not offer it the performance found in its American counterpart, the AWACS.

Beriev A-40 Albatros

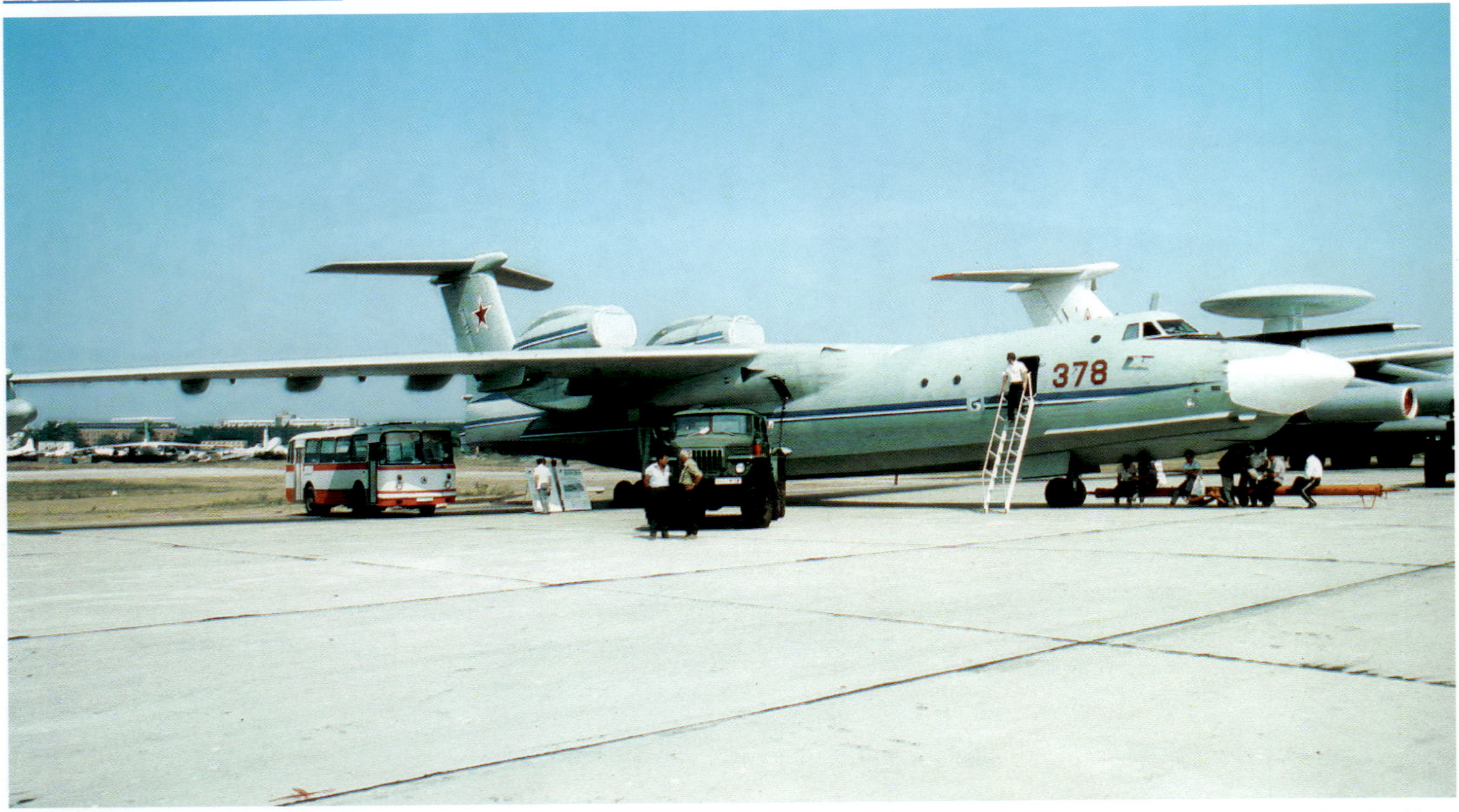

The Beriev A-40 Albatros (NATO: Mermaid) is a long range air-sea rescue aircraft, on the verge of quantity production to satisfy Russian Navy requirements.

Myasishchev VM-T Atlantik

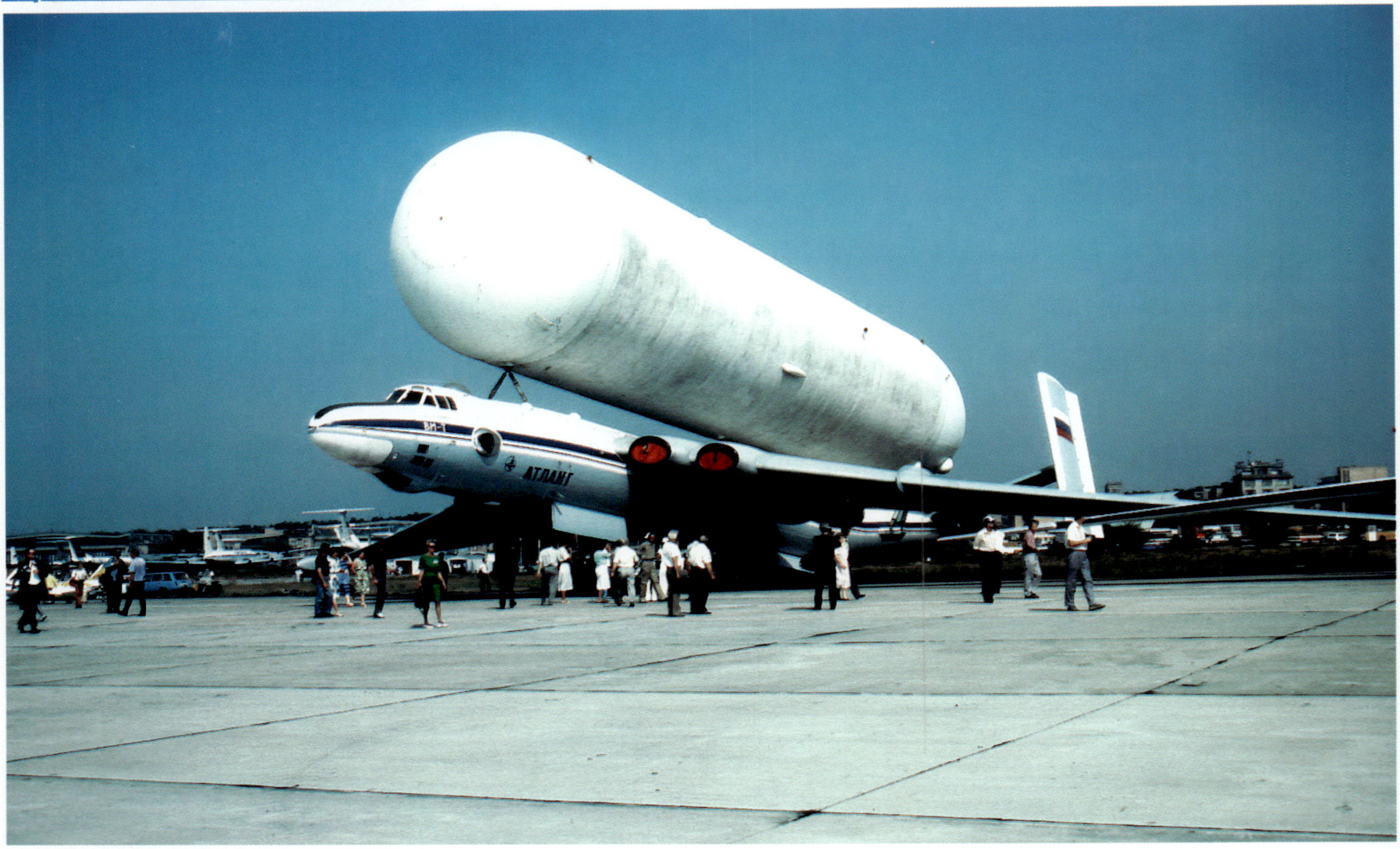

Always an imposing sight is the Myasishchev VM-T Atlantik, a version of the 3M Bison bomber modified to carry the large central fuel tank of the Energia space booster rocket system.

Myasishchev M-55 Geofizika

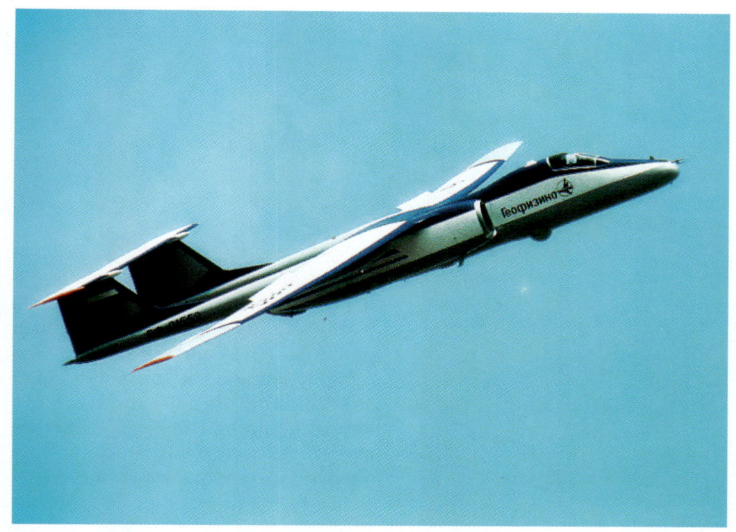

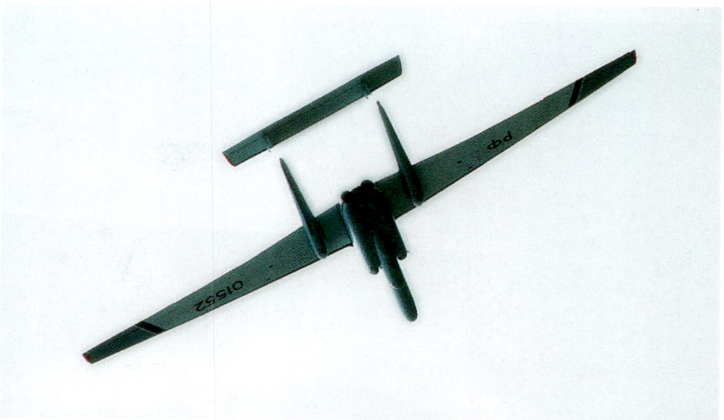

The elegant Myasishchev M-55 Geofizika is the latest incarnation of the high altitude powered sail-plane idea. It is currently being used for high altitude scientific research.

The enormous wingspan of the Geofizika allows it to operate in the thin upper atmosphere. The aircraft owes its lineage to the earlier M-17 Stratosfera. The M-17 stemmed from a 1950's KGB requirement for an aircraft capable of shooting down US Moby Dick reconnaissance balloons. But the Myasishchev bureau was closed from 1959 to 1967, and by the time it had reopened and restarted work on this project, the requirement had disappeared.

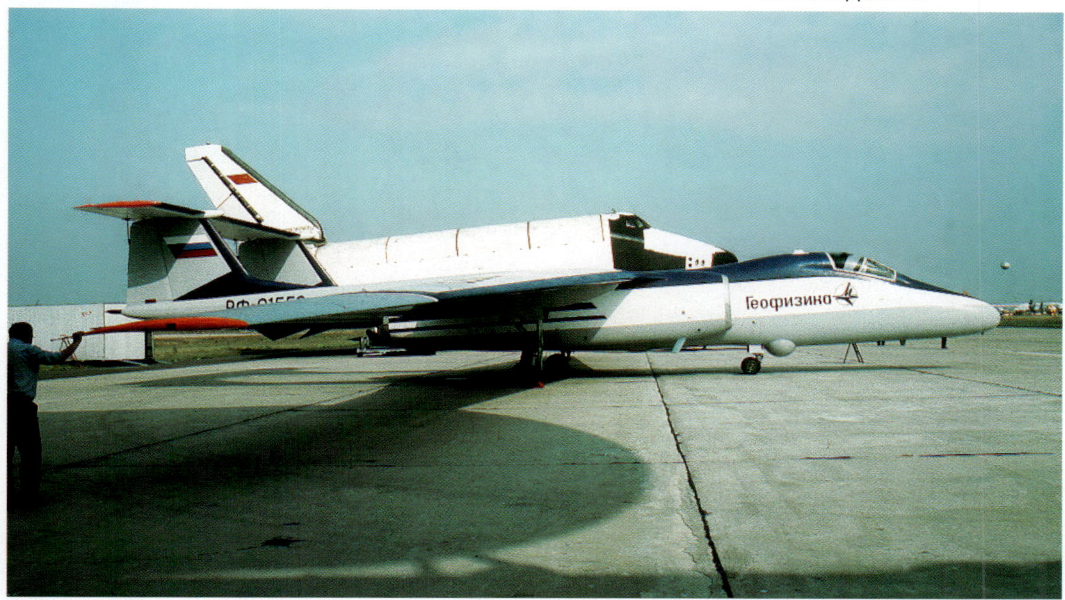

The M-55 Geofizika looks out of place and ungainly on the ground compared to its stylish performance in the air. Russia is trying to interest other countries in the Geofizika, and has reached tentative agreement with Chile.

Sukhoi Su-29

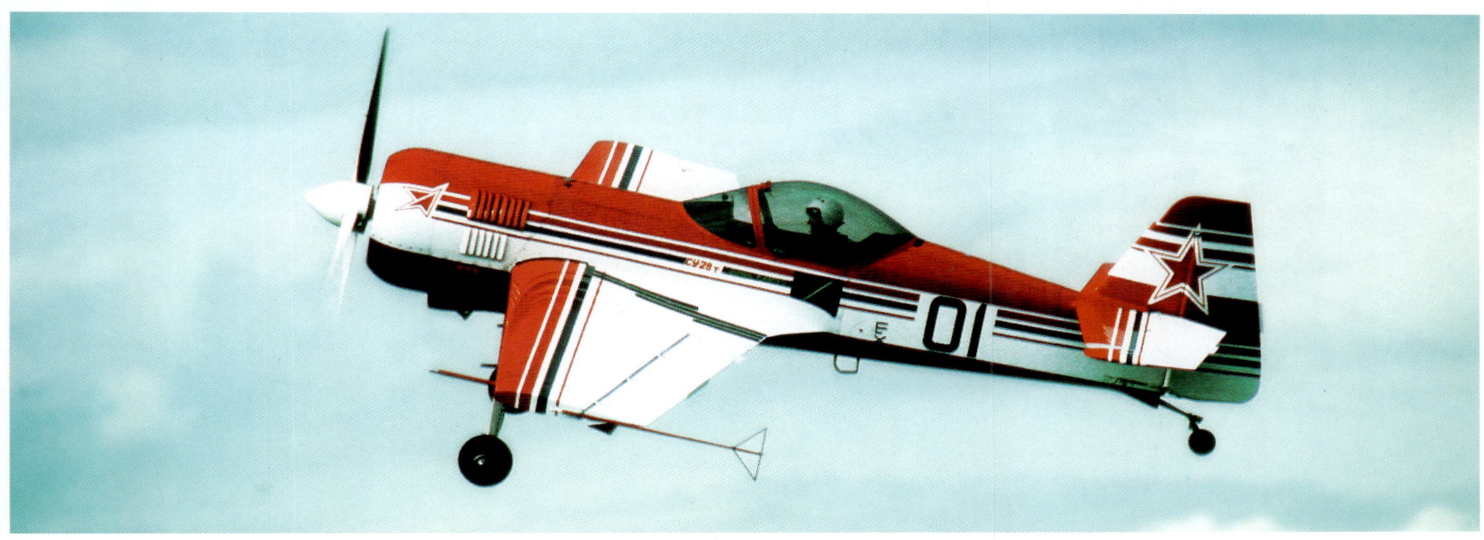

Although not a military aircraft, no one who attended the 1992 Farnborough air show could possibly omit the Sukhoi Su-29 aerobatic trainer. The outstanding performer at the display, the announcer was at a loss for word's to describe its performance. Some of the more memorable phrases were : "That maneuver is impossible!"

AVIATION WEAPONS

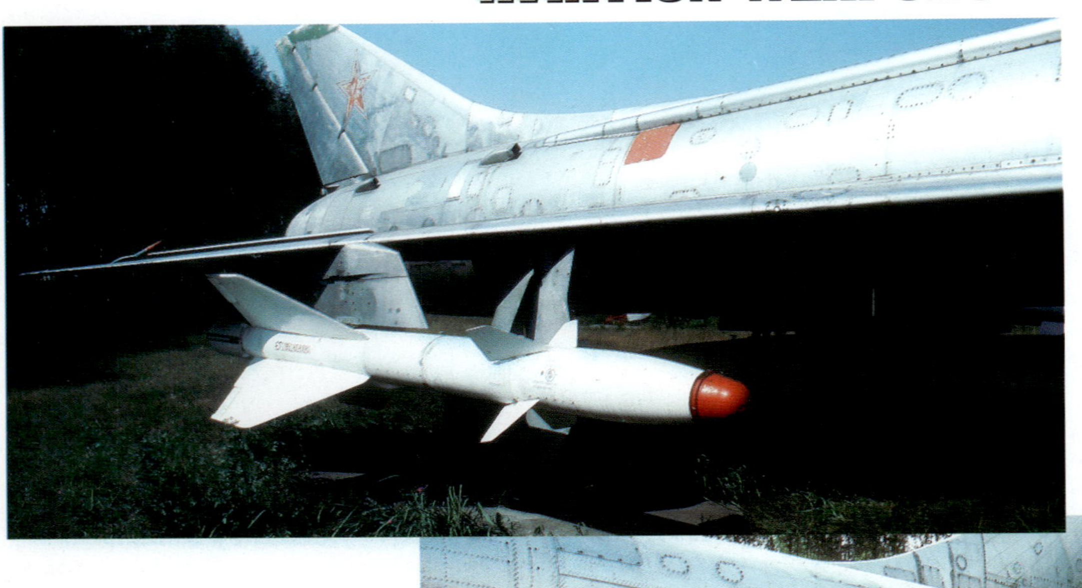

Rarely seen in close-up, the R-30T (AA-3d Anab) air-to-air missile (AAM) was used on interceptors such as the Su-15TM and Yak-28P. It was primarily intended as an anti-bomber weapon and was never used on tactical fighters. The R-30T was the infrared version of the family, and an improved version of the earlier R-8T.

The R-30R (AA-3c Anab) was among the first Soviet semi-active radar homing air-to-air missiles, an improved version of the earlier R-8R (AA-3a Anab). It was basically similar to the infrared guided version, but had a passive radar seeker head, seen here with a red protective cover.

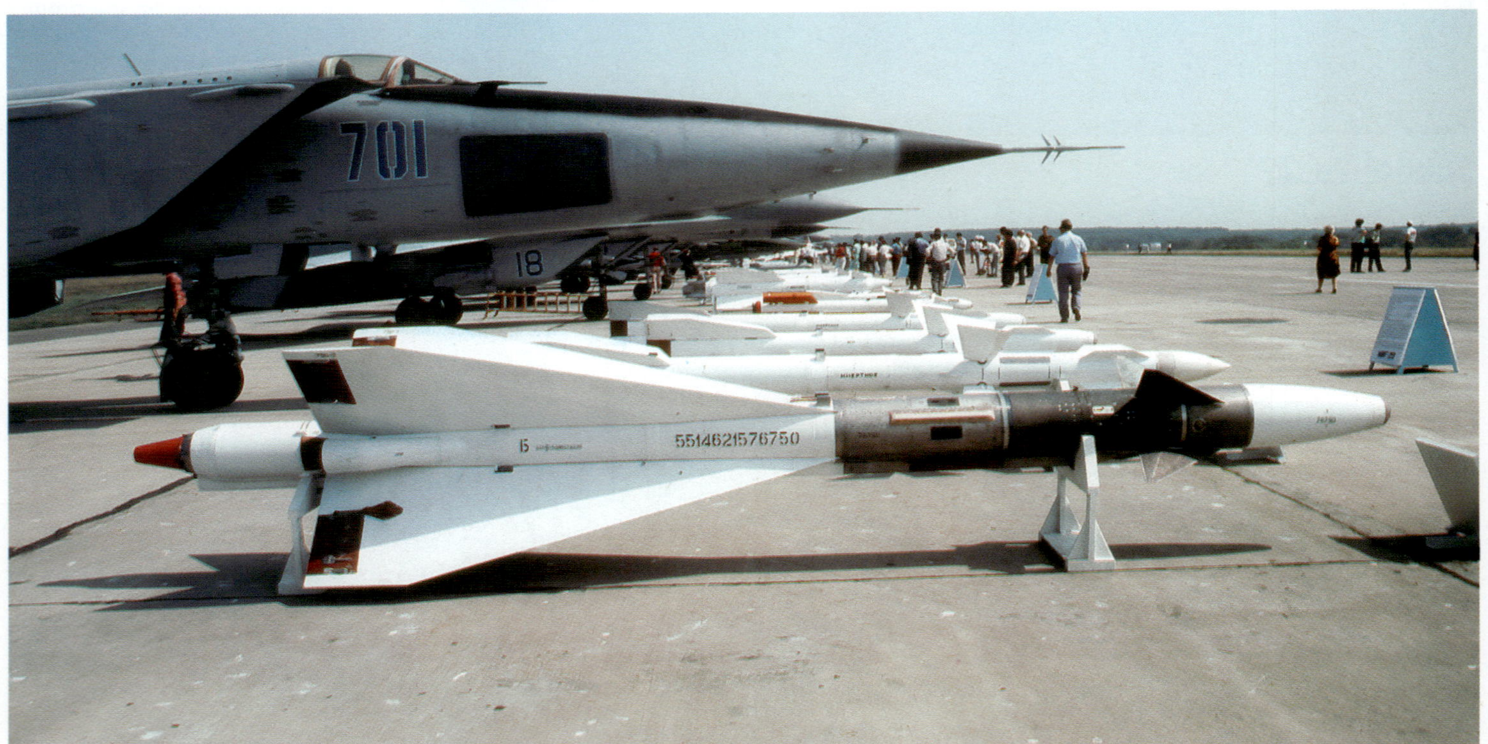

The largest Russian air-to-air missile ever built was the R-40, seen here in the R-40T (AA-6 Acrid) version. This large anti-bomber missile was developed specifically for the MiG-25 interceptor, and was late used on the MiG-31.

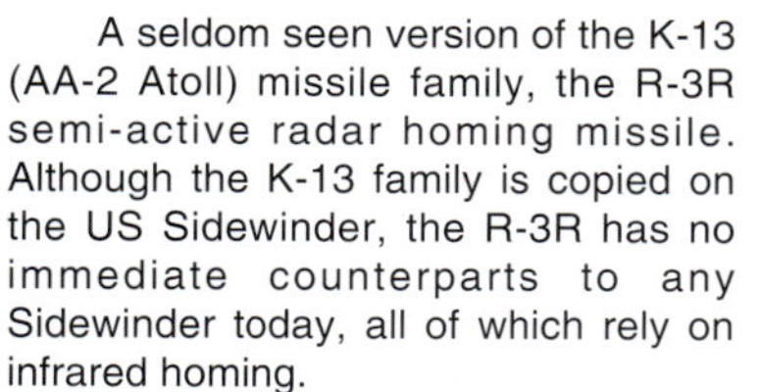

A seldom seen version of the K-13 (AA-2 Atoll) missile family, the R-3R semi-active radar homing missile. Although the K-13 family is copied on the US Sidewinder, the R-3R has no immediate counterparts to any Sidewinder today, all of which rely on infrared homing.

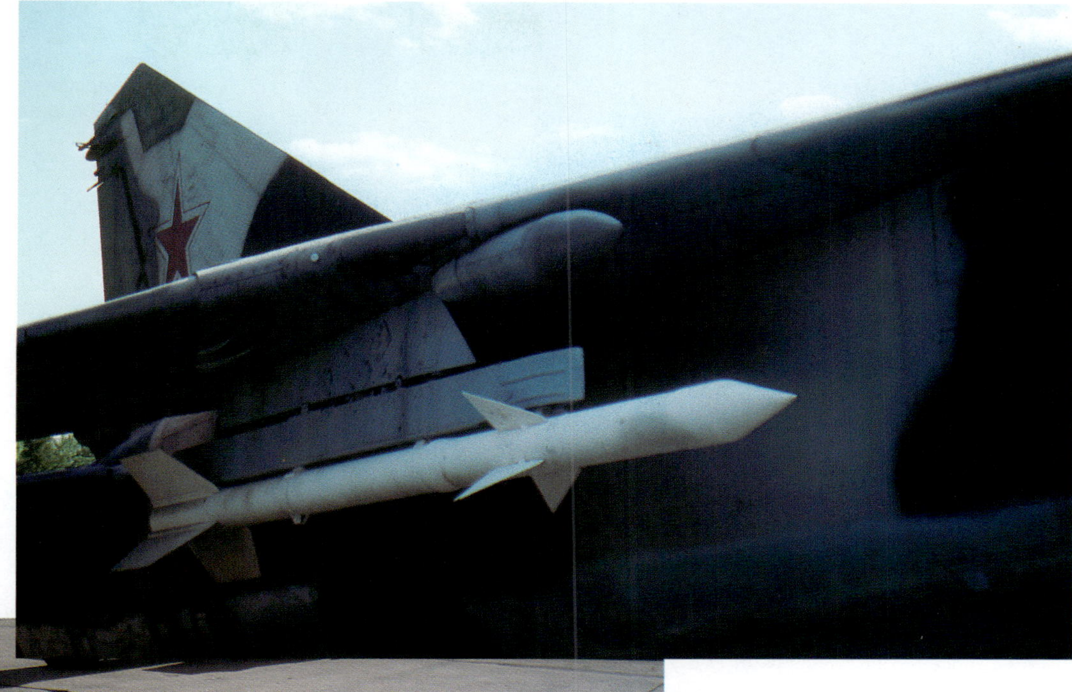

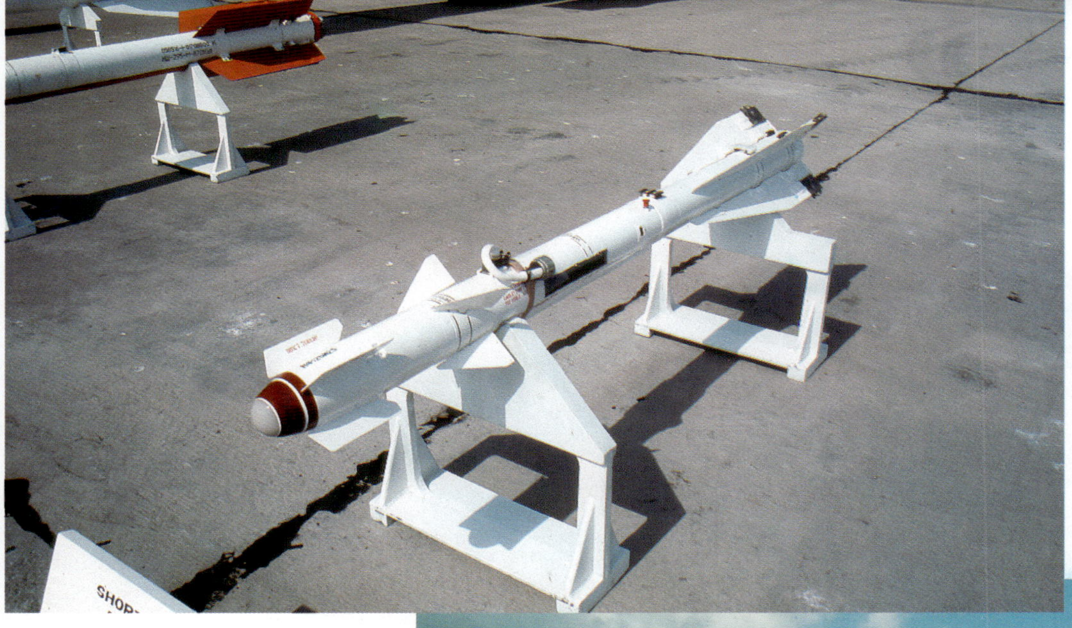

The R-60MK (AA-8 Aphid) is a small infrared homing AAM used for self-defense. Though often compared to the American Sidewinder, it is in fact a much smaller and less-capable missile.

The R-60MK is often carried on a two-rail APU-62-2 launch pylon, seen here on a Sukhoi Su-24MR.

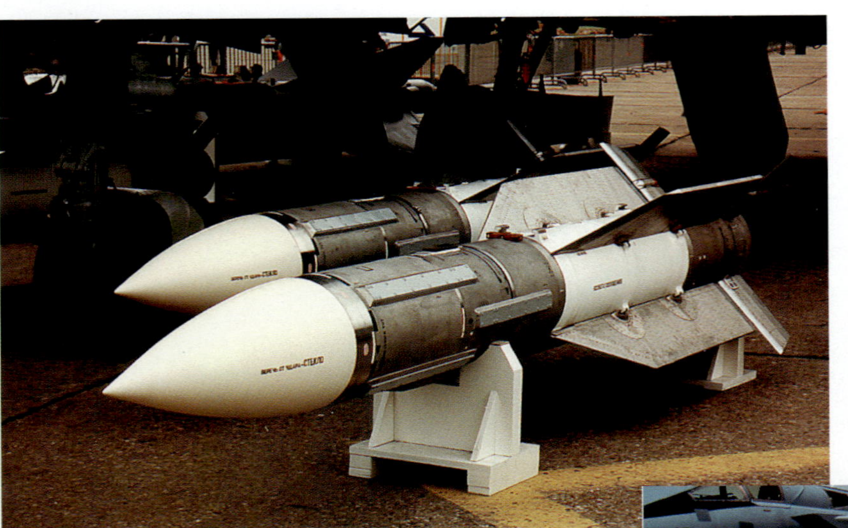

The R-33E (AA-9 Amos) is a Russian counterpart to the American AIM-54 Phoenix. It is used exclusively on the MiG-31 intercepter. Although similar in appearance to the Phoenix, it is a shorter ranged weapon due to its use of semi-active homing rather than the terminal active homing of the Phoenix.

The R-27ER (AA-10c Alamo) is part of a new family of missiles replacing the older R-23 (AA-7 Apex) on Russian fighters. The R-27E family is an extended range type, the R-27ER being semi-active radar guided and the R-27ET (AA-10D Alamo) being infrared guided. These extended range versions are intended primarily for the Su-27 interceptors, but newer versions of the MiG-29 family including the MiG-29K, MiG-29M and MiG-29S can also fire them.

The R-27T (AA-10b Alamo) is a medium range version of the R-27 family, the R-27R (AA-10a Alamo) being its semi-active radar homing equivalent. The difference between the two versions is the seeker head, the infrared guided versions having the blunt optical tip. These missiles are used on the MiG-29 and Su-27.

The R-27ET (AA-10d Alamo) is the extended range infrared homing version of the R-27 family. It is primarily used on the Su-27, MiG-29 and Yak-141 fighters.

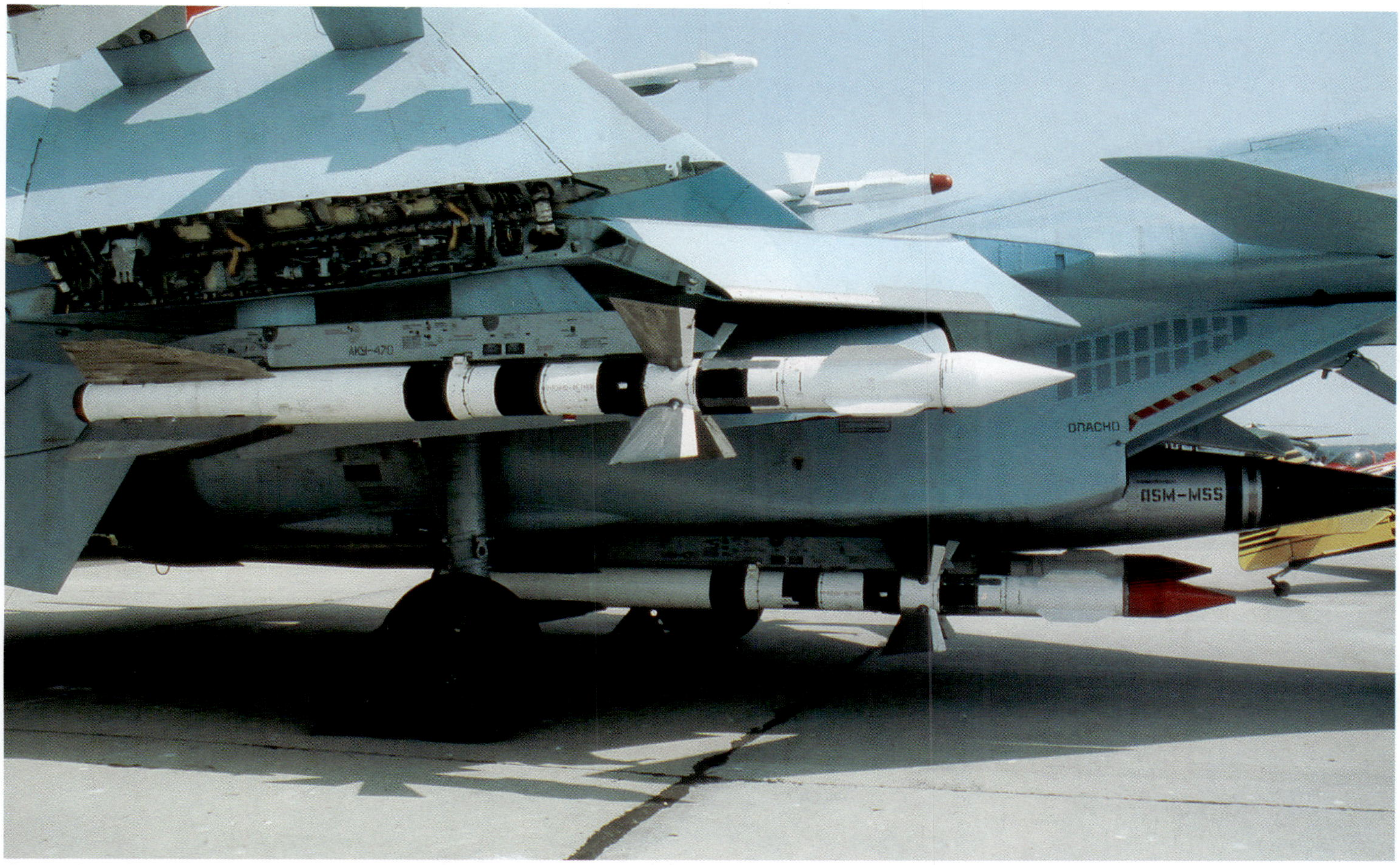

A pair of 27ER missiles on the Su-27K. These are actually UZR-27ET practice missiles as is evident from the black bands.

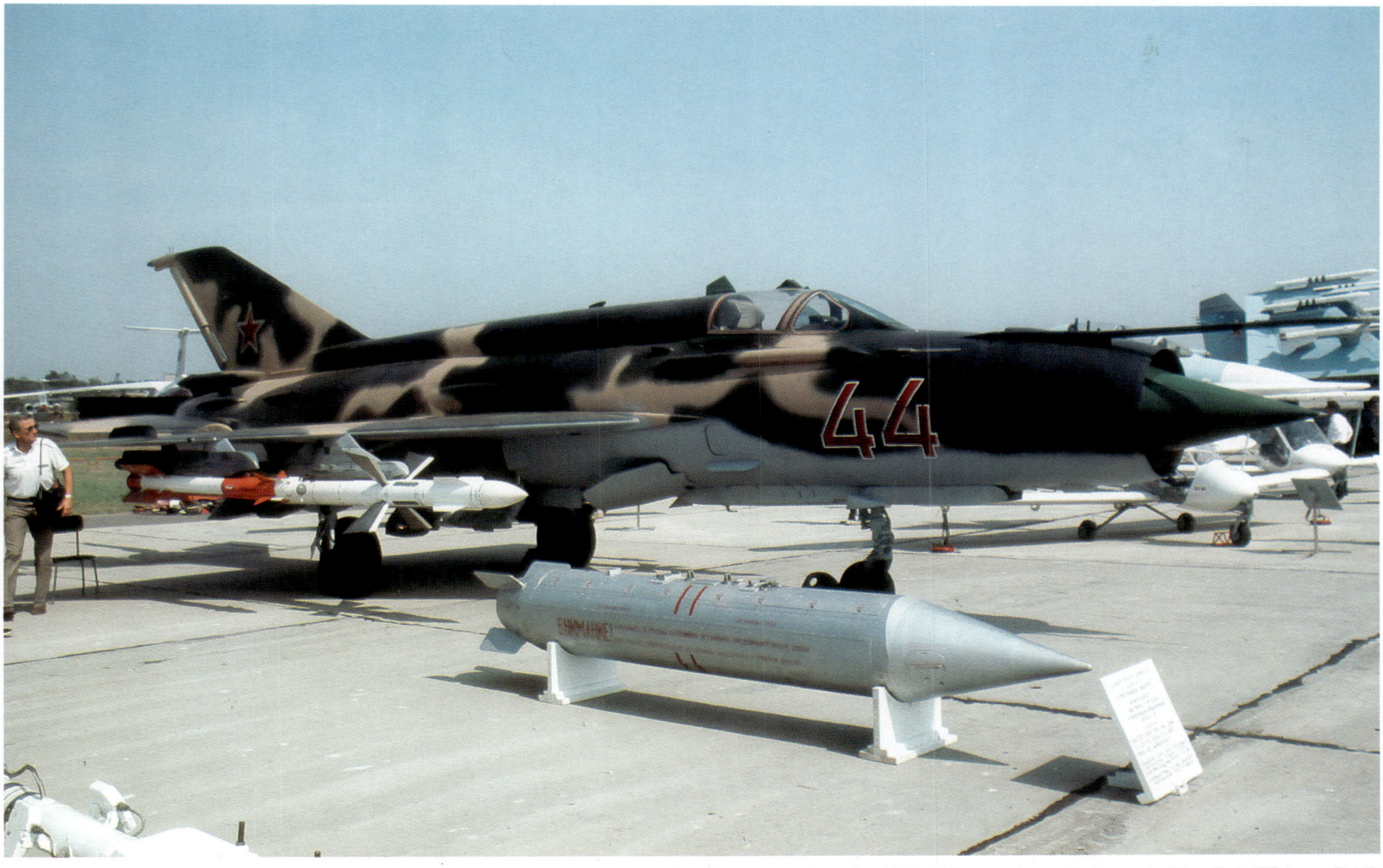

A special version of the R-27T, the R-27PS, has been developed for older fighters such as the MiG-21S seen here. Outboard of the R-27PS is an R-73 (AA-11 Archer).

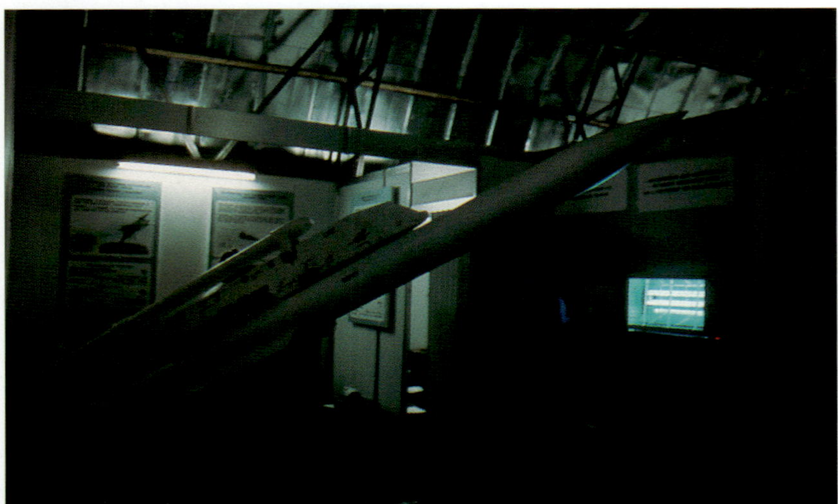

A view of the R-77 on its AKU-170 launch pylon at the Vympel display in Zhukovskiy. Vympel is the primary Russian designers for air-to-air missiles.

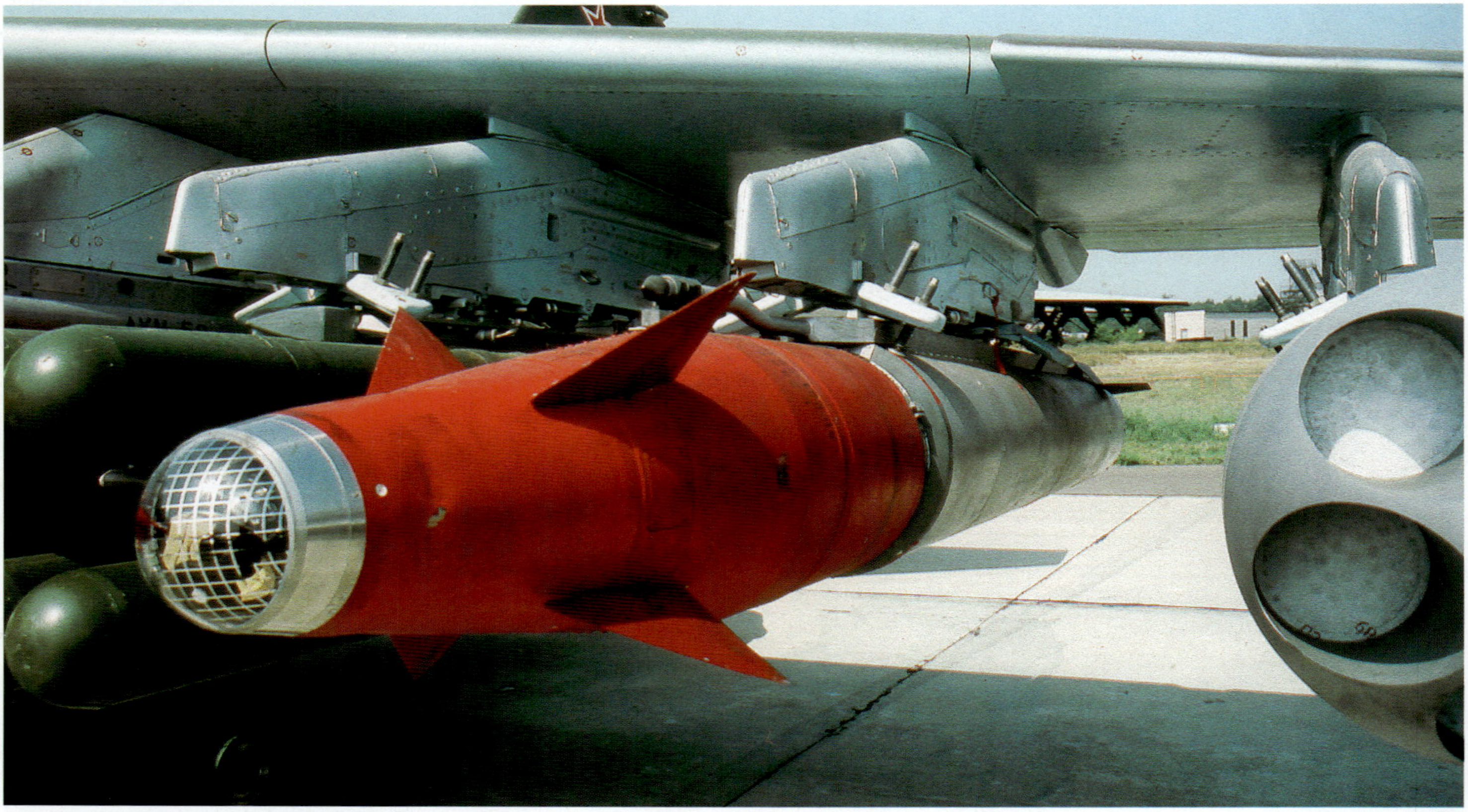

This unusual weapon is the S-25L, a laser guided version of the S-25 unguided rocket family. It is contained in a launch tube, and the fins pop out only after release from the container. This weapon is carried on the Su-25T.

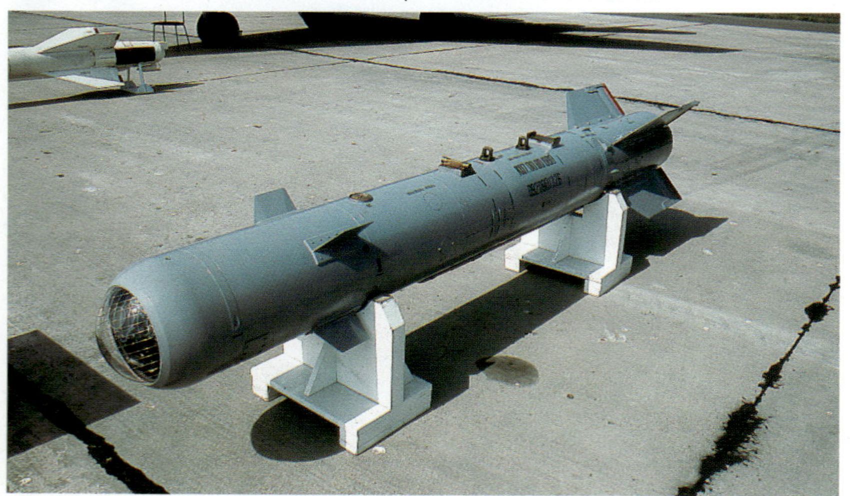

The KAB-500Kr is an electro-optically guided bomb which has a small television camera in the seeker head. It is designed to attack pin-point stationary targets such as bunkers, bridges and airfields, and was developed by Region GNPP.

Probably the best short-range infrared homing missile in the world today is the R-73 (AA-11 Archer). This missile has a new seeker comparable to late model Sidewinders, but offers significant advantages in terms of maneuverability and off-angle launch. This missile is fitted to most contemporary Russian fighter types including MiG-29, SU-27 and Yak-141.

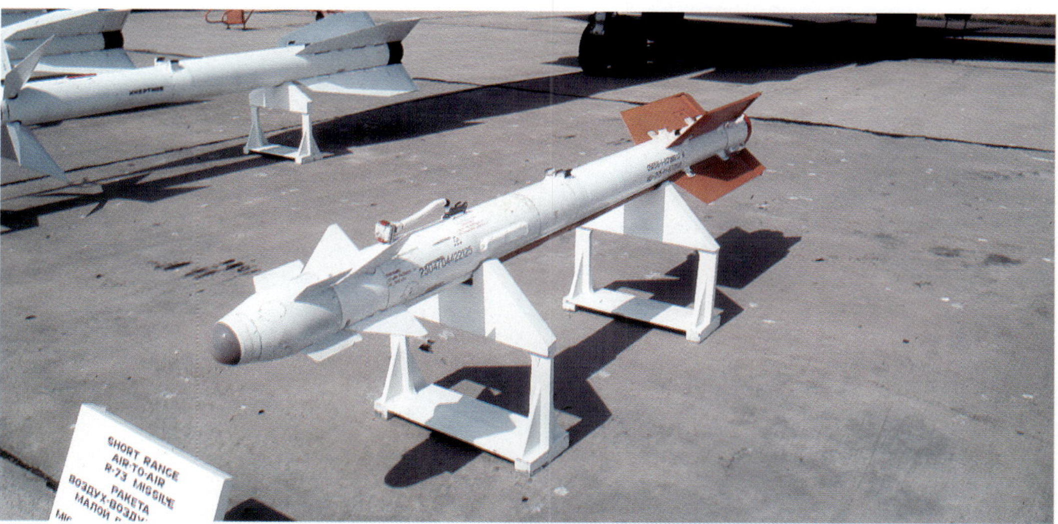

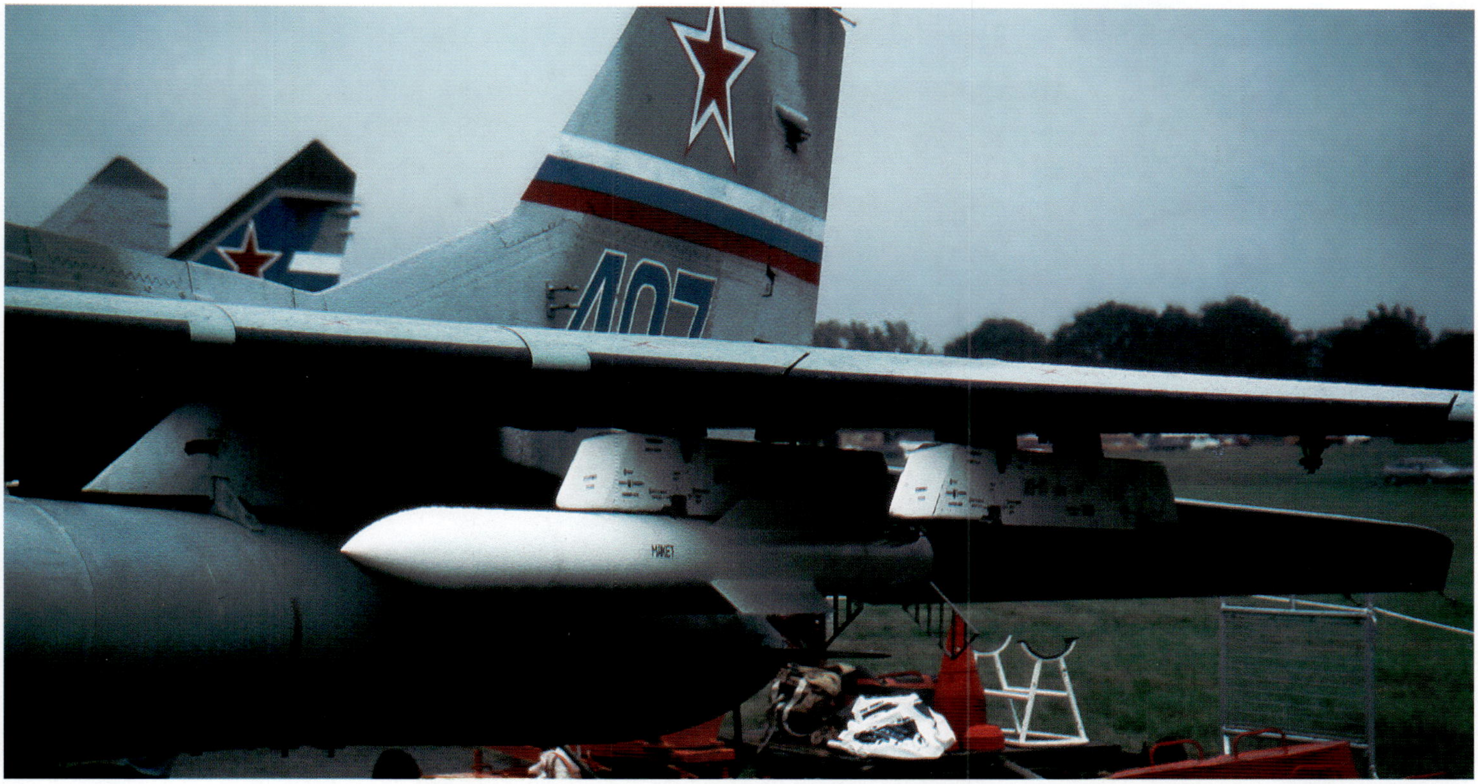

The latest Russian medium range missile is the R-77, probably called AA-12 by NATO. It is the first Russian active homing radar-guided missile, and is comparable to the US AIM-120 AMRAAM, hence its nickname, the AMRAAMSKI. One of the most unusual features of this missile is its use of rear grid fins, a feature previously only seen on Russian ballistic missiles.

The new MiG-33 (MiG-29M) fighter has an additional hard-point allowing it to carry four R-77 missiles on both wings. The unusual grid fins on the R-77 provide much superior maneuverability during high-G turns.

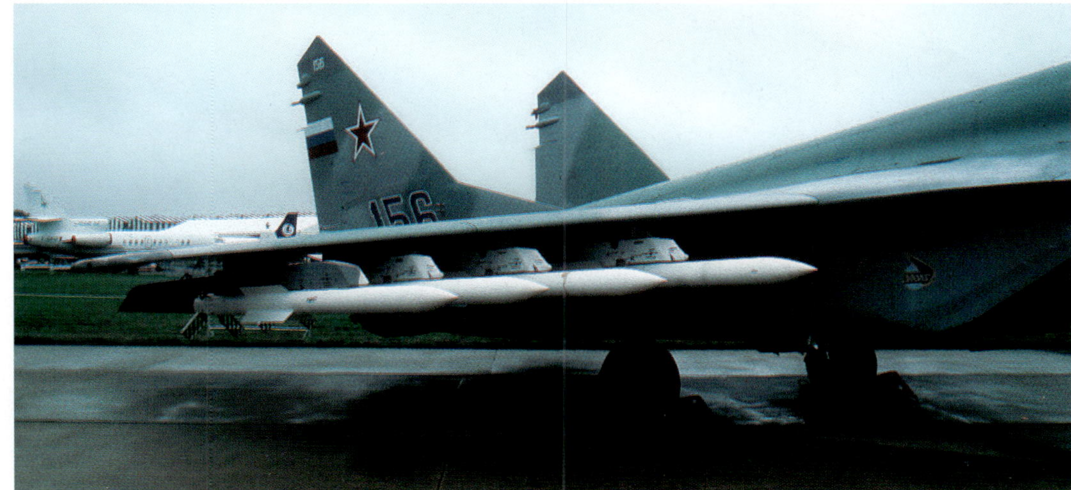

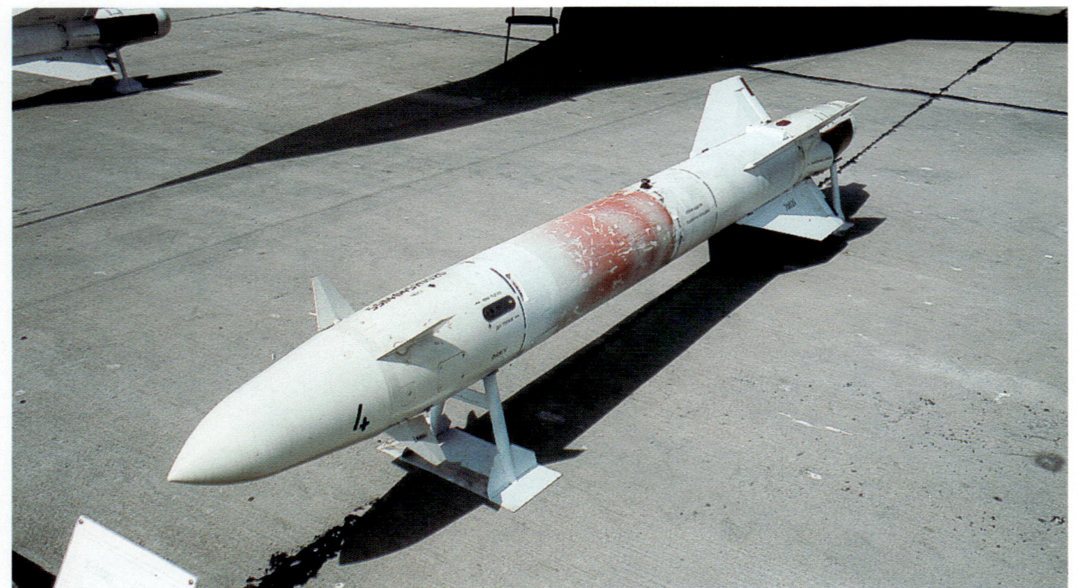

The Kh-25MR (AS-10 Karen) is a radio-command guided air-to-surface missile (ASM) similar to the American Bullpup ASM. It is used by most standard Russian strike aircraft including the Su-17/22 family as well as the Su-25 Frogfoot.

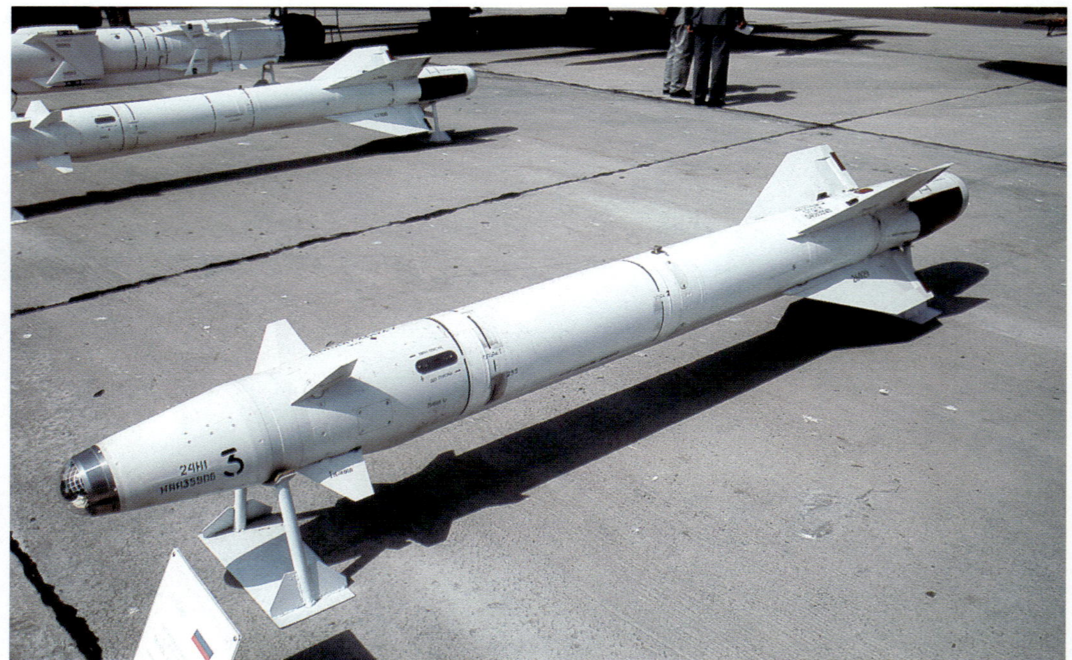

The Kh-25ML is a laser guided version of the Kh-25 (AS-10 Karen) family. It is essentially similar to the Kh-25MR, but has an alternate seeker head with an optical port at the front. It is similar to the French AS.30L in performance.

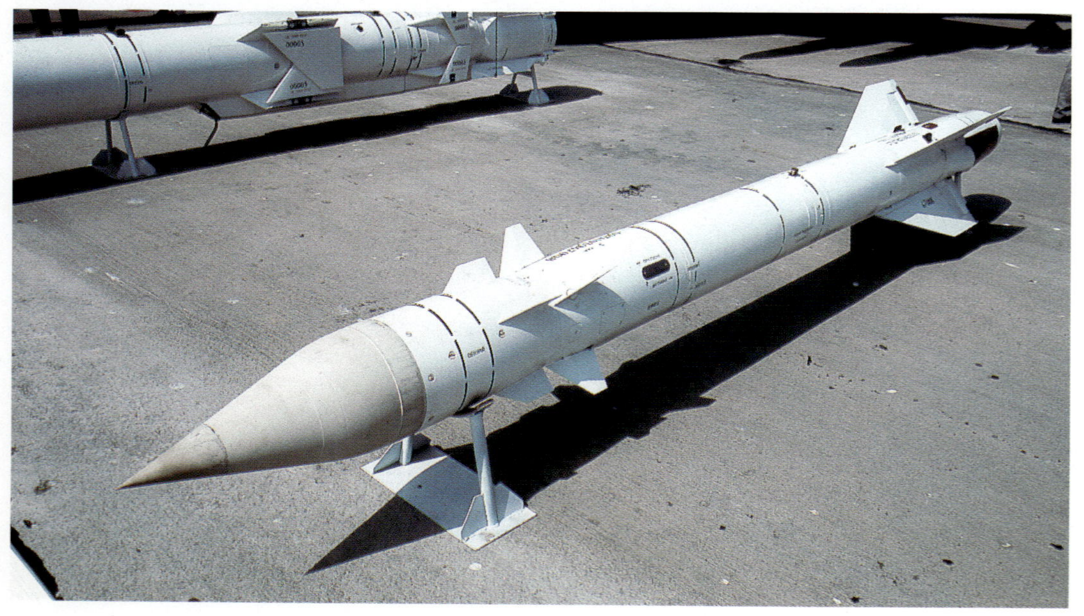

The Kh-25MP (AS-12 Kegler) is the third member of the Kh-25 family, and is an anti-radar missile with a passive radar seeker in the nose. This missile was designed primarily to attack the radars associated with the Hawk air defense missile system.

The Kh-29MT (AS-14 Kedge) is an electro-optical homing version of the Kh-25 family, and can be easily distinguished by the larger optical nose. Its American counterpart is the AGM-65 Maverick. The Kh-25L is carried by such aircraft as the Su-25T and the Su-24M.

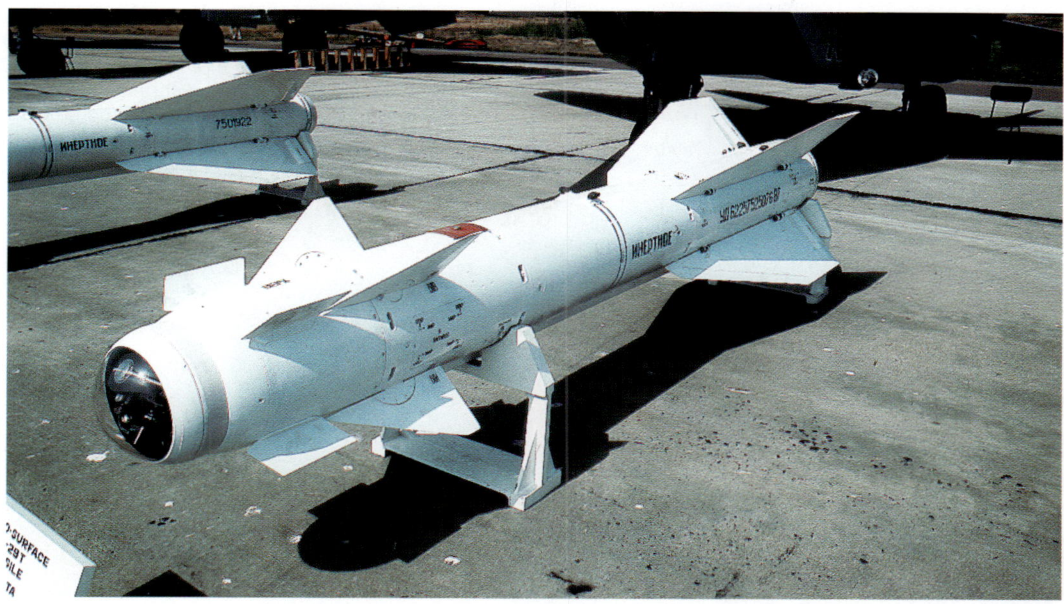

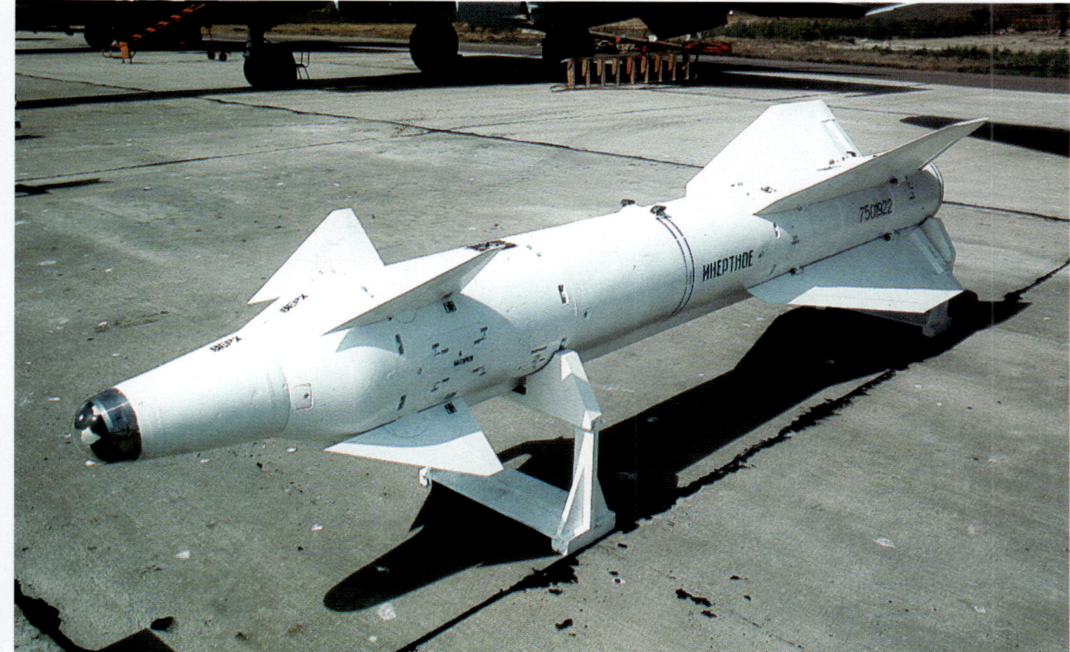

The Kh-29L is the semi-active laser guided version of the Kh-29 family of missiles. It has a smaller laser seeker in the nose, compared to the larger nose of the Kh-29MT.

The Kh-31A (AS-17) is an anti-ship version of the Kh-31 family. Externally, both the Kh-31A anti-ship missile and Kh-31P anti-radiation missile are essentially similar. These missiles use a combined rocket/ramjet propulsion system which gives them high speed and long range, up to 200km.

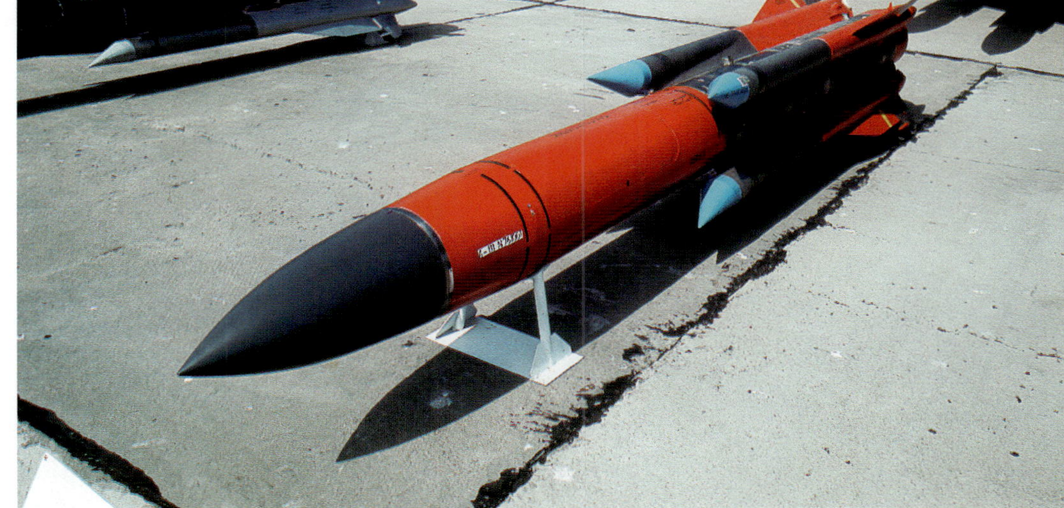

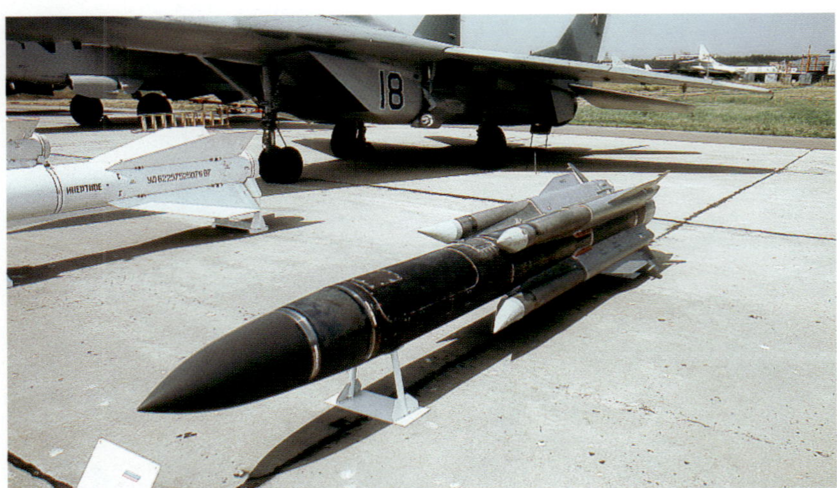

The Kh-31P is an anti-radiation version of the Kh-31 family. Two versions have been developed, a version for attacking ground based radars, especially those associated with the Patriot system, and an air-to-air version, designed to attack airborne radar aircraft such as the E-3A Sentry.

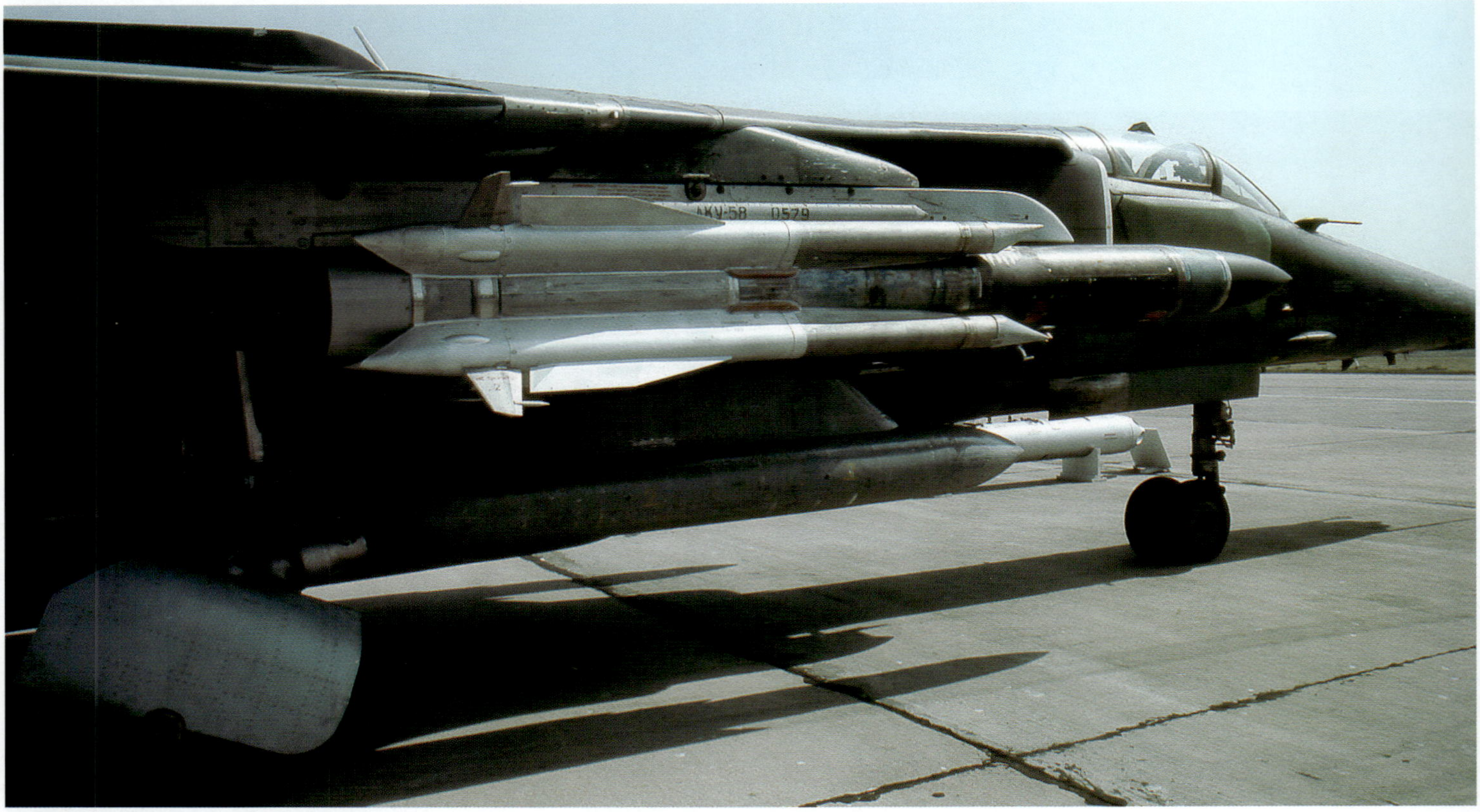

When using the Kh-31 missile, the host aircraft has to be fitted with an associated data pod, the APK-8 seen here on this MiG-27 under the Kh-31P missile. This pod provides an encoded data signal between the aircraft and missile for long-range missions, and may also contain ESM equipment to monitor the radar signals which the missile uses for homing.

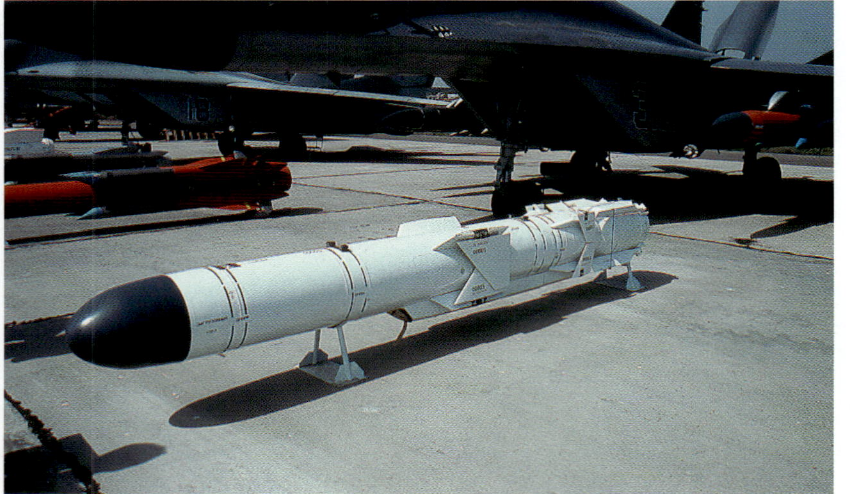

The latest Russian anti-ship missile is the Kh-35, sometimes called "Harpoonski" due to its physical resemblance to the American anti-ship missile. This is the first Russian anti-ship missile compact enough to be carried on small tactical fighters. Earlier Russian anti-ship missiles were generally intended to attack large warships such as carriers and were so large in size as a result that they has to be carried by bombers such as the Tu-16K or Tu-22M. This missile is in launch configuration with the wings folded.

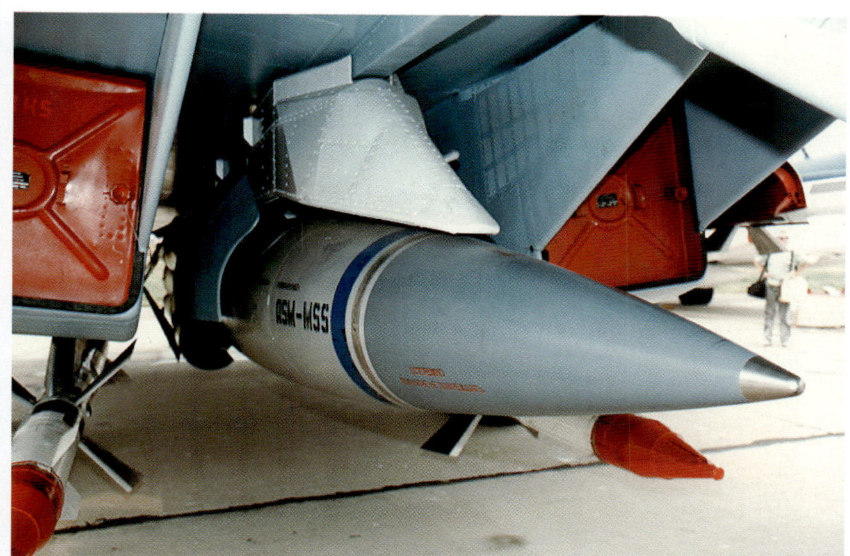

This four ton monstrosity is the Raduga Moskit (Mosquito) anti-ship missile, designed for the new Su-27K carrier fighter. The missile has a 150km range and a 320kg high explosive warhead. The shield on either side of the missile prevent it from crashing into the sides of the air intakes during release.

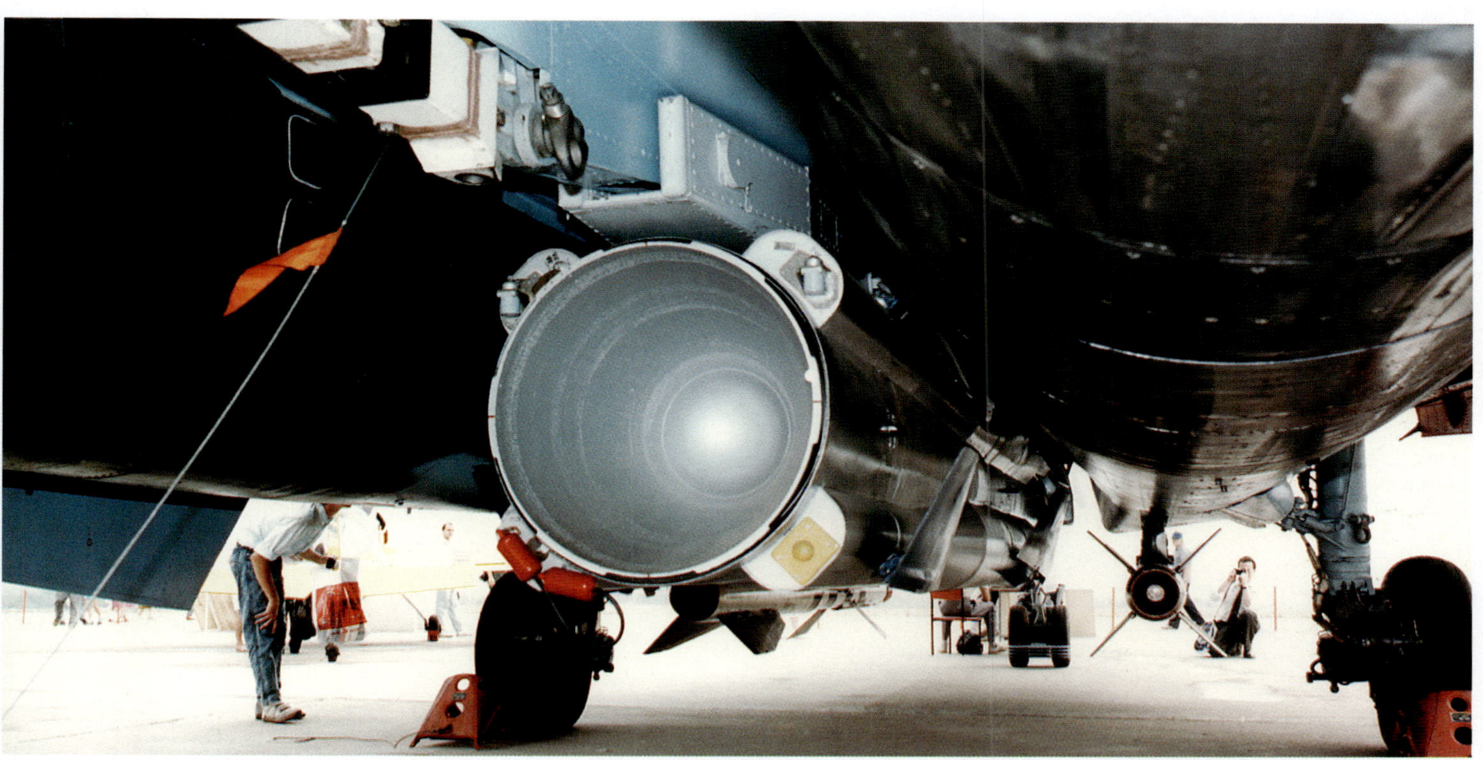

A rear view of the Moskit under the Su-27K, showing the fins folded. Also evident in this view are details of the arrestor hook on the aircraft.

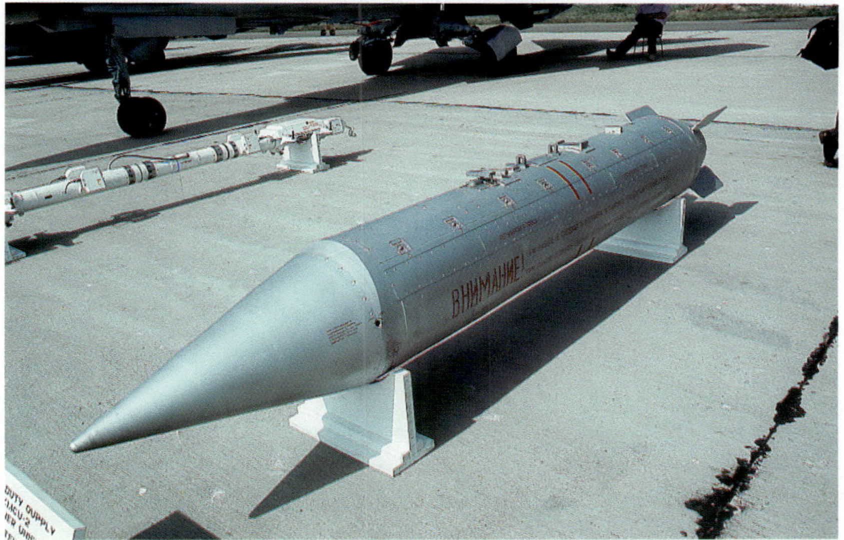

The KMGU-500 is a Russian cluster bomb unit which can contain alternate types of submunitions. The inscription on the side reads: VNIMANIE! (Attention).

The MBD3-U4-T is a standard Russian multiple ejector bomb rack which carries four bombs, usually up to 500kg. It is carried by aircraft such as the Su-17/Su-22, and Su-24.

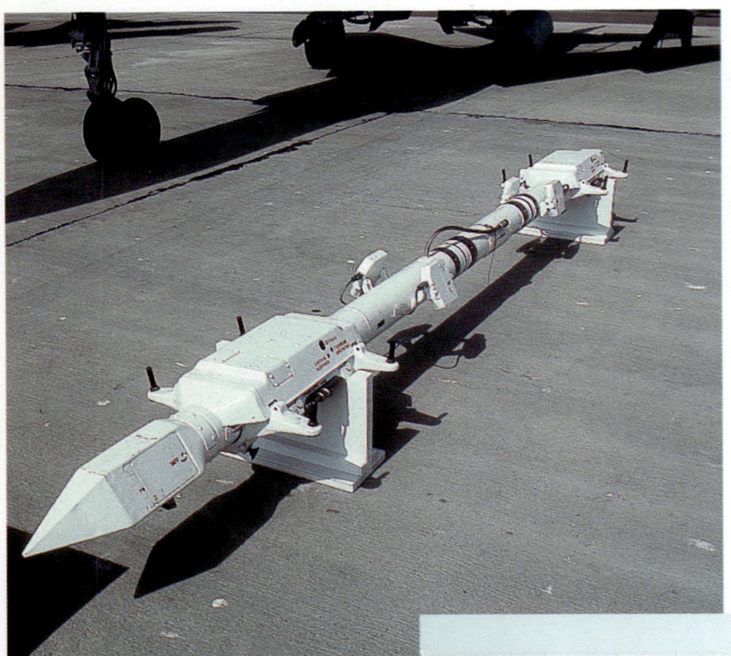

A detail view of the rear of two types of rocket pods, a B-13 launcher on the left which fires up to five of the new S-13 122mm rockets, and an O-25 on the right, which fires a single S-25L laser guided rocket. These are fitted under the wing of a Su-25T Grach (Frogfoot).

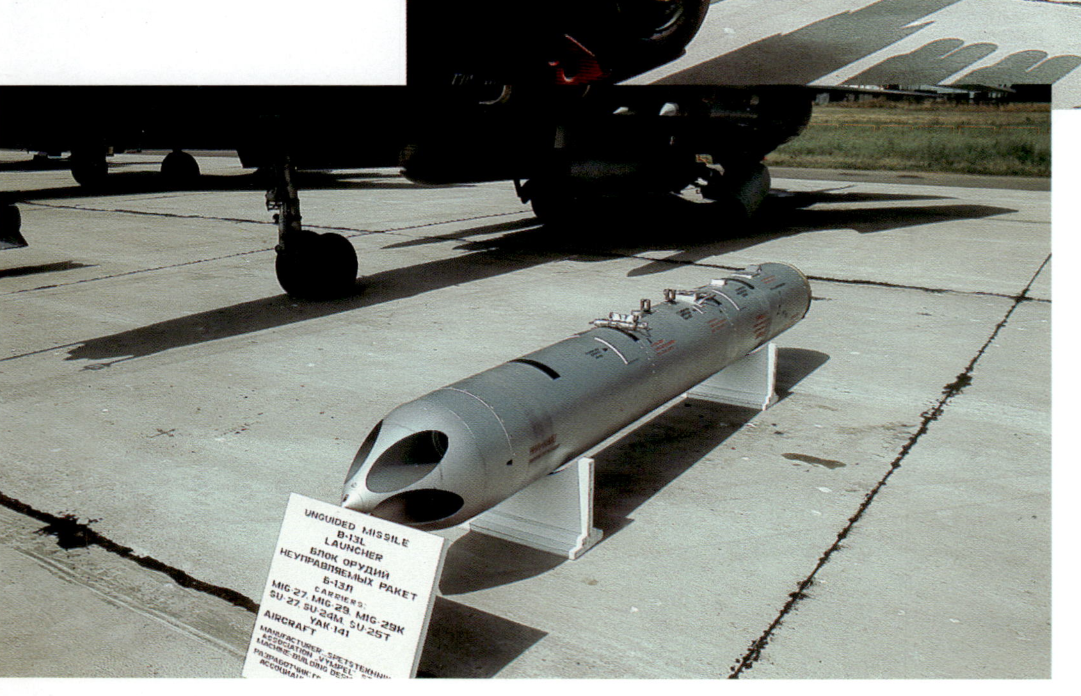

The B-13L is a new rocket pod for strike aircraft which fires the 122mm S-13 rockets. There are three different warheads for this pod, the S-13, S-13T anti-tank and S-130F HE-fragmentation rockets.

1/72 AIR SUPERIORITY SERIES

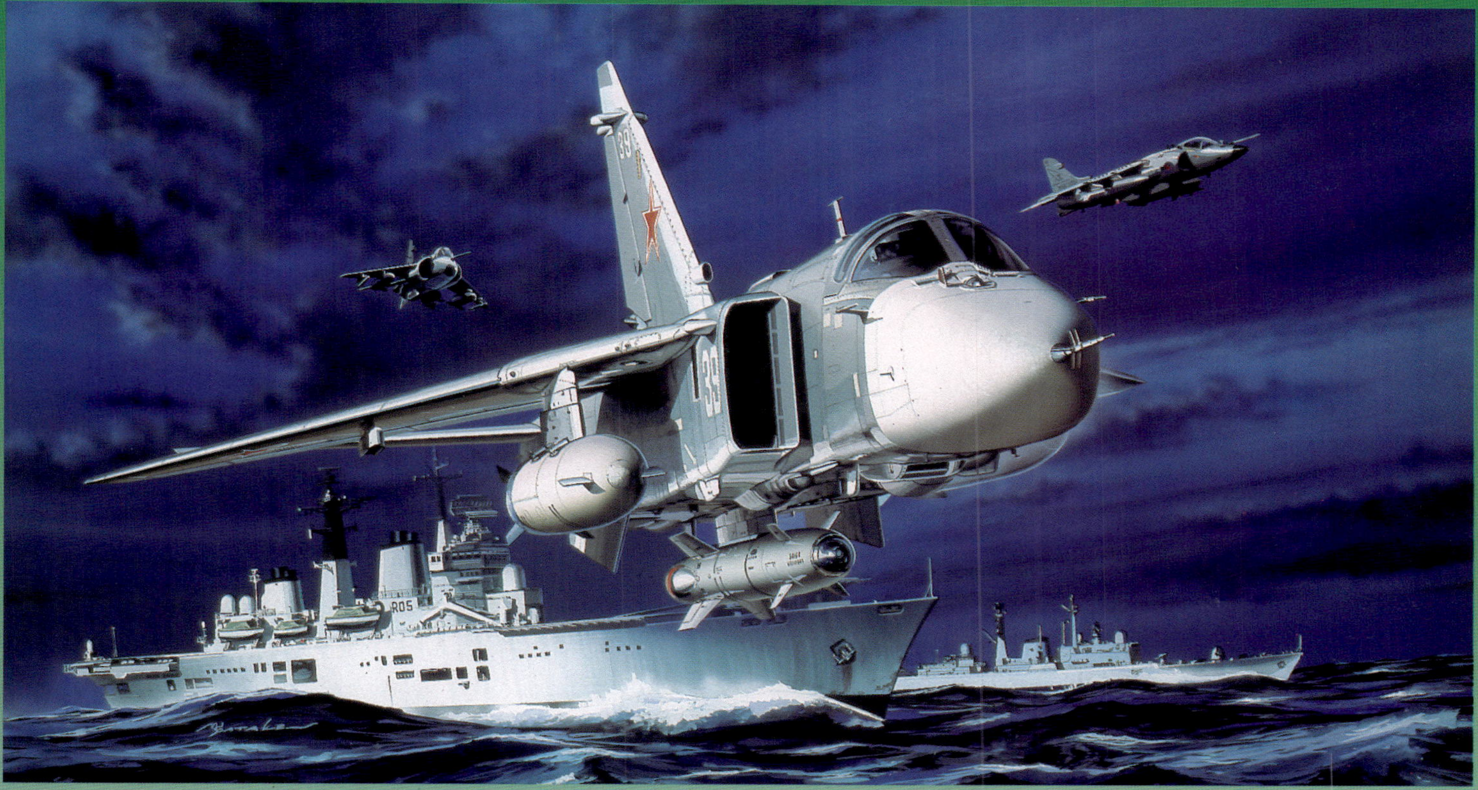

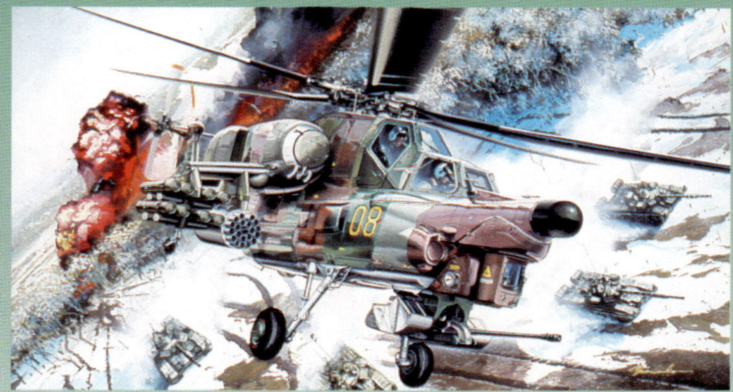

2502 SU-24 FENCER D

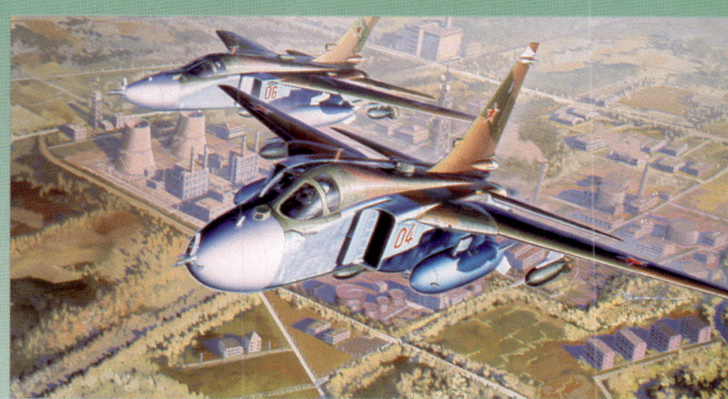

2501 MI-28 HAVOC

2503 SU-24 FENCER C

MODERN SOVIET AIRCRAFT WEAPONS SET

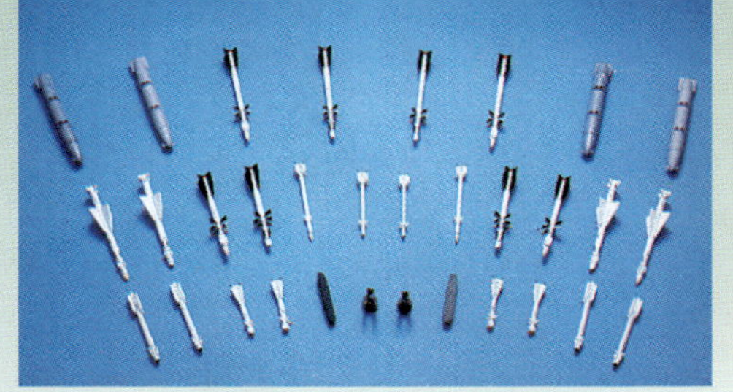

2504 SET 1: AIR TO AIR MISSILES

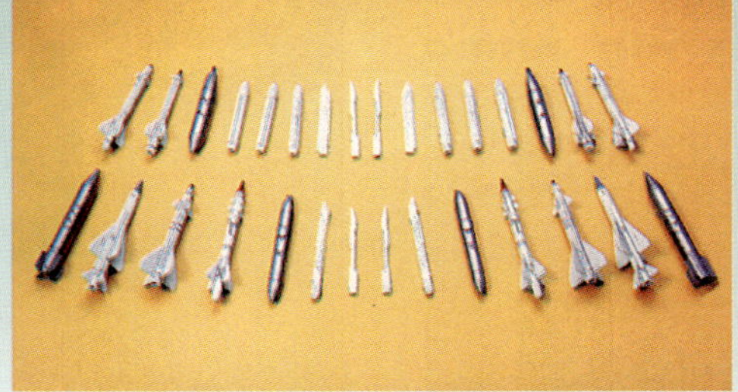

2505 SET 2: AIR TO SURFACE MISSILES

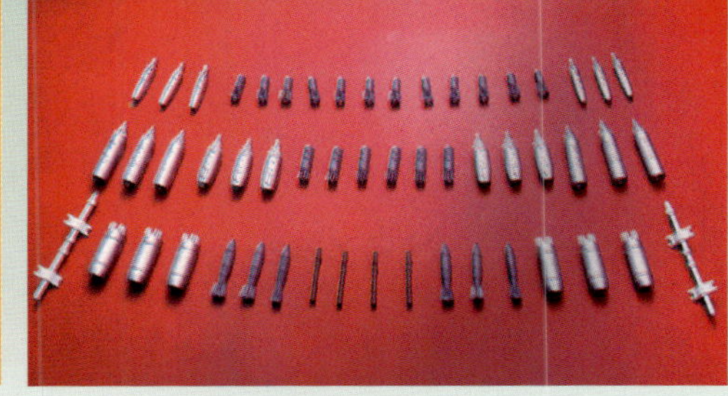

2506 SET 3: ROCKETS AND BOMBS

"STEPS AHEAD .....ALWAYS"

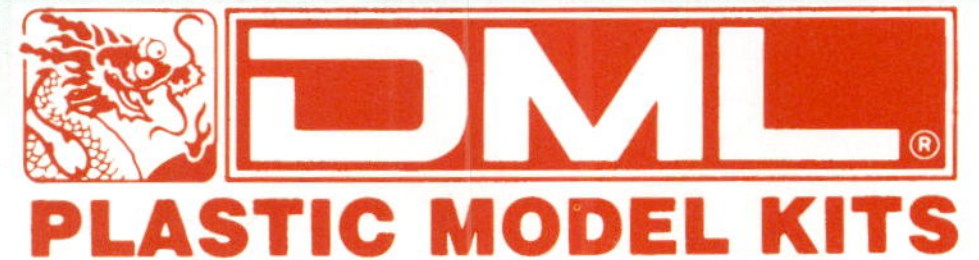

DML PLASTIC MODEL KITS

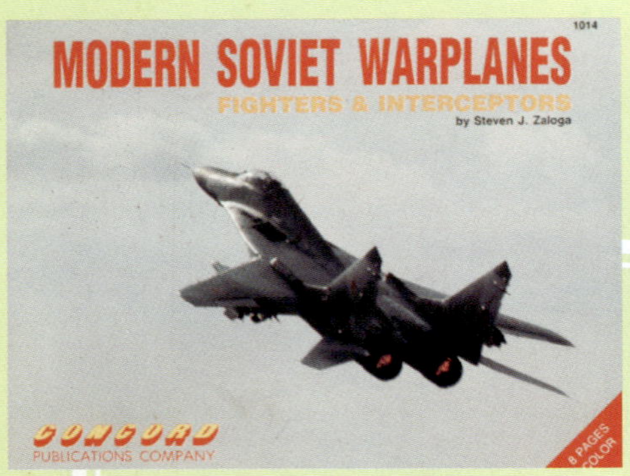

1014 Modern Soviet Warplanes: Fighters & Interceptors
by Steven J. Zaloga

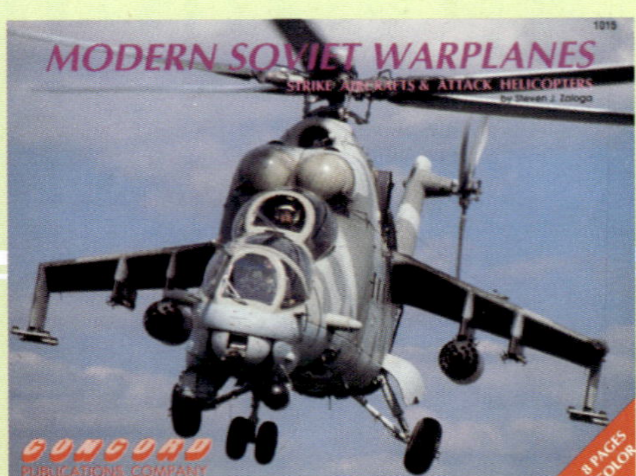

1015 Modern Soviet Warplanes: Strike Aircrafts & Attack Helicopters
by Steven J. Zaloga

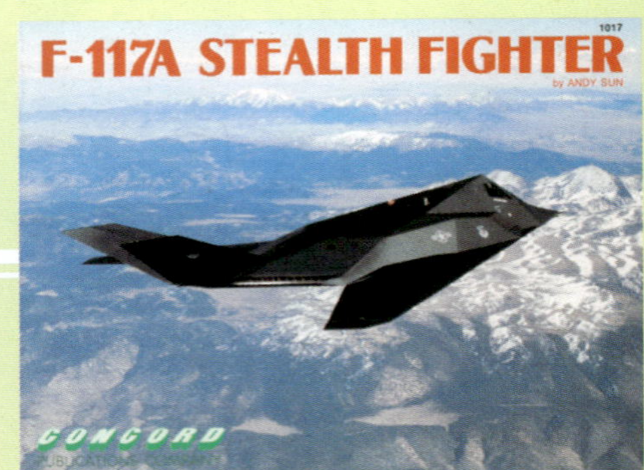

1017 F-117A Stealth Fighter
by Andy Sun

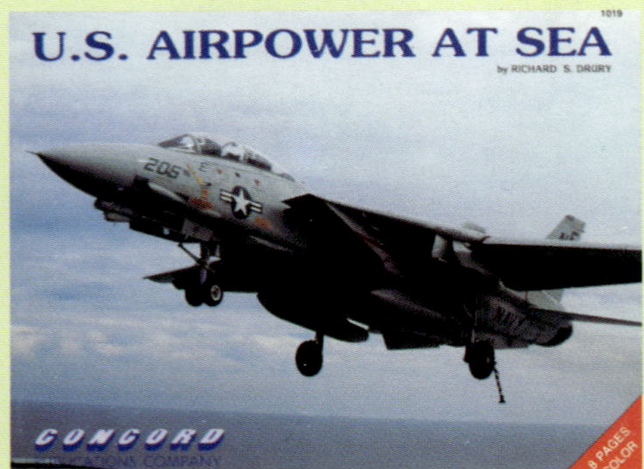

1019 U.S. Airpower at Sea
by Richard S. Drury

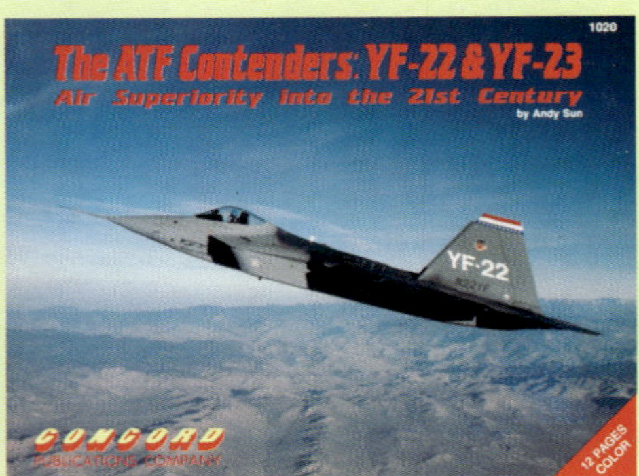

1020 The ATF Contenders: YF-22 & YF-23
by Andy Sun

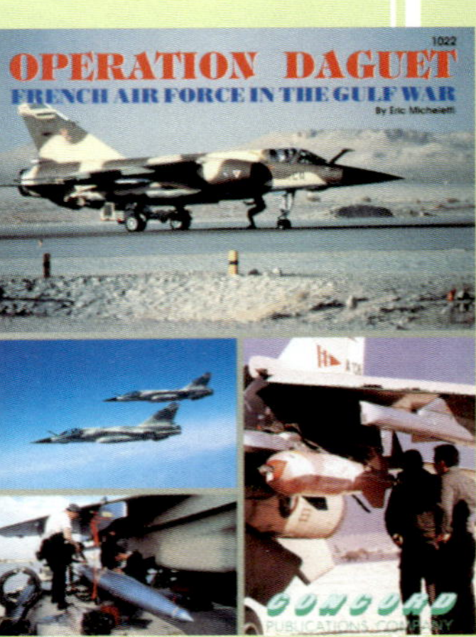

1022 Operation Daguet: French Air Force in the Gulf War
by Eric Micheletti

AN ABSOLUTE MUST FOR ALL **SERIOUS** AVIATION MODELERS AND ENTHUSIASTS.

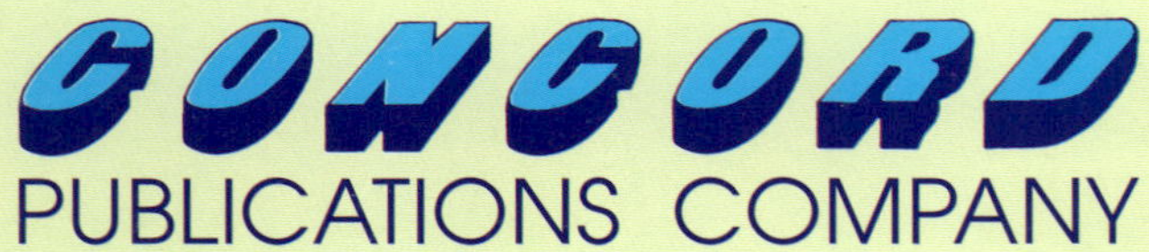

CONCORD
PUBLICATIONS COMPANY

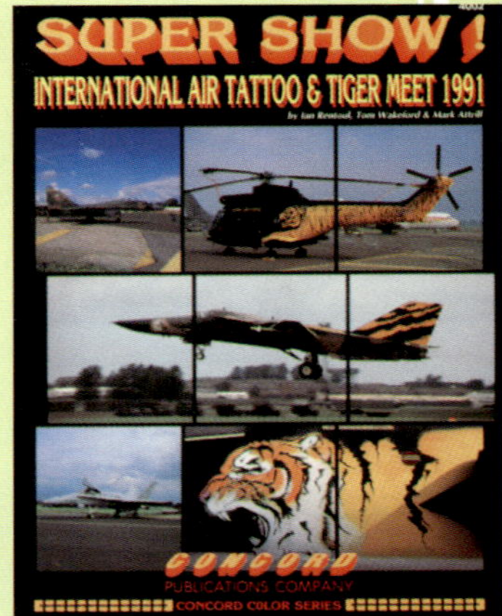

4002 Super Show! International Air Tattoo & Tiger Meet 1991
by Ian Rentoul, Tom Wakeford & Mark Attrill

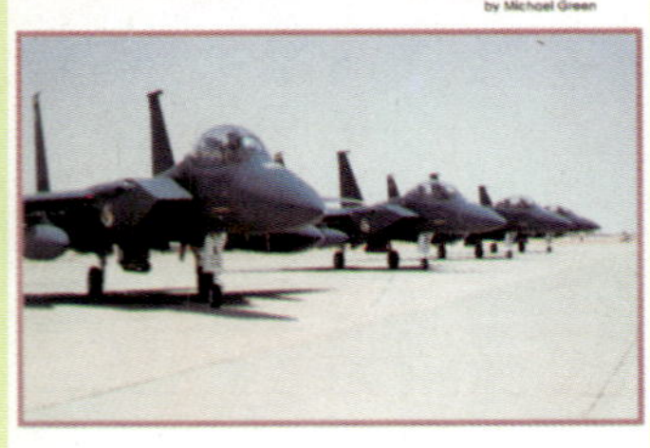

2004 U.S. Airpower in Desert Storm
by Michael Green

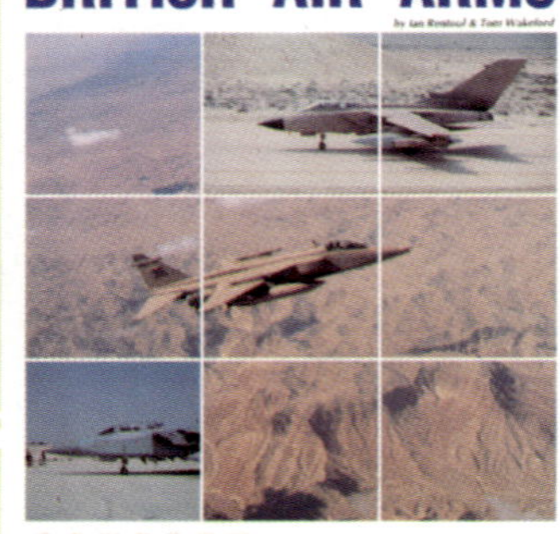

2005 Gulf War: British Air Arms
by Ian Rentoul & Tom Wakeford

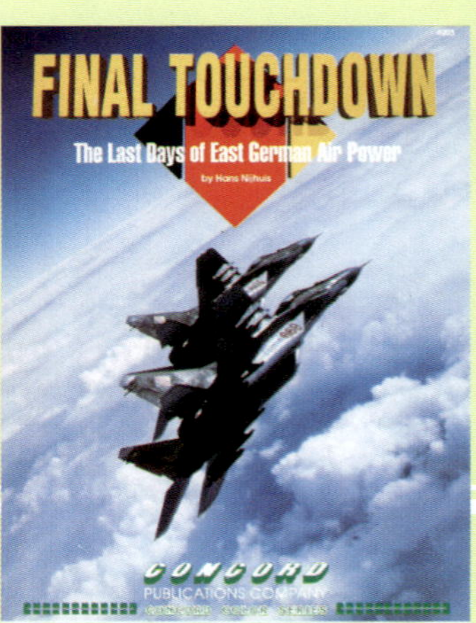

4003 Final Touchdown: The Last Days of East German Air Power
by Hans Nijhuis